Religion of Fear

RELIGION of FEAR

The Politics of Horror in Conservative Evangelicalism

JASON C. BIVINS

OXFORD
UNIVERSITY PRESS

2008

OXFORD
UNIVERSITY PRESS

Oxford University Press, Inc., publishes works that further
Oxford University's objective of excellence
in research, scholarship, and education.

Oxford   New York
Auckland   Cape Town   Dar es Salaam   Hong Kong   Karachi
Kuala Lumpur   Madrid   Melbourne   Mexico City   Nairobi
New Delhi   Shanghai   Taipei   Toronto

With offices in
Argentina   Austria   Brazil   Chile   Czech Republic   France   Greece
Guatemala   Hungary   Italy   Japan   Poland   Portugal   Singapore
South Korea   Switzerland   Thailand   Turkey   Ukraine   Vietnam

Published by Oxford University Press, Inc.
198 Madison Avenue, New York, New York 10016
www.oup.com

Oxford is a registered trademark of Oxford University Press

Library of Congress Cataloging-in-Publication Data
Bivins, Jason.
Religion of fear : the politics of horror in conservative evangelicalism / Jason C. Bivins.
p. cm.
Includes bibliographical references and index.
ISBN 978-0-19-534081-5
1. Christianity and politics–United States.   2. Evangelicalism–United States.   3. Conservatism–Religious
aspects–Christianity.   4. Horror.   5. Fear–Social aspects.   6. Fear–Religious aspects–Christianity.
7. Political violence.   I. Title.
BR516.B58 2008
261.70973–dc22   2007052826

1   3   5   7   9   8   6   4   2

Printed in the United States of America
on acid-free paper

for Nina

Acknowledgments

Over the years, I have often reflected upon what may have been my incipient leanings toward the study of religion. As a child, I was obsessed with the fantastic world of comic books, particularly Marvel Comics. In the wildness of their imaginings and the neuroses of their characters, I discovered a world both alien and recognizable. In the mid-1970s, I encountered a story, in *Marvel Team-Up*, where Spider-Man traveled back in time to engage none other than Cotton Mather in combat! As a young lad, I found this first encounter with the world of Puritan New England a disturbing one. The mad-eyed Mather terrorized the God-fearing everyday folk of Salem and, at the height of the witch trials of 1692, became so crazed himself that he dabbled with the very powers of darkness he claimed publicly to oppose. In a not-so-subtle riff on Arthur Miller's *The Crucible*, authors Bill Mantlo and Sal Buscema unfolded Mather's narrative as one of political and religious orthodoxy gone mad, yielding autocracy, insanity, and, what is more intriguing, demonism. To battle the do-gooders whom he predictably denounced as witches, Mather used the very magic he condemned to conjure a giant, fifty-foot, mohawked super-Puritan, a being so bad and nasty that even Marvel archvillain Doctor Doom aided in his defeat. Whatever its merits as popular serial art, this comic narrative marked the beginnings of my fascination with the religion of fear.

This fascination bloomed again in grad school. I was no horror freak, though one could hardly grow up in post-*Exorcist* America without seeing at least one installment of the genre's big franchises (*Friday the 13th*, *Nightmare on Elm Street*, and *Halloween*), a Stephen King adaptation (most likely *The Shining*), an *Omen*, and a spoof (anything from *Reanimator* to *The Toxic Avenger* or, more recently, *Scream*), in addition to classics of the genre. I understood why fans appreciated its formulaic qualities ("Don't go in there!"), its heightened intensity (like when my sister gripped my forearms while waiting for the inevitable "boo!" moment), and even its attention to viscera ("Dude, her intestines flew *right out* of her torso!"). My interest grew when an instrumental trio in which I performed began in 1995 to compose a score for F. W. Murnau's silent masterpiece, *Nosferatu* (a movie I begged my mother to let me watch at a Halloween series at the Silver Spring, Maryland, public library in 1975, after which I experienced weeks of paralyzing nightmares).

We were compelled by the vivid narrative, by the provocative imagery and cinematography, and by the film's thematic connections among national trauma, interwar anti-Semitism, and sexual anxiety. During the months of scoring—late at night after work and on weekends—and over the five years we performed live along with the film, we learned the effects that horror could have on audiences, the control that fear could exert, and the ways in which it can (with or without musical enhancement) push a narrative around to do its bidding: chordal substitutions can darken or lighten a mood; growing shadows can dramatize character development; and both setting and pace can heighten narrative anticipation. But to couch these basic cinematic tools in the discourse of the monstrous, the terrifying, the fearful and threatening is to charge them with a moral urgency, a fatalism, and an unease that is horror's own. This urgency and power to move is central to the religion of fear.

So, this work is bound up with my life's preoccupations, both professional and personal. Naturally, then, I have even deeper acknowledgments to offer to those good people and benevolent institutions that have helped, supported, and encouraged me over the last several years as I began, struggled with, and completed this book.

I appreciate North Carolina State University more all the time, mainly because I have such great colleagues and students. I am lucky to work in a department which is not only lively and congenial but which has proven to be richly stimulating to my thinking. My colleagues in religious studies have been immensely helpful as this work has taken shape. Bill Adler has my boundless thanks for sage advice, good humor, and reality checking. My good friend Tariq al-Jamil, now at Swarthmore, has been a part of this book since the beginning, and his fierce support has helped me during those inevitable moments when a writer's spirit sags. Anna Bigelow and Neil Schmid have been valued conversation partners, whose theoretical acumen has been helpful. While I haven't consulted Mary Kath Cunningham, Karey Harwood, and Tony Stewart about religion and fear with any regularity, I am proud to acknowledge them as fantastic and supportive colleagues. I am also thankful to the College of Humanities and Social Sciences for research support during the fall of 2003 and the summer of 2004.

Who knew that I would develop such abiding friendships and intellectual kinship with a bunch of philosophers too? John Carroll, Doug Jesseph, and Michael Pendlebury in particular have become good friends and trusted counselors, from whose humor, relative sanity, and prodigious brainpower I have benefited hugely. Of course, I would be remiss if I didn't send shout-outs to David Auerbach, David Austin, and Katie McShane. But, above all, I thank Jeff Kasser, a fellow believer in good jazz, college basketball, American pragmatism, and craft beer. Thanks for having my back, Jeff. And I am lucky to know great folks throughout my university, too many to name here. Of course, the sky would have fallen a dozen times without the steady support of our departmental anchors, Vicki Corpening, Ken Peters, and especially the incomparable Ann Rives.

This work would be profoundly diminished without the wisdom and the congeniality of my students. Thanks go to my interlocutors in my spring 2007 graduate seminar on political religions and also to Brian Collins, Emily Linthicum, and Isaac Weiner. My greatest debt here is to my undergraduate students at NCSU, from whom I have learned so much. But I give particular thanks to the "fear group" of the spring of 2005—Doc Bradley, Tim Bushnell, Aaron Chappell, Steven Cummings, Zach Gillan, Ken Peters, and Kellie Thompson—for an incredibly rich semester discussing these ideas. You guys rock.

During the research, I was fortunate to receive feedback, guidance, and patient answers from a wide range of people associated with the religion of fear. I send out a righteous "haw haw haw" to the Reverend Richard F. Lee and to Kurt Kuersteiner, esteemed ambassadors to the world of Jack T. Chick. Special thanks to Dan Raeburn—one of America's most interesting and witty cultural commentators—for graciously sending me a copy of the long out-of-print *The Imp*, no. 2, still one of the best things written on Chick. Horns out to Tom Beaujour (editor in chief of *Revolver*), Ian Christe (beast wishes!), and Albert Mudrian (editor in chief of *Decibel*) in thanks for exchanges on the relationship between American religion and metal. I am also grateful to Tom Hudgins of New Creation Evangelism in Clearwater, Florida, for his thoughtful and helpful explanations of his Judgement House outreach. Finally, huge thanks go to Keenan Roberts for lively conversation, generosity, and helpful insights into his Hell House outreach.

I have a lot of people in the field to thank for provocation, support, criticism, and cheerleading. I am especially grateful to Robert A. Orsi, not only for invaluable feedback on *Fear* during its development but also for being there. I'm also indebted to my friend Thomas Tweed, who was gracious enough to engage incisively with, and suggest improvements for, the book in manuscript form. Thanks also to the following co-travelers in the world of American religions, who have read and commented usefully on large parts of the book: Sean McCloud, Colleen McDannell, Sarah Pike, and Winnifred F. Sullivan. For feedback in the public sphere, particular thanks go to David Bains, Leilah Danielson, and Kathleen Flake. Jeffrey Robbins and Peyman Vahabzadeh gave useful feedback on a version of the introduction that appeared in the *Journal for Cultural and Religious Theory*. And for general conversational insight, tough questions, and enthusiasm related to fear, my thanks to Yaakov Ariel, Natalie Dohrmann, Jeffrey C. Isaac, Richard Jaffe, Laurie Maffly-Kipp, Maurice Meilleur, and Randall Styers.

I thank the anonymous reviewers for their insightful and helpful suggestions for improving this book. I have also benefited from the able assistance of

Meechal Hoffman and Christi Stanforth at Oxford and freelance copyeditor Merryl Sloane. Most of all, however, I sing the praises of my editor, the great Cynthia Read, for her keen eye, unflagging enthusiasm, and sound guidance throughout this process.

Of course, what would a book like this be without a few demons of its own? Books take a long time to write, after all, and it's natural for a shadow to fall or a malicious presence to crop up now and again. To them, I say, thanks for the motivation.

But thankfully my time with fear has been mostly graced and lightened by the presence of wonderful friends and family, whom I am delighted to name here. Without these folks—Alisa Ainbinder, George Baca, Martha Bausch, Marty Belcher, Anne Burroughs, Tina Caine, David Cline, Ian Davis, Jimmy Ghaphery, Shane Graham, Matt Griffin, Ted Leventhal, Bill McConaghy, Shelley Nichols, Douglas Padgett, Daniel Radosh, Eric Saidel, Hans Indigo Spencer, Eric Weddle, and Joe Wolhar—where, oh where would I be? That holds especially true for my family. You all have the patience of saints, and your love, friendship, and support mean more to me now than they ever have. My mother, Kathleen T. Noerr, and my sister, Kristina Hammond, continue to be anchors for me, two stars without whom my firmament would dissipate. I still miss my late father, Royal G. Bivins, Jr., every day, and I hope he would enjoy this book. My stepfather, Peter Noerr, is a great friend and interlocutor, upon whose wisdom and sense I rely. Jeff Hammond is not just a brother-in-law, but a great guy whom we're lucky to have in our family. Sarah Burns and Dennis Gannon hold down the Hoosier State, and I miss you both. And I'm delighted to acknowledge my local family members—Luther and Lorraine Bivins, Loretta Gibson, and Nora DeLong—here in North Carolina.

Of course, I can't imagine the pleasures—and the unpredictability—of home without the company of Otto, Stinky, and Mad Dog the cat. Pets do have a way of keeping it real. Most of all, my amazing wife, Nina, is simply beyond category, as they say about Duke Ellington's music. I will never stop marveling at how lucky I am to have met you. So much of what is good in this book, and in my life, are because of you. Most of what needs to be said is just for us, but I will say here that this book, and everything else, is for you.

Contents

SEVEN
"Like Beating the Dog":
Fear, Religion, and American Democracy
213

Religion of Fear

1

"Scary Jesus"

Locating the "Religion of Fear" in Conservative Evangelicalism

Then I saw there was a way to hell, even from the gates of heaven. —John Bunyan, *The Pilgrim's Progress*

Fear of things invisible is the natural seed of that which everyone in himself calleth religion. —Thomas Hobbes, *Leviathan*

Like so many things worth exploring, this book is rooted in memories I cannot shake. I went to graduate school at Indiana University. One of my closest friends lived for a time in a small town midway between Bloomington and Indianapolis, where his wife worked. I visited them frequently, often enjoying the winding country roads that led to Franklin, Indiana. On my first visit, my friend told me to make sure I came before dark so I could see "Scary Jesus." Apparently an image on the side of a farm building visible from the road, "Scary Jesus" was, he assured me, worth the trip. I drove slowly through the late afternoon, annoying my fellow drivers by creeping around each curve so I wouldn't miss a single barn or ramshackle building.

Finally I saw it, unmistakable in the grey drabness of the midwestern winter. A vast barn had been painted with a landscape of craggy peaks silhouetted against a fire-red (or was it blood-red?) sky. A tilted cross stretched upward, its sharp angle hinting at chaos or instability while also recalling the crucifixion on Golgotha. And in the foreground, a looming, almost threatening figure leaned outward with arms stretched and eyes blazing from within his huge silhouetted frame. This was "Scary Jesus." Could this image, whose features and aesthetic might well be lifted from some apocalyptic B-movie, be intended to intimidate drivers on the roadway? Was he supposed to stand in marked contrast to the hedonism and fornication supposedly practiced at the university? To warn all watchers that there will come a time, whose hour is not known to us, when they will be judged?

American roadways are, of course, littered with such artworks and graffiti, billboards, and signs innumerable. Some are funded by major organizations, others the work of a lone Christian with a can of spray paint or available sign

FIGURE 1.1 Scary Jesus. Courtesy Douglas M. Padgett.

space. So what was it about "Scary Jesus" that stuck with me, and what sense was there to make of the image? No observer of American religion can avoid references to hellfire and damnation, of course: these festoon many a book cover, church sign, and newsletter; they embellish Web pages and DVDs; they are both convention and curiosity. While each instance of this rhetoric or imagery draws from a common symbolic pool—one whose substance partakes equally of the thunderous rhetoric of prophetic religion and of America's love affair with spectacular violence—there exists no country road which links them all together. And yet some seed was planted that afternoon on Indiana State Road 44, as I began to wonder if impulses and images like "Scary Jesus" could be manipulable for political purposes.

I have long been fascinated by the political cultures of conservative Christians in the United States, particularly with the New Christian Right (NCR).[1] Though my previous work on political religions has not focused exclusively on this culture, these conservative evangelicals have always been the practitioners who have most intrigued and challenged me. This book examines one mode of American political religion's expression by exploring how political cultures are narrated and taught (which, throughout, I call religio-political pedagogy). How do we account for the persistence in the United States of conservative religion, by which I mean not just theologically conservative Protestantism (a category which could extend to politically progressive groups, insofar as theological norms may constitute critical principles) but, more particularly, Protestantism that has engaged political matters from a position of social and cultural conservatism? Is it simply the case that American history and culture have a deeply political edge to them, this being one manifestation among many? In part. Is the endurance of right-wing Christianity just evidence of the cyclical nature of American public life, where long periods of history are dominated by particular cultures that manipulate specific moral discourses to achieve political gains? Again, in part. But these responses fail to attend to an important range of questions concerning how political worldviews are shaped and transmitted, made both coherent and pliable enough to respond to contemporary events. How is it, then, that the deeply felt, experiential religion of American evangelicalism is so frequently linked to one set of political norms, one range of social issues, above others?

These are the questions underlying *Religion of Fear*, which interprets four evangelical popular creations—Jack Chick's cartoon tracts, anti-rock religious criticism, Hell Houses, and the *Left Behind* novels—as a way of thinking about how religio-political cultures are shaped. The book has four major components: (1) the documentation of these creations themselves, (2) the unearthing of their political dimensions, (3) the use of my two interpretive categories (the erotics of fear and the demonology within, about which more below), and (4) my own critical analysis in the book's conclusion.

The fearful and the demonic have surfaced regularly in American religion and have erupted in the cultural politics of recent decades at the intersection of popular culture, conservative politics, and evangelicalism. I call one dimension of this intersection the *religion of fear*.[2] I am not suggesting that there is a movement afoot in American evangelicalism which defines itself in these terms; nor does the religion of fear refer to a common institutional framework, distinct membership, theological core, or single political issue. As with my *The Fracture of Good Order*, I aim to map a religio-political impulse—one that is the object of much common concern—that captures important features of American life and requires new interpretive languages in order best to assess it. The religion of fear is a mode of social criticism and a political sensibility (which I often refer to as a "discourse," emphasizing its pedagogic and representational aims). Its creators are politically motivated and engaged, drawing on and influencing broader cultural transformations through a social critique expressed in popular entertainments. These pop expressions do representational and rhetorical work for readers and audiences, linking fears of damnation to a carefully identified range of sociopolitical practices and beliefs. Such links are accomplished by creating interpretive frames that identify causes for these perceived ills, invest the discourse with religious and emotional urgency, and situate the criticism in hellfire narratives that contend that America's religious and political fortunes have plummeted since the 1960s.

Fear talk is out there in our culture. We all know this. How, though, do we name and interpret it, give it a language that opens it up beyond the obvious? And how specifically can religious studies account for its presence? It is too simple to say that American fear today is simply, for example, the by-product of Bush era politics and pulpit thumping. I propose an alternative, examining the roots and resonances of a specific kind of fear talk and mapping its circulation and coalescence in a series of popular entertainments. These themes—which have shifted from obscurity to ubiquity since the 1960s—sound and resound in the deepening, thickening strain of criticism I call the religion of fear. I transcribe them in what is both an analytical and an interpretive study, documenting the criticism and later ruminating on its meanings.[3]

In exploring this political religion, I am not suggesting that this is the way all evangelicals think about public life. While fear's creators impel audiences to feel and act in certain ways, the experiences of audiences are complex and variable. Further, political ideas and issues are widely contested among evangelicals, with clear ambiguities in many individual positions. In fact, I am attempting to challenge the notion that conservative religion is a monoculture by isolating a specific political force—albeit a very powerful and public one—and seeking to generate an interpretive language appropriate to it. This requires supple thinking about the complicated negotiation of identities at work in these representations of fear and evil. These pop creations need to be brought in from the margins and given proper scrutiny, both for their significance within American evangelicalism and for their politics (only the *Left Behind* novels have generated much scholarly attention).[4] Though my interpretive focus is specific, I hope that my orientation to political religions—how they are expressed, taught, and analyzed—might be suggestive more broadly. That is, beyond what I believe is a provocative way of viewing the power and complexity of the NCR, examining the resonance among pop, politics, and religious fright may open up conversations about how we have arrived at this political moment, one characterized not only by fear but by the decline of political energy and engagement with public concerns. Tracking how evangelical fear talk has engaged contemporary politics reveals a harmonization between this political exhaustion and the religion of fear. To understand the contours of this mutual resonance, we need new conceptual terms for thinking about American political religions.

RELIGION AND PUBLIC LIFE

Meditations on religion and public life in the United States are commonplace, and they have flared up in recent decades when conservative evangelicals seem ascendant.[5] Since the 2004 presidential elections, it has become nearly impossible to avoid this subject, as Americans seem interested once again in the intersections between religions and politics. This interest circulates throughout public life, as newspapers, blogs, talk shows both "real" and "hyperreal," and books on the subject have poured out.[6]

Indeed, there are few subjects in American public discourse that have generated more interest and about which more ink has been spilled than "religion and politics." Yet the percentage of this commentary which is interesting or illuminating can be distressingly low. What is more, even in religious studies, this is a conversation that is at best in its germinal phase: while academic commentary has existed for many decades, analytic development has been slow. One large shortcoming is a failure to question what is meant by the term "political." Despite work done in political theory, postcolonial studies, and American studies, for example, religious studies seems tacitly to define politics quite narrowly. Hanging over these discussions is the legacy of "church-state" studies and meditations on "civil religion" (investigating the possible harmony between civil law and divine command, or the bestowal of faith in civil institutions themselves).[7] Aside from its privileging of a single tradition, "church-state" implies that, when we are talking about religion and politics, we are actually talking about two discrete institutions ("church" and "state"), and that what we mean by politics is government. "Civil religion" captures something of the interplay between two modes of piety or allegiance, but in too many ways figures politics as an abstraction to which intellectual assent is either bestowed or withdrawn.

Even those studies which generally move beyond these presumptions tend to cluster around a certain well-worn set of foci: the investigation of constitutional discourses about "religious freedom"; the role of specific figures or traditions in the election cycle; the involvement of religious groups in "the political process" in ways similar to lobbying or other interest groups; and various kinds of protest or social movement activism.[8] These considerations are important and have taken on renewed urgency in recent years. Yet, if these constituted the only means of engagement with religion and politics, there would be a great deal that we might overlook. It is imperative to think about American religions in explicit relation to the broad spaces, conceptions, and practices of the political which have historically taken shape in the crucible of specific arguments and struggles—over race, gender, patriotism, public speech, and so forth.

I use the term "political religion," hoping that it avoids the essentialism of "religion and politics"—as if each of these were a fixed, discrete entity—since whatever we mean by the political or the religious, it is most analytically fruitful to see them as modifying each other rather than necessarily and a priori existing separately. Despite my interrogation of "politics," I step consciously away from a similar engagement with "religion." Religious studies has long been defined by both its yearning for and suspicion of unifying methodologies. No one needs reminding that the earliest nonconfessional studies of religion were marked by a distasteful philosophical hostility to religious belief; an Orientalist tendency to rank religions according to their similarity to the master culture of "home"; or the reduction of the complex cluster of human experiences we call "religion" to but a single component of that experiential mosaic (eros or economy, for example). Indeed, even the notion that religion is a sui generis category has been assailed.[9] There is little hope of saying anything about religion that will not be dissected by eager scholars, slavering like wolves at the merest whiff of reductionism.

Such methodological suspicion has, of course, been standard for several decades and there is little about it that is radical any longer. Yet ours is a moment of theoretical openness, of hesitancy to use old categories, of new attentiveness both to the experiential grounds of religions and to new critical positions. I do not throw in my lot with any particular theoretical school (or anti-school), but I hope that this heightened self-consciousness among scholars of religion will yield new orientations to our discipline, not only ones that follow predictably cautious paths that sidestep well-known methodological sins but ones that embrace new modes of critical responsibility and political engagement as well.

I seek to do just this in *Religion of Fear*. I use the adjective "religio-political" and the noun "political religion" not to suggest that these are different religions than others (for this would surely be a different kind of essentialism). Rather, I use these terms as a kind of thought experiment to explore how particular engagements with public matters can be captured by this language. And while I focus considerably on cultural politics and contestations over power, I am not suggesting that politics is everywhere. Political religions are constituted when religious narratives conflict with those of the state or public authority, where public space (that which is not "properly" religious) is marked by differences between forms of political and religious power and through engagement with concrete issues (which, like war or abortion, are symbolically and materially invested by numerous cultures) whereby religions become politicized or are, by virtue of their speech and actions, marked as political. So, a cultural politics—rather than a merely electoral or governmental politics— can be advanced not just through conventional means but also through apparently nonpolitical media like cartoons. Political religions are thus located in multiple spaces outside of those commonly recognized: in stories, in habits of consumption, in perception, in formulating habits of thought and bodily habits.

The religion of fear's politics resonates with the larger cultures and aims of the NCR, which has both responded and contributed to American democracy's legitimation crisis. The post–World War II social contract legitimating liberal constitutionalism depended on a number of realities (the perpetuity of a growth economy, for example) whose existence is no longer certain and on consent to ideas derived from political liberalism (an atomistic conception of citizenship, a sharp boundary between public and private, and suspicion of comprehensive moral or religious worldviews in politics) which have come under attack since the 1960s, a period of instability during a broader shift from industrial capitalism to informational/consumer capitalism. American democracy has, in its efforts to maintain political order by avoiding contentious moral or religious topics, ironically fueled the very conflicts it sought to temper. Groups seeking to enact and realize specific forms of political will, to re-emotionalize or resacralize politics, have availed themselves of larger structural crises in attempts to secure cultural or political power for themselves.[10]

The religion of fear is linked to and draws from these developments. As criticism, it expresses no material support for a particular political administration or class of elites; these entertainments are not direct interventions into activism or electoral politics; and while some of fear's architects are linked—institutionally and personally—to the NCR, these popular tales do not function as legislative or organizational efforts. Its politics draw on emotional discourses—those of evangelicalism and those of the popular culture of horror—in order to commend specific cultural, behavioral, and affective responses to the sociopolitical issues it criticizes. This politics of religious fright is not so much explicitly justified as wrapped in representations that underscore the more distinctly political assertions found in these tales, helping thereby to establish modes of seeing or understanding their social and political worlds. This changes the articulation of the politics and the arena in which it is shaped; it does not diminish it.

It would be a mistake, then, to ignore or dismiss them simply because of their perceived aesthetic value or because they lack obvious links to policy. In the politically coded drama of Hell Houses, in the pages of apocalyptic novels or Jack Chick's cartoon tracts, and in the public denunciations of popular music, there is far more at work than simply Christian kitsch or crude antimodernism. Creators provide for audiences and readers an interpretive template that posits demonological causes for political decline, and they situate readers in a historical framework and define for audiences a coherent, unchanging place therein. These responses both are and are not consistent with conventional understandings of conservative evangelicals. The public self-representation of American evangelicalism has assumed two prominent and related forms since the 1970s: the growth and diversification of political organizing within the NCR and the proliferation of mass media culture sponsored by evangelicals and centered on social or cultural concerns.[11] The popular entertainments I interpret suggest a way of thinking about the links between the political programs of the former and the emotional or psychological effects of the latter.

But why fear and why now? There are many easy generalities and observations which could be made. The marriage of religion and fear in the United States is no shocking one. Who needs reminding, after all, of the ghoulish imaginations of the early English settlers in the Northeast, of the fantastic frights and visions experienced by early evangelicals, or of the antimodernist paranoia that haunted the first fundamentalists? The mingling of religions with politics and popular entertainments is not unique to our time either; it has flared up regularly in periods of sociopolitical instability when proclaiming radical change to be evil's handiwork provides—if not stability—at least some form of comfort. Even as evangelicalism—in all its complexity—slowly developed into a dominant public religious idiom, one consistently articulated response to the experience of such dislocations has been to proclaim besiegement and marginalization, to generate a sense of embattlement (both cultural and spiritual) which galvanizes responses to perceived threats while also authorizing the religion said to be at risk.[12] Efforts to clarify the distinction between the fallen world and the regenerate community have frequently collapsed the boundary separating the spheres of religion and of politics, yielding discourses ripe with what James Morone calls "a thousand angry thou-shalt-nots."[13] In Puritan New England, during the Great Awakenings, in the nativist encounter with the immigrant Other, or in early fundamentalist antimodernism, American Protestants gripped by terrors responded to their fearful Others by producing interpretations—literary, performative, political—of their circumstances which, at least in their understandings, shored up their identities and preserved some degree of social stability.

So, what distinguishes the contemporary religion of fear from earlier expressions of religious fear? First, the religion of fear is committed to (and reliant upon) a declension narrative specific to this moment in American political culture, singling out the 1960s as the moment when a previously safe and stable "Christian America" came under siege from the forces of secularism and moral permissiveness. That this tale of declension is found in a wide range of evangelical pop culture suggests some of the ways in which these entertainments resound with the political sensibilities of the NCR (and also with the widely acknowledged fear-soaked politics of contemporary America). Second, this incarnation of evangelical fear expresses its politics in a different way than its predecessors. The religion of fear dramatizes and indicts both a range of personal or theological errors (which may have political resonance) and also specific conceptions of citizenship, government, political history, and public policy. And the comprehensiveness of its political commentary is more sharply in evidence than in previous discourses; for not only are creators motivated by the sociopolitical, the cases themselves can be linked to national networks of activist and media organizations. That these political sensibilities emerge within a popular aesthetic often dismissed or ignored does not reduce the power they hold for their creators and consumers. Finally, this fear regime is distinctive in the ubiquity of the popular culture therein. As Colleen McDannell writes, American religions are "multimedia events."[14] In earlier periods, popular culture sometimes served as a vehicle for theologies of fear and redemption (Billy Sunday's mock funeral for John Barleycorn, for example, or Mason Locke Weems's gory tracts). In the religion of fear, however, the work on politics, on crafting identity and a place in the world, is driven by and situated in what McDannell calls "secular popstream culture."[15] Indeed, the incredible expansion and transformations of evangelical pop culture since the 1970s have overlapped—and in many ways resonated—with the resurgence of conservative evangelical politics since the 1970s (both in the coalescence of national organizations in the 1970s and the subsequent shifts to grassroots activism begun during the 1990s). Of course, there are many evangelical entertainments that are not explicitly politicized. But there nonetheless endures a powerful expression of evangelical pop which has engaged political matters through the register of fear and horror.

METHODS AND THEMES

How should one best focus on and interpret the construction and the use of fear in conservative American evangelicalism? (Nonspecialists may be less interested in these technical matters and should feel free to skip ahead to the next section.) Historian Paul Boyer distinguishes among three levels of "prophecy culture" that relate as concentric circles, each marking a different valence of intensity or ideological adherence: an inner circle of producers and creators, a surrounding circle of religious communities for which the discourse is meaningful, and a final circle that represents the general culture influenced by the discourse.[16] My analytical focus here is on something like Boyer's innermost circle. Fear's tales of religio-political horror are everywhere in American culture, having emerged initially from a somewhat marginal sensibility (certainly one that regarded itself as embattled and countercultural, even as it was demographically majoritarian and culturally comfortable). I make these distinctions and qualifications not simply in the name of technical detail nor to define my project into a subniche, but to make clear that my explorations of this culture are not undertaken in the name of any psychological reductionism or crude deprivation theory. I have no stake in, and indeed I find distasteful, the idea that evangelicals are reflexive antediluvians or panicky antimodernists. And in some sense, my book is not even about evangelicals as such as much as it is about the political cultures of American religions.

The religion of fear's social criticism is embodied in popular texts which—owing to the similarity of their declension narratives and their rootedness in shared themes or concerns—can be meaningfully read together. In noting that they are produced by highly visible public figures and that they aspire to codify religio-political morality for their audiences, I take it for granted that they have various degrees of success in so doing. Indeed, the sensibilities in these entertainments are contested in evangelical communities. So I choose not to focus on "how political culture gets learned," as it were: to focus on the reception and consumption of such texts would constitute a different book, with different methods, telling a different story. The religion of fear may be more influential in shaping a specific public discourse and in reflecting a prevailing political mood than in shaping the lives of "everyday evangelicals." I hope that my focus on the former may yield conversations about the latter as well.

Throughout, I draw on my own readings and experiences of these pop creations along with conversations and interviews I have had with creators, audience members, and participants (some of whom understand these entertainments as political material and others who do not). I have visited Hell Houses and Judgement Houses, transcribed and analyzed numerous Web chats and discussion board exchanges on these subjects, and have read every anti-rock book, Chick tract, and *Left Behind* volume I could find.[17] I have used multiple methods simply to bring the entertainments to life, contextualize them, and unpack their religio-political self-understandings. The cases are widely known and circulated in evangelical cultures and have obvious resonances more broadly. I read them to understand the political motivations of the teachers, not the students, as it were (or, to use a different image, while these representations aim explicitly to give audiences a road map for American politics, consumers may obviously choose not to use them).

In so doing, I follow a common way of working in the humanities. For example, even without ethnographic studies of the "consumers" of Harry Emerson Fosdick's sermons and books, we can speak meaningfully about how his preaching shaped American liberal Protestantism. And while we do not know exactly who listened to the *Old-Fashioned Revival Hour*, its heavy emphasis on certain tropes and issues—viewed in the context of the world we know existed around its audiences—allows for the opportunity to say things about its place in twentieth-century evangelicalism. So, I read the religion of fear's internal signifiers and meanings in order to think about not simply a contemporary presence but the chronological development of a certain political sensibility among conservative evangelicals in the United States. This book attempts to measure the pulse of a specific kind of religio-political sensibility, one which may have implications for thinking about American politics more broadly. Informed by a culture about which it has deep reservations, engaged with the very popular forms and demons it aims to vanquish, the lifeblood of the religion of fear is the emotional urgency its representations convey and their link to conservative politics.

I also attempt to rescue these popular entertainments—provocative sources of evidence for evangelical imaginings of political life—from the margins of academic discourse; they have been consigned there for a number of reasons, perhaps out of a condescension that seeks to melt them there like so much cultural slag or perhaps because of an academic tendency (particularly pronounced in religious studies) to treat our subjects with so much tenderness that we look away from spaces of discomfort and anger. Taken together, I hope these orientations will work together to generate an alternative narrative of political religions to stand against the thin, reductive treatises about "red state America" (referring to electoral maps, where states won by Republican candidates are colored red, often interpreted as if this expressed cultural unity among residents), "values voters," or "theocons."

I use the term "conservative evangelical" for several reasons. While many of the creators and participants in the religion of fear do embrace the theological tenets associated with Protestant fundamentalism, the term "fundamentalism" has been overused to such a degree—both in scholarship and in the media— that it has little analytical precision any longer. It would be inaccurate for me to apply this term to dispensational premillennialists, Pentecostals, and hardline cultural conservatives who may not necessarily be linked doctrinally to *The Fundamentals of the Faith*.[18] "Evangelicalism" on its own casts too broad a net, for the narratives of the religion of fear are alien to many practitioners who identify themselves as evangelicals (conservative and nonconservative). Not all evangelicals are conservative, in other words, and there are also several degrees of conservatism that exist within this complex tradition. Additionally, the culture which shapes and surrounds the religion of fear includes conservative Pentecostals (some of whom are Latino/a), for whom material evil in general (and Satan in particular) is a very real presence. Pentecostals are obviously distinct—historically, theologically, and ritually—from, for example, Southern Baptists; yet to the degree that they share a common lineage which runs through the heyday of American revivalism in the eighteenth and nineteenth centuries, and insofar as their sociopolitical worldview is frequently one that is shared and conservative, I refer to them in common with the term "conservative evangelical."[19] With Andrew Greeley and Michael Hout, I concur that both the insider view of conservatism (which sees tradition defending core values against "the onslaughts of a secular and vulgar culture") and the outsider view (seeing evangelicalism as "a dangerous juggernaut bent on undoing liberty") overlook evangelicalism's complexity.[20] Yet within this broad and complicated culture there has arisen—since the 1970s in particular—a class of highly influential religio-political elites who have been the primary architects of the discourse I describe.

The religion of fear shares some historic features with political conservatism. Fear's authors seek to defend what they regard as permanent religious truth from threats which emerge from a specific political order or fallen society. For theological reasons foremost, they cherish the freedom and sanctity of the individual (whose experience is at the heart of the evangelical religious dynamic). They believe that the universe contains an unwavering core of moral truths which ought to be enshrined in political order. Tradition and community are seen as guides for nurturing these truths. Beyond these very general features, the religion of fear rests heavily on the widespread conservative belief that America's exalted and sacred status has, since the 1960s, become compromised. Whereas the United States once prospered as a nation uniquely favored by God, this narrative suggests, hostile presences like political liberals, an "activist judiciary," and secular humanism have undermined the autonomy of families, traditions, and communities. Believing that both souls and tradition are at stake, conservative evangelicals have acted on this contention in a number of ways, from the overt political organizing of the NCR to other kinds of activism and cultural pedagogy. Yet the religious creations emerging from these communities are not mere scrims masking political maneuvering or theocratic ambition; they arise from specific religious convictions as these have been shaped by their tradition's understandings of social and political change, understandings that they aim to transmit and promote. The religion of fear is thus not simply an epiphenomenon of the NCR, even though its narrations of fear and evil clearly harmonize with the NCR's politics on a number of levels and reveal much about its lasting power and influence. There are less evident links between, and resonances with, the wider cultures of American conservatism, including, for example, intellectual neoconservatism as found in the journal *First Things*, constitutional literalism (manifested in some of Justice Antonin Scalia's Supreme Court opinions and in the legal writings of figures like Michael McConnell), and non-Christian religious conservatism. While I do not address conservatism from a position of this breadth, I do note below those instances where the religion of fear is engaged with such sources.[21]

My orientation is to what Thomas Tweed would call the "sacroscape" of evangelical fear—in Tweed's formulation, "the multiple ways that religious flows have left traces, transforming peoples and places, the social arena and the natural terrain"—in order to tease out links among the representation of fear and evil, constructions of evangelical identity, and the specific political sensibilities found in the religion of fear.[22] These links form what William Connolly calls, after Deleuze and Guattari, a "resonance machine" wherein the structural features of the "machine"—the sociopolitical context in which discourses and practices take shape—constitute a "chamber" wherein "diverse elements infiltrate into the others... [yielding a] resonance between elements that become fused together."[23] The links also coalesce in a "fear regime," which refers to the intersection of these political engagements with emotions and interpretations in an interlocking system of concepts and representations that is "administered" or distributed via consumable pop. A fear regime is similar to what Michel Foucault called an "episteme," a culturally or politically produced conception of "truth" which ties together and grounds other social discourses. The emotional resonance of these formations is captured by William Reddy's term "emotional regime," which he defines as a "set of normative emotions and the official rituals, practices, and emotives that express and inculcate them."[24] It is due largely to the sense of urgency conveyed in the emotional registers of these representations that their political dimensions can be so effectively transmitted and appropriated by audiences and consumers. In Talal Asad's formulation, these categories reveal "how contingencies relate to changes in the grammar of concepts."[25] In other words, there is a dynamic relationship between the representations and concepts generated by fear's architects and the society they seek to shape.

Recent studies of emotional cultures raise important questions about the role of emotional experiences in identity construction. I do not regard "evangelical fear" as an analytically distinct emotional category nor do I take sides in the debates, ubiquitous in the literature on emotions, which seek to privilege either the biological rootedness of emotions or their cultural boundedness.[26] Instead, I analyze the traces of emotional expression located in the political cultures of conservative evangelicalism. As Reddy acknowledges, we cannot experience anything like a "pure" emotion in culture, since we are always acting from scripts. I am interested, then, in the contexts which shape the religion of fear's scripts and their articulation within the already-politicized cultures of conservative evangelicalism. While I do not disavow the importance of the body as a locus of emotional experience, my angle of vision onto these issues is primarily cultural since I take it for granted that emotions are, if not primarily shaped by culture then certainly significantly so. Moral and emotional actors constitute themselves in what is obviously an intersubjective, historically conscious world, where the lines between culture and experience are fluid. It is this intersubjectivity, along with the intermingling of culture and experience that contributes to the formation of identity, which constitutes the starting point for my reflections on the religion of fear.

But what specifically can be said of fear? Many studies position fear as either a neurobiological stimulus intended to spur an agent to act in self-preservative ways or as one element of a specific culture's "feeling rules."[27] Not only are there many different experiences regarded as fear inducing—from the classic example of a charging bear to rather different experiences, like the fear that nobody will like this book—but these feelings exist in concert with beliefs, habits, personal history, and social expectations.[28] Emotions generally, and fear specifically, facilitate an understanding of our world and serve as means by which we formulate convictions about it. The naming and narration of fears helps to control or displace them, to police the fraught boundary between self and feared Others. Each complex engagement with a fallen world promises a symbolic resolution to conflict, accomplished by warning audiences of dangers lurking within and without. In issuing such promises, fear's architects emerge not as mere Bible-carrying thunderers but as technicians of identity who suggest that their recipes for engaging the fearful can help to establish or solidify a particular kind of religious identity or being in the world. These entertainments depict the frights of the sinning body and polis in order to commend to audiences a specific vision of American political culture and proper conduct therein. As Christian Smith writes of religious boundary making, such projects aid in "defining (creating social representations), coding (creating rules to signify identity with them), affirming (enacting and validating identity claims), and policing (protecting meaning and enforcing the identity code)."[29]

The depiction of grisly moral consequences in the religion of fear generates a set of rules for moral and political behavior, where emotional experiences are linked to a politics of prohibition and a combative orientation to pluralism is commended through images of damnation. Fear's politics takes shape through its use of the images and strategies of horror. Religious tales of terror have long served civic purposes in this haunted nation, just as the unquestioned truths of our public culture bear the imprint of shadowy histories. In *Religion of Fear*, I interpret these conservative evangelical terrors as a window onto an important and influential political religion. Politics lives and breathes in these spaces. The deeper one travels into the cultures of conservative evangelicalism, the more clearly this presence emerges.

Yet, as compelling as this presence is on its own, and as much as it illuminates some dimensions of American political religions, there is an additional—and possibly more suggestive—quality to these creations: they suggest that the identities at play in these representations, those which readers and audiences are enjoined to embrace, are torn between separatism and engagement, revulsion and attraction, darkness and redemption. From a clear sense that American culture has fallen into a morass of moral decay, sexuality, and demonic traps, the religion of fear constructs a salvation narrative. Yet its bright optimism not only depends on a deep engagement with all that is dark and unsavory, it reveals the ways in which fear's authors (both those I study herein and perhaps those in the culture more broadly) may even delight in the forbidden, the illicit, the demonic. Perhaps the persistence of such fascination with darkness suggests that the fearful spectacles may be written into evangelical identities themselves.

The rhetoric of anxiety and embattlement used by fear's authors suggests that this discourse is driven and defined by two suggestive points of instability and flux. Each of these *two instabilities* is visible in evangelical conflicts and struggles for self-definition from the past, almost as if they were ghosts that surface in fear regimes, rattling chains to draw attention to the work of self-representation. The first I call the *erotics of fear*: the desire for or fascination with that which is condemned or consigned to the realm of darkness and demonology. I use this term to describe how the religion of fear appears drawn to precisely what it seeks to drive away. Across the range of these cultural productions, the greatest energy and detail are found in representations of what is damned, demonic, illicit, carnal, and generally outside the bounds of orthodox belief and practice. In fear's handiwork, we see not only regular portrayals of "lewd" or "foul" acts but extraordinarily detailed ones, which promise documentary realism or even, significantly, the possibility of a surrogate experience. "You can practically feel the flames of Hell crackling around you," a Chick tract promises. You can see the viscera and smell the smoke of hellfire in a Hell House abortion scene. You can read in techno-thriller detail about assassinations, environmental cataclysm, or bloody warfare in the *Left Behind* novels. And you can hear anti-rock preachers painstakingly detail the demonic imagery, sexual traps, and drug propaganda that they claim characterizes heavy metal and hip-hop music. What does this fascination reveal if not an abiding preoccupation with, even attraction to, the darkness?

Second, the boundaries of conservative evangelical identity at work in these creations are porous themselves. The religion of fear is preoccupied with the symbiotic relation between interiority and exteriority, between self and Other: Chick tracts, LaHaye novels, Hell Houses, and music censors seek to delve into the thoughts and hopes and fears of both characters and audiences; they contend that demons and foul things whisper to unsuspecting innocents who consume pop culture, unaware of its taints; they labor to establish a connection, therefore, between the dynamics of popular entertainment and the sociopolitical forces which, to fear's architects, evince the real presence of evil in the world. There is, however, an irony in this aspect of identity maintenance: the very things which threaten to undermine the purity of the self, which must be expunged, are absorbed into the very cultures and symbol systems they are said to oppose. They are written into these expressions of evangelicalism, and without these Others, there could be no self. I call this indwelling Otherness the *demonology within*.

These iterations of the demonic are, in part, linguistic reminders of the forbidden, representations which conjure the image of the Other. Yet aside from this semiotic dimension of identity maintenance, there is also a revealing intimacy between orthodox and fallen. It is precisely amid the strongest efforts to clarify religious orthodoxy and identity, in those moments when the religious stakes seem highest, that these tensions and conflicts emerge most clearly; the centrality of these imaginings is ironically confirmed in the vigor with which they are denied or projected onto others. Boundaries are blurred in the very effort to clarify them.

The demons of the religion of fear are acutely real to those who produce its entertainments and to many who consume them or participate in them. But they may also be seen as what Ralph Ellison called "projected aspects of an internal symbolic process," obsessions and haunting figures which are disavowed through confessionals, testimonies, and populist narratives of good and evil.[30] Fear talk enables "a simultaneous drawing up and crossing of...boundaries."[31] It creates and participates in a symbolic-social field of contestation whose immediate referents—the practices and beliefs linked with hellfire—enable evangelicals to enact identities while also identifying with the feared through desire and pleasure, through exuberance in and exploitation of those things damnable. The demonology within is thus a register of evangelical power; but, as it makes things fearful, it also reveals the anxieties and terrors of its speakers. It suggests that, at bottom, the religion of fear's most pressing concern is that the monster may lurk within as well as without. To paraphrase French psychoanalyst and theorist Julia Kristeva, fear is at its strongest when the source of horror is the self's own alien substance.[32]

In using these categories, I am not suggesting that they are employed by— or would even be acceptable to—conservative evangelicals. Yet they are clearly features of this brand of social criticism, and they are also categories through which we may interpret and understand it. They emerge from the polysemy of the creations themselves, but can also be read as products of the creators' desires themselves. These two instabilities overlap and partly constitute each other. The nearly erotic attraction to the darkness reveals features of the demonology within, which in turn helps to explain the recurrence of the erotics of fear. The latter captures the way in which the religion of fear is externalized, while the former describes its internal configuration.

READING, LISTENING, WATCHING:
CONSUMING THE SPECTACLES OF FEAR

The links among the aesthetics of fright, evangelical piety, and social criticism shape the representation of fear and evil in each creation, though the impulses circulate beyond the examples I interpret. Although the study of American religions has benefited in recent decades from close attention to material culture, visual culture, and pop in general, there is far more to be said about evangelicalism and popular culture and about the political valences of this culture.[33] Perhaps this is because there has been a disciplinary bias against cultural works like a Chick tract or a novel about the post-Rapture exploits of the Tribulation Force. Consciously or not, the association of mass-produced religious culture with "low" religiosity still circulates in the academy.[34]

The category "popular" is hardly an adequate one in many respects, since— as Lawrence Levine writes—" 'popular' has been utilized to describe not only those creations of expressive culture that actually had a large audience ... [but also] those that had questionable artistic merit."[35] These expressions are often recognizable for specific constructions and aesthetic styles, which may lead some to overlook their importance; yet these elements are not only aesthetically central, they are also vehicles to convey meanings which have often eluded the scholarly gaze, which tends—for the methodological reasons noted above and discussed in detail in the conclusion—to give the politics of religious pop relatively short shrift.[36] Though it is right to exercise caution against reducing evangelical popular culture to politics alone, avoiding reductionism need not—and indeed should not—risk the error of ignoring the political elements in and directions of these creations. By focusing on the creations and their interpretive contexts, I hope to give readers a portrait of not only a powerful kind of political religion but a way of thinking about the ways in which political cultures are generated and circulated. I selected these four cases from a range of possible expressions of this fear regime, which might extend to David Thompson's apocalyptic films, James Dobson's child-rearing manuals, or the world of religious museums and theme parks. But since part of the work of this book is to convey the sense in which this kind of fear talk has been normalized since the 1970s, I have chosen cases which seem to capture that progression and which each embody a certain phase in the discourse's development.

In the next chapter, I explore the following questions: Who are conservative evangelicals? What is the nature of their religio-political worldview? What is their relation to previous fear regimes? What role is played by the current politics of fear? And in what ways do images of horror function in these cultures? The subsequent four chapters proceed to unpack the religion of fear's "conceptual grammar" through the case studies. Each of fear's creators intentionally produces social criticism and is conscious of his work as such. While they may not recognize it as political in the sense I put forth here, these dimensions of the works and their contexts are essential to our understanding. The creators believe deeply in their works and in many ways are acting out of care, but they are also aware of the strategic effects of their representations. First, I enter the world of Jack Chick, a "cartoon evangelist" who has been producing comic tracts for decades, hoping to convert readers who chance upon them in subway stations, restaurants, or ATM booths. Chick and his promoters claim that these miniatures are "easy-to-understand soul winning gospel tracts with a salvation message that anyone can understand,"[37] and yet the pamphlets are far from one-dimensional in their caustic denunciations of homosexuality, Roman Catholicism, and secular humanism.

The next chapter explores the religion of fear's anti-rock preaching, a wide-ranging impulse that is most pointed in its denunciations of heavy metal (particularly artists like Marilyn Manson or Slayer, thought to embody evil) and rap music (seen as the apotheosis of violence and carnality). Through pronouncements about the music's dangers, critics promote moral codes that reinscribe conservative norms regarding race, gender, and sexuality and construct interpretive frames that posit certain kinds of social change and pluralism as threats. The most prominent and long-standing anti-rock critics—Bob Larson, Jacob Aranza, and Jeff Godwin—have spent considerable time cataloging the sins, foul exhortations, and representations of sex and violence in these genres. What underlies these censorship campaigns is the insistence that real demonology is—through explicit or subliminal coding in popular music—encouraging adolescents to contribute to religio-political trends which the religion of fear frames as illicit.

I next explore a different kind of dramatization in Hell Houses. Conservative evangelicalism's answer to the haunted house, these morality plays are sponsored by local churches to illustrate to young people the dangers—not merely physical, but moral and salvific—posed by drug use, premarital sex, and other such "illicit" activities. Through sometimes surprisingly realistic portrayals of the sins condemned, Hell Houses appropriate the tropes of genre horror and use bloody corpses, gloating demons, fiery wrecks, and weeping children to shock audiences. Each scene is written into a larger narrative about liberalism's attempt to undermine the foundations of Christian America.

Finally, I explore the popular *Left Behind* apocalyptic thrillers. Co-authored by longtime NCR figure Tim LaHaye and Jerry B. Jenkins, these pulp novels dramatize a specific interpretation of sacred history (dispensational premillennialism) in which specific beliefs and behaviors (e.g., liberalism or homosexuality) determine whether or not one will be saved. LaHaye has a long history of jeremiads railing against specific features of American liberalism. With narrative strategies appropriated from conventional page-turners, LaHaye and Jenkins attempt to construct vivid depictions of the worldly misery and horror that will follow the Rapture of the faithful. Through energetic descriptions of apocalyptic violence and diligent cataloging of the sociopolitical shortcomings that will leave one left behind, the co-authors work at the boundary of evangelical identity, where demonic hordes and saintly hosts mingle.

In my conclusion, I ponder this question: what does it say about our culture that these entertainments, and their combative politics, have become normalized? I attend to the specificity of the religion of fear's declension narrative and to the understandings of political culture couched in its representations, linking these specifically to the broader antiliberalism that often permeates conservative evangelical culture. These popular creations are designed to disseminate stock portraits of "everyday" people facing questions about appropriate belief, sexual morality, wealth, pop culture, and so forth. The concerns are intended to harmonize with those of a potential audience member, and this convergence is seen as opening the possibility for evangelization. Yet written into these entertainments is a very specific political sensibility which stems not only from the religion of fear's engagements with American political culture, but from its resonance with the larger projects of the NCR. The shared sense of America's decline and fall constitutes a kind of "religious radar" which is trained on specific moral issues that, for fear's architects, crystallize larger political transformations.

These narrations of the feared require engagement and understanding, from the academy and from the culture more broadly. Such engagement will facilitate understanding not only of the new shapes of political evangelicalism and the persistence of fear regimes in American culture, but also of conservative religion's enduring fascination with fear. I argue in my conclusion that scholars of religion—notwithstanding notable exceptions like Jeffrey Stout's *Democracy and Tradition*, an important reckoning with the problems of religious commitment, pluralism, and the agonistic practices that make up democratic cultures—have been too reluctant to engage such matters critically.[38] Stout's embrace of the normative is to be celebrated and demands to be taken up not simply by those whose writing is primarily theoretical but more broadly throughout the discipline. One of the most pressing signs that such scholarly engagement is needed can be seen in the religion of fear's own development since the 1960s, from a position of relative marginality to one of ubiquity, from the cramped, sweaty offices of Chick Publications to the well-lit spaces of giant bookstores, CNN, and megachurches. The ascendance of this discourse signals troubling transformations in American life, which in my conclusion I not only document and interpret but engage critically as both scholar and citizen.

The religion of fear's entertainments possess religious, explanatory, and social power. They also establish a religio-political location, both situating and narrating. For all the instability of the boundary work evident in this culture, these discourses aim to center, orient, and root. Though it thrives in a period when conservative evangelicals are energetically recasting identities in transition, the religion of fear speaks reassuringly the rhetoric of constancy, legitimacy, and righteousness. Through the dramatization and representation of systems of the horrific, the religion of fear produces a moral code, a series of prohibitions, and a political ethos. By linking what is dark and fearful with what might be called sociopolitical fallenness, these entertainments shape an ethical-political agenda. While they are offered as exhortations to cling faithfully to orthodoxy, these are at heart monster stories intended—as the term *monstrare* signifies—to show and to warn. They are also, it should not be forgotten, extremely violent. This violence is not condemned but is instead often gleefully described or reenacted in the simultaneous censorship and firsthand experience of dark desires. As Americans continue their preoccupation with the role of religion in public life, the religion of fear suggests that political religion is not found just in the well-lit spaces of courts, lobbies, protests, and elections, but also in the dark corners and subbasements of American culture, recognizable but still awaiting excavation.

2

"A Common Thrill"

Evangelicalism and the Culture of Fear

Evil draws men together. —Aristotle, *Rhetoric*[*]

The Church has always condemned magick, but she has always believed in it. She did not excommunicate sorcerers as madmen who were mistaken, but as men who were really in communion with the Devil. —Voltaire, *Philosophical Dictionary*

We are all sensitive people. —Marvin Gaye, "Let's Get It On"

In all of the debates about whether or not the United States is a "Christian nation," some historical details get lost. Many who point to America's "Christian roots" cite not only the purported faith of the founders, but the right-living piety of the seventeenth-century New England commonwealths.[1] The Puritans are portrayed by conservative evangelicals as the architects of a religio-patriotic narrative (about the righteous "city on a hill," a beacon to the world) whose promise has been under siege since the mid-twentieth century. We are told by Thomas Babington Macaulay that "Puritans hated bearbaiting not because it gave pain to the bear, but because it gave pleasure to the spectators."[2] Yet while contemporary evangelicals often inhabit a moral universe which seems as tightly scripted—and, according to some, as dour— as that often ascribed to the Puritans, there is no denying that evangelicals can be both masters of spectacle and great revelers therein.

In this chapter, I explore the historical tributaries that feed into the religion of fear, four contexts in which its resonances take shape—evangelicalism's birth, its demonology, the horror genre, and evangelical pop—so as to situate my questions about religious politics and identity in a narrative of earlier evangelical fear regimes, a lineage that the religion of fear partly inhabits. The evangelical past is replete with demonology, though this accounts for only one part of this heterogeneous tradition. The religion of fear produces representations that share imagery and structure with those of previous eras. I am not claiming that there is equivalence between fear regimes. But in at least some sense, it is possible to read them together through their common concern with social dislocation and threats to identity, and to learn in this process what is distinct about the religion of fear.

FEAR ITSELF

Fear is, much like "religion," a category thought to be self-explanatory but which, when we press for a specific definition, proves notoriously elusive. We may know where to locate it or under what circumstances it is likely to occur; we can talk meaningfully about what it is not; and we certainly know it when we feel it. We can learn something about the religion of fear by exploring the fearful qualities of religions themselves. Though religious experiences resist post hoc descriptions, one often encounters the language of awe, of fear and trembling. Religions may of course be preoccupied with mundane matters as well as "transcendent" ones; but when they orient themselves to the "unknown," we read that "the sacred" is experienced as powerful Otherness.[3] This is particularly evident in monotheistic religions, as is illustrated in the Hebrew Bible. In Genesis, as Corey Robin points out, the Fall—which most associate with emotional states like shame or ignorance—is explained partly through recourse to fear: Adam's discovery that he is naked makes him fearful, makes him hide from God (Genesis 3:8–13).[4] More frequently, the Hebrew Bible describes a pious fear, a moral directive to remain steadfast in one's faith lest awful consequences follow. From Noah's preparation of the Ark (Hebrews 11:7) to the Egyptian midwives who refused Pharaoh's orders (Exodus 1:17, 21), from Obadiah sheltering prophets from Jezebel (1 Kings 18:3–4) to God's own description of Job (Job 1:8), fear of God (more specifically, of God's wrath) is a trait associated with the virtuous, the obedient, and the safe. As John Hollander writes, "this fear is construed as a positive state, neither enervating nor panicking, and seems a mixture of awe and apprehension."[5] In response, of course, God often consoles followers and encourages them not to be afraid.

In the New Testament, the richest source is the book of Revelation, whose landscape is overrun with monsters and demons pitted against the divine in a final cosmic battle. The vision of John is, in Timothy Beal's provocative phrasing, "neck deep in human blood, much of it spilled by God and God's sickle-swinging, plague-bearing angels."[6] Such violent imagery is, therefore, not alien to Christian tradition and self-understanding; it has inspired all manner of representations of the demonic, from the "evil" deities of other cultures to popular Gothic and horror icons. Of course, elsewhere in the New Testament, Jesus utters consolations to the disciples (John 6:20, for example).

The centrality of such sentiments to religious worldviews is well known. Indeed, one of religious studies' foundational insights holds that religions help to explain the unknown, narrate the incoherent, and sew together the diffuse. We read as early as Hume that religions consist not of a priori formulations of the divine but of experiential constructs of order that drive out fears and anxieties.[7] Freud posits that the "oceanic feelings" of religious experience are actually a function of the terror that occurs when the boundary between ego and id becomes porous.[8] Rudolf Otto describes, in a different intellectual idiom, the "bewildering strength" of "the holy," and piety's link to "the 'natural' emotion of fear": "[t]he awe or 'dread' may indeed be so overwhelmingly great as to penetrate to the very marrow, making the man's hair bristle and his limbs quake."[9]

More recently, Harvey Whitehouse contends that some "religious experience is constructed in terror," but can ultimately be used to secure social coherence.[10] Specific experiences of fear can be modeled on religious "scripts," but they may also help in the writing of religion for practitioners who thereafter experience it with a sense of urgency highlighted in the frisson of fear. Representations of fear arouse feelings that resonate with and reinforce specific patterns of social interactions and ethical norms. Though these circumstances— the totemic rite, the *mysterium tremendum et fascinans*—may be isolated ones not subject to repetition, their performance and memory may nonetheless be central to group self-understanding, including political sensibility. What relation, then, do such aspects of religious identity have to our fear-soaked moment?

"A COMMON THRILL"

How darkly appropriate it is to be writing about fear in the first decade of the twenty-first century. Amid the unrelenting flow of information to which we have all now become accustomed, there is an expectation of suddenness, a suspicion that somewhere in the tide of special reports, graphs, polls, and extended coverages (perhaps nowhere more powerfully than in that endlessly replicating index of panic, the news ticker), an event or breaking news will foretell a new terror, disease, or horrible wrongdoing. We live on guard now, as various color-coding systems inform us of the relative toxicity of our air or the degree to which we are imminently at risk of a terrorist attack. Governmental agencies have been generated to address this fear, which is assiduously documented—limned in our consciousness—in our media.

Fear chokes the very air of our culture like smog that, while it can be seen from afar, we breathe in unknowingly with deep gulps. It is no great surprise to find that American religions have been active respondents to, and participants in, our culture of fear. Since the 1990s, there have been many opportunities for Americans to reflect and pronounce on such dangerous and fearful times: Columbine, the technological dread of Y2K, Hurricane Katrina, the Virginia Tech shootings, and the attacks of September 11, 2001, loom large in these reflections. But historically, the United States has often been preoccupied with fear and monsters. This haunted nation—compelled by danger, risk, and recklessness—revels in what Henry James called "a common thrill."[11] As Barry Glassner writes, "Give us a happy ending and we write a new disaster story."[12] The seemingly bottomless American appetite for stories of epidemics, natural disasters, or mass murders is linked not to some self-destructive urge to blast identity and safety into nothingness; conversely, in some sense, these appetites work as devices of protection. The more lurid and gory the spectacle, the more we work to convince ourselves that it cannot puncture the smooth surface of the orderly everyday.

Even without catalytic events and laser-focused catastrophes like 9/11 or Y2K—the very brevity of their names exuding a sense of urgency, as if any extra syllable uttered would jeopardize our safety—we seem to live in a dystopian moment wherein Americans tend increasingly to displace substantive, material engagement with problems like the scarcity of resources or sociocultural discord onto scrims and screens. As Ulrich Beck has written, one condition of "late modernization" is "the impossibility of an external attribution of hazards."[13] In what Beck calls "risk society," our consciousness—in earlier eras shaped by external threats like invading armies or natural disasters—is now shaped by the consequences of actions we have deliberately undertaken, or especially by the avoidance of these consequences. Here, collective fears and social panics enable a kind of negative projection or transference, either directly constituting a scapegoat to alleviate anxieties or redirecting attention from the material to the symbolic. According to Mary Douglas and Aaron Wildavsky, "Dangers get selected... because they offend the basic moral principles of the society or because they enable criticism of disliked groups and institutions."[14] Thus, a culture's fears justify sociopolitical projects, explain the ambiguous, and allow anxieties to be addressed "safely," seemingly free of social or moral consequence.

Cultures of fear depend upon narrations, on vivid imagery, and especially on atmosphere, elements that help audiences to believe that the objects or events being narrated are likely. This sense of risk and urgency is central to justificatory or identity-maintenance projects. That these perceptions and engagements are so frequently located in the realm of everyday life—rather than projected onto unfamiliar or remote locales, as if the shocks and frights that unsettle our existence could not happen to us—enhances their power to frighten. Moral panics play upon already existing fears and concerns; they rely on presumptions more than facts; they dramatize and sensationalize so as to keep audiences in a state of continual alertness.

These strategies surface regularly in American history, elaborated with regard to either abstract threats—big government, international bankers, secret societies—or specific scapegoats like communists, welfare mothers, or immigrants.[15] These fears are also visible in popular culture, audible in conventional speech, palpable in the ways that citizens interact with each other. One key theme that emerges is the relation between surfaces and depths, a sense that the world as it seems is a mask for the truly significant activities and processes that are hidden and usually threatening (often, in more conspiratorial scenarios, orchestrated by shadowy villains). Whether one is convinced that the Illuminati steer political institutions from afar or is alarmed at the perceived moral degradation of society, the notion that influential persons and forces mask their true intentions is a powerful and suggestive one.[16]

In our own period, these general features have proven highly adaptive to what seems an ever-widening range of dangers and contagions.[17] As Frank Furedi and Corey Robin show, political fear can also restore order, establish allegiance and identity, or clarify the very boundaries it elsewhere seems to disturb.[18] Political fear is thus always pedagogical. Even as the world is seen as riven with dangers both observable and invisible, political fear promises safety and certainty. Even as we grow appalled that barbarians are at the gate, that permissiveness abounds, or that comfort has been given to thugs and lay-abouts, these same panics and indignations confirm the moral order being violated. Political fear goes to work when first principles are in doubt; its judgments and purposes seem to resonate with our own; it teaches us strategies of avoidance, how to avert disaster and sidestep moral corruption. And if its dramas sometimes ring hollow and the remedies enjoined seem brutal, political fear justifies itself by showing us how much worse are the demons held at bay. As Robin writes, while political fear is always theatrical and depends on the magnified projection of social anxieties, such fear also "reflects the . . . reasoned judgments of the fearful about what is good for them."[19]

These sociopolitical dimensions of fear do not overwrite fear's biology—the rising heart rate, the body's tension—but supersede the physiological with a form of sociopolitical learning, central to which is—according to Leonie Huddy—a "tendency for threatened individuals to become less tolerant of difference."[20] Political fear attempts, within the conventions of collective life, to banish terrors to the margins of culture in order to preserve necessary social myths. As Furedi has argued, in some senses this banishment actually serves "to deny the existence of the problem" at its root.[21] Political fear is thus both the subject and the object of political work. Just as the specters of evil and chaos prompt cultures of meaning to (re)construct themselves in efforts to seal off what is feared, so does the vitality of these cultures frequently depend upon constant reminders of evil and chaos. In these rituals of self-affirmation, it is often seen as necessary to restrict the range of acceptable social behaviors or to banish to the margins those whose views and practices threaten the plausibility of culturally constructed meanings. Moral panics and fear regimes, then, aim simultaneously to raise and symbolically to resolve terrors, establishing normative and behavioral guidelines which fold safety, certainty, and sanctity together.

EVANGELICALISM

In what ways has the diverse tradition of evangelicalism responded to such iterations of fear? Evangelicalism has a complicated relationship with the fearful and terrible dimensions of Christian history and cosmology. This tradition, which Randall Balmer calls "America's folk religion" and whose name refers to the "good news" spread by those who preach the gospel, has roots in the Northern European Pietism that arose in seventeenth-century Europe and in certain strands of colonial Puritanism in the United States.[22] Pietism's emphases on religion's emotional immediacy and suspicion of worldly institutions shaped the evangelical tradition in the United States.[23] These themes were appropriated by itinerants (notably the Dutch Theodore Freylinghuysen) who traveled the American colonies in the mid-eighteenth century during a period of intense revivalism known as the First Great Awakening (ca. 1730–1750). Figures like George Whitefield (whose flamboyant speaking style did much to popularize the idiom), Gilbert Tennent, and Jonathan Edwards articulated a religious sensibility that contrasted with that of the (mostly Anglican) ecclesiastical authorities of the day, emphasizing a piety which did not require the mediation of institutions or hierarchy but only an open heart and an open Bible. Using the tropes of freedom and liberty initially popularized by the Dutch Pietists and an emotional emphasis indebted to English Methodists, these itinerants described an individual encounter with the Holy Spirit that would lead to a "born-again" experience, where one realizes that one is a sinner, that one is absolutely dependent on God, and that Christ atoned for humanity's sinful nature. This idiom's popularity was fueled by its injunction to save souls and its "protest against deficient morality, intransigent ecclesiastical establishments, and worldly elites."[24]

Following the revolutionary era, revivalism increased dramatically during the Second Great Awakening during the first half of the nineteenth century, incorporating older elements of revivalism into a context shaped less by the colonial town than by the camp meeting or tent revivals occurring in the "unchurched" territories of Indiana, Kentucky, and Ohio. Itinerants like Charles Grandison Finney, Timothy Dwight, Barton Stone, and Lyman Beecher maintained the theological emphasis on God's absolute sovereignty, a suspicion of institutions, and an emotional practice, but they demanded of new converts that they save not only individual souls but also the social order itself.[25] These transformations within a now recognizable religious tradition blended familiar tropes of American individualism and self-reliance with an enduring skepticism regarding the possibility of worldly betterment.

Evangelicals subsequently assumed a place of prominence in (if not outright control of) most major denominations in the United States. Following the Civil War, the tradition developed through institution building (notably by Dwight

L. Moody), missionary work, and continued revivalism (much of it focused on social reform like the temperance movement or expressed in jeremiads like those of Muscular Christianity).[26] During this period, certain wings of the tradition became polarized in response to social, political, and intellectual developments. Both a conservative and a liberal evangelicalism became more distinct, and, in conjunction with widespread fragmentation in mainline denominations, conservatives identified themselves in opposition to new developments in social and intellectual life, such as evolutionary theory, biblical criticism, feminism, and Marxism.[27] While the tradition had always been conservative theologically, these historical developments amplified the oppositional or separatist tendencies in many conservative evangelical communities, where a sense of opposition was sharpened by an emphasis on "dependence on God, the depravity of the world and of human nature, and the harshness of God."[28] These emphases were both theological and sociopolitical and emerged as meaningful ways of distinguishing conservatives from both mainline and liberal believers, as seen for example in Moody's excoriation of America's sinning cities or Samuel P. "The Sledgehammer" Jones's fierce oratory.[29]

These tensions increased in the early twentieth century as certain conservatives underscored their insistence on the Bible's authority even further: not only did the Bible reveal God's word and reflect a permanent moral order, it was also without error or contradiction. From 1910 to 1915, a series of pamphlets entitled *The Fundamentals of the Faith* was distributed widely, which declared that there were certain beliefs (such as the literal belief in Christ's resurrection and insistence on the literal truth of the Bible) so integral to Christianity that they could neither be made concessions to modernity nor watered down.[30] Those communities professing an affinity for this orientation became known as "fundamentalists," and in 1919 they established the World's Christian Fundamentals Association. The challenge presented by this worldview seemed to peak during the infamous Scopes "Monkey Trial" of 1925, after which it seemed that fundamentalist coalitions frayed.[31] In the wake of perceived public humiliations, conservative evangelicals—the majority of whom, if not technically fundamentalists, at least identified with that movement's doctrinal and social positions—split over the extent to which the goals of evangelization could be met by engaging or separating from the wider culture. The "new evangelicalism" which arose during the 1940s and 1950s, initially represented by the National Association of Evangelicals, largely rejected separatism. Militancy remained, championed by Carl McIntire's American Council of Christian Churches, but did not gain quite the public exposure or institutional foothold that the new evangelicals did.[32]

Below, I write more about evangelicalism's development after World War Two, specifically about its politics. For now, it is enough to say that this tradition, which emerged during the eighteenth- and nineteenth-century revivals

and diversified during a period of intense conflicts with modernity, is preoccupied with boundaries: between life prior to rebirth and after; between Bible
truth and deception; between regenerate and unsaved; and between orthodoxy
and heterodoxy. Such dualisms should be seen as historically linked to the
broader affirmation that, however potent and disordering is worldly evil,
God's moral order is without ambiguity and thereby more resilient. This situates moral agency in a context where behavioral and doxological norms are
irrevocable and absolute; they cannot be altered via interpretation, nuance, or
partial convictions. While evangelicalism is not necessarily unique in the way it
privileges certitude, fixity, and commitment over ambiguity, fluidity, and
multiplicity, the shapes of this tradition's darkness and its combativeness have
often been distinct.[33]

DARK RELIGION, HAUNTED NATION

Some of American culture's most defining features concern haunting, with
tropes of punishment and damnation that resound in a lingering Gothic echo.
Ghosts and spirits have found work in the United States, in metaphysical
movements like spiritualism, in the ancestral rites of Native American traditions, in the *lwas* of Vodou and the orishas of Santería. But religious frights and
the spectral unseen have drifted through American Christianity too, in fear
regimes whose lineages teach us about the religion of fear. Colonial Christianity, for example, was not as distinct from "occult" or "magical" practices
as people—then or now—have generally assumed.[34] Indigenous religions, folk
practices, and magical beliefs blended in an admixture of right-living piety
with fear and darkness, perhaps most visible in the Puritan commonwealths of
the seventeenth century. Already committed to a stark moral universe, Puritanism's ontological certainties were framed by an unshakeable conviction
that demonic Others lurked outside and within the regenerate community: in
the "savage" New World, with its woods shrouded in mystery, its dark-skinned
natives, and its darker secrets. New England settlers responded to their un-
settling new conditions with a bricolage of the religious, the fantastic, and the
Gothic whose legacy lingers still. One need only note the titles of some of New
England's earliest religious treatises to discern the interplay between chiliasm
and fright, including *Groans of the Damned, Day of Doom, Thirsty Sinner,* and
Memorable Providences Relating to Witchcraft and Possessions.[35] Indeed, William Bradford wrote that, by 1642, "things fearful to name...have broke
forth" in the Plymouth Plantation.[36]

This burgeoning fear regime took shape in Cotton Mather's zeal for "the
workings of the 'invisible world'—a hidden domain populated by devils, spirit
forces, witches, and angels."[37] It is also evident in the diaries and doom-laden
poetry of Michael Wigglesworth, where self-loathing and sexual desire mingled

in grippingly described terrors before the divine. These Christians believed that the shadow world of spirits and demons was as real as the waking world; the devil's work was no trifling matter and, precisely because it bred such seductions and captured the imagination, required engagement and combat from the devout. Yet, in the zeal of their scrutiny, Puritans produced a body of work (which Perry Miller has called a "staggering compendium of iniquity") and a worldview that revealed fear's erotics.[38]

Evangelicals are in many ways the heirs of this religious ferment. In particular, during times of social and religious crisis, a preoccupation with darkness and demonology emerges, almost like a shadow side whose desires and fascinations are illuminated by hellfire; this darkness works in parallel to political fear, explaining, indicting, and staking out a place in the world.[39] As evangelicalism emerged in America, some children of the revivals also partook of the hauntedness which so defined the Puritans. In their own debates about identity and orthodoxy, a strain of evangelical piety emerged that yielded similar strategies of self-fashioning: a magnetic compulsion exerted by things reviled and a reliance on Others both demonic and heterodox in the construction of the self.

At the center of these processes for evangelicals were contestations surrounding both demonology and the appropriate expression of religious experience.[40] Whitefield, Tennent, and their contemporaries compelled audiences not only with larger-than-life performances but with prophetic intonations about hell and damnation. As Mechal Sobel suggests, the Others emerging from the evangelical imagination in the latter part of the eighteenth century were primarily racialized and gendered figures who manifested in fevered dreams and visions.[41] The itinerants were often nervous about the effects of such religious "enthusiasms" and believed that "raptures," "visions," and "revelations" could, if left unchecked, distract one from "real religion" or could even jeopardize the social order. Charles Chauncy noted with alarm that these effects left one "fill'd with great Anxiety and Distress... [and] an overpowering Sense of Sin, and Fear of divine Wrath."[42] Edwards, of course, believed that not only was terror an appropriate response to the divine presence but that religious pedagogy was often most true and effective when expressed in the idiom of fear.[43] In other words, debates about evangelical identity itself—those concerned with both the body and demonology—turned on the categories of fear, sin, and God's wrath.

Such preoccupation with things gloomy and occult is, of course, never simply an aesthetic predilection, never just the identification of threats, never merely a precaution; it is always also desire and fantasy at work. (In Puritan and early evangelical culture, these obsessions were interiorized, while in Hell Houses and the *Left Behind* novels, one finds few traces of the tortured conscience, of Martin Luther's *anfechtung*.) In the vividness of the imaginings of sin and in the regularity with which its critics returned to it, compulsion and attraction arose amid censorship and moral exhortation. It is with such fantasies—where longings are revealed in fears and horrors in lust—that American religions have wrestled internally. That the "Age of Reason" could yield such rich imaginings of the spectral and supernatural is no mere irony since, in Elisabeth Bronfen's apt phrasing, "the more forcibly superstition is banned to the realm of eternal night, the more persistently this repressed material returns in configurations of the uncanny."[44] In the religious imagination of the time, this supernatural doubleness or shadow side both confirmed the existence of holy power while also disrupting the social order.[45] There were violent eruptions in nature and culture alike, alarming occurrences whose signs and telltale features were documented in chapbooks, oratory, and journals, and which were occasions for naming and classifying evil so as to preserve order.

The language of evangelicalism in the early nineteenth century was a Gothic one, often overflowing with dreams and visions, spirits and magic.[46] Evangelicals were, even into the Second Great Awakening, a minority whose struggles for self-definition were coupled with struggles for legitimacy. They often alienated people with the intensity and the bodily nature of their devotions (which, at the epochal 1801 revival at Cane Ridge, Kentucky, even included some practitioners barking like dogs).[47] Yet they also, after leaving Cane Ridge's muddy fields or reflecting on the public humiliations of the "anxious bench," became known for the staunchness of their critiques of a world which seemed to them teeming with sin and demons. God's grace and the believer's joy in Christ were in some sense given clarity by a kind of social or psychological shroud that was never far away.

Even as their place in American religion grew less marginal, there persisted a sensibility tormented by the possibility that the slightest backslide or licentious thought could invoke divine wrath or alert a demon to the illicit desire that festered in the confessing heart. Yet the very presence of darkness confirmed the opportunity to do God's work. As with the Puritans, the stern warnings and cautionary tales saturating evangelical speech and writing also titillated, entertained, and provided a frisson of real fear: their goal was to arouse misgivings, self-doubt, and concerns that personal excess and passion could put one's soul at risk. Not all evangelicals situated themselves in such an overtly demonological cosmos: Francis Asbury, for example, had grave concerns about such supernaturalism.[48] But preoccupations with the demonological did not disappear; they only shifted in the evangelical imagination. As the United States became more urban, industrial, and pluralistic, conservatives managed and maintained the boundaries of their identities often with the rhetorical assistance of the languages of evil and hellfire, used to articulate a sense of perceived cultural collapse. Despite their demographic power, many clung nonetheless to a sense of embattlement in modern America, a trope which eternally recurs (as it does in contemporary evangelical culture and politics). Yet there is an irony here, for as conservative evangelicals shifted into a position of hitherto unknown political power and influence in the late twentieth century, many became preoccupied once more with a discourse of demonology. The resurgence of such criticism marks a concern about the stability of identity and social power and about the encroachment of evil—sexual, political, or ontological—that threatens to violate established boundaries.

THE DETAILS ARE IN THE DEVIL:
HORROR AND POLITICS

This brief historical tour was not meant to be exhaustive but simply to underscore how evangelicalism's construction of its Others has been shaped by sociopolitical necessity. More than a general perceptual awareness of Others, *alterity* refers to the cultural construction of a usually malevolent Other that takes place in particular cultures of meaning. These efforts are clearly at work in the religion of fear, whose specific strategies are driven by and responsive to a vibrant secular pop culture, especially the imagery and structure of genre horror. The languages and representations of fear—whether in the prophetic idiom or in the blood-red tones of slasher cinema—go to work when barbarians are at the gate, threatening to crash the boundaries of identity.

We have already seen how responses to such crises are occasions for self-definition, representational efforts that work by directing attention to objects, legitimate or not, and away from their own construction. Particularly instrumental are monster stories, bogeymen, and social interpretations of fright. There is nothing like a monster to set a culture on solid ground. The lore of cultures often recounts the defeat of monsters—whether primal ones like a demon or political ones like a tyrant—as a way of justifying the political history followed since the point of origin: "[a]fter their disappearance, human society, culture, and law begin."[49] By naming and narrating what is feared—whether indwelling presence or exterior threat—and squeezing it into conventional forms, narrators and audiences can participate in resolutions to the traumas thought to be born of this Other. These representations and narrations can achieve a clarity that is often seen as lacking in the messiness of everyday reality. There are obviously great distinctions between the "timeless" mythical material on which monster and terror lore is frequently based and the usually quite timely or topical discourses that saturate the culture and politics of fear. They are nonetheless linked: the common thread underlying ghost stories, lullabies, fairy tales, and monster movies is their propensity—whether they mean to soothe or alarm—to warn us of the consequences of bad behavior or bad beliefs. In representations of fear, hostile Others "play the part of disciplinarian alter egos."[50]

The primary strategy by which the religion of fear names its Others is through representations of demons or the Antichrist. As Bernard McGinn writes, the Antichrist is a "mirror for conceptions and fears about ultimate human evil."[51] In other words, representations of the Antichrist tell audiences a great deal about those crafting the representations; when seeking to understand a creator's cultural position, the details are in the devil. For conservatives specifically, Satan is as historically real as God is; both intervene concretely in worldly affairs, and both are associated with specific patterns of life and behavior. Thus, one's actions in the temporal realm associate one with—or tie one to—a specific realm of the afterlife and a particular set of eternal consequences.

The various conceptions of hell that populate monotheisms have a long history.[52] One finds them in scripture, of course, but most contemporary representations are indebted to the culture of medieval Europe, whose woodblock prints, paintings, and illustrated manuscripts are adorned with vivid, often highly sexualized, depictions of hell. Their pedagogic function was clearly linked to the demonstration of the horrific fates that awaited sinners and heretics. Yet the sins themselves were often lavishly detailed; the torments depicted nude bodies, gleeful violence, and representations of Satan with a vaginal entrance or a face on his groin, for example. As is well known, Dante Alighieri and John Milton established—with considerable help from the book of Daniel and the book of Revelation—some of the most vivid and enduring imagery of hell: Satan's throne and lair, lakes of fire, and the unending abyss.[53] These have over time become standard for mass representations of the fiery pits, most notably for those religious discourses which, like the religion of fear, aver the literal existence of that place of torments unceasing and seem to exult in detailed portraits thereof.

Conservative evangelicalism has often appropriated these grotesque, bloodsoaked, almost surrealist visions of hell, even if these do not speak for the tradition as a whole. American evangelicals have identified the Antichrist as, among others, a leader of the ecumenical movement, a Native American, Thomas Jefferson, Franklin Delano Roosevelt, a Jewish banker, a New Age practitioner, the pope, a freemason, a feminist, or an Arminianist. As Robert Fuller aptly reasons, "When a community . . . names the Antichrist, it reminds its members who they are and whom they must never allow themselves to become."[54] Flames leap forth and souls cry in agony when a jeremiad is necessary, where boundaries are at risk, and when internal tensions flare up. As a register of religious self-understanding, demonology and its hell are meant to soothe. But the very boundaries which devils and torments aim to mark off cannot contain the explosive creativity, doom-struck melancholy, and dark consciousness that also lurk in this tradition.

In American culture, these themes and images have frequently coalesced in an enduring commitment to the Gothic. Edmund Burke theorized that the sublime always had a dimension of terror to it since it exceeded our descriptive and analytical qualities, thus calling attention to our limits, including that final limit experience: death. Burke's sublime included all things dark and dangerous; its sinister, disturbing gravity was enough to give heft to the Gothic as a literary genre. In ever more intense, shocking, and visceral forms throughout the nineteenth century, the Gothic emerged from the Enlightenment's shadow as rationalism's repressed Other, combining overwrought sentimentality with rationalism and inexplicable frights with science. Setting and mood were the key ingredients to Gothic texts, and they have been appropriated by contemporary horror film and fiction: darkened moors, ruined abbeys, locked doors, ancient manuscripts or gloomy portraits, and forbidden desires given vent in the deep of night.[55] The Gothic's exploration of—and reveling in—the hidden side of "proper" society, the secret yearnings of men and women, the sexual longing and barely contained violence that lurks beneath social convention all have kept audiences on edge, in what Ingebretsen calls "a continuous oscillation between reassurance and threat."[56] This sensibility not only confirms specific anxieties and fears but also audiences' great interest in the ever more lurid depictions of sex and violence that serve to document this shadow side.[57] The Gothic, then, is the kind of "safe" exploration of—and indulgence in—social taboos that is so commonplace in contemporary horror and in the religion of fear. The scandalized reader (or viewer) is also titillated by these materials, as we see in the erotics of fear where every high school is a Columbine, every date a rape in waiting, and every weekend drive ends in a drunken wreck.

These characteristics are common to horror-driven entertainments, social strategies of identity construction, and religious representations of evil, all trained on the resolution of sociopolitical crises. But the religion of fear has expertly appropriated the tropes, images, and techniques of pulp horror (primarily its cinematic expression) in particular. In horror, America's Gothic preoccupation with haunting is transformed through a fixation on the figure of the monster, which can embody and constitute the racial, sexual, political, or religious Other.[58] When monsters are narrated as threatening the inviolable boundaries of identity and society, horror's formula succeeds by establishing, threatening, and reclaiming the purity of a community in a haze of blood and gore. Horror is therefore, as Ingebretsen suggests, a preservative and conservative genre: "it tells a story, explains that story, and draws moral conclusions, simultaneously."[59]

Horror's instant popularity at the dawn of the film age was due in no small part to its ability to serve as the screen on which social anxieties were projected. Its formulas and conventions promised that viewers too could triumph over their terrors, could safely repress once more what had returned unbidden in the night. Modern American life is indebted to horror's formulas too. Not only have they generated an iconography, they also show how deeply American culture is shaped in lurid spectacles or grotesqueries which seem to manifest as frequently as popping flashbulbs. Our fascination with monster movies and gore is simply one aspect of the deeper cultural well from which the religion of fear drinks. One need only leaf through an issue of *Fangoria*, bravely rent one of the many *Faces of Death* videos (compilations of footage of actual death scenes) in circulation, or spend time with video games like *Silent Hill* to appreciate this.

The continuum of freak shows and monster movies is in many ways a public spectacle of inversion, the scarred side of the coin or the mirror we convince ourselves shows another, not us. As Leslie Fiedler wrote, our culture "at times seems a chamber of horrors disguised as an amusement park 'fun house,' where we pay to play at terror and are confronted in the innermost chamber with a series of inter-reflecting mirrors which present us with a thousand versions of our own face."[60] Ironically, the prosperity of the 1950s fed the hunger for horror. After the genre's popularization in the 1930s and subsequent struggles with censorship, post–World War II America was hungry for blood and monsters. Fifties monsters—whether they rose from the deep or raged from a laboratory—often expressed social anxiety about the nuclear power which, in nearly all narratives, spawned them. Pulp magazines, movies, and comic books proved resilient as vehicles for the social transference of anxiety about race, the state, war, and other problems. The life of tranquility and abundance so regularly portrayed in 1950s entertainment was, when seen through the lens of horror and monster fantasy, if not an illusion then at least a site of social ambivalence: the two most enduring sources of terror in this period were radioactivity and "the visitor from beyond," both clear indices of Cold War anxiety.[61] No matter how well manicured the suburban community, how stable the political order, or how fixed the moral identity, these narratives seemed to suggest, something foul lurked below or within.

The religion of fear embodies this ambivalence and this horror-derived sensibility, but also appropriates the techniques and strategies of post-1960s horror which, beginning in the Vietnam era, began to explore both interiority and a kind of social realism (the zombies in George Romero's films were inspired by makeup artist Tom Savini's memories of the fields of dead in Vietnam).[62] Horror again became a vehicle for psychological transference, both therapy and abjection. Following this period, horror began to focus on serial killers, revenge fantasies, and sexual morality, themes of disorder and depravity to some extent reflected in the New Christian Right's ascendance during the same period. And recently, the idiom has become reenergized once more, continuing to explore not only social deviance and monstrous violence but devoting considerable energy to epidemics, terrorism, and environmental cataclysm.

This is a genre that promises what Marina Warner calls "the ambiguous satisfactions of scariness," pleasures manifestly at work in the religion of fear.[63] Just as surely as horror narratives are set in motion by the carnal id, so is the religion of fear given life by its desires. The creepy thrill of a Hell House or the lurid assertions of a Chick tract are not, according to most cultural scripts, supposed to provide pleasure (bodies wrecked and blood spilled should not provoke laughter). Yet they do so, not only insofar as pleasure or laughter are frequent responses to the shock of the horrific but also, importantly, because pleasure confirms that these horrible events are not happening *to us*, that they are make-believe.[64]

Thus, the compulsions, desires, and fascinations that these representations seek to displace inevitably return in vicarious experiences and representations which promise the erasure of these desires even as they deliver a surrogate thrill. These experiences seek to resolve social tension and deflect attention away from it. Death and sex and violations of social order are, when written into the fabric of horror's moralizing narratives, safe to explore and even experience vicariously. Desire is thus, even when expressed in a litany of repudiations, a central part of the religion of fear. Sin and seduction exert a kind of magnetic pull, continually orienting the reflections of creators and, it is hoped, audiences.

THE EVANGELICAL MEDIASCAPE

Finally, let me briefly discuss the means by which such tales of religio-political horror are spread. Clearly, this is done most effectively through popular entertainments. Evangelicalism's religious radar has often stayed locked on wayward youths, whose easy seduction and errant tendencies are believed to risk larger compromises with worldly and supernatural evil.[65] Nominally seeking only to dramatize the objects of its concern, the religion of fear's criticism also reveals the sweaty fascination with the "impure" at the heart of most censorship campaigns.[66] One of the most powerful means by which fear's claims are advanced is through tropes that posit children or adolescents as victims. The construction of such a moral panic reflects the cultural mood and anxiety of its architects, for whom moral topics like teen sexuality, drug use, and abortion are seen as evidence of evil's encroachment into everyday life. While the religion of fear demands that materials deemed too violent, sexual, or irreligious be kept away from young audiences, its creators understand that popular entertainments address a need felt by young consumers. Based on such recognition, contemporary evangelicals have, since the 1960s, developed a pop paraculture that allows adolescents to enjoy entertainments resembling those of "secular" culture while lacking any "harmful" influences. So even when evangelical discourse condemns popular culture—as in the Southern Baptist Convention's well-known denunciation of the Disney Corporation's "immoral ideologies such as homosexuality, infidelity, and adultery"— there has been a consistent engagement with the power of pop.[67]

While evangelical media and popular culture are neither intended as nor devoted to direct political advocacy, the success of criticism like the religion of fear has been aided significantly by the growth and influence of evangelical media, which can help to shape conservative political culture and reinforce its norms. Popular culture did not spring forth from evangelicalism fully formed in the contemporary period: dating back to the revivalist heyday, evangelicals have been keen to use dramatic or theatrical techniques, popular writing, mass communication, and other strategies to attract and maintain audiences.[68] But while these tactics have often caused concern to those practitioners wary of excessive engagement with the "fallen" culture, this propensity reveals evangelicalism's adaptive nature and its continual wrestling with the society it seeks to transform.

This does not signal a conflict between worldliness and separatism so much as it represents different styles of worldliness. Emerging initially from print and radio cultures, evangelical pop constitutes an important part of the American religious landscape, one which is ever more central to the development of young evangelicals' self-understandings.[69] Although the blurring of the boundary between righteous community and fallen world remains problematic for some evangelicals, the producers of popular entertainments mostly (if begrudgingly) embrace the tools of culture in order to combat the taints of culture. As Hendershot writes, "[C]onsumers use Christian media not as tools of salvation but as safeguards against secular contamination."[70] As any observer of American Christianity knows, these media can be very far ranging and creative, including not just film and music but creations as far-flung as Christian skate parks, Christian versions of YouTube (Godtube.com), and, in at least one community of which I know, a Christian appropriation (called *Goof Troop*) of the MTV show *Jackass*.[71] This evangelical marketplace has expanded exponentially since the 1970s, when the conservative engagement with popular culture was enhanced by a political sensibility that emerged from the NCR and also was abetted by the considerable disposable income possessed by middle-class evangelicals.[72]

In the context of a highly developed media culture—including over 200 Christian TV stations, 1,500 Christian radio stations, and a vast print media and Web network—the religion of fear has gained an audience. These media do not, of course, overlap everywhere with the more ideologically driven voices, but they do so with some regularity; and, importantly, they provide arenas in which these voices may be heard and distribution channels through which they may be disseminated.[73] They help to constitute for consumers what Pierre Bourdieu referred to as a habitus: a "system of structured, structuring dispositions...which is constituted in practice and is always oriented towards practical functions."[74] These dispositions are registered not only in people's patterns of consumption—the way they participate in a symbolic as well as a material economy—but also, according to Bourdieu, in their modes of perception, classification, and distinction.[75] Perhaps such processes are especially powerful in the United States since, as Wade Clark Roof writes, "beginning with the post–World War II United States, personal identities came to be linked more to lifestyle and consumption" than with traditional forms of affiliation.[76] It is through these activities that popular media and entertainments, which are both rooted in and reflect everyday existence, are made meaningful. They situate agents in what Bourdieu referred to as a "field of power," both in terms of a hierarchy of subject positions and in terms of control over discourses or representations.

Prior to the work of Raymond Williams, Stuart Hall, and the Birmingham school of cultural studies, it was long customary to denounce not only the "low" creations of popular culture but their cultural and political effects as well: Henri Lefebvre described the cultural impoverishments that accompanied the consumer revolution; and Frankfurt school theorists, particularly Theodor Adorno, decried the banality and apolitical tendencies of the "culture industry." Other theorists link such creations to rootlessness: Guy Debord, responding to the epistemic and ontological shifts accompanying mass media saturation, described the hypertrophy of the visual; while Jean Baudrillard went further than Debord in suggesting that nothing is left of sense and significance beyond pure simulation.[77] Yet religions are not simply subsumed in the marketplace but can be partly constituted through consumption and exchange; the resulting forms need not be discounted as mere epiphenomena of economic power. Indeed, the fields of social interaction in which religions participate are increasingly defined by exchanges of production and consumption, in face-to-face interactions as well as in the faceless ones of cyberspace.[78]

Though religions exercise their creativity and agency within often constraining conditions, this does not entail that agents' intentionality is compromised or illegitimate. Cultures, and their various configurations of power, are always unsettled and polysemic. Religions use popular entertainments to evangelize, insofar as media generate broad audiences and provide easily accessible worldviews; these entertainments draw upon the shared habits of perception available in culture and contribute to those habits. American religion thrives in this mediascape,[79] "where it can respond in innovative ways to changing social realities and to people's own recognized, but changing, needs and preferences."[80] Popular entertainments contain multiple meanings and yield divergent interpretations, depending on which audiences are involved in appropriating them. Rather than being faced with totalism, consumers of these entertainments employ "the willful, creative twisting of language to suit the needs of the situation."[81]

Interestingly, the religion of fear manifests this creativity precisely in rejecting mainstream popular culture in favor of its own creations. Where cultural studies scholars like Stuart Hall and John Fiske rightly call attention to the indeterminacy of media entertainments, they often conclude from this that popular culture therefore possesses a "liberatory" potential insofar as audiences can interpret pop in ways unintended by producers.[82] The religion of fear does not seek "subversive" or "counterhegemonic" readings of mainstream pop so much as it advocates a rejection of conventional narratives in favor of its own creations; its representations may be experienced as liberatory, but only in the sense that they clearly distinguish orthodox from fallen.

The religion of fear's representations are effective to the extent that they insist on their own singularity of meaning: they help to establish and negotiate social and perceptual space, both through their emotional valences and in their capacity to aid in the symbolic resolution of sociopolitical conflicts. These materials entertain, they teach a specific religiosity, and they reinforce identification with conservatism. The simultaneous fascination with and revulsion of what is fearful defines this culture, as does its incessant need to display what is feared. The very scenes of horror are, in Clark's words, "marshaled for the purposes of encouraging moral fortitude among the faithful."[83] This tradition runs deep in American evangelicalism, but the psychosocial and political dynamics of this process are assuming provocative forms in the two instabilities.

The religion of fear is squarely within the long tradition of evangelical darkness, a tradition which radiates with Gothic intensity and speaks a language of doom. Yet it is just as clearly born of the period when evangelicalism embraced the bright optimism of American religio-cultural stability. Deeply concerned about what it sees as the fearful effects that modern society has on children in particular, the religion of fear acts on this concern by seeking purposefully to terrify. The result is often dazzlingly energetic and creative, a suspension of the taken-for-granted in moments when—as pages turn, as oratory and music are heard, as frights leap from shadows—mundane reality seems suspended. Yet its very spectacular qualities facilitate a return to conventional life, a reestablishment of boundaries, and a vigorous assertion of order.

The frights are not propagandistic, but they are politically coded. While they may not be designed to generate political ideologies or programs directly, they are created out of sociopolitical concern and they underwrite antiliberal politics. And while they do not speak for all evangelicals or even all conservatives, their voices resound loudly. Chick's cartoons, anti-rock/rap censorship, Hell Houses, and the *Left Behind* novels assume that their audiences consist of both the unconverted and the saved. Yet none of these creations takes a "mustard seed approach," waiting patiently for faith to blossom. They are proudly direct and confrontational, seeking to alarm in God's name. They are horror tales, and they capture the complicated experience of a culture which feels politically and religiously embattled. Through blood, shock, death, and destruction, the religion of fear ushers into being a world whose very terrors announce its redemption.

3

"Jesus Was Not a Weak Fairy"

Chick Tracts and the Visual Culture of Evangelical Fear

Even though the Antichrist's tyranny and deceit are to be feared, the prospect of his imminent appearance is also a source of hope and even jubilation. —Robert Fuller, *Naming the Antichrist*

Jesus Christ can be your most loving friend . . . or the most frightening enemy in the universe. —Jack Chick

At first glance, the small pamphlets are relatively unassuming.[1] Approximately three inches by five inches in dimension, roughly the size of a note of currency or an old flip-book, they comprise about twenty small pages of black and white cartooning in a fairly antiquated graphic style. These tiny comics can be found in almost any imaginable public space: on college campuses, at nightclubs, draped atop street signs, under windshield wipers, deep in subway stations, on laundromat dryers, and at rest areas, placed atop men's room urinals. The illustrated tracts are populated with sinners and the pious, with Jesus and Satan, and with exclamatory denunciations of a vast catalog of wrongdoings. In their succinct and inflexible narrative form, they suggest that seemingly innocuous life choices (presumably those faced by a reasonable cross-section of the people passing through these public places) can have eternal, usually infernal, consequences. Taken as a whole, the tracts yield a vision of America in religious, cultural, and political decline. They insist, in the face of this morass, that not only must one bow before the correct deity, one must fraternize with the right people, listen to the right music, and avoid certain habits of thought and practice in order to avoid the fiery depths. The casual reader is meant to see that the illustrated characters—all of whom do things we have done, or could see ourselves doing—are beset by demons, cast out of heaven, and filled with unending anguish. For over forty years, Californian Jack Chick has produced these works, which are as popular and widely known as they are scorned. We encounter them as subculture, and indeed Chick's work was begun at the margins of American religion. Somehow, though, he has become an indelible presence over the decades. Like a substratum of soil, Chick's themes and concerns emerged early in the religion of fear's development, nourishing and enriching it.

VISUALIZING DAMNATION AND REDEMPTION

Public, visual religious interventions in the United States are common, however urgently they present themselves. Yet some specific images precipitated my thinking about the visual culture of evangelical fear. During a period when I spent considerable time driving long distances, I began to notice a proliferation of billboard messages produced by the organization Godspeaks.[2] These billboards were all black, and each featured a different text in bold white letters. They were "quotes," ascribed to God (clearly a specifically Christian deity, though the hope was presumably that the messages would resonate with drivers from many traditions) and apparently aimed at an audience of people who, from what the messages suggested, possess an identifiable group of problems and anxieties. What seemed most significant was the fact that they were often issued as warnings, some of them quite fearful. Situated at particularly well-traveled spots on major interstates and in cities (I first saw them in North Carolina between Chapel Hill and Winston-Salem on I-40 West), many were couched in a folksy, comforting idiom: "I love you and you and you and you and...," "Turn life's cares into prayers," or "God answers knee-mail." Others were focused specifically on aspects of car travel: "My way *is* the highway," "Need directions?" or the somewhat darker "Will the road you're on get you to my place?" and "Keep using my name in vain, I'll make rush hour longer." The most memorable, however, were those that were overtly threatening: "You think it's hot here?" "God grades on the cross, not the curve," "Don't put a question mark where God put a period," "Have you read my #1 best seller? There will be a test," and the widely known "Don't make me come down there." More recently, a new wave of billboards contains more overtly political messages, such as "One nation under me" and "The real Supreme Court meets up here."

Expressed in a familiar, even casual tone, the warnings seem to reveal much about those subjects and anxieties which can lead practitioners to embrace a discourse of fear (particularly those willing to link it to terrorism and national tragedy, as Godspeaks does in other literature). Vehicles are, after all, spaces of solitude nestled into large, moving crowds of metal; they are also, increasingly, spaces of rage. I had begun work on this book and began to think seriously about graphic representations of fear such as these. In this context, the importance of Chick's tracts seemed undeniable. I had known of Chick tracts for decades, having stumbled on them throughout my travels in the United States in addition to encountering them in the world of comic fandom.[3]

As I began the research for this book, I was given a tract called "Eat, Drink, and Be Merry" from Tract Ministries of Canton, Ohio. This piece was something of a Chick spin-off (of which there are many, including parodies), sharing with Chick's little jeremiads a declamatory social criticism and a fright-filled cosmology couched in comic art. This holiday-oriented tract was framed by a crude portrait of an innocent reveler (iconically represented with a sequined mask and jester's hat) unaware of the robed specter of death hovering just behind him. Inside, merry making was described as risky and, in a Gothic update of the temperance impulse, the tract specifically condemned the way Americans are drawn—like moths to a flame—to the local watering hole or liquor store. Little did the cartoon partiers in this tract know, however, that each belly-up to the bar could be their last before their judgment. Would the besotted be ready, or would they, in apparently the only other option, be met with flames and the lake of fire? The text inscribes the uncertainty of life in the starkest and most fearful of terms:

> For some people, the pleasures and tragedy from the night before will burn like a hot iron in their memory. Maybe it will be the twisting steel and flying glass of a car wreck. Maybe the sound of a shot from a gun echoing in the night that stilled a life. Yes, life is uncertain, death is sure, sin is the cause, Christ is the cure.

Clearly, such messages aim first to reorient viewers' perceptions and, second, to establish a sense of urgency within a framework that is both colloquial and emotionally vivid. Such instantiations have a long history in American public culture, one that encompasses far more than "Scary Jesus" and Jack Chick. Indeed, in recent years, conservative Christian cartoons have become more commonplace. The Web site www.raptureready.com—the butt of many a liberal blogger's snarky joke—features dozens of political cartoons, while the indefatigable Hal Lindsey has recently sponsored the creation of Oracle cartoons at www.oneimage.org. An additional improvisation on the style has recently been generated by the organization the Truth for Youth, which has produced (by late 2007) ten manga-influenced comics on "hot" topics, including Internet porn, homosexuality, rock music, evolution, safe sex, abortion, school violence, peer pressure, drunkenness, and drugs.[4] Cultural theorists have often explored the predominance of the image in late capitalism, yet have rarely acknowledged how American Christians have regularly engaged their culture by using the pictorial register as well as the textual.[5] In addition to religious paintings, decorative art in homes, Bible illustrations, and so forth, the tradition of pamphleteering—of which Chick can reasonably be seen as a part—is a well-established one in Christian history.[6] In the 1600s and 1700s, pamphlets were widely used in Europe and in the American colonies; as movable type became commonplace, this technology was eagerly appropriated for purposes of proselytization.[7] These traditions of evangelization often incorporated emotional strategies lifted from genre writing and art, generating vivid grotesqueries meant to dramatize the condition of damnation. Tracts and pamphlet literature have often been well suited to these tasks and continue to this day, from the local to the international level.

In addition to the oft-cited doom-struck poetry of Puritans such as Michael Wigglesworth, an underrecognized figure in the deep history of American religious fear regimes is Mason Locke Weems. An Episcopalian known mostly for his fabrication of the story of George Washington chopping down the cherry tree, Weems was also the author of multiple religious tracts which included gruesome graphic portrayals of the fates awaiting sinners. In "The Drunkard's Looking Glass" (1812), for example, Weems showed a besotted horseback rider's accident, which left the man with one of his eyes "cleanly knocked out of its socket; and, held only by a string of skin, there it lay naked on his bloody cheek."[8] Many of Weems's other writings—such as "The Devil in Petticoats" (1810) and "God's Revenge against Murder" (1820)—feature portraits of the sinning body's destruction, "with engravings of shattered skulls and strangled corpses, their tongues bulging."[9] Weems's work can be seen as part of the broader tradition of American Christian tract literature, which was advanced and institutionalized with the 1825 founding of the American Tract Society (an organization that was highly influential in the temperance move-ment, among other reformist impulses). As R. Laurence Moore explains, the development of religious moralistic literature between the nineteenth and twentieth centuries necessitated—much against the initial wishes of many authors—the embrace of not only modern marketing and entertainment techniques but also what Moore calls "moral sensationalism" or "moral pornography."[10] This culture is still a vital one in American Christianity and extends to hundreds of tract organizations throughout the United States.

With the development of mass entertainments over the last century, par-ticularly during the period since the late 1940s, visual culture in the United States has—from the dawn of television to the limitless depths of cyberspace—become increasingly dense and rapid in its circulation, as well as compre-hensive in its presence.[11] From the inescapability of public advertisements to the ubiquity of portable devices like the iPhone, it appears that no dimension of daily life escapes the dominance of the image. American religions have naturally been participants in these complicated processes, and the visual registers of religious sensibility and practice have expanded and transformed too.[12] Visual expressions of religion are quite widespread and can include visual media (film, television, and cyberspace), material objects or spaces (sculpture, architecture, shrines), public religious displays (from public rituals to specifically religious modes of comportment to the recognizable trios of Bernard Coffindaffer's crosses), and graphic art (such as illustrated Bibles, graffiti, the increasingly elaborate conflicts emblazoned on bumper stickers and fixtures, and Chick tracts). Within this range of expressions, the image can be a powerful vehicle for or component of religious pedagogy. As David Morgan writes, "[T]he act of looking itself contributes to religious formation and, indeed, constitutes a powerful practice of belief."[13] Images can help to concretize ways of viewing the world; they may serve as the objects of ritual, the media of religious feeling, vehicles through which different religious spaces or times are connected, or reminders of the shapes and boundaries of various spheres of human existence, from the intimate to the societal.

In accomplishing these functions, images and representations of religion can—even when not assembled into a narrative form—address social concerns and crises as well. Clearly, religious imagery and representation are not alone in their ability to serve such functions, but they are frequently understood to have significance or meaning beyond those of nonreligious art. Morgan suggests that art's engagement with social concerns is best accomplished when images are "submerged and naturalized."[14] Yet this seems to assume that imagistic pedagogy works best when social and political "information" is concealed. Such functions, in fact, vary from period to period and work to work, depending largely on the aims of the artist. Consider, by way of a very brief example, the difference between Victorian paintings such as William Powell Frith's *The Railroad Station* (wherein the class system is normalized and naturalized, given tacit endorsement by the artist) and 1930s social realist paintings like Philip Evergood's *The Strike* (which is aggressively open in its political commentary).[15] Further, even in representational art which, like cartooning, calls attention to its own form and avoids naturalism, such functions can be approximated through the adoption of narrative. Cartoons are meant to be disseminated and consumed as entertainments; this does not exclude their capacity to function as representations or interpretations of the real, but simply distinguishes cartooning from, say, iconography or realist painting. Cartoon art is linear and narrative in a way that suggests it can be particularly well suited to not only entertainment but to crafting representational frames for understanding the self and its social-cultural milieu.[16] Mass-produced, readily accessible creations like Chick tracts can contribute readily to these projects: indeed, despite those who would dismiss his work on the basis of its apparent aesthetic value, Chick's tracts have for decades been widely disseminated and highly influential in evangelical cultures, even if his perspective is not wholly normative.

"THIS WAS YOUR LIFE!"

Jack T. Chick himself is as reclusive as his tracts are ubiquitous in evangelical cultures.[17] Other than a series of cursory remarks given to his local paper in 1997, and secondhand accounts filtered into various publications, Chick's last recorded interview occurred in 1975. My repeated attempts to contact

Mr. Chick all met with failure, though his staff was quite friendly and informative. I was, however, fortunate enough to speak with people who have met him on multiple occasions. Further, after many months of what I thought were promising exchanges with his representative, Chick refused to grant permission for his cartoons to be reproduced in my book. I received a cordial letter stating, "For many years, his policy has been to never allow his drawings to be used as a part of someone else's publish [sic] work. He has made only one exception to this in all of his years of publishing. . . . He will not do it again." I encourage readers to consult the various Web sites I list in order to view the material.

A lifelong Californian, Chick was born April 13, 1924, in Boyle Heights, California.[18] A sickly child, Chick was nonetheless active in his Alhambra high school's extracurricular life. He came of age during the 1930s and 1940s, the so-called golden age of comics. Initially captivated by standard images of airplanes, soldiers, and men in tights, Chick is remembered as having been so obsessed with sketching that he failed the first grade. He subsequently became preoccupied with theater, joining his school's drama club and eventually pursuing this interest courtesy of a two-year scholarship to the Pasadena Playhouse School of Theater. After a stint in the Pacific during World War Two (where Chick was one of the only survivors of the horrific battle at Okinawa), Chick returned to the Pasadena Playhouse and there began cartooning regularly.[19] It was also at the playhouse where Chick met his first wife, Lola Lynn. He recalls being exposed to the gospel courtesy of his in-laws (Lynn's family were fundamentalists by most accounts) and, while on his honeymoon, by the Reverend Charles Fuller's *Old-Fashioned Revival Hour*.[20] Chick was for a time an independent Baptist, and for a long time he attended a church pastored by Roland Rasmussen. According to some accounts, Chick ultimately had a falling out with the church based not only on the messages articulated in services. According to the Reverend Richard Lee—a longtime acquaintance of Chick's and an Assemblies of God preacher who uses Chick tracts in his ministry—Chick disliked "the power they had, backed up by institutional authority." For decades, Chick has declined to profess allegiance to any one denomination because he "doesn't want to be under the control of anybody."[21]

Beginning in the late 1940s, southern California enjoyed an economic boom that included considerable investment in the aerospace industry. Chick took a job as a technical illustrator at El Monte, California's AstroScience Corporation. During this period, Chick read Charles Finney's *Power from On High* and "became convinced that the evangelical church needed to be shaken out of its complacency."[22] During this period, Chick listened to Bob Hammond's missionary radio show *The Voice of China and Asia* and was fascinated to learn how Maoists "came up with the idea of using comic books as Communist propaganda."[23] Chick became consumed by this idea, seeing in it a perfect strategy to use, inverted, for anticommunist and pro-Christian purposes.[24] At night, he began work in his kitchen on what would become the first Chick tracts. His supervisor George Otis encouraged him to pursue his cartooning and even made several loans to Chick (along with the $800 credit union loan that Chick recalls as being hugely instrumental in his "origin story").

The Chicks transformed their kitchen into a production company, and eventually Chick's first cartoon ("Why No Revival?") was published in 1961, followed quickly by the first proper tract, "This Was Your Life!" in 1964. Once described as "a masterpiece of shorthand horror," this tract established a narrative and stylistic template that has remained largely unchanged.[25] Chick's art is unashamedly cartoony: the spare, black-and-white layouts and stock composition resemble Saturday morning cartoon animation more than the detailed rendering one often finds in mainstream comics. In Chick's cramped panels, wide-eyed and wide-mouthed characters interact heatedly with their faces contorted and bodies elongated or abstracted in what might almost be an Archie Comics knockoff. Yet the grim backgrounds and dark tableaux of sin and depravity clearly evince a style much closer to the shocking gore found in Al Feldstein's and William Gaines's EC Comics of the 1950s (the "haw haw haw" laughter that Chick uses is, as Richard Lee pointed out to me, also derived from EC).[26] Sinners are depicted vigorously, energetically, and at great length: they have personalities and foibles, in contrast with the flat piety of the saved; they sweat, carouse, swill liquor, flout convention, and brim with lust. In so many Chick works, and as is common in the religion of fear, the sinful acts that constitute a wasted life are documented in vivid detail as they lead to the inevitable discovery of salvation (or the consequences facing the unsaved).

Chick's sensibilities coalesced during a period when many evangelicals sought to move closer to the cultural mainstream. The "new evangelicalism" of the post–World War Two period prized its distinction from "secular culture" but moved comfortably therein. Chick, however, clung vigorously to a combative idiom as a way of marking his distance from a culture he found increasingly alien. Though not affiliated with Carl McIntire's American Council of Christian Churches nor Billy James Hargis's Christian Crusade, Chick's evangelism shared with those organizations a militancy and an oppositional sensibility. This was a transitional period for Chick, when he saw a golden age of American cultural and political power—which dovetailed with righteousness and rectitude in his eyes—begin to erode from within.

Chick formally incorporated Chick Publications in 1965 in Chino, California (the distribution is handled from a warehouse in Rancho Cucamonga, a town which was once—in another of the strange connections one finds in American subcultures—home to Frank Zappa). Using bold text and screaming capital letters to keep characters on message, Chick has focused his social criticism on "youth at risk." From the outset, he has doggedly pursued his documentation of a once-stable Christian America under attack and in decline. Beginning in the 1960s, it "looked to him that the world was going to fall apart . . . chaos, out of control."[27] Distancing himself explicitly from those who would respond to such trends by working within and accommodating to mainstream culture, Chick has avidly scanned the cultural landscape and rendered his findings in the form of panic frames describing various cultural trends as traps to lure unsuspecting youths from lives of secure piety into the hazards of fallen secular culture.[28]

The religiosity expressed in these tracts is squarely in the traditions of muscular Christianity ("Jesus is not a weak fairy," according to Chick) and combative evangelicalism, which seek to wrestle publicly with sin.[29] Indeed, according to Dwayne Walker (probably the last person to interview Chick), a sign on Chick's office door reads "The War Room."[30] Chick's worldview is also highly conspiratorial (Dan Raeburn calls him "the Thomas Pynchon of fundamentalists").[31] Secret plots unfold everywhere; backstage machinations are revealed behind every worldly institution; evil and sin abound. And despite the comforting familiarity of the cartoon tropes found in these tiny works, they can be genuinely frightening. Daniel Clowes, a renowned indie comic artist, claimed that in college he devoured eighty Chick tracts in a single setting. He confesses, "By the end of the night I was convinced I was going to hell. I had never been so terrified by a comic book."[32] Such recollections are quite common: one young fan admitted that he "still has nightmares featuring specific Jack Chick tract characters and plots" while another recalls, "when I was young . . . we all use[d] to freak out at the Jack Chick tract that showed people wearing the 666 on their foreheads."[33] Despite the seemingly narrow and unmarketable idiom of the tracts, Chick claims to have sold over 500 million of them collectively.[34] While his work has been banned in some countries (including Canada), Chick and his followers have used both conventional and unconventional methods to ensure the tracts' distribution.[35] While they are disseminated through channels that are customary for evangelical literature— they are distributed by tract leagues around the country, used in church services and Sunday schools, distributed by the box to missionaries, and placed in libraries and bookstores—they have also been left on movie theater seats, dropped from planes, and stuffed into bottles to drift across the seas, for example.[36]

Far more elaborate than the well-known tracts are Chick's full-scale comics, *The Crusaders* (begun in 1974 and illustrated by Fred Carter, an African American from Illinois whose artwork was uncredited until well into the 1980s, as Carter apparently believed that God deserved sole credit).[37] With much more detailed and stylized artwork and lengthier narratives, this series afforded Chick the opportunity to explore in detail ritual murders, plotting witches, the seduction of "cults," and the evils of rock music, among many other topics. Ito remarks that not only do *Crusaders* books provide details of sins innumerable, but "the books' sexual overtones—as well as scantily clad biblical sirens like Eve, Delilah, and Semiramis—have led critics to describe Carter's work as 'spiritual porn.' "[38] The Crusaders are Chick's version of a superhero team: ex–Green Beret Timothy Emerson Clark and his African American partner James Carter, a reformed drug dealer whose street smarts are now used in the Lord's service.

In *The Crusaders*, Chick first introduced his readers to Alberto Rivera, a purported former Jesuit who "revealed" to Chick "proofs" of the many allegations about Roman Catholicism that Chick has made over the years, ranging from suspicions that the Vatican is hatching plans for global supremacy to assertions that Catholics were involved in both the Holocaust and Jonestown (in "Double Cross," Chick described Jim Jones as "a powerful warlock and a well-trained Jesuit"). Ito also claims that, under the influence of Rivera, Chick actually quit the Christian Booksellers Association in 1981 because he believed the organization had been infiltrated by Catholics. In fact, the organization had begun debating the merits of Chick's claims about Catholicism. Mark Noll writes, "Protestants from very many backgrounds joined Catholic spokesmen in denouncing the books; the Christian Booksellers Association . . . expressed its regret over the publications; and evangelical journalists contributed much of the hard information that exposed the comic books as fraudulent."[39] While the final Rivera book was published in 1988, and Rivera himself died in 1997, this facet of Chick's work has continued to provoke controversy. This is no anomaly, for Chick has often been linked to, or declared his admiration for, controversial figures. He supported a minister named Tony Alamo in 1984, even though the latter had been accused of child abuse, tax evasion, and stealing his late wife's corpse. Many of Chick's antiwitchcraft comics are based on the allegations of Johnny Todd, a self-proclaimed "former Grand Druid" whose "insider knowledge" led him to avow that Satanists in America routinely sacrificed humans in their rituals.[40] More recently, Chick has consulted Rebecca Brown (a physician who claims that her hospital was once commandeered by witches) and Daniel Yoder (who alleges the existence of a rabbinical cabal with global financial ambitions).[41]

Chick's wife, Lola, died in 1998 and his daughter in 2001. The cartoonist now lives in Glendora, California, and has remarried (to a much younger Asian-American woman). As of 2002, Chick Publications—"sandwiched between a hardware shop and a carpet store," according to Ito—employed thirty-five people and made somewhere in the neighborhood of $3 million annually (primarily through sales to churches and youth groups). Though in relatively ill health of late, the elderly Chick is seemingly impervious to the criticism his works have generated and apparently prefers to live in seclusion as much as possible. His assistant Karen Rockney claims, "There are many people who wish him harm," and even the offices of Chick Publications reflect a paranoid sensibility (with large signs reading "Please Do Not Enter Unless Invited").[42] Still producing tracts regularly, Chick also sponsors newsletters on current events and books written by sympathizers; in 2003, he completed his film *The Light of the World* (which conveys Chick's reading of the Bible by slow-photographing over 250 oil paintings mostly crafted by Carter).[43]

On the most general level, Chick spends a considerable portion of his energies documenting the handiwork of Satan, seeing his infernal handiwork in every salacious lyric, fornicating movie, pornographic Web site, or, most of all, false faith.[44] Indeed, Chick once declared that "[w]e can pretty well tell how effective a new tract will be by the intensity of spiritual warfare that we go through while making it."[45] He has often recounted the various difficulties suffered in producing his tracts, seeing the devil's handiwork in every bump in the road (Chick attributed a stroke he suffered upon completing "Where's Rabbi Waxman?" to Satan).[46] More specifically, however, his art reveals a fascination with—and horror in the face of—competing religions, which he heatedly, and repeatedly, denounces. Chick once despaired, "I have a large map on the wall at home, and sometimes I feel so heavy-hearted at the mul-titudes who will pour into the lake of fire from Africa, India, Southeast Asia, China, Russia, etc."[47] In this area, too, Chick has gathered around him several closely trusted "experts" upon whom he relies for his information on "cults" and "false religions." These figures—Bill Schnoebelen and the aforementioned Rivera and Todd—have assisted Chick in projecting an authoritative denun-ciation of non-evangelical traditions. Chick has also regularly consulted "cult-busting" organizations, such as the Watchman's Ministry and the Institute of Contemporary Christianity. And Chick's works have on occasion been cited as a resource by other evangelical media outlets. Additionally, Chick has often cited "canonical" texts such as Hal Lindsey's *The Late Great Planet Earth*, as well as various creationist textbooks (many sponsored by the Institute for Creation Research, co-founded by Henry Morris and Tim LaHaye). As one sees throughout the religion of fear, Chick and his colleagues have an intimate relationship—via avid study and precise observation—with precisely those things they find most objectionable.[48]

Of great importance is Chick's newsletter *Battle Cry*. Here, in rapidly published salvos from the trenches of the "culture wars," Chick's worldview and his reactions to contemporary events (and his critics) are readily avail-able.[49] The sense of embattlement is palpable, as Chick is convinced not only that American culture is a battlefield between the devout and the demonic; he has also long contended (as is now commonplace in the religion of fear and in the broader culture of American political religions) that Christians are victims of outright bigotry and hostility. Decades before it became commonplace to hear dispatches from the "war on Christmas" or the "judicial war on faith," Chick's newsletter articulated such a siege mentality in a slightly more topical format than in his tracts. Yet for all the steady growth and visibility of Chick Productions, for every book, newsletter, and video released, every salacious detail harvested from a decadent culture, it is the simple cartoon tract which has endured as Chick's most powerful medium of communication. What is it about this genre that generates such powerful reactions?

THE SEDUCTION OF THE INNOCENT

The explosion of cultural studies in recent decades has led to a renewed academic interest in popular culture, including musical subcultures, genre fiction and movies, fashion, and sports, among other topics. Comparatively little attention, however, has been paid to pulp art, comic books, and graphic novels.[50] Yet these creations are suggestive in their capacity to reveal important features of social history and of the norms and anxieties circulating outside of their panels and pages. Below, I provide a brief account of the genre's history, so that unfamiliar readers might get a better sense of the creative context of Chick's works and the dynamics which make them effective.

From their inception in what were once quaintly known as the newspaper "funny pages," comics or sequential art have been as maligned as they have been popular. Though most readers might understandably associate the genre with its iconic superheroes, comic strips and books were seemingly tailor-made for the exploration not just of muscle-bound heroism but of subcultures, satires, and fantasies both morbid and sexual. Before the birth of the modern comic book in the late 1930s, some of the earliest cartoon art consisted of political satire of the sort produced by Honoré Daumier in the nineteenth century. By the 1890s, early serials—like *The Katzenjammer Kids, The Yellow Kid, Little Nemo,* and *Mutt and Jeff*—began to appear in major newspapers and were often collected in pulp magazines. The ribald humor, seedy street life, and mischievous antics often depicted were associated frequently with the instability of the new urban, immigrant, industrial America, all realities enjoyed by these comics' readership, assuming they were kept at a safe distance (as they were in the comics medium).[51]

The later mainstreaming of comics paralleled the degree to which the medium became more "wholesome" and closer to the self-understandings of post-Depression Americans. The first feature-length comics were instrumental in this transition, and their costume-clad superheroes often embodied the collective aspirations of both readers and creators. The publication of *Action Comics,* with its flagship character, Superman, was clearly the single largest factor in popularizing DC Comics. Much has been made of the fact that Superman's creators, Jerry Seigel and Joe Shuster, were second-generation American Jews whose heroic imaginations explored both their own outsider status (Kal-El was an alien after all) and the American dream.[52] The DC roster—including Wonder Woman, the Flash, Green Lantern, and Captain Marvel, among others—ranged from masculinist fantasy to pro-war propaganda to what Bradford Wright calls "a passionate celebration of the common man" engaged in "[m]orality tales attacking the evil of greed."[53] Others, like Batman, represented a darker and more vengeful take on these same source materials, one in which childhood trauma was linked to the obsessive pursuit of justice. There was, then, a rich psychosocial vein in the genre from its earliest phase.

It was with the advent of the Timely/Marvel group that vigorously pro-war propaganda comics became popular (notably in *All-Star Comics*, which regularly featured Captain America battling Nazis and "Nips"). World War Two comics proudly backed the war, never questioning the rectitude of the federal government; if governmental injustice existed, it was seen as the result of local thugs and corrupt officials perverting basically sound ideals and procedures.[54] Also unquestioned was the use of racial stereotyping in the comics, evident not only in the malicious anti-Asian caricatures found in the pro-war comics but also located in the genre more widely as, well into the 1950s, one frequently encountered superheroes (even Sheena the [Caucasian] Jungle Queen) putting down a "Zulu rebellion" or "Arab uprising."[55] One sees here the way in which comics—like film or music, for example—use certain representational types to construct a social symbology for readers.[56]

Concerns about moral purity have accompanied the genre's development and often crept into the stories themselves. The genre came under scrutiny, and later outright attack, when its explorations of fantasy and adventure were deemed too racy for susceptible young readers. Even as well-groomed superheroes were upholding a postwar vision of prosperity, education, and order, into this vision crept concerns about atomic power and communism and about seditious threats to a stable society. Following World War Two, American home structures changed and children spent more time with each other, a trend which facilitated youth marketing. As youth culture became more profitable, and comics more prominent, criticism of the genre bloomed. For example, Sterling North, writing in the *Chicago Daily News*, called comics a "national disgrace," which traded in "mayhem, murder, torture, and abduction...voluptuous females in scanty attire...a strain on young eyes and young nervous systems," all claims which would be routinely invoked in the future.[57] The "juvenile delinquent" became a fixture in public criticism, depicted as an otherwise well-meaning American youth who, seduced by the lures of pop, did wrong things.

Publishers reacted to the growing outcry by creating editorial boards to ensure that their books—now extending to romance comics and diversions like teenaged gadfly Archie and Casper the Friendly Ghost—were "wholesome." The more pronounced these efforts became, the more comics seemed preoccupied with increasingly detailed explorations of the very threats and wrongdoings under apparent scrutiny. In the context of well-meaning titles like *Crime Doesn't Pay*, one might encounter vivid renderings of sadism, knife fights, and bondage, for example. There was a growing sentiment after World War II, which in many ways presaged contemporary arguments about violence in television and video games, that comics either produced violent impulses in children or heightened extant propensities to act out violently. As Wright documents, in September 1947, a Pittsburgh jury blamed the influence of comics when a boy hanged himself; in May 1948, two Oklahoma boys stole a plane and flew it for 120 miles (they claimed to have learned how by reading comics); and in August 1948, three Indiana youths strung up another child and tortured him with matches.[58] While many acknowledged the patriotic virtue of Superman and his ilk, there were growing concerns about crime comics, monster comics, and especially the fantastically gory titles from the notorious publisher EC Comics.

Into this collective panic dropped Dr. Fredric Wertham's *Seduction of the Innocent*, a scathing condemnation of comic books that was central to later congressional hearings scrutinizing the genre. Wertham objected to comics on nearly every level: for their ideological implications (in his judgment, superheroes were neofascists), their glorification of violence, and their stimulation of sexual appetites (via portraits of buxom heroines or seductively clad females in need of rescue). These arguments resonated with post-Marxist critiques of mass culture (e.g., those of Theodor Adorno), yet in the United States they also dovetailed with 1950s patriotic anticommunism and the impulse to purge society of corrupting impulses. Wertham claimed that comics were morally base, "sexually aggressive in an abnormal way," and that they made "violence alluring and cruelty heroic."[59] While he stopped short of positing a causal link between comics and delinquency, he claimed that the genre's powerful influence merited serious sociopolitical concern.

This critique helped to legitimate the Comics Code Authority (CCA), which came into existence following the congressional hearings and mandated that no comic could be published without being inspected and embossed with the organization's infamous stamp of approval. After the mid-1950s implementation of the code, it became less common to find in comic books the severed heads, grisly battle scenes, sex, and torture that readers continued to crave.[60] The gory horror which had served as a key index of American anxieties was no longer a comics mainstay, so readers' fears were reflected in a new range of subjects—communist spies, alien invaders, and grotesqueries created in atomic experiments gone wrong—from which the medium formed an "escape valve of mordant humor and therapeutic social cynicism."[61] Comic books remained big business, and—following horror cinema's trajectory—they gradually lost their status as targets of outrage as social opinion was deflected onto new dangers like rock music. With the advent of a new wave of super-heroes (courtesy of Marvel Comics, whose stable included Spider-Man, the Hulk, and the X-Men), the psychosocial dimension of comics resurfaced along with a pronounced inclination toward social commentary. The heroes of the 1960s and 1970s were known as much for their (relative) psychological complexity as for their social relevance, as these super-beings fought not simply super-villains but drug dealers and explored not merely dastardly plans for world domination but the ethics of Vietnam. The mainstream comics industry had mostly accepted the CCA and pushed forward into new realms of marketing and cultural ubiquity.

It was in reaction to the constraints of the code, and to what many creators lamented as the staid formula of the superhero book, that independent comics began to proliferate in the late 1960s. Most of Chick's admirers situate him squarely (if awkwardly) in the comics underground. The best-known exam-ples of indie comics included R. Crumb's sexual neurotics (including the horny exploits of his characters Mr. Natural and Fritz the Cat) and Gilbert Sheldon's trio of pot fiends in *The Fabulous Furry Freak Brothers*. Since the early 1970s, most major innovations within comics have occurred in inde-pendent books, including *Cerebus the Aardvark, Grendel, Sin City, Hellboy*, and *Top Ten*, among many others.[62]

Comics thus constitute one of the more significant and influential visual media and popular entertainments of the last century.[63] They remain vastly popular, and their development can be read as social and cultural history: amid the tights, capes, and giant sound effects are creators' hopes and anxieties as well as specific representations of history, politics, and social norms. Co-mics are also a powerful means of communicating these representations to readers. They can both reflect and shape audiences' understandings of them-selves and their sociohistorical position. Aside from the specific aesthetic syntax of the medium itself—its stark lines, its reliance on panels, its hyper-bolic rendering of the human body—the way narrative is constructed in comic art is significant for understanding its impact. In this, the appeal of comics lies not only in their widespread accessibility and the ease with which they can be consumed; it lies also, significantly, with their formulaic properties. This refers in part to the "ways in which specific cultural themes and stereotypes become embodied in more universal story archetypes."[64] Superman, for example, represents mid-twentieth-century conceptions of heroic masculinity, while Marvel's Punisher, a vigilante who targets mobsters, is seen as anticipating the militarism and disdain for public authority that characterized post-Vietnam American pop culture. The formulas are also, however, narratological ones in which extant social or material conflicts can be resolved in the realm of the fantastic and/or the aesthetic by rendering these conflicts using archetypes and ideals which resist ambiguity and fluidity.

The visual style of comics helps to convey a sense of one-dimensionality, which can help to underscore authors' intended meanings.[65] The visual constitutes a kind of symbolic code that helps readers to familiarize themselves even when dealing with unfamiliar subjects; this code can resolve what seems to elude meaning or fixity. Comics scholarship has tended to focus not only on strategies for reading but on the polysemy of comics qua popular texts. Indeed, comics' rhetorical or symbolic typologies may express what cultural theorists are fond of referring to as "oppositional culture."[66] So, for example, each bong hit inhaled by a Freak Brother playfully skewers the ideal of comics as sanitized children's entertainment, while the cartoon erotica of *Omaha the Cat Dancer* can both convey disdain for the obscenity charges often used to constrain comics art and also represent a different expression of the fantasy endemic to the medium.

Chick's works, however, convey a different sense of opposition. In many ways, the tracts express a tension one finds throughout the religion of fear: these creations express a sense of embattlement, of cultural orthodoxy at risk, even as they defend a vision of normalcy which can only with difficulty be regarded as oppositional.[67] In his denunciations of secular and liberal cultures, one senses Chick's revisionist understanding of a prelapsarian Christian America and his graphic narration of religious nostalgia. The very fluidity and polysemy that often inheres in texts—whether serial art or not—is what Chick seeks to resist, using stock symbols and stereotypes (often quite hostile ones) to seal his art off from ambiguity. Chick's self-understanding, his evangelical sensibility, and his place in American culture are reflected in his brief, blunt morality tales.

"JESUS WAS NOT A WEAK FAIRY"

Chick's tracts proclaim their ultimate goal to be the salvation of the individual, doubting reader, who will presumably go on to aid in the work of exposing and challenging social evils.[68] And readers do certainly encounter Christ, God, heavenly hosts, and so forth with great regularity. In these panels, jagged lines convey the brightly shining lights of heaven; soft double hatching is used to delineate billowy clouds; and the denizens of heaven are bedecked in flowing robes, with anonymous facial features, neat haircuts, and discreet robes. Jesus frequently graces the end of a tract, appearing to the newly repentant as if he had just stepped out of Warner Sallman's *Head of Christ*. When the crucifixion is depicted, one generally sees it only silhouetted from a distance; the custom in Chick's corpus is to show the suffering of the damned in visceral detail while tastefully limning the trials of the righteous. Chick only occasionally draws God, heavily anthropomorphized but with no facial features save an oval head suggestive of a comic book android.

These light-bathed images of goodness, order, and salvation serve as necessary pressure releases from the intense violence and carnality found in the majority of Chick's work. The gory details of the fallen world and its manifold traps are documented in great specificity, as indices of social ruin. One sees the backsliding human body subjected to a wide variety of techniques of destruction: people are burned, overrun by poisonous snakes, stabbed, ripped apart by cannibals, and dragged by drooling demons into the maw of hell. The innocent make their way through a world boiling with evil, its odds stacked heavily against the triumph of the good: the people we encounter in our everyday lives fume behind our backs, they seethe with indignation, they bristle at righteousness, and they conspire to tempt, sully, lure, and entrap. For heaven's sake, Chick becomes a cartographer of hell. In defense of the good book, Chick writes a chronicle of damnation.

American culture constitutes one massive slippery slope, in Chick's estimation; its promises are gateways to pain, its gaudy entertainments are ruses masking some nefarious evil. In response, Chick sees his works as tools for evangelism, and his publishing company has for decades encouraged their widespread distribution as a witnessing tool: promotional literature recommends leaving the tracts in the rented shoes at bowling alleys, inside video or DVD cases at rental stores, in libraries and hospitals, in stores' dressing rooms, or in planes' seat pockets. This particular strategy of proselytization has, not surprisingly, been controversial; one of Chick's responses has been regularly to feature outrage over any censorship of his work in the tracts themselves (indeed, rich meta-references abound in his corpus).[69] Widely available and widely known by evangelicals, and purchased in the hundreds by churches, the tracts are also distributed internationally and have on occasion even been used by public officials (for example, by police officers investigating "Satanic panics" in the 1980s).

Catholicism

Something about the period artwork actually connotes 1950s whitewashed illustrated Bibles, with their blond airbrushed Jesuses, combed hair, and spotless robes. Against this aesthetic, Chick's vivid depictions of "cults" and their evil doings are shrouded in sweaty anguish and eros, in darkness and ill intent. In addition to "mainstream" traditions, Chick frequently goes after New Age and Wicca (claiming that goddess religions identify the Virgin Mary with Isis or Hecate) and frequently traces both traditions back to the influence of Catholicism (in Chick's world, many enemies are linked in a conspiracy that is ultimately of Catholic provenance).

Indeed, of all the "false" religions to fall under Chick's withering caricatures, Catholicism has endured the most consistently stinging denunciations.

One of Chick's most steadfast contentions holds that the Roman Catholic church is the "whore of Babylon" referred to in the book of Revelation. For Chick and his supporters, Catholicism—and the Jesuits in particular—play the same role in American religious and political culture that the Illuminati or the "shadow government" do elsewhere in the broader culture of conspiracy theory: Catholics are behind more sinister plots and are responsible for more social misery than any other institution. Chick's regular attacks on Catholicism have aroused some of his work's most intense criticism. Some critics compare Chick's publications to earlier periods of anti-Catholicism: Mark Massa sees Chick as an heir to Puritan fears of "popery" and nineteenth-century nativism; David Bennett describes Chick's Alberto series as "Maria Monk returned in 1984"; and Mark Weitzman links Chick's creations to a recrudescent anti-Semitism.[70] Chick, however, has remained unbowed. Indeed, he has written, "the whore of Revelation is the Roman Catholic Institution...[but] I love the Catholic people enough to risk my life and business...to pull them out of the false religious system they're now serving."[71] In 1991, a number of Oceanside, California, citizens complained that tracts proclaiming that the pope was Satan were left under the windshield wipers of their parked cars.[72] Fairport, New York, Catholic Mike Gallagher was outraged when a teacher at his daughter's Christian school distributed some of Chick's anti-Catholic tracts to her students.[73] William Putnam was livid when a couple passed him one of Chick's anti-Catholic tracts in public.[74] Many such reports have been circulated over the years, including allegations that tracts have been left inside books in Catholic bookstores.[75] Some Christian retailers continue to stock Chick tracts (though many more refuse to do so because of Chick's teachings regarding Catholicism).

These denunciations of Catholicism are premised on a distinction between Catholics and "real" Christians. "Are Roman Catholics Christians?" is the most reviled of many anti-Catholic tracts, containing Chick's distillation of the theological differences supporting the above distinction. He focuses on Helen, a devout "citizen of two countries": her country of birth and the Vatican (a dualism which Chick often invokes, articulating hoary anti-Catholic concerns that the Vatican demands allegiance that might otherwise be given to other, more "godly" nations or institutions). He claims that the Catholic clergy is illegitimate because the term "priest" was "taken" from Judaism; the hierarchy is never mentioned in the Bible; and its existence functions solely to seduce the weak with institutional and liturgical bedazzlements. Chick then goes on to "rip away Rome's false mask" by explaining (or rather, he does not so much explain as he repeatedly asserts in bold text) that the Eucharist, like many features of Catholicism, is not Christian "ACCORDING TO THE BIBLE" (for example, "Helen doesn't realize that the Pope is only a man dressed up in a religious costume"). Critics and defenders alike continue to debate these claims, particularly on listservs and message boards (a vital resonance chamber for all American religions, not just the religion of fear).[76] For example, one writer defended Chick's "accurate" teachings on Catholicism by proclaiming that Christ did not found "HIS CHURCH" upon "Peter the DENIER."[77]

These are all themes elaborated elsewhere in the Chick corpus, which often uses unsubstantiated historical claims and "evidence." One of Chick's overarching concerns about Catholicism is its purported link to "occultism," a network of associations which Chick believes proves that Catholicism is not "real" Christianity. For example, in "The Death Cookie" and "Man in Black," Chick contends that the communion wafer's symbol "IHS" is not a contraction of the Greek name for Jesus but in fact "stands for Isis, Horus, and Seb the gods of Egypt." He claims that the roots of transubstantiation lie with Egyptian priests and that the first pope was under the direction of Satan. Such assertions are linked to Chick's contention that the Roman Catholic church is involved in global conspiracies designed to manipulate minds. Among the most effective tools at its disposal, Chick argues, is the creation of additional "false" religions. In his book *Four Horsemen*, Chick claims that Catholics stand behind the machinations of the Illuminati, the Council on Foreign Relations, international bankers, the mafia, the Freemasons, and New Age. In another book, *The Force*, Jesuits are said to have helped create Jehovah's Witnesses, the "Moonies" of the Reverend Sun Myung Moon's Unification church, the Church of Jesus Christ of Latter-Day Saints, and Christian Science.

Catholicism's greatest triumph in this area, Chick writes, was its role in creating Islam. In "The Deceived" and "The Storyteller," Chick writes that seventh-century Catholics manipulated Muhammad into creating Islam, which thereafter was used to persecute Jews and to facilitate the pope's "conquest" of Jerusalem. In Chick's account, Khadijah was a Catholic operative who was ordered to leave her convent to marry Muhammad and to advance the Vatican's plans: "They used two dark religious forces, 'Allah' and the 'Queen of Heaven' to make us slaves." Further, "[t]o destroy true Christianity, Satan moved his murderous religion from Babylon to Rome." "The Deceived" shows two Muslims converting to Christianity after reading a Chick tract exposing Islam's "fraud," while "The Storyteller" asserts that the Vatican faked the 1981 assassination attempt on Pope John Paul II in order to create the illusion of animosity between Catholics and Muslims (and thereby to deflect potential attention from their collusion).

Chick's concerns about American sovereignty find their way into his anti-Catholic tracts, emerging both in his interpretations of the historical past and in his engagement with contemporary challenges (such as his vigorous anti-communism or his post-9/11 musings). In tracts like "The Poor Pope" and the book *The Big Betrayal*, one is told that Jesuits fomented the fires leading to the

Civil War, supporting the Confederacy and ultimately arranging to have Lincoln assassinated. Chick also claims in "The Godfathers" that Catholics established the Ku Klux Klan (a claim made despite the Klan's history of anti-Catholicism) and that Jesuits assisted "Marx, Engels, Trotsky, Lenin, and Stalin" in devising and spreading communism. According to "Macho" and "Fat Cats," this latter endeavor has been underwritten by liberation theology, which Chick denounces as a front for communism. And in "Ivan the Terrible," a communist character named Ivan schedules a lunch date with a pious Christian whom he openly mocks. In response, the Christian articulates Chick's understanding of the Catholic/communist plot, whereupon Ivan converts (with the rapidity one sees from most of Chick's cartoon converts when bluntly confronted with truth). In many of these narratives, like "The Poor Pope," the Catholic hierarchy is shown as fat and sweaty, part of an institution whose bloated wealth comes from its involvement in gambling, booze, and prostitution.

In "Holocaust," Chick claims that the Vatican once sought to kill all Jews and extremists, ultimately planning to mastermind the Holocaust as a means to achieve these ends. Chick argues that "Hitler, Mussolini, and Franco were backed by the Vatican for the purpose of setting up a one-world government to usher in the 'Millennial Kingdom' under Pope Pius XII." Indeed, many of Chick's end-times tracts prominently feature Catholics. Fred Carter's marvelous illustrations depict in detail the hooded masses who worship the horned god disguised as the pope. In "The Beast," Chick's end times reveal the pope as the Antichrist (in "Is There Another Christ," Chick denounces the theological legitimacy of the papacy by claiming that the pope sees himself, in his capacity as the vicar of Christ, as an *alter Christus*). In "Here He Comes," the false prophet of Revelation is referred to as the "Jesuit General." This tract illustrates such conspiracies with intense scenes of carnage, including a sequence depicting the severed heads of those who have refused the mark stacked in front of a guillotine. And in "The Only Hope," Chick warns of a future where people will be unwillingly tattooed with the number 666 and where the ecumenical movement ultimately will sponsor support for the Antichrist. In this grim future, the pope will make television commercials urging people to accept the mark. To buttress these claims, the artwork vividly portrays plagues and curses (poisoned water, seas of blood, plagues of locusts) afflicting the damned and grisly scenes of Satan's minions (horned demons, goat-headed malevolents, zombies, and werewolves) torturing and slaying at will before the final battle with Jesus. And in "The Last Generation," Chick adopts the postapocalyptic idiom, warning of a future totalitarian state headed by the pope and wherein Jesuits at the United Nations ensure the compliance of all citizens with this institution's infernal power. Like many conservative evangelicals, Chick believes that the United Nations rests on no proper political authority and that its existence serves merely to undermine American political autonomy. In this tract, "true Christians" become fugitives from the oppressor state. A monocled figure is shown, along with a sinister-looking Asian assistant, torturing a Christian who refuses to apostatize; in response, the Asian exclaims, "@!!!**! Take this heretic away. Dispose of it, or use it for food."

One key area of contestation between Chick and Catholics centers on the King James Bible.[78] Chick regularly asserts that the King James translation is under attack from hostile practitioners and that failure to defend its orthodoxy will pave the way for manifold theological errors. All other translations, Chick fears, are linked to Catholic conspiracies. Catholicism's primary historical evil in this area was, for Chick, its longtime resistance to using any text other than the Vulgate. In "The Attack," he asserts that Catholics have long tried to suppress the distribution of the King James text, initially by murdering translators. One panel depicts a darkened room wherein a cabal of Catholic priests announces, "we must destroy the credibility of the King James Bible"; elsewhere, a footnote pronounces that "Jesuits were sent to infiltrate all Protestant theological seminaries and Bible societies" in order to legitimize their "impure" translations of scripture. This theme is pursued in "Kiss the Protestants Goodbye," as one is told that Catholic designs on the King James Bible are metonyms for the institution's larger plans for domination.

Chick's collected depictions of Catholicism suggest that he views the tradition as one which will stop at nothing to infiltrate worldly institutions, to pursue its global hegemony, and to weed out all opponents. In his portraits, Chick regularly moves among theology, institutional critique, and denunciation of specific practices. He alleges in "My Name . . . in the Vatican?" that the Vatican houses a supercomputer containing the name of every Protestant for reference in future persecutions (persecution and murder, Chick warns, are par for the course for the Catholic church, which he claims killed 68 million people between 1200 and 1808). Elsewhere, he cautions that Catholic practice cannot save the sinning soul: in "Last Rites," Henry is killed in a car wreck but, after receiving last rites, is told by God himself that Catholic "works" cannot prevent him from going to hell; the cop protagonist of "Murph" is shot on duty and renounces his Catholicism when Murph's witnessing partner out-theologizes a bumbling priest; and in "Man in Black," an evangelical persuades a suicidal Catholic to abandon the church.

The crowning work of Chick's animosity toward Catholicism is his series of full-length comic books based on the allegations of Alberto Rivera.[79] These books constitute Chick's very own *The Da Vinci Code*, exposing "Rome's innermost secrets," its aggressive and often militaristic pursuit of its aims, its use of occult powers to deceive, and the Vatican's consort with demons. In these books, Chick reiterates many of the claims made in his tracts, yet it was the story surrounding the books' key "informant" that proved so controversial and so illustrative of Chick's sensibilities. Alberto Magno Romero Rivera (1935–1997) was from the Canary Islands. During the course of his relationship with Chick, Rivera contended that he had trained as a Jesuit in order to infiltrate the Vatican and discover its secrets. He boasted of having been so successful in his subterfuge that he actually became a bishop (all the while secretly worshipping as a born-again Christian, although Rivera also once claimed that he embraced Protestantism while recuperating at a sanitarium following his break from the Catholic church); he finally left the church (but not before rescuing his sister, who he claimed was being held against her will in a convent near London).

Beginning in the 1970s, Chick harvested Rivera's tales and published all of his allegations in *The Crusaders'* Alberto series. These comics garnered attention outside of Chick's usual readership. Most notably, Gary Metz published a scathing indictment of Rivera in *Christianity Today* in 1981.[80] Metz revealed several incidents from Rivera's past that called into question not only his knowledge of Catholicism but his general reputability. At the time of the article, Rivera was being sued by a Los Angeles Baptist congregation from which he had borrowed and not repaid $2,000, claiming that he understood it to be a contribution to his ministries. Such incidents were littered throughout Rivera's narrative. In 1967, he had studied at the Church of God of Prophecy's Tennessee headquarters, where he collected donations for a college in Spain. Church officials had concerns about Rivera's activities and, upon contacting the Spanish college, learned that Rivera had only been authorized to collect for a brief period of several weeks. College officials also claimed that Rivera had identified himself as a Jesuit, yet had offered no proof of this affiliation. Ultimately, the Church of God of Prophecy, having discovered that Rivera collected additional money for nonexistent Spanish parishes, wrote to the Department of Justice and reported Rivera for writing bad checks from a closed account. Following this incident, two warrants for Rivera's arrest were issued in Florida in 1969 (one for credit card fraud, another for unauthorized vehicle use). Metz also determined that Rivera's sister was never a nun, but had simply been working as a maid in a private home in London. Further, there was no record of Rivera's ordination as a Catholic priest (his only "proof" was part of his false passport documentation); indeed, Rivera actually fathered two children in the mid-1960s, when he was purported to have been living a life of celibacy.[81] Chick has generally interpreted such critical reportage as evidence of the conspiratorial forces seeking to undermine him.

The Vatican's Moon God

Culled from his interpretations of Catholic history, Chick's portraits of Islam are linked to an array of conspiracies and heterodoxies. In "The Pilgrimage," a prosperous middle-aged Muslim, Dr. Abdul Ali, is returning to London from his tenth *hajj*. In a typical Chick gesture, there is a horrible plane crash and all passengers and crew are killed. Dr. Ali meets an angry Jesus, who vehemently denounces Islam (actually claiming at one point that "Allah is a satanic counterfeit"). In 1994's "Allah Had No Son," Chick depicts interreligious encounters between Christians and Muslims. A God-fearing father (a tourist in the Middle East, drawn standing before minarets) answers his son's good-natured question about the dozens of prostrated believers, "What are they doing, daddy?" His father responds, "They're praying to their moon god, son." An irate Muslim confronts the tourist but, upon taking tea with his insulter, his temper cools. The evangelist explains that a Catholic conspiracy was behind Islam's origin and that the Vatican agent Muhammad actually selected Allah from among 360 "pagan idols" housed in the Ka'aba, calculating that Allah would be most useful in the manipulation of the faithful. During this exposition, the tract casually makes several incendiary claims: "Muhammad sent millions to Hell," "Muhammad lied through his teeth," and "He was no prophet." The erstwhile Muslim quickly converts and hurries off to witness.

In "The Promise" (2001), regular Chick character Bible Bob Williams travels to Israel and witnesses an intifada attack on a public bus. A stereotypically swarthy Palestinian opens his jacket to reveal explosives taped to his chest, exclaiming, "Death to all Jews! This is for Allah and his prophet Muhammad!" Bob witnesses to the grief-stricken survivors, explaining that all the carnage occurred because Abraham fathered Ishmael and Isaac, thereby sowing the seeds for Islam's violence (a historical claim in apparent tension with Chick's claim that the Vatican invented Islam). "Who Cares?" from 2002, is Chick's response to the September 11, 2001, bombings. It focuses on an American Muslim family's reaction to the attacks. The mother is concerned that angry mobs might unfairly attack her son Omar, who is headed to work at the "Jiffy Mart." "May Allah protect you, son," she says to Omar, who replies, "If he doesn't . . . I'm toast." At work, Omar is indeed attacked by thugs exclaiming, "Get the lousy camel jockey!" Bible Bob shows up and helps Omar to the emergency room. When Omar awakes, Bob explains the difference between fake Christians (who beat people up) and real ones (who do good works). Having gotten Omar's attention, Bob explains that, while the Qur'an acknowledges Jesus as a prophet, it never said anything about Jesus lying. Jesus, therefore, must have been telling the truth in his message of salvation, even according to the Qur'an. When Bob asks Omar if Allah sent anyone to die for his sins, Omar realizes Jesus' unique claims to divinity and converts.

In the August 2001 *Battle Cry*, Chick included a cartoon depicting the United Nations poised to make an assault on the world, stopped only by God's arms. Beneath this tableau, an elderly woman exercises her freedom by handing out a Chick tract. The subsequent issue, released just before 9/11, featured the headline "Muslim Countries Becoming Bolder in Persecuting Christians." Chick's accompanying cartoon featured a grisly scene where a scimitar-wielding Muslim pauses before beheading his next victim to shout at a news crew, "Stop that camera! We're doing this for Allah!" His colleague—training a submachine gun on a line of perspiring Christians (a man standing next to the basket of severed heads has a "Jesus" sweatshirt on)—grumbles, "This is OUR religious freedom! Why are you persecuting us?"

The Chosen People

The relationship with Judaism expressed in Chick's work is, like that in much of conservative evangelicalism, a complicated one.[82] Despite the overarching conviction that only those who know Jesus will enter the kingdom of heaven, there is a respect bordering on reverence for Judaism which one can occasionally discern in the tracts. This sensibility stems not so much from admiration for Judaism's practices as for its historic location at the center of biblical narratives past and future. In "Love the Jewish People," Chick narrates his support for the state of Israel, owing to its centrality in biblical narratives and in the prophetic future yet to unfold. Along the way, he denounces countries like Egypt as "backwards" for enslaving Jews. In "Support Your Local Jew," Chick argues that the historic mistreatment of Jews is a mistake (all nations which have done so, he shows, have faded into obscurity). He warns the United States against making this mistake (in, for example, overdependence on Middle Eastern oil). This tract has been reissued as "Jeopardy," where the Vatican is blamed for the Holocaust and Jews are warned, "don't die in your sins...become a Messianic Jew."[83] In "Where's Rabbi Waxman?" the titular character is asked why he believes Jesus is not the messiah. In a gesture Chick returns to regularly, in what may be the flip side of the religion of fear's concern for youth at risk, a young student is seen teaching the jaded (and misinformed) adult about Jesus: the student shows the rabbi the relevant scriptural passages and, when he cannot convincingly discount the texts, Waxman begins sweating and panicking. Ultimately, Waxman goes to hell, after God has explained to him that all scriptural prophecy comes true. Converted Jews, however, go to heaven (a narrative outcome which Chick believes proves that he is not anti-Semitic).

The Exotic East

Chick devotes comparably little energy to Asian religions in his work.[84] Only two tracts have engaged the "idolatry" of Hinduism and Buddhism. In "The Traitor," Chick engages Hinduism through an exploration of Kali worshippers (who are shown sacrificing children). In a corrupt northern Indian town, these Kali worshippers bribe officials, exploit the masses, and even kill those who will not do their bidding. Kali herself rides into town on a tiger, surrounded by Thuggees, a spectacle to which an alarmed Chick responds that "[t]he power of Kali is stronger than any god in India, including Shiva, Ganesh, and Hanuman." A mad-eyed high priest tries to have a resistant Christian killed, but the hesitant demons whom the priest attempts to command turn instead on him (Chick repeatedly reminds his readers that demons fear true Christians). The high priest, having witnessed this religious power, ultimately becomes saved himself. The Crusaders story "Exorcists" occurs in India and condemns both Buddhism and Hinduism: regarding Hindu deities, Chick says there are "300 million and all of them are Satanic." The characters Raj and Santosh discover an "idol" and promptly get bitten by a poisonous cobra. In Chick's world, there is at times a quasi-magical understanding of religious efficacy, where bad beliefs bring instantaneous bad luck. They seek immediate help and, although Raj dies, Santosh encounters a local missionary, the Reverend Hayes, who escorts him home and theologizes along the way. Santosh concludes from Hayes's focus on the devil that Satan is more powerful than God; upon arriving at this conclusion, Santosh becomes possessed and ultimately can only be saved by the Crusaders. In the tract "The Tycoon," the central character, Yut Suvarnin, is a wealthy man who is naïvely regarded as a saint by Buddhists. Suvarnin openly dismisses these practitioners as gullible (though he himself claims to follow Buddhism for expedient purposes) and similarly shrugs off the Christian who hands him a Chick tract (and who is subsequently beaten by other Buddhists). Laughing, Suvarnin tosses the tract from his limousine window and dies shortly thereafter in a grisly car crash. Jesus actually confronts Yut, tells him that he cannot be reincarnated, and condemns him for worshipping idols to advance his profit margin. Lastly, Chick's *Light of the World* film has a sequence devoted to "false religions" and claims, "Satan has multitudes following the teachings of Buddha," an assertion punctuated by the kind of cymbal crash used often in kung fu movies.[85]

Cults in Our Midst!

Chick has focused regularly on the "problem" of "cults" in American society. His attention began in the 1970s, doubtless informed by the wave of "cult busting" that was attending the resurgence of new religious movements in the United States. Beginning in this period, many organizations (like the Christian Research Institute, the Watchman Fellowship, and the Spiritual Counterfeits Network) linked the popularity of cults to the decline of American morality and the rending of the social fabric begun during the "permissive" 1960s.[86] The Crusaders issue "Angel of Light" is a broad-brush reading of "false religions" (here grouped together under the heading "Luciferianism").[87] Responding to a rash of Satanic abductions and murders in their town, the

Crusaders bemoan the fact that many preachers, in urging love and tolerance, underemphasize the reality of hellfire. The Crusaders describe "Satan's system" in detail, focusing on its "five major fronts: through religion, the occult, finance, politics, and lodges." The Crusaders are especially critical of Mormons, Masons, Jehovah's Witnesses, and Catholics, although most other traditions are discredited as "Baal worship":

> Asia goes down the tubes with Eastern religions. Africa goes down the tubes with Voodoo, Islam, etc. In the Western world, many liberal "Christian" pastors don't believe the Bible, or they laugh at hell.... The cults and sects are flourishing and man is so confused he doesn't know what's going on ... but Satan does!

Within this system, there is a hierarchy of demons, each in charge of a particular domain of sin (just as one sees in the tract "The Assignment"): "Addiction & Partying" (which includes "Caffeine" as a "sub-sin"), "Mental Illness," "Murder" (which improbably lists "Gossip" as one of its "sub-sins"), "The Unspeakable Demon," and "Sexual Lust." Sins are self-replicating in Chick's world, all eventually linking up to one another in the complex machinery of his conspiracy theory.

In "The Crisis," Chick takes aim at Jehovah's Witnesses. His main source for this tract (and a related article in *Battle Cry*) is ex-Witness Paul Blizard (now an ordained Southern Baptist). It opens with the portrayal of an innocent little girl needing a blood transfusion but, since her parents are Witnesses, she is denied one (the chaplain and the doctor exclaim, in Chick's customarily gory prose, "we're going to have a little corpse on our hands"). Chaplain Barnes confronts the parents, contending, "I believe there are several verses in the Bible to show Jesus is God almighty. Can we look at them?" As with Catholicism and other "false faiths," the implication is somehow that groups like Jehovah's Witnesses ignore (or reject) Jesus rather than simply having different understandings of his divinity. Barnes goes on to reveal that Jesuits actually maneuvered to create the New World translation of Jehovah's Witnesses (he frets that "maybe the Watchtower is tied closer to the Vatican than you've been led to believe").

Chick has devoted perhaps surprisingly little of his work to the Latter-Day Saints. Despite occasional dismissals—such as a May–June 2001 *Battle Cry* article tellingly entitled "Mormons Maneuvering to Appear More Christian"— Chick has only produced one anti-Mormon tract, "The Visitors." Here, the devout Janice is shocked to learn of her Aunt Fran's new friendship with some local Mormons. Janice questions her aunt's LDS friends about doctrines like exaltation. The tone of the tract is clearly derisive, as Janice snorts at their answers, finding it laughable that these beliefs are held without "proof," simply because of tradition or because Mormon sources have claimed them to be so. Janice explains that Mormons actually participate in idol worship, revering beings who mask the presence of the demon Baal (an accusation Chick regularly directs at his targets). Chick occasionally uses *Battle Cry* to issue his thoughts on this tradition: the May–June 2007 issue promotes Chick associate Thomas F. Heinze's book declaring that the Book of Mormon is "pure fiction."

Chick has occasionally trained his sights on Freemasons, the subjects of much conspiracy theory. In "The Curse of Baphomet," a seemingly casual meeting between friends reveals that Alex is a Mason, to which his Christian friend Ed responds, "I had no idea you were into witchcraft." After a heated argument, Ed claims that the Masons actually worship Baphomet (high-level Masons conceal this from low-level participants like Alex). Ed produces a document written by Alex Pike, whom he refers to as "Grand Commander Sovereign Pontiff of Universal Freemasonry" (like Tim LaHaye, Chick often depicts his opponents using the pomp and language he believes are characteristic of Catholicism), which claims, "The MASONIC RELIGION should be, by all of us initiates of the high degrees, maintained in the purity of LUCIFERIAN doctrine." Ed also carefully analyzes the Masonic symbolism on the one-dollar bill. This tempered encounter with a reasonable Mason contrasts with "Good Old Boys," where deranged Masons infiltrate a Christian congregation and machine gun all of the parishioners (to the stock comic book sound effect "buddabuddabudda").

Metaphysical new religious movements do not usually surface on Chick's radar unless they are associated with "occultism."[88] In the anti–New Age tract "The Trap," Robert is a spirit medium who channels a being named Seth and is eager to spread his ideas about "ascended masters" at a party. The host's brother, however, has recently been saved and confronts Robert. After he patiently explains that, in the New Testament, one can find evidence of true miracles and ascensions (as in the story of dogs licking Lazarus's open wounds), most of the partygoers are anxious to get saved.

"One Giant Coven"

On the theme of "occultism" in general, Chick concludes that its popularity in American society—seen not only in the actual presence of witches but also in popular entertainments and in celebrations like Halloween—is another sign of the culture's steady decline and its need for salvation. To some extent, this material harmonizes with Chick's general cultural criticism, but it also constitutes a distinct subgenre. "Bewitched," from 1972, is a cautionary tale wherein Chick warns readers to be on guard against that which seems most innocuous; when we take things for granted, he suggests, our discernment and resistance are weakest. As an example, he cites the 1960s television show *Bewitched*, which "paved the way for all of our occult and vampire programming viewed by MILLIONS today." The popularity of such shows also familiarizes and numbs young people to occult "recruitment tools," such as Ouija boards, "spiritism," and astrology. In Chick's world, exposure to these ideas may induce a mindset that facilitates acceptance of ecumenism and one world government (again, one finds stock elements of conspiracy theories underwriting Chick's depictions of religious conflict). Additionally, "occult" entertainments are seen as gateways to both "goddess worship" and drug abuse (as in the vivid and very dated acid flashback scene in "Bewitched").

"Satan's Master" is a Rebecca Brown tract from the mid-1980s (along with "Poor Little Witch"). It centers on the activities of a coven's "high priestess," who recruits four little girls whom she ultimately orders to be killed. The first to go is Ann, who, as punishment for muttering a criticism, is thrown from a third-story window by the demon Ri-chan (her body is shown already limp as shards of glass rip her face and blood seeps from multiple wounds). Ri-chan is then sent after an evangelical ex-witch, a task which so enrages the demon that, unable to locate his quarry, he turns on the priestess who summoned him and kills her instead. The third girl, Hannah, believes she is a "white witch." Yet there is no such thing as benevolent magic in Chick's world, and we see Ri-chan choking her to death while boasting, "You little fool. We demons supply the power behind ALL forms of witchcraft." The fourth girl seeks out an apostate witch, Judy, so that she, too, can be saved.

In "Poor Little Witch," Mandy is the child of a single working mom (representations of single mothers are, in Chick tracts, inevitably linked to their children's endangerment). Absent the guiding force of an available parent, Mandy is unwittingly lured into witchcraft. However, after seeing a ritual involving drinking a freshly slain infant's blood (elsewhere, Satanists are shown gnawing on severed fingers), Mandy understands the dangers of occult dabbling and is eager to be saved. In "Somebody Goofed," Chick again asserts that drug use constitutes a slippery slope toward the embrace of religions like Wicca (regarding this connection, one character exclaims, "Wow! What a drag!"). In "The Thing," a young Mexican girl named Maria is possessed by a demon named Verono because she "loved astrology and ouija boards—she studied palm and card reading!" Not only does Chick contend that there is no such thing as a "good witch" or "good magic," he also opposes other comic books and cartoons, claiming that Saturday morning animated shows are "pushing the occult and rebellion" while mainstream superheroes use "occultic powers" to accomplish their deeds.[89]

One of the most fertile breeding grounds for the occult is, in Chick's estimation (shared throughout the religion of fear), Halloween. Chick's classic interpretation of this holiday is the tract "The Devil's Night." Here, an unthinking mother parades her doe-eyed daughter before a display of the myriad props of Halloween: pumpkins, gravestones, dangling spiders, flittering bats around a Dracula figure, and a pointy-hatted witch. The daughter, Buffy, is frightened while her mother seems exuberant. The next day at school, in a class taught by Ms. Henn (whose face resembles that of the witch), we meet Li'l Susy, a young Christian who is nervous about dressing up for Halloween. Li'l Susy confides to her grandfather that she doesn't want to dress up like a witch. Citing Romans 13:1, Grandpa enjoins Susy to respect her teacher's authority but claims that there are "all kinds of costumes" she could wear. Susy dresses as Santa, which enrages her teacher. Buffy confides in Susy, telling her that she is also afraid of Halloween (whereas her mother, who "watches all the vampire shows," loves it). Susy tells Buffy that Halloween is scary because "it belongs to the devil...and all the witches love it" (we presume therefore that the two mothers and Ms. Henn are witchy). Susy's historiography derives from her grandfather, who informed her that Halloween comes from "old England," whose people "didn't know God" and "lived in fear." What is more, "[t]he pagan priests were in control, and these men were totally evil. They were deep into the occult and were the priests of Satan." These same pagan priests, we are told, invented the practice of trick-or-treating by going door to door and asking for sacrifices for their gods (when residents could offer none, trick-or-treaters responded, "Then we'll take the child!" who was then ritually sacrificed). Buffy expresses her relief that such practices are consigned to the dark ages of history, but Susy informs her that such sacrifices still take place (usually dogs and cats but, Susy ominously notes, "Lots of kids disappear before Halloween.... That's why kids have to be so careful"). What follows is the fascinating scene of a grade-school child evangelizing one of her peers (and we are also shown, in a classic Chick meta-reference, that Susy's Grandpa, instead of giving trick-or-treaters candy alone, actually slips in a Chick tract, "The Little Ghost"). Such active engagement remains commonplace for Chick's supporters. During the 1990s, for example, the morning after each Halloween parade in Chapel Hill, North Carolina, found streets and parks littered with tracts.[90]

In related tracts like "Boo!" we find exuberant depictions of demonology and evil rendered more powerful through Chick's appropriation of horror cinema devices. The setting is a Halloween celebration—involving the sacrifice of a cat—at "Camp Basil Bub." Satan himself appears wearing a jack o'lantern on his head, and he kills the assembled masses with a chainsaw (an iconic horror trope). Here, the reader again encounters Chick's history of Halloween. A pastor tells an innocent named Joey that the Druids (whom Chick draws carrying a staff topped by an Egyptian ankh) invented Halloween ("Those guys were really spooky"). Joey's pastor tells him, "As we get closer to the second coming of Jesus, Satanism will increase. SO WILL HUMAN SACRIFICE!" In "Happy Halloween," children attending a haunted house are so terrified by the horrible sights therein that they scurry madly from the house, one of them actually dashing into the street and being run over by a car. In "The Little Princess," Heidi is a dying seven-year-old who just wants to dress up as a princess for Halloween. Her neighbor Millie Smith puts a Chick tract in Heidi's bag, resulting eventually in Heidi's entire family getting saved (Heidi herself dies and goes to heaven). And in "The Trick," it is again asserted that Druids are Satanists who put poison or razor blades in Halloween candy. In one incredible panel, a metonym for Chick's understanding of American society's unceasing terrors, a nice-looking suburban couple hears a child screaming somewhere in the night.

Chick's most recent interventions into the dangers of occultism have focused on popular entertainments once again. Chick has engaged such matters with renewed vigor, explicitly in response to the popularity of the *Harry Potter* books and the film adaptations of *The Lord of the Rings* (both of which portray magic being used for positive and negative ends alike).[91] Chick has released a DVD denouncing the Potter phenomenon, *Harry Potter: Witchcraft Repackaged*, and has written in one of his open letters, "In public schools, teachers are allowed and even encouraged to teach the religion of Wicca to their students through the 'Harry Potter' books . . . [which] will cause a tidal wave of warlocks and witches covering the land."[92] The lead character in "The Nervous Witch" (2002) is named Samantha (another possible *Bewitched* reference). Heedless of the dangers she courts, she is shown gleefully casting a circle and boasting, "WITCHES RULE! God is dead and the churches are powerless. Old 'Bible boy' won't stand a chance against our black arts!" Such rhetoric, typical of the comics medium, reveals how Chick imagines the speech and practice of cult members. Samantha is confronted by "Bible Boy Bob," who tells her about the witch of Endor in the Bible. As Samantha slowly discovers that she has been duped into trusting in magic, Bible Bob reveals further that among those perpetrating mistruths about magic are false Christians who enjoy the *Harry Potter* novels and who believe in spirit guides (who are actually demons). Chick associate David W. Daniels situates Potter's popularity in a larger context wherein fantasy fiction has blurred the once-clear boundary between good and evil (Daniels has also cited the "Zen spells" shown in *Star Wars*).[93]

In "The Broken Cross," the Crusaders travel through youth culture to expose the Satanic conspiracy that they contend has infected all worldly and church authority. This moody noir tale opens with a fourteen-year-old female hitchhiker being abducted by a vanful of Satanists, who use a syringe to drug their victim, next seen on an altar of sacrifice as cowled worshippers raise high their knives to begin the grim ritual. The Crusaders find her corpse and are shocked that it is completely bloodless. Clark and Carter investigate the matter but encounter resistance both from local police and from a self-identified liberal Christian, who calls the Crusaders religious bigots. This characterization signals that Chick is aware of the rhetoric used by his own critics (indeed, Chick's promotional literature takes on these issues). The liberal preacher is later seen lighting a "devil candle" for revenge. The town turns out to be rife with these sorts of people, but ultimately the Crusaders manage to convert enough citizens to turn the tide. The issue's most memorable scene features Clark and Carter on a relaxed walk with teenaged Jody, who proudly announces that she is a witch ("I dig the power!"). Jody "tried the church scene" but, along with "about 80% of my school," she was given "everything I wanted" by Lucifer. However, she soon found herself "afraid of everything" and at length accepted the Crusaders' invitation to pray and accept the gospel. Ultimately, the Crusaders unite the town in a ceremonial burning—common during the 1970s and 1980s—of all occult objects and entertainments. Chick promises at the end of this issue, "If you want real power, turn to Jesus."

Chick frequently addresses these issues in *Battle Cry*, even suggesting that there will be "One Giant Coven in the Last Days."[94] Reacting to a rash of vampire entertainments (like *Buffy the Vampire Slayer*) in the early 1990s, the December 1993 *Battle Cry* featured a piece ("Vampires: Hollywood Is Pushing Them . . . but Are They Real?") written by William Schnoebelen, an evangelical who—on his complicated religious journey—claims to have been a Mormon, a Satanist, a Mason, a Wiccan, and a vampire. He warned against taking the occult lightly and believing too quickly in anything coming from Hollywood (since the 1970s, there has been an intensification of Christian conservative rhetorical constructs of Hollywood, rendering it a symbolic fusion of Babylon and Weimar Berlin).

"Christless Graves"

At the heart of these portraits of "false" religions is an understanding of the necessity of conversion and its centrality to the evangelical born-again experience. Representations of conversions occur throughout Chick's social criticism; the sweaty repentant of "This Was Your Life!" appears, multiplied and in different locations, throughout Chick's corpus (in canonical conversion tracts like "One Way," "The Great Escape," and "The Word Became Flesh"). Social hardship and temptations may vary, but the dynamic between the sinner's conscience and a loving God, Chick suggests, is a constant (if continually under threat). Indeed, the very premise of Chick tracts—that compact, disposable salvation literature can and should be distributed everywhere—testifies to this worldview.

Consider some examples of Chick's conversion strategies, which rely on exegesis, public shame, and prophetic warning. The popular "The Sissy" recalls Muscular Christianity—ascendant from the late nineteenth to early twentieth centuries, under the leadership of celebrities like Billy Sunday, and reemerging since the 1970s, most obviously in the Promise Keepers movement—and is apparently often left at truck stops.[95] Hirsute trucker Duke thinks that only weaklings worship Jesus ("In my book, any man that turns the other cheek is a chump!"). A tougher trucker, a Christian, embodies Chick's assertion of Christianity's superior power and soon confronts Duke by explaining, "Your house is on fire. You're going to hell on a greased pole and Satan is laughing his head off." This last vivid image exemplifies the strengths of Chick's creations: their rich and vengeful depictions of sin's consequences, rising up when least expected, like the former ninety-eight-pound weakling confronting the bully who once kicked sand in his face. In "Back from the Dead," for example, a man wakes up in a morgue (a scene in many horror films) and tells the assembled onlookers what hell looks like. Chick illustrates these descriptions with gruesome drawings of a disheveled man swarmed and overrun by mewling, drooling demons. When the newly saved patient is up and about, he consults a priest and is shocked to learn that many people actually discount the reality of hell. The preacher explains, in a critique echoed throughout these creations, how Christians who deny hell's existence have sinfully strayed from literalism. He also enumerates a long list of all the sins and false religions which jeopardize the undecided ("No church, saints, Buddha, Mary, Confucius, Allah—No religion can save you from going to the Lake of Fire. Only Jesus can!"). "Flight 144" replays an oft-repeated theme, as missionaries returning to the United States brag of their "works" while on the plane home; the plane crashes and the missionaries are shown burning in hell. In "The Great Ones," Chick explains that even those with vast worldly success cannot be spared unless they are saved. And in "The Assignment," Chick documents what is behind these many pitfalls and traps: Satan assigns different demons to various domains of life, where the demons battle with angels for the souls of humans. No area of existence is spared the ravages of spiritual combat; no space of human activity lacks the trace of demonology.

Some conversion tracts deal explicitly with methods of evangelism, often coupled with portraits of military activity both hostile and benevolent. "Kings of the East" (1975) is thick with Cold War panic, directed specifically at China's growing might, which Chick believes will fulfill the prophecies ushering in the end times. The tract establishes the futility of realpolitik engagement with the Chinese government and concludes by showing Jesus appearing before the unsaved: "Jesus cuts them to shreds. The blood in this 130-mile valley is 4-feet deep up to the bridle of horses. The greatest slaughter in human history, 1/3 of the world's population is gone." Similarly, the 1970 tract "Kiss India Goodbye" warns that the "Red Chinese" plan to build a highway through India to facilitate China's plans for world domination. The only way to stop this, Chick warns, is to deluge India with gospel literature. About the doomed Indians, Chick claims, "One of their gods is a cobra. We MUST tell them about

Christ! Beloved—the heathen are going to hell!" The Crusaders also engaged Cold War themes. "Operation Bucharest" is set behind the iron curtain, where the reader encounters communists arresting Christians, beating children, and confiscating Bibles. Rather than pursuing accommodation, the Crusaders attempt to smuggle Bibles into Soviet bloc nations, sneaking into Romania carrying microfilm Bibles stuffed into cigarettes by fellow members of the "Christian Underground"; the now-ubiquitous theme of persecuted Christians had begun to take shape in Chick's tracts. The Crusaders travel in an orange VW Bug and disseminate the Gospels to any people they encounter. They are identified and betrayed by the Jewish spy Gertrude Levits, but they ultimately succeed in converting many citizens. "Scar Face" pursues Cold War and colonialist themes in an espionage fantasy wherein the Crusaders match wits with Chinese operative Lu Fang (the chief of "Oriental Intelligence" and a member of a secret society called the Golden Dragon Organization). And "Hey Joe" is addressed specifically to military personnel, geared toward keeping troops focused on piety while away from home and hearth.[96]

"The True Path" is designed to convert Native Americans (often depicted as quasi-literate and alcoholic), who in this tract are lured into a building that advertises a "free gift"; the building turns out to be a church, and the gift is the gospel. "The Breakthrough" both argues for and partially exemplifies the "Wordless Gospel" that Chick deems necessary to establish communication between evangelists and "natives"; according to Chick's official explanation, "Wycliffe Bible translators are working diligently to crack the tribal languages," but the "Wordless Gospel" will have to suffice until the completion of that task. Chick describes New Guinea natives—who come across as representative of all indigenous peoples—as brutal and uneducated, and bemoans the fact that "[a]s the decades roll by, these tribes slip into Christless graves." In "The Last Missionary," there are more colonialist representations of indigenous religions (here shown as face painters carrying skulls). But this only opens onto a larger worldview where, for Chick—like Hal Lindsey and others—promoting the gospel abroad also advances the purposes of Americanism.

American Decline

It is in Chick's general social criticism, however, that one witnesses often the most vivid displays of the two instabilities and fear's declension narrative. Many of these date from the early to mid-1970s, and they fuse cult scares, anxiety about sexual permissiveness, and conspiracy theory. In these narratives, matters of comportment, consumer habits, sexual morality, politics, and belief collapse into one another. For Chick, all social ills constitute a single force with palpable, anti-Christian meaning. "Operation Somebody Cares" (1970) is an illustrative screed against backsliding America, which focuses on a secret meeting of a group called Instant Anarchy Inc. Its members are drawn in a way that almost parodies Gilbert Sheldon's Freak Brothers: one character resembles Allen Ginsberg wearing a hammer and sickle armband; another is a heavily muscled African American dressed in a dashiki; and the third conspirator is a greasy, pot-smoking peacenik. These three are shown conferring in Satan's shadow, proclaiming, "Let's pray that . . . Operation 'Somebody Cares' Doesn't Catch On!" Referring to one of Chick's cartoon missionary endeavors, this sequence clearly positions the counterculture—unpatriotic, godless, lawless—against wholesome, chaste, and lawful evangelistic activities. Another panel reveals a "Communist Time-Table for the U.S.—1973," with hairy thugs breaking into suburban homes, starting fires, grabbing women and children by the hair, and gunning down resisters. "The Poor Revolutionist" portrays a future where hippies have helped communists to invade the United States, only to be lined up and executed by their would-be saviors. "Psssssssst! Isn't It Time??" (1973) is filled with scenes of reefer-puffing children on school playgrounds and raincoated perverts dashing out of XXX theaters to chase little girls through the streets. "Only a revival could slow down this juggernaut!" Chick exclaims.

"Soul Story" (1977) resembles a blaxploitation film. The Fred Carter–penned cover features a militant, bell-bottomed, Afro-sporting bad-ass with an automatic weapon on one arm and a Pam Grier–like vixen on the other. Hard thug Leroy Brown gets out of jail and confronts the rival who stole his girl and his gang. Leroy is dressed in stereotypical pimp garb and confronts his usurper, calling him a "stupid jive turkey" before beating him mercilessly. After Leroy's grandmother dies (having attempted, without success, to witness to Leroy) and his girl is gunned down during a funeral drive-by, Leroy attempts to seduce his ex's best friend, who responds by trying once more to convert him. As Leroy mulls over the proselytization, a gang war (an obvious touchstone for broader social panic) erupts. He dies in the girl's arms but, in a stock resolution to social anxiety, goes through a deathbed conversion.

Youth Gone Wild

Like so many of the religion of fear's creators, Chick focuses on the dangers bubbling up from various youth cultures. In these endeavors, Chick strives—as do his fellow critics—to keep abreast of developments within youth culture. He has consistently produced antidrug tracts, each significantly attempting to adopt the language of that which it denounces. In "The Hunter," the pushers who prowl American streets at Satan's behest refer to smoking "happy powder" and conspire, "One drag on that primo and you're mine, stupid!" "Bad Bob" is an early 1980s drug tract, where the title character was once a town's main pusher. A typically grimy hippie type drawn with a dash of biker flare,

Bob is described by his clients as "crude, rude, and socially unacceptable, but we just love him.... He can get us acid, smack, dust, coke, speed, and black beauties." Yet since even the worst of society's dregs has the potential to be saved in Chick's world, the tract concludes with Bad Bob converting in prison. "Party Girl" illustrates the dangers of bacchanalian events like Mardi Gras by suggesting that Satan's minions have arranged for "drugs, alcohol...the hottest groups...and low grade condoms" to be made available.

The 1980s and 1990s tracts of this nature exchange hippies for skate punks and metalheads. In "God with Us," for example, the ubiquitous Bible Bob encounters an unruly mob of young layabouts, all of whom are heavily pierced and bedecked in leather (one has a tattooed forehead, while another wears white corpse paint makeup resembling metal musicians). Bible Bob contends that, in flirting with these styles, the youths are exposing themselves to multiple social "sicknesses" (including homosexuality, which Bob explains using the well-worn phrase "God created Adam and Eve, not Adam and Steve"). In "The Choice," a committed Christian youth tries to convert his wayward friend by describing the manifold social forces working in unison to prevent people from accepting Christ: one panel depicts a teacher next to a portrait of an ape named Daddy, with the caption "Satan also uses education. Many think they are too smart to accept this one truth"; another panel portrays peer pressure, showing a clean-cut youth surrounded by angry-looking mohawked punks. "No Fear?" documents the link between metal music and teen suicide, while "Dark Dungeons" aims to establish a link between "witchcraft" and the once-popular role-playing game *Dungeons and Dragons*.

The most vivid of Chick's anti-rock tracts is "Angels!" which takes on the seemingly wholesome Christian rock phenomenon.[97] Even this music, Chick claims, uses its hypnotic sexual beat and ear-bleeding noise to make listeners "slave[s] to rock!" The Green Angels are a Christian rock band, whose agent is named Lew Siffer. Siffer brags of controlling billions of souls with rock music, explaining that the genre's development since the 1950s reached its apex with heavy metal, which he boasts is the genre best suited "to destroy country, home, and education." After the band signs a contract in blood (having admitted that their faith was not ironclad), they become a "SINsation." The center of this tract shows demons flying out of Marshall stacks into the audience, as the band sings, "We're gonna Rock, Rock, Rock Rock with the ROCK!" At the height of the band's fame, calamity erupts with Chick's typical causal bluntness. Band member Bobby marries another man and promptly becomes HIV-positive. The other musicians die one by one: one from a drug overdose and another, memorably, from vampirism. The only band member to escape does so with a Chick tract slipped to him by a caring fan.

In "Spellbound," the Crusaders attend a guest sermon given by a former "Druid High Priest," who describes a highly organized shadow organization whose goal "was to destroy Bible believing churches and make witchcraft our nation's religion." After explaining pentagram signals and other forms of "occult" communication, this preacher goes on to claim, "The most powerful spells hitting Christian homes come through rock music.... That's why we must burn those records, tonight!" When this injunction is opposed by Penny, a rock fan who believes that her records are innocent, the preacher then describes the Satanic/Druidic roots of rock music: "The drumbeat [played on drums covered with human skins] was the key to addict the listener ... a form of hypnotism.... the same beat the Druids used is in the rock music of today." The Beatles deserve particular condemnation, he claims, because "they were able to turn our young people on to the eastern religions ... [after which] the floodgates to witchcraft were opened." Rock music also contains coded demonic and/or Druidic messages (a close companion to allegations, popular in the 1970s and 1980s, of backward masking).

Sinning Body and Mind

As further evidence of America's cultural decline, Chick criticizes psychiatry ("The Mad Machine") and sexual promiscuity. In "That Crazy Guy," we meet a swinger named Craig who is on his way to pick up Suzi for a date (Craig's car has a bumper sticker that reads "Do It in My Datson" [sic]). Suzi is warned beforehand about Craig's promiscuity and receives admonitions from a friend about birth control and venereal disease. She ultimately learns that she is HIV-positive. Though Chick's work is littered with exuberant depictions of temporal misery and moral backsliding, he is ever eager to point out that things can always get worse. So it is that, when Suzi learns of her fate, her pious physician convinces her to convert so that she may avoid a fate "far worse than AIDS." In "Caught!" Bible Bob shows the reader an adulterous couple followed by four demons, an angel, and a dog as they creep into the "Motel Delight" for their liaison. Chick has also long articulated his concerns about spousal and child abuse through his tracts as well, penning miniature theodicies that portray the eventual (if not always temporal) rectification of such injustices. In "The Secret," a formerly abusive husband converts while in jail. Upon coming home, he makes amends and lives a blissful, devout twenty years before dying of heart failure.[98] In "Somebody Loves Me," one of Chick's tracts for young children, a boy is shown being beaten by his drunken father, thrown out of the house to become homeless, and ultimately becoming saved. And in "Lisa," a down–and-out husband—who is unemployed and whose wife is a nag—sits at home watching pornography all day. As ever, Chick draws conclusions and establishes links for readers. We learn that this pornography soon gives the father sexual ideas about his daughter. When he is discovered by his beer-chugging neighbor, the latter agrees not to alert the authorities as long as he can participate in the abusive activities. The family doctor discovers that the daughter has herpes. When the daughter reveals to the doctor what has been happening, he defers to an authority higher than the temporal and decides to convert the father rather than calling the police.

Of the sins of the body, however, Chick devotes most attention to homosexuality. "Sin City" recounts the biblical story of Sodom as a warning from God against the "promiscuous" and "sinful" lifestyle of "the gays." "Wounded Children" documents what Chick describes as Satan's most effective carnal temptations: homosexuality, masturbation, and sexual fantasy. In "Doom Town," Chick blames contemporary homosexuals for outpourings of biblical wrath such as those seen at Sodom. Although the possibility for redemption always exists in these tracts, Chick is rarely compassionate in his portraits of the backsliders who do not repent. The detailed depictions in "Doom Town" of children who have been molested suggest that all gay people are child molesters: "Even children were not safe from their perversions." The scene then shifts to a contemporary gay rights rally where a Christian is witnessing about the lessons of Sodom (Chick's eye for detail is sharp, as the placards at the rally feature contemporary slogans like "Hate is not a family value"). At this rally, Chick's gay activists issue a call to "poison" America's blood supply with HIV-positive blood. Copies of these tracts, along with "Where's Rabbi Waxman?" were sent to various student and administrative groups at Dartmouth College in 1999.[99] This hyperbolic rendering of identity politics and sexuality, shot through with the threat of terrorism, underscores Chick's demonological orientation to his religio-political Others.

One of his most popular tracts on this subject is "The Gay Blade" (originally published in 1972), which predicts a future where gay couples can legally marry, where gay people occupy prominent media positions, and where they have achieved social acceptance. Throughout, Chick depicts gay males as hostile and dangerous but also feminizes them persistently (starting with the lavender and purple cover emblazoned with a silhouette of a limp-wristed man in bell bottoms and puffy shirt). Chick revisits the biblical story of Sodom, seeing in it a key to understanding the preponderance of "homosexual rape" (a subject he also heatedly explores in "Trust Me," which features a prison rape scene). After the Sodomites are blinded by angels, Chick depicts what Kuersteiner describes as a "perverse parody of 'Dawn of the Dead' . . . [where] blind homosexuals spend all night outside groping for the back door."[100] Later tracts register a changed global sensibility and Chick's awareness of new threats. In "Going Home," a white doctor dying of AIDS is in Africa treating dying AIDS patients (Chick captions these panels with a stern warning: "The US could be like this in just a few years"). Chick holds out the possibility that those who "renounce" their homosexuality, or who contract AIDS through means other than sexual activity, can go to heaven (as does Peter, a saved African who dies from AIDS and is escorted to heaven by a black angel).

"Wounded Children" (1983) is perhaps Chick's most aggressive tract to engage this subject. David is a young gay male who desperately wants to be straight but cannot. He is depressed, nearly suicidal, and frequently taunted by an invisible demon. He goes on dates with women, one of whom is shown responding positively to David's sensitivity. (David, however, thinks to himself, "Oh, honey, you just don't know. I'm really your sister.") We learn that David "turned gay" when he saw dirty pictures in books his father had hidden. He soon began to play with dolls and subsequently found himself "facing Demonic forces coming at him using subliminal mind control through the power of suggestion." David relocates to the big city and quickly moves in with another gay male (who, like all of the gay males in these tracts, is in a constant state of sexual arousal and sleeps around widely). David and this man soon break up, and David is left to meet the consequences that, inevitable in Chick tracts, await him. The scene shifts to a pickup truck filled with hooligans going "queer hunting" ("We're gonna find us some fags to play baseball with, and bust their !@#&**! heads!"). Chick usually takes pains to condemn this kind of behavior, doing so through the model Christian characters around whom most tracts revolve. Yet Chick's gay tracts frequently use terms such as "homo heads" and "in-your-face fags," language which—even if it is only used by cartoon characters—has an edge that is lacking in many other tract subjects. (One Chick supporter responded to critics by defending "Jack's attempt to reach out to the homo community with our Lord Jesus Christ's wonderful plan of salvation").[101] Additionally, the homosexuals attacked are shown to deserve some kind of punishment (usually far worse than their physical assaults, and usually not in the temporal realm). David sees the ruffians beating his ex-boyfriend and leaves quickly to avoid being beaten himself. Wracked by guilt after his ex dies from his injuries, David goes to drown his sorrows at a local tavern simply called "Gay Bar." He is met by an ex-gay preacher (drawn with permed hair and a turtleneck), who ultimately converts a number of patrons, including David. These tracts are very popular among Chick's supporters: a Chick Internet bulletin board, for example, is filled with years of commentaries and anecdotes from those who distribute or have been saved by the tracts (including Tom A. of Dothan, Alabama, who boasts of keeping the back seat of his car filled with tracts, including "Doom Town" in particular).[102]

Chick has continued to keep abreast of current developments in this area. The March–April 1993 *Battle Cry* proclaimed with alarm—initially in response to the then oft-cited book *Heather Has Two Mommies*—"Two Cities Approve Homosexual Recruitment in Public Schools." Similarly focused on the educational sphere as a "recruitment" area, the September–October 2000 *Battle Cry* warned, "Homosexual Teachers 8 Times More Likely to Molest Students." In recent years, many more articles have been published: "Professor Gets Threats for Study Showing Homosexuals Can Change," "Sodomites Declare War on Boy Scouts," "Gay Teachers Emboldened by Marriage Law," "Schools Pressured to Tell Students Sodomy Is OK," and "Youngsters Being Taught to 'Construct' Their Gender," among others.

Despite the centrality of abortion to conservative evangelical politics, only two tracts and six *Battle Cry* articles (including "Aborted Baby Parts for Sale") engage the subject. "Who Murdered Clarice?" opens with surgeons in a darkened room, huddled over their task. This scene is quickly followed by a portrait of abortion rights supporters going to hell. In "Baby Talk," premarital fornicators Ashley and Eric are punished with a broken condom and are launched headfirst into the abortion debates. Eric's doctor is a witnessing Christian, who explains to the couple that public schools are hotbeds of immorality, where condoms are distributed after sexually explicit "education" classes and abortions are encouraged by amoral teachers. Chick thus folds together concerns about public education, premarital sex, and a broken judiciary which legalizes practices that he considers abominable.

Abortion is not the only issue regarding which Chick articulates his concern about public education. The teaching of evolutionary theory in public school classrooms has been one of the most enduring concerns of conservative evangelicals, surfacing in public discourse not just during the infamous Scopes "Monkey Trial" but in a vast array of public activism in response to Supreme Court decisions like *Epperson v. Arkansas* (1968) or various perceived local offenses.[103] Chick first engaged the issue in 1969's "Creator or Liar?" which purports to be an overview of Christian history and is designed specifically to refute supporters of evolutionary theory. "In the Beginning" denounces contemporary Christian histories and cosmologies which diverge from literalism, in addition to repeating Chick's denunciation of Darwin's legacies. In this tract, a character named Jason tells Bible Bob that dinosaurs lived 145 million years in the past. Bob responds by asserting that, in actuality, God created all dinosaurs approximately 6,000 years ago (within the time frame of biblical history) and that "evolution is the religion of scientists who laugh at God." Similarly, in "Earthman," Chick writes, "The world teaches that man is just a highly developed primate. We are told this took millions of years through the process of evolution. Most people believe it! But now, top scientists denounce evolution as a bad joke. Yet godless media and public school teachers keep pushing it." In some of these tracts, Chick draws panels that feature dinosaurs lumbering through Eden.[104] As ever, these tracts fold together hot-button social and moral issues (of the sort frequently politicized by the NCR) with rhetorical frames and categories like "godless media" or hostile educators.

In "Hi There," Chick attacks nonliteralist readings of the Bible with a seemingly improbable scene where secular humanist construction workers debate cosmology. They are heard saying, among other things, "God is dead," "We evolved from apes," "Preachers are all hypocrites," and "The Bible was written by a bunch of Jews, and is full of contradictions." Once they resume work, the most ardent secularist—Charlie Conners—encounters the Grim Reaper high up on an iron girder. The Reaper says, "Hi there. . . . We have an appointment," whereupon Charlie tumbles toward the earth, his pinwheeling body an object lesson for Chick's understanding of biblical history. Charlie lands impaled on a spike, and as he dies in pain he mutters, "[H]elp me . . . I . . . uh . . . I'm starting to bur . . . ugghhh!" And in "Big Daddy," a stereotypical professor (who, like many of Chick's academics, resembles Allen Ginsberg and is perhaps meant to look Jewish) stands before a portrait of an ape with a banana, entitled *Our Father*. This professor is, we are told, attempting to force Darwinian theory upon his students. One student, however, is versed in creationism and proceeds to humiliate his professor. In an oft-repeated Chick fantasy, the student then becomes the teacher and reveals the truth of creationism to all assembled. (Richard Lee even recalls using Chick tracts in his high school Bible study group, and eventually mustering up the courage to give out some of Chick's antievolution tracts in his science class.)[105] This tract is one of Chick's most enduring and, like many popular pieces, has been revised according to contemporary style (early versions incorporated now-dated language, with students responding to the good news by exclaiming, "Far out!" or "That's too much!"). In the Crusaders story "Primal Man?" Chick's hero is a creationist anthropologist who tries to convince television executives to give him air time so that he can debunk evolutionary theory as "one of the cruelest hoaxes ever invented." Chick cites writings from both *Scientific American* and San Diego's Institute for Creation Research (co-founded by longtime Tim LaHaye associate Dr. Henry Morris) as proof that, for example, carbon dating is inaccurate. Once again, the story line suggests that deviation from an earlier period of American decency and triumphalism ushered in this rash of immorality and heterodoxy. This story weaves in Chick's customary assertion that not just evolutionary theory but also the libidinous lifestyle of the 1970s ("We're Christians, Tommy!" "What a bummer! I thought we'd go out swinging tonight with some chicks!"), when this issue was released, stands in contradiction to Christian devotion. Chick regularly trawls the newswires for instances of these conflicts, which he documents in *Battle Cry*. He wrote in March–April 2006 that "there is enough evidence [of intelligent design] to choke a horse. It's evolutionists that must go by faith alone." In May–June 2007, Chick claimed, "the evidence is piling up on our side" in contrast to "the evolutionists' sinking ship of faith."

This sense that public spaces and institutions have been usurped by forces hostile to Christianity is a persistent feature not only of Chick's work; it is also linked to one of conservative evangelicalism's most productive arguments of the last two decades. Charges of "anti-Christian bigotry" have become a commonplace in the NCR declension narrative, from Ralph Reed's mid-1990s protestations that Christians simply want a "place at the table" to more recent denunciations of an "activist judiciary." There is a sense among many critics that, in the name of defending First Amendment rights, America's courts are protecting "minority" religions while crowding the Christian majority from the public sphere. This sensibility is evident in 1991's "Sin Busters," for example. Striking a dystopian note, which both recalls the discontent following the Supreme Court's *Stone v. Graham* (1980) decision and anticipates Alabama judge Roy Moore's 2004 protests against the removal of the Ten Commandments from his courtroom space, Chick portrays jackbooted government thugs arresting a teacher for putting the Ten Commandments on the class bulletin board.[106] One student explains to the class (and to the government agents, who do not even recognize the Decalogue) that these laws are hidden due to "the evil world system that now controls most schools."

In "It's the Law" (2001), an irate teacher screams at her student, "You flunked! I gave you an 'F'! How DARE you write about the 10 Commandments?!" Recalling Chick's assertion elsewhere (specifically in "Don't Read That Book," which alleges that Satan conspires to keep people from reading the Bible) that forces are marshaled to make an unfair assault on Christians' rights to exercise their religion, Bible Bob responds to this scenario by conducting a history lesson. He explains to the teacher that the Gospels have helped to deliver humanity from times of darkness and religious backwardness (he proffers as an example the Egyptian worship of Horus). He eventually converts the teacher, who goes defiantly before the school board to announce that she will be teaching creation science. In "The Trial," young Anna witnesses to one of her classmates on school property. The latter's outraged parents immediately contact the ACLQ, which is only too eager to "attack" this purportedly innocent expression of devotion (as many conservatives believe the American Civil Liberties Union is wont). The ACLQ representatives refer to the gospel as "hate literature." A liberal reporter corners Anna and shrieks, "You have been charged with a major hate crime! Your hateful words have inflamed the entire community!" The supporters of the ACLQ are depicted as standard Chick rogues: Catholics, Muslims, beatniks, a Hasidic Jew, and pointy-headed liberal intellectuals. Chick exacts the vicarious revenge so prominent in his tracts by showing that, years later, these accusers have their real trial on the day of judgment. These themes surface regularly in *Battle Cry* articles like "Danger of Hate Speech Laws Becomes Apparent," "Worldwide Drive for 'Tolerance' Does Not Include the Gospel," "Religious Freedoms under Attack" (where laws against hate speech constitute "a small step to arresting bold pastors for speaking biblical truth against sin"), and "Is This Hate?"

Chick's world seeks to close itself off to outsiders. The impermeability of its boundaries, however, depends not only on the existence of such outsiders (those with "false" faiths or those who are politically abominable) but on their proximity to the very orthodoxy they are said to threaten. In his vigorous engagement with myriad demons, Chick renders his own identity as an engaged evangelical more coherent and densely encoded; he also commends such an identity to his readers. Visible within the crowded writing and packed panels of Chick's work, then, are the erotics of fear and the demonology within.

"LIKE HAMBURGER ON THE CROSS": CARTOON INSTABILITIES AND CHICK'S POLITICS

In "Who Murdered Clarice?" Chick writes, "Jesus Christ can be your most loving friend...or the most frightening enemy in the universe." This Christology is perhaps an apt summation of Chick's worldview, encompassing both his social criticism and his strategies of evangelization. The tracts aim to teach by generating a way of reading politics and society through the lenses of a very distinct, and highly combative, religious sensibility. We see these elements manifested in the narrative form of the tracts and comics: they begin by establishing sociocultural problems, which are then explained as religious through the representational frames, links, and conclusions that Chick establishes. Thereafter, a twofold approach to the problems is offered: grisly doom or salvation. We see them reflected in the tracts' strategies of demonization, their representations of victims, and in the conversion tactics they commend. Perhaps most vividly, these elements are manifest in the tracts' tone, both visual and verbal.

In reading this tone for an understanding of its contexts—the sense of soteriological urgency which drives Chick the social critic—Michel de Certeau's understanding of "popular texts" is helpful. Building on the work of Henri Lefebvre—whose "regressive-progressive" method focused on entertainments both "high" and "low" (from Brecht to Chaplin) as "texts" that captured the experience of alienation at the heart of modernist universalism—de Certeau built upon the now-conventional observation that popular entertainments can serve as instruments of social power.[107] His orientation to "everyday life" saw popular texts and creations not simply as blank slates upon which power wrote scripts to be followed but as part of a more complicated articulation of identities in relation to institutions, ideologies, and histories. Critical challenges to everyday life—not just those mundane practices and habits of consumption that exist outside of "official" institutions but areas of social intersubjectivity—yield an unstable identity defined by an awareness of its own constraints, perhaps even of the futility of trying to overcome such limits. As social criticism, Chick's tracts constitute such a challenge, which is never as flimsy as the paper on which it is printed. Chick's tracts move in this space defined by critical possibility and constraint, keeping their Others both at a distance and close at hand. One could almost say that these complexities manifest what de Certeau called "the metaphor and drift of the doubt which haunts writing," the understanding that there is no doing away with demons without using the language and the ideas of demons.[108]

The tracts wrestle with these processes, seeking to draw boundaries around protean culture just as Chick frames his cartoon panels. Chick writes himself into and out of fallen America, making connections and establishing resolutions that are as succinct as a thought balloon, as emphatic as a trio of exclamation points. The social and cultural history of Chick Productions is a marginal one, both insofar as Chick has doggedly maintained his status as an underground artist fighting "the world system" and also in the sense that his important contributions to evangelical popular culture have gone largely unacknowledged by scholars of American religions. Yet his sensibility is a powerful one in its widespread accessibility, its longevity, and the influence it has had on several generations of American Christians. No matter how fervently one might seek to ignore them, Chick tracts keep turning up, often in the oddest of places: during my research, one young woman told me that when she was doing missionary work in Santa Cruz, California, she was given several tracts by a homeless man (convinced that his ultimate redemption from a hateful world awaited him) in a park.[109]

What do we gain from examining these miniature screeds, produced in the hundreds of millions yet seemingly below the scholarly radar? How might this reading of Chick's tracts facilitate understanding of the religion of fear, of combative evangelical political religion? Scholars of religion tend to work with an implicit, rarely acknowledged range of class and taste distinctions, often avoiding the subcultural. Chick's creations might easily be mistaken for diversions, pop ephemera with as much substance as a McDonald's hamburger. Yet these diversions are nearly as ubiquitous as the burger (and indeed, the two American staples often meet on common ground—one young man with whom I spoke recalls his father handing Chick tracts through the cashier window on trips to the local drive-thru).[110] These ubiquitous entertainments continue to provoke debates and scorn that abet their longevity and centrality.

Despite the apparent simplicity of the form and its reliance on stock thematic material and caricature, Chick tracts are hugely suggestive. They promise neither community nor an arena for practice, but they do generate a way of seeing American culture, an opportunity for meditation on spectacularly documented sins and on possibilities for redemption. As de Certeau writes, social texts like these aim not simply to communicate to audiences but to shape them: "[t]he image of the 'public' ... is implicit in the producers' claim to inform the population, that is, to 'give form' to 'social practices.' "[111] Chick's tracts both reflect and craft a specific range of conservative evangelical (self-)understandings and sociopolitical beliefs. His political sensibilities are not those that can necessarily be mapped onto electoral strategies, institutional preferences, a theory of democratic participation, or any such conventional way of thinking about political religions. Since these are comics, after all, the standard ways of thinking about political religions fall short. Yet the tracts take as their touchstones a vision of social, religious, and political declension that falls squarely within the NCR's larger narrative and that highlights sins that are in many ways interchangeable with those enumerated by conservative evangelical activists. Indeed, Lee has remarked, "When there's a state of societal normlessness, Chick's commentary/response is to fight the system." In this sense, Lee continues, "Chick's work is countercultural."[112]

As one of the earliest, and most enduring, creations in the religion of fear, Chick's tracts articulate the hopes, concerns, and anxieties of this fear regime quite vividly, establishing one of the earliest soundings in its resonance chamber. Their repetitive formulas promise to resolve social complexity; their identification of the demonic inscribes religio-political conflict within a salvation narrative that looks outward to a cosmological point beyond social confines and also invests the everyday with religio-political significance. The polysemy of popular texts acknowledged by interpreters like de Certeau and John Fiske is certainly evident in these Christian comics.[113] For Chick's intentions and interpretations are not simply downloaded into readers' brains. Readers fashion a wide range of interpretations of the tracts, with some reading them as courageous and necessary—one young woman who had attended the first *Left Behind* movie reported that she and her friends left tracts on their seats because "this movie is just not doing the job"—while others regard them as delightful kitsch.[114] Reception aside, Chick's work makes clear that he sees no ambiguity of meaning in the tracts. He intends them to constitute a closed system, visually representing a stark and combative world whose very flirtation with ambiguity requires a muscular reproach, one whose Christianity is shown by the tracts as sufficient to address any sociopolitical problem.

These combative comics—both fully underground and defiantly protective of religious and cultural "normalcy"—are not intended to be read as fiction. Rather, they represent a stage in the establishment of what Talal Asad would call the "conceptual grammar" of the religion of fear.[115] Chick's highly scripted social criticism shapes and disseminates a portrait of American history, politics, and religion that enshrines a combative conservatism. Indeed, his confidants affirm that, for Chick, liberalism is to blame for many of the ills documented in the tracts: "people are looking more towards government and less towards the church" and are turning their backs on what has historically served America well: "conservatism, pull yourself up by your bootstraps."[116]

Chick fervently believes that American history has strayed from its providential goal, that the struggle between good and evil is manifest in even the most seemingly mundane acts, and that American society is overrun by hostile beings. Yet, in his work, these evils are a source of energy, even excitement. While it may be going too far to suggest that Chick retrospectively announces his own desires via tract depictions of sins, there is little denying that by far the greatest energy and the most intense art is reserved for moral filth. The tracts overflow, in other words, with the erotics of fear.

Over nearly a half century, forests have been felled to produce panel after panel crammed with exuberant depictions of ruined lives, brought low by sin and depravity. The corpus as a whole constitutes a detailed catalog—filled with exclamatory depictions—of sin, leading to a fateful choice where one either converts (in brief and without much detail) or burns (at length and in great detail). Chick's work falls, like much of the religion of fear, squarely in the horror genre. It shares this popular aesthetic insofar as its moralism and its sense of justice brutally meted out are also revenge stories, where the function of the *monstrum* is to execute God's terrible judgments on the wicked. The living are carried off to hell, much as corpses carry off the living in the medieval dance of death, in an idiom that blends intense piety with a robust sadism.[117] Much of Chick's work focuses, in Lee's estimation, on two central themes: "I used to be one" and "tables turning."[118] The latter theme is particularly suggestive in light of the tracts' horror dimension, since so many of Chick's writings can be read as revenge fantasies. Chick has written openly on multiple occasions about the need to tilt the balance of power away from Satan and the "world system" and to counter a permissive society's unjust marginalization of religious truth. Toward this end, the tracts show, in Lee's words, "Jesus coming back and killing everybody [in] very graphic and bloody detail . . . but it's good revenge because it's God doing it."[119]

The erotics allow readers to examine sins (albeit cartoon ones) in detail, perhaps even to identify with them for a time before renouncing them. Early versions of the well-known tract "The Beast," for example, feature tellingly exuberant renderings of the sexual revolution: males making out in the corner of a bar and topless waitresses strutting between beer brawls. Such prurience emanates from the pages of Chick's work as a whole: the sweating sinners in Chick's panels cannot control their urges, whether in living rooms blue-lit by the flicker of video porn, flesh pressed together in a drunken cab ride, lesbian teachers seducing students at all-female pajama parties, or nervous runaways lured into the world of free love, skin mags, and gay bars. Chick shows all this and more in what Raeburn calls "pure sadomasochistic fantasy with an emphasis on rhetorical foreplay leading up to the inevitable seduction and submission to Jesus Christ."[120] It is not just the nearly encyclopedic representation of sin that confirms the erotics, but Chick's exuberance and brio in these depictions. Lee suggests that it is likely that Chick enjoys writing about the dark side, while stopping short of glorifying it. While one could easily attribute these features simply to Chick's ministerial zeal, one also cannot help but note how consistently lurid and gory the tracts are. And fascinatingly, Lee reminds me that the goriest thing Chick has ever shown was Carter's drawing of Jesus in "The Gift": "like hamburger on the cross."[121]

More than this fascination and preoccupation with rejected materials, Chick's work manifests the demonology within by laboring at the boundaries of evangelical identity. Chick aims to commend a specific way of thinking and acting as a Christian, one whose rejection of wickedness is accomplished precisely by an engagement with the demonic. What would Chick's art look like without the devil? Would its panels be as blank and featureless as his infrequent renderings of God? Would their dialogue then be as terse and formulaic as the conversion literature on the final page of each tract? The intimacy or proximity of evil is necessary for crafting the identity of Chick's religiosity, perhaps even of his Jesus, who will be either "your most loving friend" or "the most frightening enemy in the universe." Indeed, Chick's visual style depends in part upon a reference library that includes, among other sources, horror movies like the entire *Friday the 13th* series.[122] The delights of the visual as manifested in fear's erotics also become a fierce demonstration of the pedagogical, in some ways a near recrimination which confirms the existence of these pleasures.

Read in light of the erotics and the demonology, Chick's exuberant trawling through the swamps of a sinning America emerges as a necessary part of the orthodoxy he commends to readers. "I want to shock people," Chick has said. "I want to make them physically sick when they see this."[123] The vast demonic population uncovered in his social criticism is as integral to the identity he commends as is Christ; each forceful displacement of the demonological is only made possible by an intimate inspection or a vicariously experienced graphic representation of evil. Cults confirm and sins solidify in a pious demonological dance between good and evil. The single-mindedness with which Chick has, for much of his lifetime, pursued his demons confirms their sacred importance in his universe. Chick's stern warnings and denunciations demand, and depend upon, contact with all that is foul and wicked.

The intermingling of the erotics and the demonology yields a sensibility that is also violent. As Raeburn has shown, Chick's writings are shot through with not only theological rebukes of the enemy but also with military rhetoric. His tracts are "ammunition" used by "God's army" of distributors to "smash the gates of Hell." Indeed, Chick once wrote in an open letter published in *Battle Cry*, "When I go out, I want to go out with honor, and I want to take as many with me to Christ as I can."[124] Chick also reportedly said in parting to Jimmy Akin, "We're in the war."[125]

The naming and vivid portrayal of these threats facilitate, in Chick's view, their ultimate defeat, the rewriting of the declension narrative so that the permissiveness of liberal society—the sins of the body, the lure of popular cultures, the incursion of false religions, and the politics of information being waged in public schools and the media—can be contained. Chick sees the tracts not only as models for understanding these forces but also as tools for rolling them back. While some critics denounce Chick's use of "stupid and offensive stereotypes," others defend this mode of communication as a way of confronting readers with the "blunt message" of the Gospels.[126] With the urgency of the apocalyptic and the gritty focus of the documentary, Chick absorbs the very culture he criticizes, using the tools of one of its most popular entertainments to attract an audience he hopes to rally.

For Chick, Christ is there amid demons; the very proximity of the redeemer and the deceiver, or the demonology within, is for Chick a signal of Christianity's glory. Even in the lowest place, a sinner can be raised up; the light of the world may shine on even the most wayward, provided s/he has an open heart. Still, there is little denying the militancy of Chick's social criticism; indeed, as he writes in response to those who denounce his creations as "hate speech," "[t]rue hatred stands in selfish silence as hell's population grows."[127] Lee supplements this sentiment by saying that those who denounce Chick's work as "mere" hate speech "haven't looked at the testimony of Scripture, which is almost the same thing."[128] But amid his panoramas of lust, greed, and violence are the lost souls Chick seeks to reach. The aim of his art, finally, is to convert. There is even, despite the tracts' strongest tendencies, an occasional political quiescence that finds its way into Chick's world: he sometimes refers to Christ's love as "The Great Escape" from a doomed world. Though violence, gore, and carnality occupy the bulk of his work, Chick's motivation is care for the wayward, however odd this may seem to readers.

The final page of every Chick tract contains a brief set of instructions on how to be saved. As in the conversion scenes frequently rendered in the tracts, this final page is somewhat formulaic. After pages spent energetically, hyperbolically documenting evil, the reader's journey concludes with the enumeration of a series of steps—the kind of formula Americans seem to love—to be taken before and after salvation. "The Bible says there's only one way to Heaven!" stands emblazoned on the top of the page (glossed by John 14:6). "Nobody else can save you," Chick warns, but he then offers a four-step program for redemption. The convert must then enter the world—which writhes in torment and is roiling with sin—armed with Chick tracts, which even angels in heaven recommend as proselytization tools. Steadfast and resolute, those forgiven by Christ's love are instructed to keep in their hearts the prayer through which they initially confessed their sins and their need for forgiveness. Yet, even here, at the moment of redemption's promise, something emerges almost like an overtone series detectable in the melody of Chick's prayer. In this prayer, written into the back of every tract, two words are highlighted, words that stand out from the others to establish the horizon of Chick's Christology and his understanding of a world ruled by evil: *precious blood.*

4

"Runnin' with the Devil"

Conservative Evangelical Fear and Popular Music

Oh, no! No!! Please, God, help me! —Ozzy Osbourne, "Black Sabbath"

Rap is really funny, man, but if you don't see that it's funny, it will scare the shit out of you. —Ice-T, interview in *Rolling Stone*, August 1992

If you can scare someone, you know you have some control over them. —Tom Araya of Slayer

I came of age in the 1980s, at the apex of Reagan era conservatism, with its whitewashed veneer of smiling optimism and its wondrous array of subcultures. Two of the most influential musical cultures to flourish during this period—heavy metal and rap—were also those that attracted (and, significantly, continue to attract) the most intense scrutiny from religious critics. It was common to hear of communities riven by the horrific discovery that teens were performing dark rites in the local woods, smoking pot and drinking beer, or experimenting with gender roles and sexuality; inevitably, a (usually religious) authority figure would denounce the demonic influence of the heavy metal music which had presumably pushed the impressionable teens to commit such acts. Beginning in the same period, and intensifying during the 1990s, a similar (and often explicitly related) moral outrage accompanied the critical engagement with rap music. Though the discourse was rarely openly racialized, the denunciation of the genre's purported violence and carnality was often a register of racial panic.

These accusations are part of a larger morality play throughout American pop cultural history. And they represent an important iteration of the religion of fear, articulating its declension narrative and social convictions through engagement with music most foul. They also show the ways in which such moral condemnations require an intimacy and familiarity with this music that reveal fear's two instabilities. Metal and rap musicians, of course, delight in and court such outrage avidly (after all, this is generally a surefire way to increase downloads or record sales). And the fact that each of these rich, diverse genres is frequently maligned as musically (as well as morally) base only enlivens the debates that continue to proliferate among religious critics. As this mutual exchange of derision rose in pitch between the 1970s and the 1990s, themes and concerns which had begun to foment in Chick's work were presented to a wider audience by fear's flamboyant anti-rockers.

Public Christianity in the United States—and evangelicalism in particular—has long been deeply engaged with popular entertainments. While Christians have defined themselves over and against popular culture in diverse ways, critics have historically maintained vigilance against the possible seductions of leisure time and the "taint" of fallen cultures, even as they have frequently appropriated from these media strategies of communication which have advanced the causes of evangelicalism.[1] The relationship between "the church" and "the world," then, has been a creative and unstable one, which has endured as one of the key axes along which American evangelicals have crafted their identities, including in the enduring tradition of anti-rock. Beginning in the 1970s, peaking in the 1980s, but very much still a part of public culture, the religion of fear's anti-rock preachers saw in the popularity of rock music a series of social dangers and widespread falsehoods—most powerfully expressed in heavy metal and rap—that captured for them the larger process of sociopolitical decline. In this chapter, I first describe the emergence of this discourse, focused mostly on the careers of Jacob Aranza, Jeff Godwin, and Bob Larson, the most widely known and influential preachers in this idiom: these three have produced more books and recordings—and have spoken far more regularly, over longer periods—than other anti-rock preachers. Additionally, their arguments have over time produced an interpretive template for thinking about the "dangers" of popular music. Thereafter, I describe heavy metal and rap and the panics surrounding these genres, since an understanding of the history of these musics is needed to contextualize the criticisms thereof. I conclude by analyzing the politics of religion, fear, and sound. The demographic influence of these preachers has surely waxed and waned over the decades, yet they have helped to shape an identifiable strain and stage of development in the religion of fear. As I show below, these efforts have directly and indirectly contributed to numerous censorship initiatives on the national and local levels, have played a role in widely documented court cases in recent decades, have fashioned powerful interpretive frames in the wake of events like school shootings, and have posited specific links between pop music and areas of social concern like gender, new religions, and public order.

PREACHAZ WITH ATTITUDE

The rich history of American popular music is unimaginable without the accompaniment of its critics. Since the late nineteenth and early twentieth centuries, when the blues and jazz were beginning to coalesce from various strains of African American vernacular music, music located at the social margins has attracted panic and criticism in roughly equal measure. When jazz emerged, as mysterious then as the legacy of Buddy Bolden is now, the *New Orleans Time-Picayune* wrote in 1918 that "[o]n certain natures sound loud and meaningless has an exciting, almost intoxicating effect, like crude colors and strong perfumes, the sight of flesh or the sadic [sic] pleasure in blood. To such as these the jass [sic] music is a delight."[2] Music promoting cathartic release, ecstasy, or passion is often stigmatized as licensing hedonism or disregard for authority, as manifesting darker qualities like the hypnotic, the seductive, the animal, or even the demonic, all of which have historically placed the censorious on alert. Music which evades the normative boundaries established by prevailing conceptions of "good" or "appropriate" listening— perhaps meaning background music, or at the very least "pleasant" and nonthreatening music—has tended to draw the interpretive gaze of moral authorities: its rhythms or volume may enact unbidden physical transformations, seducing listeners into actions they might normally forswear; its lyrics may either directly invite lawlessness or consort with evil, or these lyrics may mask a hidden agenda, which works its way into the listener's subconscious.

Inevitably, these suspicions often have a social critical edge, as concerns about wayward youths become prisms for larger understandings of perceived cultural crises. Such a critical impulse is, in its milder forms, a perennial feature of American public discourse.[3] Yet, in its more intense or alarmist expressions, it reveals acute cultural or religious anxieties particular to specific historical moments. Allan Bloom, writing on the eve of the so-called culture wars, lamented that American youths "have as their heroes banal, drug and sex-ridden guttersnipes who foment rebellion not only against parents but against all noble sentiments."[4] In 2002, talk show host Bill O'Reilly railed against the alliance between Pepsi and Atlanta rapper Ludacris, whose Dirty South rhymes (like "I Got Hoes") O'Reilly found offensive and inappropriate for the Pepsi Corporation's youth marketing.[5]

Denunciations of this general ilk have been issued by American Christians since rock's inception. Some critics have focused their concerns on album cover art (some of whose more renowned targets have included the Beatles' infamous "butcher" cover to *Yesterday and Today*, the Dead Kennedys' *Frankenchrist*, and Jane's Addiction's original *Ritual de lo Habitual* cover), on the purported sexuality of this originally black music (whose "hypnotic" beat might overcome adolescent listeners), or, more enduringly, on the evil inherent in the genre. Beginning with a 1952 campaign against Johnny Standley's "It's in the Book," conservative evangelical screeds denouncing pop music— whether or not such music purports, as Standley's had, to be in the service of the church—have persisted. While 1950s preachers like Frank Garlock—who once announced that "Rock music is the Devil's masterpiece for enslaving his own children"—may have believed themselves to be entering a new struggle, musical evil has been on religious radars for centuries: the medieval Catholic church condemned the tri-tone interval as demonic; nineteenth-century fiddlers were thought to be playing the "devil's instrument"; and 1920s jazz saxophonists were accused of playing the "devil's flute."[6]

When Elvis's music began to appear on jukeboxes in the 1950s, campaigns like Garlock's proliferated. Alongside the general cultural criticism and audience enthusiasm evoked by certain white performers'—notably Elvis's and Jerry Lee Lewis's—appropriation of black music, also at work in the critical reception of early rock music were anxieties surrounding integration and civil rights.[7] National public attention to anti-rock criticism rose when the 1960s "Ban the Beatles" program established one of the first mass record-burning campaigns in the United States (occasionally, in a dark ritual gloss, effigies of the Fab Four were also burned). By the end of that decade, when some musicians—such as Arthur Brown, the Rolling Stones, and Black Sabbath, among others—had actually begun to incorporate Satanic imagery into their music, a growing number of preachers began to generate a rhetorical tradition that would in time coalesce as part of the religion of fear. Among the most important was the Reverend David A. Noebel, then dean of the Colorado Christian Crusade Anti-Communist Youth University and author of, among other works, *Rhythm, Riots, and Revolution; Folk Music and the Negro Revolution; Communism, Hypnotism, and the Beatles; The Beatles: A Study in Drugs, Sex, and Revolution;* and *The Marxist Minstrels: A Handbook on Communist Subversion of Music.*[8] In many ways, Noebel, who would later co-author *Mind Siege* with Tim LaHaye, set the tone for much subsequent anti-rock writing, blending academic aspirations (his books are heavily footnoted, drawing on sources like Aristotle and B. F. Skinner) with conventional religious exhortations. In 1971, Garlock again came to prominence for a pamphlet (published by South Carolina's Bob Jones University) which declared that rock stood opposed to America's long-standing traditions of Christian decency and that rock's "revolutionaries" sought "to tear down everything that Christianity has built up in the United States."[9] In 1975, the Reverend Charles Boykin of Tallahassee claimed that 98 percent of unwed mothers became pregnant because of rock music's influence (rock's "seductive" melodies and "pounding" ostinati purportedly awaken young people's sexuality).[10] The Peters brothers— authors of *Why Knock Rock?* and *Hit Rock's Bottom* and co-founders of Truth about Rock Ministries—organized huge record-burning rallies in Minnesota in 1979. Though isolated local events had occurred previously, these burnings became widespread and highly publicized in the wake of this rally. Over the next several years, there were larger public record burnings in Des Moines and Keokuk, Iowa; Salinas, California; Lynnwood, Washington; and elsewhere. Teens reported that they felt "closer to God" after the events and had become convinced that rock musicians "cause crime and drug abuse."[11] It is this implicit social criticism which has been amplified so suggestively by Aranza, Godwin, and Larson, as they have persistently generated symbolic and rhetorical frames for their audiences, drawing together the scattered threads of social chaos into a coherent sonic enemy. During the course of my research, I tried on multiple occasions to contact each of these three individuals. Godwin has no e-mail address and my letters to his post office box in Bloomington, Indiana, went unanswered, sent back to me unread. Aranza's assistant, Kathy Poche, at Our Savior's Church in Louisiana, spoke with Aranza on my behalf, but he politely declined to speak to me. After repeated attempts to contact Larson, his assistant agreed to accept a list of questions from me via e-mail; no answers, however, were given.

What brought fear's anti-rocking into focus in the 1970s was not simply the moral and sexual anxiety that have long surrounded popular music. The occasion for rock music's emergence in this fear regime—with all of its institutional connections and political resonances—was the allure and shock of "occultism" that seemed to surround rock after the 1960s. As the New Christian Right began to surface in American politics, it was against the backdrop of these record burnings and public denunciations of rock music, which had become occasions for the expression of discontent rather than mere censorship campaigns; themes of social decline, amoral government, and illicit entertainment resonated in both discourses. Additionally, it was during this period that evangelicals began more concertedly to create alternatives to "secular" rock music, films, and other entertainments. The crucial issue for critics was the way in which they saw pop music as undermining "proper" social, sexual, and religious norms.

These concerns had explicit political valences, and it would be wrong to see them simply as side shows or occasions for derision. The political dimension of this critique arose first in the fervid opposition to communism (which this discourse often linked to juvenile delinquency, another of the era's overriding concerns) in the 1950s: Noebel claimed that rock was spawned by Soviet Russia, "an elaborate calculated scientific technique aimed at rendering a generation of American youth neurotic through nerve-jamming, mental deterioration, and retardation."[12] From such roots, a distinct critical discourse coalesced in the early 1970s, as Larson, Aranza, and Godwin began to outline the links among perceived cultural decline, occult influences, and popular music, generating a sounding chamber within which these disparate themes harmonized. As music historian Ian Christe has said about the scope of their criticism, "[i]f even 2–3 [audience members] in every zip code believed heavy metal fans were literally agents of evil—their numbers and donations were sizeable on a national level."[13]

The most important figure during this period was Larson, a former musician from Nebraska whose long career as a youth minister and cultural critic has been marked by his eagerness for the spotlight and his vitriolic criticism. Larson was an active rock musician in a teen band called the Rebels until he was converted by country musician T. Texas Tyler, and later he was persuaded to enter the ministry by David Wilkerson, author of *The Cross and the Switchblade*.[14] He became a prolific author and made his name denouncing rock, publishing his first book, *Rock & Roll: The Devil's Diversion*, in 1967, and following its success with a steady stream of anti-rock manifestos (1971's *Rock and the Church*, 1972's *Hippies, Hindus and Rock & Roll*, 1983's *Rock*, and 1987's *Larson's Book of Rock*, among others), which he continues to issue. In Larson's writings, one finds perhaps the clearest expression that rock music constitutes a prism through which to view larger processes of social decline (a degeneracy Larson claims was catalyzed by "acid-headed, freaked-out rock singers who tell [listeners] to hate the police, alienate themselves from all adults, blow their minds on drugs, and destroy the American system!").[15] Anti-rock criticism flared up again dramatically in both the mid-1980s (when the frenzy surrounding "backward masking" eventuated in congressional hearings on parental advisory warnings) and the late 1990s (when widespread concern followed the Columbine High School shootings), in each instance shaping and framing interpretations of sociopolitical events through specifically crafted anti-rock preaching.

From the 1950s through the 1990s, there was an increasingly steady and widespread sense among social-critical evangelicals that popular entertainments were either themselves concealing a demonic agenda or were at least inducing consumers (specifically adolescents) to engage in actions that were jeopardizing both society and their salvation. As important as were criticisms of popular music's bacchanalian tendencies and its purported sponsorship of false ideologies or religions, the 1970s saw an upturn of concern that within the music itself were coded hidden messages of evil. Bellingham, Washington, preacher Billy Farrar received notoriety for citing the presence of Satanic messages in popular music, actually claiming that the theme song to the television show *Mr. Ed* contained one such directive.[16] On January 14, 1982, the Praise the Lord (PTL) television network aired a report wherein William H. Yarroll alleged that a majority of rock artists both practiced Satanism and invested their music with subliminal messages via backward masking.[17] There were multiple legislative responses to allegations such as these, including official denunciations by Louisiana senator Bill Keith and the Arkansas state legislature and a 1982 attempt by a California legislator to pass a bill banning backward masking. Other critics of backward masking included California state representative Phil Wyman (who claimed that rock's secret messages transformed one's "inner brain"), the Reverend Donald E. Wildmon (who, in 1976, formed the National Federation for Decency), and minister John Hurt (primarily a critic of television).

The most influential witness to the existence of backward masking was Jacob Aranza. A self-described former rebel and a longtime youth minister, Aranza was affiliated with Larson's anti-rock ministries in the 1970s and later served as a consultant for some of Jack Chick's music-related tracts. Aranza now serves as the Hispanic Ministry Center's national youth communicator. He has also worked with the Billy Graham Crusade, Campus Crusade for Christ, Promise Keepers, Men of Integrity, and Youth for Christ. Based in Lafayette, Louisiana, his Aranza Outreach has since the early 1990s shifted his idiom of adolescent concern, focusing less on the dangers of rock than on the merits of premarital abstinence (see his *Making a Love That Lasts* and *Reasonable Reason to Wait*). Aranza is still cited by organizations—like Focus on the Family and the American Family Association—that distribute materials "rating" various "secular" entertainments, a practice that goes back several decades.[18] Moreover, each of these expressions of concern stems from a shared understanding of American cultural decline, one in which habits of consumption and gender/family norms serve as windows onto larger processes of degeneracy.

Aranza articulates the declension narrative as seen through rock history in his widely read *Backward Masking Unmasked*: "In the 50's it brought a new way of dressing and a new way of talking. In the 60's it brought in loose morals, a devastating lack of respect for authority, and drugs. . . . The mid-sixties to early seventies could best be described as the 'if it feels good do it' decade."[19] Like fear's other critics, Aranza isolated a range of sociopolitical ills and linked them to rock's purported celebration of demonology and false beliefs. Grouping a range of concerns—from occultism to drug use to sexual perversion—together as part of a larger "youth rebellion," Aranza vigorously documented the messages he claims to find both explicit and latent in rock music. While some critics have focused on the alleged sexuality of rock rhythms, Aranza focused on its lyrical content. His writings contain multiple references to coding, secrecy, and hidden forces, oft-repeated themes in the religion of fear. Aranza contended that a vast proportion of rock verse "intentionally means something else played backwards."[20] These messages, he claimed, can resound powerfully in the listener's subconscious because they are targeted at what he calls the mind's "reticular activating system."[21] They are understood to be harmful not just to the individual but, owing to the aggregate of individual instances of demonic influence, to the culture as well. Aranza's ideas still have passionate defenders, some of whom proclaim that America can be defended by revealing the "truth" of Aranza's revelations concerning the links between rock music and "persons like Anton Lavey [*sic*]."[22] And themes originally articulated by Aranza continue to resonate in contemporary discourse: Steve Bonta, director of communications for the Constitution Party and a steadfast cultural critic, describes the inexorable development from sweaty 1950s boogie to the "freak show" of 2000s rock by decrying the triumph of radical individualism, "stripped of all personal associations with family, community, and religion." "Winning the culture war," Bonta continues, "requires us . . . to understand the baneful effects of the 'diabolical bawling and twanging' of today's popular music."[23]

The overriding concern for early anti-rockers was that unsuspecting listeners were being exposed to both explicitly destructive lyrics and latent messages. President Ronald Reagan picked up on the increasingly heated public discourse about rock's purported dangers and, echoing larger concerns about liberalism's "permissiveness," claimed, "[t]he First Amendment has been twisted into a pretext for license," the pursuit of which without limits can bring harm to the innocent.[24] On May 31, 1985, the Parents Music Resource Center (PMRC) issued a document proposing a ratings system to be used by the Recording Industry Association of America. The PMRC was formed during the spring of 1985 by the wives of prominent politicians, and its orientation to rock music reflected many of the themes that fear's anti-rockers had been developing since the 1970s. Owing to the widespread publicity attending the group's press releases, these themes resounded in public discourse. The proposed ratings systems (along with a recommendation that brown paper wrappers be placed over "distasteful" record covers) singled out four "destructive" content areas: X was for records with excessively sexual content; D/A denoted specific references to drugs or alcohol; O signaled the presence of occult themes; and V designated extremely violent lyrics or images.[25]

These were all areas of concern long articulated by fear's anti-rockers, who had succeeded in partially normalizing such claims. The PMRC also sought the option to ban some records outright, but in its September 1985 manifesto, "Rock Music Destroys Kids and We've Had Enough," it settled for ratings and restrictions. The congressional hearings of late 1985 made for compelling political theater, not least because of memorable exchanges between Senator Al Gore of Tennessee and, among others, Frank Zappa.[26] Here, the PMRC proffered as evidence "the Filthy Fifteen," described as the most noxious examples of the categories in the proposed ratings system. The list cited supposed exhortations to violence ("We're Not Gonna Take It" by Twisted Sister, whose cross-dressing lead singer, Dee Snider, delivered testimony at the congressional hearings), odes to masturbation (both Cyndi Lauper's "She Bop" and Prince's "Darling Nikki"), and occult fascination (metal groups Venom and Mercyful Fate).

One of the first speakers to address the PMRC was Jeff Ling, a self-described failed musician leading a youth ministry in northern Virginia. Ling presented the group with his oft-used slide show, which featured images of "offensive" album covers and reproductions of rock lyrics designed to underscore to his audiences "the horrors of rock music and its message to young people."[27] Ling argued that rock music (regarded as a singular, pernicious entity) contributed to antisocial behavior, the perversion of moral norms, and the proliferation of anti-Christian beliefs. In his address, Ling cited a wide range of culprits, improbably including the Mentors (whose misogyny, whether tongue-in-cheek or not, is certainly offensive but whose influence is decidedly minimal), but he spoke with particular concern about metal and punk as genres (significantly, he mistook the Dead Kennedys' "Nazi Punks Fuck Off" as a pro-Nazi song).[28] Such occasional oversights proved no deterrent to positing a link between rock and threats to religio-moral purity. Indeed, as Mary Whitehouse proclaimed at the 1987 Conservative Party conference, "You've got to get away from this silly business of having to prove things. We've got to start using our common sense and human experience. Then we might get somewhere."[29]

What followed this convergence of criticism was the development of an increasingly intimate, and publicized, relationship between rock music and its detractors. At times, there seemed almost to be a coordinated effort between musicians and critics, with new causes for alarm—Madonna's "Like a Prayer" video, Sinead O'Connor tearing up a photograph of the pope on *Saturday Night Live*, Marilyn Manson ripping Bibles onstage—seeming to sprout up regularly. And in some cases, critics like Larson began to follow bands around like the most devoted of fans, paying a kind of inverse homage to the music's power by praying for bands during performances in public displays of the fascination the most vehement critics have for the music.

During this period, several lasting anti-rock themes crystallized, one of the strongest of which was an overarching concern that rock fomented rebellion against "legitimate" forms of authority. Beneath broad-brush denunciations, one finds multiple contentions that the standards of decency and propriety once thought to have shored up a prosperous and stable social order were now jeopardized by rock's bacchanalia. Jeff Godwin—one of the most active of all anti-rockers and a self-described former metal musician—attested that rock had "smeared smut" in American culture and had "preached rebellion, hatred, drug abuse, suicide, fornication and the dark things of Satan for too many years."[30] In the midst of one of his detailed typological readings—wherein, for example, Godwin exhaustively catalogs fire imagery in the lyrics of groups ranging from the Rolling Stones to W.A.S.P. to Bananarama, and links these images to biblical passages foretelling doom—Godwin meditates on rock's roots in spurning parental authority.[31] Rock is a by-product of the crisis of the American family, he muses; since rockers were raised so poorly, they spread their evil without conscience. He singles out Dee Snider who, because he rebelled against his father, "became dead meat for Satan" and helped to produce "a bone-chilling fright fest of a record, dripping with evil chaotic revolt against all authority."[32] To address such concerns, there even arose organizations such as California's Back in Control Training Center, which sought to "de-punk" or "de-metal" teens (which makes for vivid comparison with those institutions that now try to "cure" homosexuality).[33]

The center was endorsed by Larson's ministry as well as by the PMRC and Phyllis Schlafly of the Eagle Forum (additionally, some evidence suggests that the Los Angeles Police Department helped to run the center for a time).[34]

This broader degeneracy and challenge to order are, according to fear's anti-rockers, felt acutely in specific spheres where they must be contested. Chief among these are concerns about gender roles and sexuality. These anxieties harmonize with many of the criticisms introduced into public discourse by conservative evangelicals beginning in the 1970s: movements for women's liberation (and the proposed Equal Rights Amendment) contributed to social disorder by reallocating "traditional" gender roles in a way that led to domestic instability; the altering of public school curriculums, specifically resulting in the introduction of federally mandated sex education classes, in the eyes of critics, remanded a "traditionally" parental task to public authorities and resulted in unchecked and immoral representations of sexuality; a tolerance of "deviant" lifestyles (sexual promiscuity, homosexuality, bisexuality, and transgendered persons) increased even as religious expressions in public life suffered from illegitimate persecution; and there was an overall relaxing of social standards which once used to limit the representations of sexuality in public discourse and entertainment.

Aranza pursued such themes vigorously, positing a causal link between the increase of sexual activity before the age of sixteen and songs like Olivia Newton-John's "Let's Get Physical," which he contended "set pornography to music."[35] Indeed, popular music's lyrics read like a laundry list of sexual perversions to Aranza, who cited Daryl Hall's bisexuality, Robin Gibbs's softcore porn drawings, and Debbie Harry's *Playboy* pictorial as evidence that these musicians embodied sexual and social norms that might incur harm on adolescent listeners.[36] For Larson, too, many rock records glorified the various elements of the "rock lifestyle," from "sadomasochistic fantasies" to "demonic overtones" to "smoking pot and sleeping with groupies."[37] Such exaltation of sexual play strikes at the heart of the nuclear family, according to the anti-rockers. They suggest that such exaltation does as much damage—to both the individual soul and the social order—as the celebration of the occult. It is said that rock musicians reject "godly" models of male-female relationships, forgoing love in the name of sex, the intimate details of which Larson in particular chronicles throughout his corpus, particularly when he analyzes the lyrical "subtleties" of songs both obscure (Jay Ferguson's "Thunder Island") and commonplace (multiple entries from Led Zeppelin, whose links between automotive imagery—a female's "transmission" or "pumping gas"—and sex Larson documents in detail).[38] His criticism brims with the erotics of fear, as he exhaustively catalogs libidinously themed record covers (featuring women licking ice cream cones or strawberries, displaying lingerie-clad women or glimpses of buttock and breast, or depicting S&M imagery).

Just as Aranza promised to reveal the hidden messages encoded in rock lyrics, Larson promised to teach his audiences a catalog of rock slang so that they could understand the details of what is objectionable. According to Larson, "'funky' refers to sexual odors; 'gig' is a reference to sex orgies; 'groovy' is the description of the physical position of intercourse; 'groupies' are prostitutes who ply their wares in the company of rock stars; 'get off' signifies the goal of lovemaking."[39] To fear's anti-rockers, most dangerous is rock's playfulness regarding sexual identity. Aranza wrote of his shock upon seeing a young punk woman, whose dress he found horrifying because it manifested (via safety pins and anarchy buttons) not only a general antiauthoritarianism but a rejection of conventional gender norms.[40] Such gender play reveals the porousness of boundaries that the religion of fear seeks to keep solid, privileging fixity over fluidity in its interpretive frame.

Larson contends that this litany of gendered and sexed ills constitutes a slippery slope at the bottom of which sits acceptance of homosexuality. "The Gay Revolution is upon us," he writes, "and many a father who hoped his son would be a football hero, now discovers he would rather frequent a gay disco."[41] To Larson, all rock music reflects this cultural "perversion," as manifested in both playfulness with gender (Larson cites the Kinks' "Lola," cross-dressing by the Mothers of Invention, the Who's drummer Keith Moon wearing a dress, and the glam personas of the New York Dolls and the Tubes) and in the openly gay or bisexual practices of stars like Lou Reed and David Bowie (who Larson claims wander through "a nightmare world" and suffer "the lonely Saturday nights that a perfumed homosexual spends").[42] Larson's supporters frequently point to the methodological or scientific legitimacy of his claims, invoking—as Aranza and Godwin do elsewhere—a kind of rhetorical creolization, where the claim that Larson "studied medicine before becoming a popular rock musician" is invoked to legitimize his assertions that rock promotes an antiauthoritarian "cult" and reduces women's "self-esteem" by flouting gender roles (effects made possible, we are told, because listening to rock actually transforms the listener's neurology and thereby alters behaviors).[43]

Godwin's 1980s writings on rock are perhaps the most vivid in this entire genre, brimming with purple prose that blends shock, social panic, and near awe. His lectures and writings foreground the dangers in rock's purported glorification of illicit/immoral sex. Godwin contended that lustful indulgence actually served "to spread demons," which "are a venereal disease in the truest sense." Such hedonism also served, Godwin continued, as a gateway to drug addiction since narcotics are "a basic part of satanic rituals and devil-orgies."[44] The sociopolitical dimension of his claims was sharpened in Godwin's more targeted statements, which focused on specific artists. For example, he alleged that David Bowie's open bisexuality "okayed the rebellion against God's law for the natural use of man and woman."[45] Several pages of intense discussion were devoted to Little Richard (to whom Godwin referred as "this black god"), documenting Richard's childhood cross-dressing, his volleys "between sexual deviance and religion," and his time spent "hanging out in a public men's restroom, looking for 'action.' '" In typically elaborate prose, Godwin summed up Little Richard's sins by asserting that "Hollywood mansions, mountains of cash and big-finned Cadillacs merged with a brutal whirlwind of hotel room orgies and bisexual depravity as he blazed a trail of sin from coast to coast."[46] More generally, Godwin noted that "the frequent screams punctuating most Rock tunes ALL come from the homosexual penetration of the male."[47] He also wrote lengthy descriptions of "sordid" videos by groups like Whitesnake, whose videos feature Tawny Kitaen, the length of whose miniskirts Godwin documented and whose "sex-soaked 'acting' " Godwin claimed "has lust-witch written all over it."[48] Though nominally aimed at highlighting the social effects of such purported license, the majority of the critical prose catalogs the salacious details of the sins themselves.

An additional major area of concern that emerged in this formative period was the preponderance of non-Christian (or, in the ears of some critics, anti-Christian) beliefs audible in rock music. These tended either to be "occultic" (often a euphemism for explicit devil worship, though for Larson, Godwin, and Aranza an infernal hand guides all "pagan" religions) or popular non-Western or "pagan" traditions. Larson's *Hippies, Hindus and Rock & Roll* was one of the first texts openly to engage this concern. The book was premised on Larson's belief that hippies use "an underground network" consisting of "separate cultures" seeking to counter "the state values of the West."[49] Beginning to sense that political institutions and norms were being undermined from within and without, Larson slowly began to develop an alternate mode of engaging social calamity. Folding together disparate causes and effects in a single interpretive frame, Larson warned that the flower power of the "summer of love" had been replaced by a more confrontational and militant culture (Larson mentions yippies and the New Left). He went on to suggest that Asian religions constitute a front which, just like rock, is used to "indoctrinate" the unsuspecting into a world system promoting evil.[50]

Of special import to Larson was Hinduism, which he saw celebrated by rock's superstars in this period. Larson traveled to India and engaged in research, coming away with some alarmist conclusions about the nature of Hinduism. These illustrate not only Larson's social position (he reports that, during his travels, he was disappointed by "the third-rate Grand Hotel" and also shocked by the public display of Shiva lingams) but his broader religious sensibilities.[51] Conceptually, Larson found Hinduism problematic because— on his reading—it denies evil in its assertion that God is everywhere. This leads to what he believed was Hinduism's "disregard for human life... [and its] fatalistic attitude."[52] From these stem alleged practices Larson found shocking: the purported worship of cow dung; a celebration of drug use as part of "orgies of eating, drinking and illicit sexuality by Shiva worshippers"; and a preponderance of cremation which, for Larson, suggested that Hinduism was a religion of death, which may be the false religion of the last days.[53] Larson feared that artists like the Beatles (whose George Harrison studied Transcendental Meditation, an improvisation on Hinduism led by the Maharishi Mahesh Yogi) and the Beach Boys (whose Mike Love extolled the virtues of meditation) might encourage young listeners both to stray from "truth" as he understood it and also to popularize behaviors such as those Larson found questionable.

Larson's recent writings continue to bemoan the presence of new and non-Christian religions in American culture, and they claim rock's alleged promotion of these faiths. Many of his writings read like advice literature to concerned parents, with Larson promising—in a trope often used in the culture wars—to decode "the warped concoctions of Hollywood and New York writers."[54] Such contentions attribute responsibility for what Larson believes to be a moral vacuum opened up in youth cultures (a waywardness exemplified by "rampant" sexuality and cavalier attitudes toward authority) to the celebrated lifestyles of popular rockers, who are linked to a variety of new religious movements that Larson suggests are covertly Satanic. The bulk of his 1980s texts enumerated these connections, highlighting these themes in ways that resonated with then-prevalent social allegations of Satanic ritual abuse.[55] Larson posited links between rock and popular games (including Ouija boards and role-playing games) thought to be gateways to occultism. He attributed responsibility for the spread of Satanism to problematic song titles, litanies of which appear in his books (Larson condemned the Rolling Stones alone for *Goats Head Soup*, *Their Satanic Majesties Request*, and "Sympathy for the Devil"). Most frequently, Larson chose to proffer as evidence of his claims excerpts from rock lyrics: he noted ominously that Queen "declare[s] that Beelzebub has a devil put aside for them" while Heart "sing[s] of the sinister pleasures of a 'dirty demon daughter.'"[56] Most damning, in his interpretation, were lyrics revealing rock's veneration of "cultic" figures: the Eagles "worshipped" drugs in lyrics influenced by Carlos Castañeda; Fleetwood Mac's "Rhiannon" celebrated a "Welsh witch"; both the Strawbs and Todd Rundgren paid homage to Ra; and the Moody Blues' "In Search of the Lost Chord" was apparently a Swedenborgian fantasy. Larson buttressed these allegations with documented links between musicians and "cults": Yes and Paramahansa Yogananda, Seals and Crofts and the Baha'i, Donovan and Transcendental Meditation, Carlos Santana and Sri Chinmoy, Deep Purple and tarot cards, Joni Mitchell's belief that she has a muse, Dr. John and Vodou, and Earth, Wind & Fire's Maurice White (who Larson claimed "believes he possesses occult powers from previous incarnations") and Buddhism.[57] Larson has continued to address these subjects in his writings and on his radio program: recent programs have addressed the Church of the Sub-Genius (whose satirical origins Larson seems to have overlooked) and allegations that Hindus have occasionally eaten the flesh of infant corpses ("If you have a weak stomach or if you have small children, this is something you may not want to hear.")[58] Other associations Larson has noted recently include Britney Spears' "Hindu blessing" for her child, Michael Jackson's purported "embrace" of Islam (and his desire to write music for the pope), Madonna's interest in kabbalah, and George Harrison's "last occult act," praise for the Maharishi Mahesh Yogi.[59]

For Aranza and Godwin, too, rock's associations with cults is paramount among the genre's sins, symbolizing for them a broader social permissiveness and the ways in which political authorities can no longer be trusted to address potential sources of harm or wrongdoing; ministries such as theirs, they believe, should not be necessary in a responsible polity. Aranza cited the connection between "The Beast" Aleister Crowley and Led Zeppelin guitarist Jimmy Page as particularly noxious because, according to Aranza, Crowley advocated writing and speaking backward. Aranza further cited David Bowie as boasting about his use of "Tibetan spiritualistic chants" on "Young Americans."[60] Aranza added to Larson's list of "cultic" rockers jazz saxophonist Ornette Coleman (whose inclusion stems presumably from his occasional association with Jerry Garcia and not from his notoriously difficult theory of "harmolodics"), and to the list of maligned traditions he adds ISKCON and Jehovah's Witnesses.

Privileging order and domesticity in his allegations, Godwin warned that such "cultic" venerations jeopardized American homes, where abominations lurk unseen and can only be purged through the vigilance of educated parents and citizens. Such calls to vigilance again reflected the period's growing discontent with or distrust of external authorities, whose alleged failure to protect the innocent contributed—in fear's critical vision—to a broader dissent from governmental authority. Godwin situated such claims in a broader historiography of the genre he believed to be one "massive cult dedicated to" Pan and which is "[r]ooted in the Druid demon worship of Celtic England and baptized in voodoo ceremonies of Africa and the Caribbean."[61] Each of these religious expressions is for Godwin ultimately steered by Satan, for whom rock is only the latest and most successful tool by which to spread evil (succeeding to the extent that it is not recognized as demonic). The music's unique power is owed to "Satan's special beat," which Godwin claimed originated with Vodou practitioners, whose rhythms are transferred, unaltered, to rock.[62] He warned that the beat's hypnotic power results in "an instant loss of two thirds of . . . normal muscle strength" while similar weakening occurs "[a]bove a certain decibel level."[63] These historic roots are currently, Godwin asserts,

metastasizing and are expressed in multiple traditions practiced and celebrated by rockers. Like Larson, Godwin finds "the demons of Asia" to be of
particular concern.[64] Whether Buddhism ("a totally anti-Christian pagan
cult!"), Transcendental Meditation, or Asian-inspired expressions of New Age,
Godwin finds the result—when combined with rock's power—to constitute a
movement which "is coming at us like an unstoppable, monstrous, bone-
crushing steamroller . . . [whose] intent is to wipe Bible-believing Christianity
off the face of the earth and replace it with a Satanically-controlled one world
government."[65] As with Chick's work, this criticism shapes an understanding
that all social ills constitute a single Other whose malefic will is expressed on
the broadest social level as well as the smallest individual level.

Unlike the other cases I examine, fear's anti-rocking is not a product to
consume so much as an explicit commentary on a range of musical products
(though there are many books and DVDs for sale in this world). Its practitioners are myriad, and the peak period of the 1970s and 1980s produced
numerous figures and texts which have influenced the discourse: in addition
to Larson, Aranza, and Godwin, a comprehensive discussion might reasonably
discuss Michael K. Haynes, D. L. Michelson, and William J. Schaefer, among
many others.[66] And even after the formative decades, this idiom has thrived in
the post-Columbine period in multiple local ministries throughout the United
States.[67] Nonetheless, the three figures noted above and discussed throughout
have engaged popular music most consistently, have shaped the discourse
most tangibly, and have been most explicit in detailing the music's sociopolitical (as well as its religious and moral) dangers. Thus, the religion of fear's
declension narrative, its fusion of fear and politics, and its two instabilities are
more crisply manifested in these authors' works than in others. These themes
emerge most sharply in the criticisms surrounding popular music's most
maligned genres, metal and rap, the specifics of which define the religion of fear's politics most clearly. Below, I discuss these genres—and their
detractors—as ways to bring these issues into sharper focus.

RUNNIN' WITH THE DEVIL: HEAVY
METAL AND MORAL PANICS

What is so frightening about long-haired men in tight trousers playing very
heavy music through walls of amplifiers? This question, obviously, resorts to
stereotype. But on what is it premised? Surely, the elephantine feel of metal
music, or the speed of some of its varieties, has the ability to compel, even to
seduce a listener. Indeed, metal's very aggression is one of its central attributes.
Yet beyond the spectacle or the possibility of violence, images of rebellion and
the demonic have accompanied metal since its inception and are central to the

specific critiques constructed in the religion of fear. Metal bands wear clothing that suggests that they ride with outlaw bikers (Motörhead), that they come from another planet (the Dutch band Ayreon or the carnally obsessed Gwar), that they may be a different, perhaps evil species (the masked Slipknot and Mortiis), or that they are emissaries from an infernal realm (far too many bands to mention). Many musicians wear elaborate makeup in an attempt to mark their difference from the everyday (not just the candy-coated hard-rock band KISS, but the more musically and aesthetically challenging King Diamond, Emperor, and Kreator); most have elaborate stage productions which display Egyptian tombs, the shattered ruins of national icons, haunted mansions, or bondage parties; metal bands purposefully choose offensive names (from Rumpelstiltskin Grinder and Goblin Cock to Necrophagist and Face Down in Shit); and the dramatic accoutrements of metal—upside-down cross microphones, pentagrams, monsters like Iron Maiden's infamous "Eddie," cowls, pitchforks, and candelabras, just to name a few—are ubiquitous. While many bands reject such imagery as juvenile, distracting, or even morally dubious, these are not the musicians who attract the scrutiny of the religion of fear. Interestingly, most conservative evangelical critics of metal choose, whether purposefully or out of ignorance, not to engage the explicitly atheist and anti-Christian subculture of "black metal," particularly the Norwegian variant which, in the early 1990s, was actually responsible for several church arsons and a handful of grisly murders. The homegrown Jeremiahs tend to focus on popular acts like Marilyn Manson, whose showy demonology they believe popularizes a blend of sexuality, rebellion, and substance abuse.

The term "heavy metal" is thought to have originated in the '60s classic rock song "Born to Be Wild" by Steppenwolf, though there are those who claim it was first popularized by William S. Burroughs in his novels *The Soft Machine* (with the character Uranium Willy, the Heavy Metal Kid) and *Nova Express* (where the term refers to hard drugs, associated with "The Heavy Metal People of Uranus").[68] Musicologist Robert Walser writes that " 'heavy metal' enjoyed centuries of usage as a term for ordnance and poisonous compounds."[69] The two bands that truly forged the genre, however, were the heavy-riffing Led Zeppelin (a blues-based power rock band whose combination of dark imagery and hypnotic syncopation at extreme volumes proved to be a lasting influence) and, especially, Black Sabbath (the doom-laden Birmingham quartet, fronted by Ozzy Osbourne, whose detuned guitars, ominous moaning, and generally cavernous sound is acknowledged as the ur-music of the genre). Metal "began to attain stylistic identity in the late 1960s as a 'harder' sort of hard rock, and a relatively small but fiercely loyal subculture formed around it during the 1970s."[70] It was distinct in its severity, its resistance to some of pop music's conventions (catchy hooks or choruses), and particularly its images of rebellion and occultism.

FIGURE 4.1 Gwar. Courtesy Jason Nelson.

Many of the stories that circulated about metal bands like Black Sabbath were variations on rock 'n' roll urban legends.[71] By far the most shocking allegations at the dawn of the metal era were those focused on the practice of Satanic rituals by the genre's leading bands. Led Zeppelin guitarist Jimmy Page was openly curious about magic, secret societies like the Hermetic Order of the Golden Dawn, and the infamous Aleister Crowley (whose mansion Page purchased). The band's rumored dabbling in the dark arts was a common topic of conversation, and some suspected that their fame was achieved through a Faustian bargain. By far the most scandalous claim was that secret messages were buried in the band's songs themselves. The hoary anthem "Stairway to Heaven" was the first song to be charged with having "backward lyrics" featuring illicit messages. According to critics, one passage played backward (at one time accomplished by manually redirecting a turntable) revealed the lyric "Oh here's to my sweet Satan. The one whose little path would make me sad, whose power is Satan. He'll give you give you 666, there was a little toolshed where he made us suffer, sad Satan."[72] These backward lyrics do not make much sense, of course, but that was perhaps not the point for their critics.

Black Sabbath has long used dark, demonological imagery more overtly (although Osbourne and guitarist Tony Iommi profess that they are Christians preoccupied with worldly evil and darkness).[73] While, at times, Sabbath's music has linked evil with matters like warfare and political corruption ("War

Pigs"), the band has more consistently identified evil as a moral condition. In their gloomy music, one encounters an obsession with the dynamic between wickedness and redemption, the horrors of a fallen world, and the real presence of evil therein. Decked out using the tropes of pulp horror novels, the band is acknowledged for appealing less to the good-time hedonists of the so-called counterculture than to a more downtrodden, cynical audience whose vision of the world in the early 1970s was—perhaps appropriately, given the mounting evidence of political corruption, a protracted energy crisis, creeping postindustrialism, and brief, brutal wars—darkening steadily.[74]

This neo-Gothic sensibility appealed to 1970s audiences, both for its dystopian register and for its theatricality. The more commercial hard rock of KISS and Alice Cooper helped to pave the way for the genre's enduring appeal. With "corpse paint" makeup, elaborate personas, and bombastic stage shows, these two acts conferred upon the occult or Gothic tropes of Zeppelin and Sabbath a kitschy, almost cartoonish quality that proved immensely successful. Cooper (born Vincent Furnier, a Republican and Christian) was a master stage performer, who used the imagery of horror cinema to create a persona which shocked 1970s parents: he toyed with gender, was rumored to have eaten live chickens onstage, used blood and fire in his stage act (which also depicted gallows and guillotine scenes), and gave his albums titles like *Killer* and *Welcome to My Nightmare*. KISS combined the cross-dressing appeal of bands like the New York Dolls with a mythos fusing Marvel Comics heroism with monster movie kitsch. Dressed in black and silver costumes, platform boots seemingly made out of dragon's teeth, and elaborate makeup, KISS (whose name was thought to be an acronym for Knights in Satan's Service) spat blood and fire and seemed to be followed wherever they went by pyrotechnic explosions and moral panics alike.[75] It was in response to this very success that both acts became the subject of intense critical scrutiny, becoming central to boycotts, record burnings, and protests.

Metal bands carefully marketed their images as hedonists, with tales of chemical excess and sexual conquest fused with an air of social rebellion. While metal receded to the commercial margins by the end of the 1970s, its fiercely loyal fan base slowly evolved into the subcultures that have attracted the religion of fear's attention. The subsequent decades saw the emergence first of the musical polar opposites: the New Wave of British Heavy Metal (NWOBHM) and the slickly commercial "glam metal" or "hair metal."[76] The well-heeled and resplendently coiffed practitioners of hair metal seemed far less threatening than the crusty, leather-clad misanthropes of the NWOBHM. Yet while the latter (and its offspring, like thrash and, later, black or death metal) were the focus of insider metal culture, it was the former (owing to its widely accessible air of hedonism and rebellion) that was in the crosshairs of the critics.

With some exceptions, those bands that continued to trade in the demonological idiom remained more or less firmly located within one of metal's subcultures, while those with a more epicurean bent achieved success and popularity. In response to the slick sheen of hair metal, numerous underground metal scenes proliferated in the 1980s and 1990s. Among the most important was thrash metal, which appealed not only to staunch headbangers who despised glam but also to punks disaffected by Reagan era politics (consider Megadeth's "Peace Sells...but Who's Buying?" or Anthrax's "Imitation of Life").[77] While critical attention was trained on moments of spectacle like Ozzy Osbourne's public micturition and Judas Priest's purported links to teen suicide, American and European metal were developing ever more intensely aggressive and misanthropic variations such as black metal, death metal, and grindcore.[78] Each of these genres has developed countless variations since the early 1990s, alongside new idioms ranging from the complex math metal to the dirge-like doom metal.[79]

Much of the criticism surrounding metal has focused on its fans, metalheads (or, as they are often affectionately called, heshers or headbangers). Adolescence is, as seen above, a key cultural battleground for the religion of fear; the audiences usually associated with heavy metal are seen as either sources or objects of the dangers posed by the music. Fans of the genre are a diverse lot, yet critics see in them a common exposure to risks like the aggression of the music and the "angry, lonely, defiant" musicians.[80] For listeners disaffected with various social conventions or sources of authority (ranging from family life to ideology to religious beliefs), metal fandom is often socially integrative even as it can be said to promote individualism or even isolationism.[81] The music often provides opportunities for engaging in behaviors (such as the violence of a circle mosh, a modified form of older "slam-dancing" where audience members either careen off each other or move as one in a circle located in front of the stage, an area known as the "mosh pit") or discourses (ranging from bloody fantasy epics to hostile anti-Christian diatribes) that fit uneasily with everyday patterns of social interaction. Metal's grim worldview is attractive to its adherents both in its sensationalism and in its distance from social convention. Metalheads manifest the spirit of Holden Caulfield in their dismissal of the "falseness" or "superficiality" of conventional society and especially religion (social conventions are often homologized with the term "conformity"). As Jeffrey Arnett writes, it is through fandom that "they see themselves as participating in a brave effort to expose this falseness."[82] Many expressions of these efforts come through the articulation of alternate social worlds; these worlds may consist of sword and sorcery valor (Dio) or sociopolitical criticism (Napalm Death or Lamb of God), but they all bear traces of what Walser identifies as metal's key elements—its rebelliousness, its promise of an alternative identity and community, and its discourse of alienation and nihilism (all of which are regarded as deviant by metal's critics).[83]

These genre fundamentals attracted critical attention from metal's earliest days. In the early 1970s, several metal groups tried, unsuccessfully, to make a name for themselves by publicly courting spectacle and outrage. The group Coven, for example, actually staged a black mass at many of their concerts.[84] It was Black Sabbath, though, that first drew the critical gaze to metal in particular. The group was often accused of associations with the "black arts" even though, as bassist Geezer Butler acknowledged, the group "only do[es] two numbers about black magic in fact, and they are both warnings against it."[85] They frequently received, and declined, requests to play for covens and at black masses. These sorts of allegations, however spurious, established a public link between metal and explicit demonology. The band was also frequently followed by witnessing Christians. Drummer Bill Ward recalls that he was "afraid that some of these people who said they had relationships with Jesus were going to pull the trigger."[86]

Amid all of the anti-rock religiosity of the 1970s and 1980s, criticism of metal was particularly withering. Baptist Jeff R. Steele found the music to be nothing but "sick and repulsive and horrible and dangerous," constituting what is essentially an attack on "Western civilization" itself.[87] Metal was depicted as especially threatening because of its harsh sound, regarded as hateful and mean of spirit, and its associations with violence, occultism, sexual perversion, and substance abuse. When the focus of the criticism became more specific—alleging that metal concerts might erupt in mass violence, for example—it was often on the basis of "anecdote and insinuation."[88] The most avid and prominent critics, it should be recalled, inhabited a universe where evil was not simply an abstraction but a material reality manifesting itself in both the power to steer innocents toward wrongdoing and the material presence of demons. Thus, when panic swirled about adolescents playing *Dungeons and Dragons* in the 1980s, when young people swallowed shotguns whose spent shells were found next to Judas Priest LPs, or when inexplicable phenomena were simply attributed to "the occult," there was a ready-to-hand interpretive breadcrumb trail leading back to heavy metal. Fans of the music delighted in the criticism, of course, since many wanted to smash the very social conventions that critics defended. To this end, fans wore pentagrams on their clothing and skin; concertgoers joined together in shouting "Hail Satan!"; and headbangers "threw the goat" (raising the pinky and the index finger in *il cornuto*, the metal salute) as often as possible.

Emerging from the culture of record burning in the 1970s—which constituted their own "ritualistic nighttime conflagrations," in Christe's description—the mutual dance of criticism and musical response seemed exemplified for a time in the multiple high-profile trials that occurred between the 1980s and the 1990s, all of which sought to indict heavy metal as complicit in the harm or death of adolescent "victims."[89] These cases had predecessors in the 1980s allegations that serial killer Richard "the Night Stalker" Ramirez had been inspired by AC/DC. The trials were not orchestrated directly by Larson or similar critics, but they regularly articulated the religion of fear's rhetoric and interpretive frames. The first case occurred in 1988 when attorney Kenneth McKenna argued that Ozzy Osbourne's song "Suicide Solution" had induced a California teen to kill himself. The young man had indeed committed suicide while listening to Osbourne's *Speak of the Devil*, though the song in question was not on said recording. McKenna rooted his prosecution of Osbourne in the claim that "Suicide Solution" contained a backward message urging the listener to "get the gun and shoot it" (the song's lyrics caution against drug and alcohol abuse). McKenna lost this trial, but his efforts were approved by Larson and others. In 1991, he brought a suit against Judas Priest. Two Nevada teens had gone on a drinking binge and had listened to Priest's *Stained Class*. They then went to a playground, where each shot and killed himself with a shotgun. McKenna insisted that backward masking had convinced the teens to enter into a suicide plot. In these charges, McKenna did not root his case in the recording's lyrics but instead blamed the band's alleged efforts at "mind control," support of "cults," and criminal negligence for the well-being of their listeners. As in the writings of Aranza and Larson, McKenna's case blended the discourses of social deviance, hidden powers controlling the young, and wrong religions. McKenna lost this case as well, but initiatives such as these contributed to anti-rock discourse's post-PMRC reinvigoration, which was avidly embraced by Larson in particular.[90]

The public discourse that took shape in the wake of these trials influenced Larson's interventions into similar events during the 1990s. Larson became reenergized in his contests with rock following the rash of "Satanic ritual abuse" scares from the mid-1980s, and he has since pressed forward with new allegations and assertions about the power of rock. Though he did not abandon his concerns regarding sexuality or challenges to authority, for example, he came to argue forcefully that it was the spread of Satanism which paved the way for these other developments. He had, by the end of the Reagan era, built a media empire which included not only dozens of publications (ranging from books to newsletters) but also radio and television shows for national audiences, a sign of both Larson's and the religion of fear's enduring power. His radio show *Talk Back* has been broadcast internationally for over two decades, at times to as many as 200 stations; Larson is active on the lecture circuit, where he still delivers jeremiads denouncing pop culture (as ever, Larson keeps up to date); and, in addition to his regular television appearances (from *Larry King Live* to *Dr. Phil*), Larson's self-produced videos are available via Dish Network, Clear Channel, podcasts, and many other media.

He claims to have had his concerns about rock renewed during the late 1980s following a series of "disturbing" radio call-ins on his show *Talk Back*. Recounting these exchanges, Larson wrote that disobedient teens like "David" and "Lars" manifested "bravado," "inexpressible anger," and a need for "attention," qualities adduced to many of the characters discussed in Larson's anti-rock texts.[91] In order to address his growing concerns, Larson again sought detailed understanding of popular music. What resulted was one of the crowning moments of his career-long opposition to metal: he actually accompanied the infamous band Slayer on its 1988 European tour. Bob Guccione, Jr., of *Spin* magazine facilitated the assignment, which Larson described—using language more commonly reserved for eager fans—as a "once-in-a-lifetime opportunity to go behind the scenes on a rock 'n' roll tour."[92] The mixture of such exuberance with pronouncements that Slayer "exuded the embodiment of evil" and uttered "snarls of contempt for decency" reveals Larson's own erotics of fear.[93]

Throughout his account of his time with Slayer, Larson reflects not only most of the themes which recur throughout his criticism but also displays a surprising intimacy with the genre he befouls so ardently. Albert Mudrian, editor in chief of *Decibel Magazine*, told me, "I wouldn't be surprised if Larson and his like-minded peers know more words to *Reign in Blood* than you or I do."[94] In addition to his descriptions of German audiences (a "beer-buzzed, wasted bunch" wearing grimy jean jackets emblazoned with images of the demonic, all painstakingly enumerated in the text), Larson goes into considerable detail describing Slayer's concert sets. As is customary of his work in this field, Larson does indeed know all of Slayer's songs (he lists "Hell Awaits," "Black Magic," and "Evil Has No Boundaries" as set staples) and recites specific lyrics at length (including the Slayer mantra "Crucify the so-called Lord!" and several verses from "Necrophiliac").[95] Though Larson demonizes Slayer by associating the band with Nazism (a charge frequently leveled against this band) and marvels at the spectacle of a circle pit, where "metal maniacs thrust satanic salutes upward and slam-dance to the fastest rhythms in rock," he also relishes the details and the experience of hanging out on a rock band's tour bus (cataloging postconcert beer binges and late-night horror movie screenings, among other details of sordid life on the road).[96] Larson even knows enough about metal's subgenres to state that the band combines black metal with speed metal. He attempts simultaneously to demystify them for their worshipful fans (they are, in Larson's eyes, just regular people who buy postcards of the Rhine and miss their families) and to document the threat they pose. In a causal statement that sums up much of Larson's criticism, he asserts that Slayer's "themes of the occult and violence encourage self-destruction and selfish rebellion."[97]

This particular episode in a colorful career merits such lengthy discussion because it quite vividly illustrates the moth-to-flame attraction that Larson has to this Other. For Larson, Slayer is merely the worst instance of a socially and morally destructive genre. In recent texts he explains, for the benefit of concerned parents and citizens, how to spot "Signs of Satanism," among which he lists "fantasy role-playing games," "preoccupation with psychic phenomena," "addiction to horror movies," "obsession with heavy metal," "affinity for satanic paraphernalia," "inclination to write poems or letters about Satanism or to sketch designs," and even "involvement with friends who dress in black."[98] Larson's August 2000 "Family Alert" update announced the availability—as part of his series "Freedom from Family Curses"—of two new videos, *Harry Potter Hogwash* and *The Curse of Rock and Rap* ("exposing the X-rated influence of rock and rap music"). Among related infernal associations, Larson condemns Halloween, which he links to the "witches sabbat," and shock cinema, another genre entertainment with which Larson is intimately familiar. He provides his audiences with a debunking of the facades he contends metal bands construct to conceal their intentions. For example, when Ozzy Osbourne sang that war is the "ultimate sin," Larson explains, "he ignores the need for personal morality based on religious imperatives," and thus this well-meaning claim is "as potentially emotionally damaging to teenagers as overt lyrical invitations to evil."[99] Larson has sought to "expose" these issues by reading metal lyrics at length over the airwaves, paying metal artists to accompany him on speaking tours (for example, Vince Crowley of Archeron appeared at Larson's Satanic Panic tour stop in Dallas), and regularly inviting metal artists onto *Talk Back* radio.[100] Larson has invited not only Christian metal band Stryper but also Trey Azagthoth of Morbid Angel, Glen Benton of Deicide (who has an inverted cross burned into his forehead and who Ian Christe says "had a great symbiotic relationship" with Larson), and Oderus Urungus from Gwar.[101] John Swick recalls that, after a Larson diatribe, one musician took umbrage at Larson's characterization "and said something to the effect of 'C'mon Bob, it's not like we're going out and killing people and eating babies and stuff.'" Urungus protested, "HEY! Speak for yourself!"[102]

Larson is also quite familiar with other subcultures, including American Satanism. Larson has met with and hosted musician/performance artist Boyd Rice, an avowed Satanist, on multiple occasions. Rice has been on *Talk Back* many times and has hosted Larson for dinner parties as well. Rice recalls that Larson usually travels with an entourage, something Larson also does when attending death metal concerts in the Denver area: "My roommate goes to these death metal concerts . . . and he sees these really weird people standing up in the back. And when the lights come on and it's time to leave, it was Bob Larson and his little entourage—the gals that look like [women] you'd see at the mall or something, all done up."[103] Throughout his detailed examinations of King Diamond, Venom, and others, Larson uses his considerable familiarity with the subject to warn that teens exposed to metal will find themselves consorting with demons and committing acts of violence: "Whatever the real intentions of black metal bands," he writes, "the shocking reality is that their teenage fans often interpret satanic songs in the most gruesome way imaginable."[104] So too does Larson himself.

Larson's critical discourse began to circulate widely once more in the 1990s, as he appeared on numerous television and radio programs to articulate his rock jeremiad. The idiom also was appropriated by a fresh wave of like-minded preachers, including Michigan's Redge Peifer. In 1991, Peifer published *The Rock and Roll Nightmare*, where he wrote, "Satanic covens work hand in hand with the production of a lot of these HEAVY METAL and PUNK ROCK records and tapes. These workers of iniquity and evil put a satanic curse on these records asking Lucifer to draw people into drugs and the occult as these people listen to this wicked music."[105] As criticism gathered momentum, much of the anti-metal indignation came to focus on a small handful of 1990s bands: Nine Inch Nails (NIN), White Zombie, Gwar, and especially Marilyn Manson. Members of the scatological Gwar were arrested on multiple occasions for "obscenity" (perhaps unsurprising since their concerts include effects such as spraying audience members with fake blood and semen). Similar allegations were made repeatedly against Rob Zombie (whose White Zombie album *La Sexorcisto: Devil Music* drew considerable attention) and Trent Reznor's bondage-heavy NIN. All of these acts had concerts canceled, multiple protests and boycotts staged, and lawsuits threatened.

But the critical gaze focused most intensely on Canton, Ohio's Marilyn Manson. First arrested in 1994 in Jacksonville, Florida, for "obscenity," Manson (Brian Warner) became a nearly ubiquitous presence both in the headlines and in the conservative evangelical imagination. Dozens of performances on his 1997 *Antichrist Superstar* tour were picketed by conservative religious groups. Officials at New Mexico State University canceled a show under pressure from protesters. Petitions to cancel shows also occurred in Utica, New York; Richmond, Virginia; and Washington, DC, among other venues, with Syracuse's mayor proclaiming that it was his moral obligation to prevent Manson from performing.[106] Oklahoma City's city council pronounced Manson's music "obscene" and forced the state fairgrounds to install monitors for the performance. Anchorage's city council warned promoters that they could be held legally liable for any damages or lawsuits that occurred. Manson was charged with "fourth-degree criminal sexual conduct" onstage in 2001 in Clarkston, Michigan.

What exactly did the group do to merit such responses? Manson's comportment included androgyny, bondage gear, Nazi paraphernalia, and inverted crosses, among other accessories. He played the role of televangelist, military officer, and demonic scourge, defacing portraits of religious and political leaders and tearing up sacred scriptures, much to the titillation of audiences. He and his band members combined the names of actresses and serial killers (e.g., Twiggy Ramirez), they performed S&M onstage, they cross-dressed, they threw meat into the audience, they were open drug users and Satanists, and they enjoyed mixing religious symbolism into their burlesque (at one Salt Lake City concert, Manson tore page after page from the Book of Mormon, saying, "He loves me, He loves me not"). And he was once accused in Jacksonville, Florida, of inserting props, which police mistook for artificial penises, into his anus and then urinating into the crowd.[107]

The hue and cry surrounding artists like Manson focused, in ways reminiscent of Larson's and Godwin's earlier engagements, not just on the music but also on its listeners. At a Fort Worth, Texas, meeting at the 1998 Crime Prevention Resource Center conference, it was suggested that Manson's fans be forcibly hospitalized for their own good. An additional proposal recommended the creation of "a computerized database for law enforcement agencies that would monitor the Internet traffic, and musical proclivities, of suspicious youth."[108] In these panics, we see a dramatization of risk, a rhetorical and sometimes legal struggle to keep boundaries—of "decency," among other things—from being "violated." Images of sickness and contagion occasion a criminological response here, underwritten by a religious legitimation.

Related to these concerns was the 1996 documentary *Paradise Lost*, which investigated the 1993 murder of three West Memphis, Arkansas, boys.[109] Police investigated teenagers who wore black T-shirts and who manifested other traits often discussed by Larson and his fellow critics. Such a focus on clothing, comportment, and tastes in entertainment, long advocated by Larson and others as indices of a person's involvement with the demonic, became commonplace in the anti-metal criticism of the 1990s. There were numerous clothing bans in public schools: in 1997, a Braunfels, Texas, teen wearing a Marilyn Manson shirt was arrested for obscenity; that same year, Milwaukee schools banned Goth fashions and rap T-shirts, while in Fayetteville, North Carolina, eighteen students who protested a ban on Manson, 2pac, and Wu-Tang shirts were suspended; in 1998, a Zeeland, Michigan, student was suspended for wearing a Korn shirt and a Westerly, Rhode Island, student was suspended for wearing a White Zombie shirt; in 1999, the town of Portsmouth, New Hampshire, implemented a school ban on Goth and Manson attire; and in 2000, Northwood, Ohio, police officers confronted a student to tell him it was forbidden to wear his Insane Clown Posse shirt.[110] Mudrian told me that, in 2004, "Lamb of God was unceremoniously yanked from a show with Slipknot and Shadows Fall at Los Angeles' Great Western Forum [owned by the Faithful Central Bible Church] in response to the band's name and its former moniker, Burn the Priest."[111] As recently as 2007, Raffi Khatch-adourian's *New Yorker* piece on American Al Qaeda noted ominously that Adam Gadahn—the first American to be accused of treason in a half century—

had been a death metal fan in his teens.[112] To be sure, there are not always evident causal links between anti-rock preaching and such initiatives. But the shared observations and critiques can be meaningfully read together as participating in a shared anti-rock tradition and constituting a discursive resonance chamber.

The 1999 shootings at Columbine High School in Littleton, Colorado, energized anti-rock preaching once again.[113] In the wake of these incidents, there arose intense anxiety about the power of certain kinds of music (specifically, the Gothic/industrial music associated with the "trenchcoat mafia"), the result of which was a social (and often religious) panic that convinced parents that their children were unsafe in public schools. Shooters Eric Harris and Dylan Klebold were quickly associated, because of their dress and their musical tastes, with Marilyn Manson, and an attempt was made to establish that Manson's infernal music had inspired the shootings (as it happens, Harris and Klebold did not care for Manson and instead preferred Rammstein and KMFDM). Yet for several months following the Columbine incident, a concerted effort was made by religious groups to cancel as many Manson concerts as possible: in Atlanta, a group called "Be Level-Headed" lobbied to cancel a local hard rock festival; Focus on the Family's Bob Waliszewski claimed that "Marilyn Manson and gangsta rap could be linked to Columbine and other incidents of school violence."[114] School administrators across the United States hastened to implement dress codes such as those noted above (extending not only to rock T-shirts but even to banning black clothing, portable music devices, trench coats, and piercings).

These responses constitute the deep pool of cultural panic from which the religion of fear drinks and to which it contributes. The convergence of religious and moral discourse, behavioral monitoring, and metal help to constitute the resonance chamber for fear's anti-rock preaching. However shallow the waters seem, however distant the resonance's echo, the arguments return. Larson, who for a time had devoted less energy to the devil's music, was reenergized by the Columbine incidents. The music's threat now had become so dire, in Larson's eyes, that he sought to popularize the Antirock Pledge he had written during the 1980s (including "I will abstain from voluntarily listening to rock music," and "I will destroy all rock records and tapes in my possession").[115] Larson was convinced that demons had forced the hands of Klebold and Harris. Columbine happened, Larson said, echoing broader antiliberal claims, because Bible reading and prayer in public schools were ruled unconstitutional; additionally, he claimed, "[t]he kids who got shot were Christians. The kids who shot them were not Christian. It's like—duh, excuse me, there is a message here. The kids who got shot were not listening to Marilyn Manson and playing Doom."[116] Drawing on the increasingly influential notion that Christians are persecuted in a regime dominated by "secular liberalism," Larson conveyed his idealized

FIGURE 4.2 Marilyn Manson. Courtesy Jason Nelson.

picture of a Christianized polity by delineating youthful monsters. Because evil and demons are literally at work in American society, Larson believes that it would have been ethically permissible (even obligatory) to have lynched Manson before a Columbine could take place.[117] Such assertions represent both a critical engagement with political processes and a sense that conventional political authorities can no longer protect us from harm.

The anti-metal discourse that Larson and others had nurtured for decades had blossomed once again into a series of warnings and, in several cases, legal actions which together posited a link among sociopolitical disorder, religious heterodoxy, and metal music. The discourse—generated and extended by the religion of fear—drew on panics both marginal and systemic, often yielding assertions like those of Dr. Dale Griffis, who claimed on the television program *20/20*, "We have kids being killed. We have people missing. We have all types of perversion going on, and it's affecting America."[118] In at least the last part of the statement, Griffis was correct.

"POSITIVE RAP IS BORING"

In 1990, Chuck D—the lead rapper in the once infamous Public Enemy—declared on the record *Fear of a Black Planet*, "Elvis was a hero to most, but he never meant shit to me. Straight up racist, that sucker was simple and plain. Motherfuck him and John Wayne."[119] The group modeled its militaristic image on the Nation of Islam, and its often scathing social commentary (here concerning white pilferings of black popular culture) garnered them considerable critical attention.[120] This particular intervention mocked the release of a Presley postage stamp, and PE's dismissal of "The King" led to outrage in newspaper editorials, radio broadcasts, and even political commentary. This was, however, simply one episode among many in one of the most intense early phases of rap criticism, a preoccupation which surfaces regularly in American public discourse.[121]

What is so frightening about young African American males (and occasionally females) wearing athletic clothing, displaying garish jewelry, and glowering into cameras while posed next to cars, in front of abandoned buildings, or in sumptuous penthouse suites? This question too is rooted in stereotype, but what is the cultural history of such imagery? Rap music, regarded by many as the most significant popular musical innovation since punk rock, has a complicated history relating to African American vernacular music, to the postindustrial city in America, and to a precisely articulated style of verbal expression and comportment. As Nelson George writes, the African American pop vernacular upon which rap drew took shape between the 1930s and the early 1970s, from the decades immediately following the era of minstrelsy and early jazz through the era of rhythm and blues, soul, and funk.[122] It was in the specific location of the South Bronx in the 1970s that rap emerged. Following the multiple musical innovations of the late 1960s and early 1970s—which ranged from obvious examples like James Brown and Sly Stone to the slightly more marginal innovations of Funkadelic (the fuzzed-out underbelly of the more commercial Parliament) or, more important, Gil Scott-Heron and the Last Poets—the intersection of African American and Puerto Rican culture in the Bronx produced a number of vibrant "street creole" musics.[123] Rap was also shaped by the emergence of graffiti culture and breaking (or breakdancing).

With roots in a wide array of black vernacular cultures—toasting, playing the dozens, signifying, and folklore—rap from its inception manifested what John Szwed calls "a social mix in which a community's ethos could be affirmed or where new and even forbidden ideas could be tested."[124] The older forms of oral expression share with rap a concern to narrate what is forgotten, outlawed, or "nasty"; they also share the formal properties of "rhythmic talk…stress and pitch…[and] cadence-counting chants."[125] The "nasty" talk of signifying tales and outlaw legends like Stagolee began to resurface in the late 1960s, as artists like the Last Poets and Scott-Heron sought to remake pop music and poetry for what Nelson George calls a "post-soul" generation.[126]

As George writes, rap raided earlier forms of black music (most obviously in the form of sampling) as a way of refashioning black identity for an age of low expectations: rappers "came of age in the aftermath of an era when many of the obvious barriers to the American Dream had fallen…but new, more subtle ones were waiting."[127] Early acts like Coke La Rock and Luvbug Starski were obscure, but the new genre was soon popularized by Afrika Bambaataa, DJ Kool Herc, Soulsonic Force, and Grandmaster Flash.[128] The music itself consists not only of sampled, decontextualized, and remixed excerpts from older forms of black music (a Jimmy Nolen guitar chord from a James Brown single, a Temptations bass line, a Lee Morgan trumpet break), it also rarely (in this period at least) featured live instruments being played. Subsisting on the restructured possibilities of everyday electronics—the turntable, the mixer, the microphone, and the amp—rap could be jarring and dissonant. It constituted what George calls a "continuous sound environment" marked by what Tricia Rose identifies as the three primary characteristics of rupture, layering, and flow.[129] The first single to break out of this local scene was the Sugar Hill Gang's iconic "Rapper's Delight," which facilitated rap's first commercial success and was quickly followed by Kurtis Blow's "Christmas Rappin'" and Grandmaster Flash and the Furious Five's "The Message." As the first wave of rap (including notables like the Fat Boys and Run DMC) was documented, it benefited both from the entrepreneurialism of figures like Fab Five Freddy and

Russell Simmons and also from the occasionally considerable support of white record company executives.

As the idiom gained popularity, it became known not only for its distinctive sonic imprint but for the "B-boy" culture that surrounded it (including breakdancing, specific modes of dress, ghetto blasters, and graffiti).[130] Though rap music enjoyed white sponsorship and audiences from its inception—some of which can be seen as a kind of voyeuristic interest in the blighted landscapes from which rap emerged—it was only with the commercial explosion of the genre beginning in the mid-1980s that it attracted significant critical scrutiny.[131] Even as rap was being celebrated by listeners as "party music," the genre was also developing its long-standing documentary tendencies (e.g., "The Message") in a way that proved disturbing to some critics. Whereas early rap did not refer overmuch to the heroin empires of 1970s urban America, which had fueled gang culture to some degree, the widely discussed popularity of cocaine in its various forms in the 1980s played to white audiences' appetite for spectacle, fear, and fascination with black outlaw culture.[132] Rap music began to discuss "freebase" and "crack," then-new terms seen by outsiders as linguistic windows onto a foreign, dangerous subculture.

The emergence of crack was, according to many interpreters, coextensive with the development of gangsta rap as a subgenre. The drug itself was said to have been nicknamed after blaxploitation film characters or P-Funk songs, and soon became referenced in rap music itself (first in Grandmaster Flash's "White Lines" and Toddy Tee's "Batteram").[133] This kind of reportage proved unexpectedly appealing to white suburban audiences. Artists like Boogie Down Productions, Schoolly D, and Public Enemy introduced new narratives into rap, documenting crime, poverty, incarceration, and "thug life" in general. A "direct by-product of the crack explosion," this new documentary strain in rap evolved—from the late 1980s to the mid-1990s—into the grim, rough-edged gangsta idiom heard in Niggaz with Attitude (NWA, which included famous alums Dr. Dre and Ice Cube), Ice-T, 2pac, the Notorious B.I.G., and the Wu-Tang Clan, among others.[134] White audiences have, of course, long been fascinated not simply by black culture but by black outlaws. In addition to the archetypes noted briefly above, post-1960s popular culture has traded heavily in icons like the pimp and the gangster: characters derive both authenticity and allure through challenges to authority; the narrative appeal of fugitive life or jail life reveals not just an idolization of outlaw masculinity, but a near romanticization of social misery. As authors like Richard Slotkin have shown, the veneration of rebel figures runs deep in American history, but in anti-rap criticism, these icons are racialized as threats to social order.[135]

From its inception, gangsta rap openly courted such attention, eliciting both shocked condemnation and voyeuristic desires. Public Enemy became known for their militant politics and social scorn. Outspoken social critics, several of the group's members wore militaristic clothing that resembled both the Guardian Angels and the Nation of Islam (NOI). Lead MC Chuck D famously and repeatedly referred to rap as "black people's CNN," and he articulated an explicitly political sensibility that fused black nationalism, sympathy for the NOI, and a concern to document the struggles of city-dwelling African Americans.[136] NWA, in contrast, was not so programmatic in its antiauthoritarianism, tending instead to celebrate the "thug lifestyle" as a countersign to a social order that seemingly tolerated institutionalized racism. This model proved by far the most prominent and the most successful, and its central tropes—automatic weapons, "hoes," crack, and ghetto nihilism—proved to be hugely successful in the 1990s. It may be possible to read in this spiking popularity a parallel to the cultures of militarism that thrived in the 1990s, from the commercial cultures of blockbuster cinematic violence to subcultures ranging from "weekend warrior" paintball games and war reenactments to the aggressively separatist militia movements.[137] The genre's greatest exposure came during the infamous East Coast/West Coast wars of the mid-1990s, when West Coasters (including 2pac Shakur, associated with Death Row Records) clashed heatedly and publicly with East Coasters like Notorious B.I.G.[138]

Considerable attention was given to gangsta rap in this period owing in part to an extant tradition of media attention being summoned at key moments of panic and outrage surrounding rap music. Most notable was the Florida obscenity trial of Luther Campbell and 2 Live Crew, whose lyrics were thought to be too salacious for public consumption.[139] There was also an outcry against Public Enemy member Professor Griff's blatant anti-Semitism ("why do you think they call it jew-elry?") and against Ice-T's song "Cop Killer" (performed with his band Body Count and attacked by former vice president Dan Quayle).[140] Overlooked in much of this reportage is the fact that central to gangsta is a critical impulse that both constitutes a "ghettocentric identity" and targets "deindustrialization, rightwing policies, and market liberalization."[141] Eithne Quinn's study of gangsta rap explores this duality effectively, not only by documenting gangsta's roots in black working-class youth communities (or communities of extreme poverty) but also by showing that the genre's popularity contributes to a "politics of redistribution" (where more black people are involved in the recording industry and its profits than before) and a "politics of recognition" (which she claims raises "questions about cultural identity and political orientation through its textural practices").[142] As Quinn and others show, beneath gangsta's confrontational rhetoric (NWA's defiant "Fuck flippin' burgers!" or Wu-Tang's "First things first man you're fuckin' with the worst, I'll stick pins in your head like a motherfuckin' nurse"), its often grisly documentary streak (Biggie's "After the hit, leave you on the street with your neck split, down your backbone to where your motherfuckin' shit drip"), and its gallows humor ("Guess what, motherfucker? You just won the wet t-shirt contest!" Ice Cube exclaims just before gunfire explodes), there is a seldom acknowledged articulation of a specific social location.[143] These elements are largely seen by critics as expressions of danger and eruptive violence rather than constituting a critical discourse.

Against the open-endedness and social criticism which interpreters like Quinn and Szwed locate in rap, the music's critics seek to establish interpretive closure. As Adam Krims notes, some criticism of rap has focused on its sensual or bodily pleasures: rap as a "sonic force" provides "deep visceral pleasures" to listeners.[144] Additionally, some diatribes against the music have focused on the alleged incomprehensibility of the lyrics. What Krims calls "reality rap," however, has received by far the most attention from critics, particularly from the religion of fear's anti-rock preachers. Krims's term refers essentially to gangsta or other subgenres which produce "[r]epresentations of gang/street life . . . [including] boasts about physical/violent/gun prowess, boasts about the 'hardness' of a particular location (e.g., Compton, Houston, or some borough of New York), [and] narratives of criminal life."[145]

From its inception, rap generated a more intense critical scrutiny than even metal had attracted. As of 2001, 59 percent of rap records carry a warning sticker, while only 13 percent of metal records do (this despite the fact that some unlabeled metal records contain images which might turn the stomach of even a hardened horror film buff).[146] Rap music has attracted the considerable indignation not only of fear's anti-rock preachers but of a broader range of critics, including pundit George Will, who described the music as a "slide into the sewer."[147] Rap has served, even more effectively than metal, as an all-purpose scapegoat. There are many examples of this. Consider that, in response to the 1989 assaults on joggers in Central Park, blame was more or less arbitrarily assigned to rapper Tone Loc (whose "Wild Thing" was a party anthem that year).[148] These and other sensationalist stories (e.g., a *New York Post* headline declaring "Rampaging Teen Gang Slays 'Rap' Fan") proliferated from the late 1980s through the mid-1990s, and they "fed easily into the white fears that black teens need only a spark to start an uncontrollable urban forest fire."[149] As Rose demonstrates, rap was being constructed not simply as an epiphenomenon of an "urban crisis" involving drug use and gang violence but as a causal factor in the creation of this "crisis." This discursive construction also extended to the ways in which concerts were promoted and reported. Following an incident at the Nassau Coliseum in 1988, it was asserted in many public forums that violence was either more likely to occur at rap concerts than elsewhere or that rap audiences were potential powder kegs of social disorder. As John D'Agostino wrote in a 1990 *Los Angeles Times* article, Public Enemy's audience was "a single-minded moveable beast. Funk meets Nuremberg rally."[150] Around the same time, *Penthouse* wrote that "Flavor Flav and Chuck D spew boastful bile about gang violence and the pleasures of misogyny."[151]

While such claims might seem superficially to echo Larson's concerns about Slayer audiences (whom he also likened to proto-Nazis, ready to erupt in violence), the anti-rap idiom is substantively different insofar as it is racially coded, masking its concerns about race in a revealing rhetoric of crime and disorder. Barry Glassner writes, "By the late 1990s, the ruinous power of rap was so taken for granted, people could blame rappers for almost any violent or misogynistic act anywhere."[152] African American critics of the gangsta genre often included other rappers, who believed that groups like NWA were pandering too much to the salaciousness of white listeners.[153] Such claims, however, usually went unnoticed in the wake of larger social panics surrounding the music. There were numerous bans implemented throughout the United States (such as a 1990 Tennessee ban on the sale of NWA's *Straight Outta Compton*). Ice Cube's 1991 *Death Certificate* was protested by Korean-American and Jewish-American groups for its offensive lyrics, in response to which the state of Oregon passed a statute making it illegal to display the rapper's picture in any record store.[154] These efforts represented a diffuse impulse which sharpened quickly in reaction to the aforementioned "Cop Killer." Upon the song's 1992 release, a national outrage ensued: police officers protested tour stops (it was not uncommon for off-duty officers to rush the stage at NWA and Body Count concerts); President George H. W. Bush and Vice President Dan Quayle routinely denounced the song in campaign speeches; Charlton Heston and the National Rifle Association pressured Warner Brothers to reprint the album without "Cop Killer"; many national chains returned crates of the record to their distributors; and Focus on the Family actively publicized the song to law enforcement communities.[155] Focus on the Family's magazine has also regularly published articles seeking to educate parents about the popular culture to which their children might be exposed: rap's "lurid lyrics" have regularly been singled out for condemnation.[156]

As was the case with metal in the 1980s, rap in the 1990s opened up an opportunity for the construction of a powerful screen against which were projected interpretive frames that displaced concerns about the erosion of urban social safety nets onto vilified black males and popular music. In 1994, House Commerce, Consumer Protection, and Competitiveness Subcommittee meetings were held to "discuss the necessity of rating gangsta rap records," and these hearings featured loaded testimony linking rap with urban violence and increased drug use. Immediately following these hearings, then Georgia representative Newt Gingrich urged supporters to boycott radio stations which played any rap music at all. William Bennett and C. Dolores Tucker went further and stated their desire to stamp out any rap which was "blatantly pro-drug" or "obscene."[157] Bennett pronounced that "nothing less is at stake than civilization."[158] Their injunctions were later supported by Senators Joseph Lieberman and Sam Nunn. Such social panics emerged once again in April 2007, in the aftermath of radio personality Don Imus's firing following his characterization of the Rutgers University women's basketball team. Imus's defenders suggested that his language was no worse than, and in some ways drew upon, the idiom of hip-hop. Following this assertion, rapper Russell Simmons said, "Comparing Don Imus' language with hip-hop artists' poetic expression is misguided and inaccurate and feeds into a mind-set that can be a catalyst for unwarranted, rampant censorship."[159]

This cluster of anti-rap initiatives drew upon the kinds of allegations central to the religion of fear in order to defame the genre as a whole. Indeed, during this same period, fear's anti-rock preachers were framing rap music as a religio-political source of panic. Godwin called rap music "Heavy Metal's ugly young cousin," a music filled with "hypnotic, street-wise chanting" whose "mindless monotony either mesmerizes you or drives you out of the house."[160] He focused on rap as spectacle, making much of the gold chains and track suits once worn by rap artists and issuing tabloid-ready alarms about the links between rappers and gangs like the Crips and the Bloods. Whereas the religion of fear expresses its anti-metal sentiments in a discourse about occultic disruptions of the psyche and their social consequences, its anti-rap sentiments trade in the language of crime and disorder which threaten moral safety and uprightness, a contrast highlighted by Amy Binder and Robert Glassner. To critics, demons craft each genre, but listeners respond differently. In Godwin's criticism, there is also what may be a tacit theory of the city at work, when he claims that "[t]he base elements of personal revenge, lustful greed and blood-boiling violence are central to most of this music—a simmering match set to the short fuse of urban unrest."[161] With the careful documentation and prurient fascination that are central to the erotics of fear, Godwin occasionally refers to the possibility of "demonic infestation" as a result of exposure to rap ("the beat," after all, stems from "voodoo" and can, along with rap's "monotonous" lyrics, "hypnotize" the listener).[162] More frequently, he indulges in vivid descriptions of the "[v]iolent riots and stabbings" he deems likely to occur at concerts, which become scenes of "beatings and blood-letting... [b]usted heads, bloodied faces, broken ribs and even gunshots."[163] The music itself pushes listeners to act in such fashion, according to Godwin, who notes ominously—after detailed exegeses of Schoolly D and Run DMC lyrics—that such violence has begun to creep out of concerts and into city streets (he blames a rash of teen murders in Baltimore on rap music).[164]

Larson has appropriated these arguments in his recent reengagements with pop music. One Larson fan and advocate contended that, for Larson, "[i]nterest in rap took the place of interest in death metal" during the 1990s, when Larson began to insist that the rap genre itself is misbegotten and lacks artistic merit.[165] Citing Snoop Dogg and other gangsta celebrities, Larson—

who has also had rap artists like the Geto Boys on his radio show—claims that the rap scene consists merely of "screwed-up people screwing up other people" and promoting "attitudes that the answer is in the barrel of a gun."[166] Such assertions are reflected in the public interpretation of events such as a 1998 school shooting in Jonesboro, Arkansas, where two white students opened fire at their school. In the wake of this incident, and others like it, it was widely believed that rap music and rappers themselves had directly inspired the shootings.[167]

Like many of the white suburbanites who comprise a major part of rap's audience, Godwin and Larson believe that the genre is defined by harsh reportage and lyrical shock tactics. Clearly, much "reality rap" reflects some of its creators' circumstances, and the critics at times confuse documentation with endorsement. What emerges from these claims about rap music is the sense that what both audiences and critics fear in rap is precisely what draws them to it. Indeed, the religion of fear itself abundantly manifests one of the traits it so fervently denounces in rap: an affinity for and reliance on violent imagery. These critics, then, are engaged in what Tricia Rose calls an "ideological recuperation" of black music, wherein genre music becomes interpretively and ideologically overdetermined (here, through alarmist statements about black sexuality, violence, revenge fantasies, and drug culture) as a means of allaying the perceived threats this music signals.[168] Of course, the articulations of these "threats"—and the overdetermination they provoke—are also expressions of the erotics of fear.

The intense visualizations of black culture (particularly poor black urban culture, which anti-rap preachers mostly decline to engage) both provoke and panic, and they confirm that the critical gaze "is more easily drawn to acts, images, and threats of black male violence than to any other form of racial address."[169] This voyeuristic dimension of criticism—where ghettos and gangs and drugs are described vividly prior to denunciation—is central to the erotics of fear as well. These elements make for compelling narrative and enable critics to intone warnings about the social disorder sown by black youths (one of the dominant themes of anti-rap preaching) while focusing their concerns mostly on the effects of this disorder on rap's listeners and consumers.

"WHAT'S WRONG WITH ROCK MUSIC? EVERYTHING!"

What are we to make of the sinister plots that snake unseen through the music industry, the hidden messages whispered by rock's demons, the shaggy rebellions encouraged by heavy metal, or the thug life that rap promotes?[170] Sustained engagement with this particular strain of the religion of fear reveals an alarming portrait of American culture under siege, a canvas teeming with Bosch-like details of evil, violence, and lust. The streets of hip-hop America run red with the blood of gangsters and innocents alike; knives and "gatts" (guns) are brandished at rap shows, while any innocent citizen may be gunned down on a sidewalk, the victim of a beat-driven drive-by; and males are socialized by this music to care more about "bling" than about "bitches and hoes." Metal, meanwhile, is believed to urge each unsuspecting teen to burn an upside-down cross into his forehead like Deicide's Glen Benton; the visual landscape of American metal is dotted not with signs of virtue and order but with pentagrams, tombstones, and leather; with each double kick-drum blast beat or thrashy riff, some dark god is summoned or school terror plotted.

These allegations might seem preposterous, and in many quarters may elicit snorts of dismissal. Yet, over time, they have coalesced as a meaningful sociopolitical framework and a significant part of the religion of fear. Critical discourse about music—its origins and its effects—confirms that music is both a product of a social world (with all of its assumptions) and also serves as a projection of a particular world's interpretations. A central feature of the religion of fear's interpretive frame, and a key motivating factor behind its cultural construction of rap and metal, is the contention that young souls risk corruption (and possibly damnation) by contact with certain products of fallen, secular culture. While there is no single demographic for either heavy metal or hip-hop broadly construed, critics of these genres worry that the musics promote alienation and rebelliousness while denouncing "traditional" religious morality and social norms.

The religion of fear's engagement with popular music generates neither a free-standing narration of demonology (like Chick tracts) nor pedagogic entertainments (like Hell Houses). Rather, this discourse is primarily reactive or interpretive. The particular dimensions of antiliberalism revealed here are a concern about society's permissiveness regarding popular culture, panic about the glorification of sex (and its impact on gender roles and domesticity), an imperative to combat occultism (felt acutely in heavy metal and its purported threat to the unstable listener), and a worldview defined by the specter of racial chaos (embodied in rap music). These musics are framed as criminal or deviant and are linked with pluralism and urbanism. Against their influence, fear's anti-rock preachers position a specific kind of religious authority.

One level of response to this situation involves the reader or listener in a politics of consumption and commodification. After all, many of these texts encourage boycotts and putting pressure on record companies. While stopping short of encouraging direct action, Larson is convinced that protests, boycotts, and even bans are moves of strength in spiritual warfare, aimed at preventing noxious ideas from circulating and demonic artists from gaining popularity.[171] (There is an irony in this, because Larson gives those he denounces so much airtime and gives his audiences extended opportunities to listen to the music he finds so objectionable. By way of example, one young listener thanked Larson for exposing him to "cool bands"—like Danzig and Pantera—that got no mainstream radio play and for mentioning belief systems, like Wicca or Masonry, of which he had not been aware.)[172] Beyond these actions, themes of warfare abound in this criticism, a symbolic response more aggressive than suggesting a simple change in consumer habits. Fear's anti-rocking is linked clearly to a larger narrative about the decline of the family, the rise of secular humanism, and anti-Christian "bigotry." For critics like Larson, rock is a prism through which to articulate anxiety about pluralism and a permissive society.

There is, of course, a larger story to be told about the debates within these communities regarding the merits of contemporary Christian music (CCM). Tom Beaujour, editor in chief of *Revolver* magazine, told me that he sees the rise of Christian metal and hardcore in particular as reactions against decades of anti-rock preaching. The music sponsored by largely Christian labels—like Tooth & Nail and Solid State—is, in Beaujour's estimation, desexualized and features intentionally vague lyrics (so as to broaden appeal). Most of these artists, Beaujour continued, believe that their music has to be even better than that of "secular" artists if they are to compete: "the rhetoric has been perfected," and bands exist more or less comfortably in the world, seeking to create an alternate scene instead of railing against it.[173] Mudrian believes that Christian rock music (metal and other genres) is unlikely to attract as much critical attention as its nonreligious counterparts, because "it's not really as sensational as metal bands screaming about Satan, burning down churches and toasting inverted crosses into their foreheads." The focus on such sensationalism, Mudrian speculates, constitutes a way "to deflect people's attention from real political issues."[174] However, the rise of CCM has indeed provoked considerable debate in the critical community. Some critics, such as Larson, are open to sponsoring Christian alternatives to secular music. Early CCM artist Larry Norman once indirectly chastised Larson in the 1972 song "Why Should the Devil Have All the Good Music?"; perhaps this was the beginning of Larson's recalibration (indeed, he has since recorded his own albums in this vein).[175] There are just as many who, like Godwin and Terry Watkins, believe that all rock music carries a demonic taint to it; this orientation contends that any music possessing rock's structure or dynamics should be forbidden, regardless of whether or not its message is ostensibly uplifting.[176] Both sentiments can be found among young evangelicals (one young woman recalled her friend's insistence that "the Lord didn't want Christians listening to rap"), of course, and it will be fascinating to see the ways in which these arguments develop in time.[177]

Godwin has been the most forceful contemporary critic of CCM, applying many of his familiar themes and charges to the growing genre. His 1997 book *What's Wrong with Christian Rock* was published by sympathizer Jack Chick. Godwin has also released several videos and DVDs containing his anti-CCM sermons. In a recent piece, "Ageing [sic] Hippies and a Dead-End Dream," Godwin posits that CCM is simply part of a long-standing development shared by all expressions of rock music, part of a steady social decline both mirrored and shaped by such popular musics. He argues that the development of rock from the 1950s through the rise of CCM has generated the viewpoint that "God is love, man." Such a failure to appreciate the stern father figure God and the necessity of rule morality has facilitated, in Godwin's reckoning, the triumph of liberalism in the political sphere and CCM in the music sphere (exemplified specifically by CCM's roots with the Jesus People USA). Godwin suggests that free love, New Age, and corporate power have colluded in portraying God as the "Big Democrat in the sky" rather than "Lord and Master of His people."[178] Godwin's updated criticism blends conspiracy theory with a representation of God that positions itself against therapeutic culture. He has been active in bringing his anti-CCM message on the road since the early 1990s, particularly in the Midwest and the Northeast, where he has garnered both praise and vilification. Just as Larson continues to invite metal musicians to appear on his radio show, Godwin seeks out debate with his Others as well. Even early in his career, Godwin boasted:

> I have personally met a great number of the Rock stars. They have ALL agreed to serve Satan in return for money and fame.... I attended special ceremonies at various recording studios throughout the U.S. for the specific purpose of placing satanic blessings on the Rock music recorded. We did incantations which placed demons on EVERY record and tape of rock music that was sold. At times we also called up special demons who spoke on the recordings—the various backmasked messages.[179]

More recently, Godwin has engaged famous CCM artist Glenn Kaiser (of the Rez Band) in debate. Some supporters seek to emulate Godwin and "proudly carry the banner forward for the cause, shining Light into those dark corners of the world."[180] Yet many who might regard "secular" pop music with suspicion stop well short of attacking CCM (Godwin, many detractors note, even went so far as to single out wholesome Amy Grant). While Godwin's viewpoint is not normative, then, his discourse is nonetheless part of an active and enduring debate.[181]

By projecting images of the demonic into metal and rap, fear's purveyors both delineate the horrible within pop music and also link this discourse of fright to social concerns about rebellion against authority, non-Christian sources of meaning, illicit sexuality, violence, and recreational drug use. Metal and rap then become ideological constructs which serve to articulate the religion of fear's declension narrative and politics of restoration, drawing these themes together in a more public, recognizable, and widely circulated form than in Chick's subcultural missives. The anti-rock preachers' attempts to contain and counter the messages and consequences they locate link up on an additional level to the sociopolitical discourse of censorship. While this discourse has links to the above concerns about consumption and distribution, it has far more to do with the dynamics of socialization and control over interpretive frames. Audiences are constructed as either potential victims (who are "subjected to" themes which should be regulated) or instigators of harm.[182] Artists are constructed as either dupes or conniving, libidinous plotters. Larson, Godwin, and those who share their concerns (such as Steve Peters, who is proudly carrying the torch into the twenty-first century) seek, through the projection of such interpretive or ideological frames on metal and rap, to render the music as a cultural text whose meanings are unambiguous.[183] And while it is clear on some level that both genres take pride in the very airs of defiance that so incite fear's anti-rock preachers, the interpretive responses generated reveal more about the critics than about the music under scrutiny.

By engaging media with countermedia, these social critics construct ideological portraits of hot-button morality issues that are also central to the NCR's political worldview: challenges to conventional gender roles, questions about social or political authority, and the diminution of religion's role in everyday life and social institutions. What is more, this critical discourse not only links popular entertainments to sociopolitical concerns, it also—as Amy Binder suggests—serves as a mode of socialization or political pedagogy that audiences may absorb into their standard modes of perception and behavior.[184] By situating these musics in sociopolitical frames for interpretation, fear's anti-rock preachers also establish templates for listeners to reason analogically and make comparisons. As Binder writes, these frames "are abstractions that writers and their audiences use to make sense of their experiences."[185]

On one level, then, this discourse explains social disturbances like teen suicides and positions its adherents against multiple constructions of danger. On another level, anti-rock preaching reveals the erotics of fear and the demonology within. The impulse to catalog the sinful and present it as evidence, to troll deep in the murky waters of corruption, characterizes the entire tradition of such preaching and nowhere more so than in the influential figures in this chapter, in whose criticism fear's erotics are central. These rock jeremiads depend upon an infinitely detailed and often extremely imaginative taxonomy of gore, moral failure, hedonism, heterodoxy, and social calamity.[186] This marks a fascinating irony, as it registers an important similarity with the music under attack: both metal and rap have historically been fascinated with extreme images, particularly those depicting bodily destruction, horror, and gore. Additionally, the centrality of the demonic to this discourse is apparent. But the religion of fear keeps its demons close only to deny them, revealing the centrality of what Ingebretsen suggestively calls "a complicated dance of *fort, da*: be driven away, stay close."[187] To fear's preachers, turning one's back on sin is nearly as bad as wallowing in it. To avoid the latter, they maintain a proximity, even an intimacy, with their demonic Others.

The anti-rock narration of fear suggests that, in the eyes of Larson and others, post-1960s society has become so permissive that, even in the seemingly innocuous arena of musical entertainment, dark forces can gather. In its defense against these forces, the religion of fear articulates an understanding of public life where religious practitioners are engaged (through criticism, censorship, and evangelization) but are also continually under threat (from, for example, urban disorder or psychic frailty); an understanding of sexual and gender roles that cleaves firmly to that of the "golden age"; and an ambivalence toward public order (which, on the one hand, is so bureaucratically distant that it permits "abominations" in the name of free speech but which, on the other hand, is a necessary enforcement tool).

So, in forbidding and demonizing these two musical forms, a specific cultural politics is advanced and boundaries drawn. Fear's anti-rock preachers construct an encyclopedia of rock demonology which limns what is acceptable behavior and identity. Drinking deeply of the forbidden in order to deny it, the anti-rockers throw themselves into the crossing sound streams of deep, subwoofing bass and overdriven guitar crunch in order to sound out a threnody for a fallen America. This sad song achieves its effects not just through piety and purity but, at its core, from its monsters and its sins. Though critics worry that such foul musics have replaced America's Christian heritage with its opposite, the two traditions are coexistent, codependent: these demons are never fully driven out but, like an endlessly glitched compact disc, return to infinitely reassert their place of prominence in this discourse.

5

"Shake 'Em to Wake 'Em"

Hell Houses and the Conservative Evangelical Theater of Horror

When you're pointing people in the direction of the cross, when you're helping them understand that they can walk away from the pain and the guilt and the heaviness of sin, you're not hurting them. . . . Sometimes you've got to shake 'em to wake 'em. —Keenan Roberts, *CNN Newsnight* (October 31, 2005)

Anglo-American culture seems to be governed by the perverse belief that portrayals of the body's abuse or destruction are harmless, even fortifying, while those that show the body in pleasure act like poison. —Walter Kendrick, *The Thrill of Fear*

Your emotions make you a monster. —Dead Kennedys, "Your Emotions"

It is October 2006, and my wife and I are deeply lost on dark country roads somewhere outside Elon, North Carolina. The directions we have been given to this year's Judgement House (a new production featuring a high school athletics theme) are apparently faulty and—in a metaphoric association that is not lost on us—we are wandering in darkness. We were disappointed to learn that the annual productions in Durham and Garner, much closer to our home, were not being sponsored this year. Tiffany Garrison of the Altamahaw Pentecostal Holiness Church mentioned that people from Virginia and Georgia had traveled to her Judgement House. We wondered as we drove farther if these productions—such an indelible part of America's evangelical landscape for over a decade—were beginning to wane in popularity. But, in October 2007, there were again multiple productions in our area, and it appeared that the enduring fascination that this day of darkness holds was in no danger of abating.[1]

Halloween has, like other holidays in the United States, been divested of its historic and etymological status as a "holy day." Certainly, it has been some time since the dominant public understanding of holidays in the United States was oriented exclusively (or even primarily) toward their religious dimension. Leigh Eric Schmidt has written of the ineluctably consumerist qualities of Easter, Valentine's Day, and Christmas, among other nominally Christian holidays.[2] Halloween, while certainly not understood as a day of particular sacred significance for Christians, has in recent decades become the subject of intense religious (and commercial) scrutiny and activity. Referred to variously as All Hallows' Eve, Samhain, and the Devil's Night, its origins are—like those of other holidays—often inscrutable. Augustine Thompson writes that pre-Christian Celtic cultures celebrated a minor festival on October 31, but that the holiday's longevity is due to its proximity to the Feast of All Saints on November 1, which Pope Gregory III moved from May 13 in order to coincide with the anniversary of the dedication of All Saints Chapel in Rome.[3] Elisabeth Nixon suggests that the holiday has historically been in continual contact with Christianity, through "failed Celtic-Druid's [sic] acceptance of the Roman Catholic Church's All Saints' Day and All Souls' Day; gradual acknowledgment by the Church of the pagan Samhaim [sic]; its official transformation into All Hallows' Eve, and its final re-presentation into Halloween."[4] Additional accounts suggest that it was on this eve that all of the disembodied spirits of the previous year's dead rose up in search of living bodies to possess for the coming year. Boundaries were blurred, and for a night the realm of the dead seeped into that of the living. The living, seeking to ward off these spirits, assumed the garb of ghosts and demons to deter the would-be possessors and then gathered outside their homes making noise and commotion to scare the spirits away.[5]

Though the specifics of earlier beliefs and practices may be blurred, the annual ritual of dressing up and mischief making survived long enough to be brought to the United States by the millions of Irish immigrants who fled their homeland during the potato famine of the 1840s (though it is believed that the actual practice of trick-or-treating derives from the ninth-century European custom of "souling," where itinerant Christian beggars received "soul cakes" from the houses of strangers).[6] It is, of course, a long way from wandering ascetics and spirit possession to the commerce-drenched landscape of contemporary Halloween, with its smiling, pudgy ghosts, bobbing for apples, sugar-crazed children, and parades of costumes tied in with the latest blockbuster film (Shrek, Spider-Man, and Frodo compete with traditional ghosts, werewolves, and witches). Despite being surrounded by familiar narratives and conventions—in both doggerel and well-regarded tales of fright like Washington Irving's "The Legend of Sleepy Hollow" or stories by Edgar Allan Poe—this holiday has long been a magnet for social concerns, few of them initially having to do with paganism. In the American popular vernacular, Halloween is associated with dressing up, suspending social conventions, overindulgence, and a rash of slasher movies sharing its name. Yet it has also continually generated fears of risk and defilement, ranging from well-known panics about razor blades in candy bars and one-time concerns about the flammability of costumes to the recent preponderance of safety guides, daylight trick-or-treating, and consumer-based trick-or-treating like Malloween.[7]

Yet other presences have recently emerged in conjunction with this darkest of holidays. When leaves fall and days shorten, America seems to turn black and orange for a time. While the mischief and role playing of Halloween are often seen as playful frights, no more threatening than its consumerism or orgies of eating, many conservative evangelicals have since the 1970s made the holiday a source of concern: it has been denounced as a pagan incursion into Christian America, a gateway into a world of demonology, a cover for the popularization of Satanic entertainments, and a night when children are at risk of bodily harm or abduction. Such concerns circulate throughout public discourse, and indeed throughout the religion of fear, and one response to them has taken shape in conservative evangelical improvisations on the haunted house. Such efforts occurred as early as the 1970s, but since the early 1990s they have become surprisingly popular and explicitly sociopolitical in tone. Creations like Hell Houses and Judgement Houses are morality plays sponsored by local churches to illustrate to young audiences the dangers—not merely physical, but moral and salvific—posed by drug use, premarital sex, and other "illicit" activities or beliefs. Relying on intense and graphic dramatizations of car crashes, abortions, gun violence, and other incidents of shock, these productions use the techniques and narrative strategies of genre horror in order to explore a different kind of demonology, one which creators believe is erupting into social and political life. As Hell House creator Keenan Roberts told me, "sin always brings about damaging consequences, the kind of thing that is just reeling out of control" in American life.[8]

Below, I tell the story of these creations in the context of this book's concerns, peering into the dark corners of this religious imagining of social life and reading its frights for an understanding of the politics produced therein. In my research, I have drawn from local Hell Houses and Judgement Houses (primarily the Bethel Christian Center, Durham, North Carolina; and the Garner Free Will Baptist Church and Victory Fellowship Church, both of Garner, North Carolina); read scripts for the productions as well as multiple reports in journals; studied dozens of recorded and filmed performances (including George Ratliff's well-known *Hell House* documentary); toured multiple "virtual" Hell Houses; and interviewed both sponsors and audience members (including Roberts and Tom Hudgins, founder of Judgement House). My accounts draw on all of these sources to generate a composite picture of these provocative religious creations. We see in their popularity and assertiveness an important moment of transition in the religion of fear, when this pop demonology began to erupt—with all of its viscera and its idiom of cultural concern—into national consciousness, generating not only social criticism but genuine thrills that appealed to believer and unsaved alike.

HELL'S ROOTS

Hell Houses[9] began to appear regularly in conservative evangelical churches in the 1990s, yet they drew on older traditions. In the early 1970s, Lynchburg, Virginia's Reverend Jerry Falwell established a precedent for the Hell House. Gordon Luff, Falwell's Liberty University's youth ministry coordinator, had attended a dramatization called *Scream in the Dark* in 1970 in Bakersfield, California. Luff was impressed by both the fundraising and ministerial potential of these productions and presented the idea to Falwell.[10] At this time, Falwell was known among evangelicals as the outspoken leader of Lynchburg's Thomas Road Baptist Church and author of texts like *Church Aflame!* which called for a newer, more aggressive and engaged evangelical style. By the end of the 1970s, he was recognized and reviled as the most visible public figure of the NCR, an image that lasted until his 2007 death, and as president of the influential Moral Majority. Yet in 1972, the Thomas Road Baptist Church Youth Department and Liberty University were searching for new forms of outreach and ministry that would get the attention of a youth culture they regarded as endangered. Taking the cue from Luff, one result of this evangelistic makeover was the first *Scaremare*, a dramatic play designed to illustrate the consequences of sin with documentary realism in the context of a haunted house. Early versions of the production were certainly tame by the standards of contemporary Hell Houses: they featured conventional haunted-room props, ghosts leaping from dark spaces to startle attendees, and a concluding crucifixion scene, without much in the way of explicit shock and gore. But Falwell's production was rooted in a concern that conventional celebrations of Halloween inured young people to the presence of evil in the world and also constituted a sign of Christianity's waning cultural influence.

Falwell believed that Halloween had potential value insofar as it "does remind the general public of the reality of Satan," but he saw alternatives as necessary to combat the holiday's negative effects, particularly the way it brought children into contact with "evil spirits and those things pertaining to the netherworld."[11] This evil was, to Falwell, manifesting itself in American society through temptations, wayward politicians, and broken homes. *Scaremare* would focus on themes of "death and preparation for eternal life," hoping to connect with teenagers through an idiom they understood, bringing them the gospel before they fell prey to sin.[12] *Scaremare* sought to plant a question in the minds of its young attendees: "If I die tonight, where will I go?"[13] Themes of uncertainty and risk abound in *Scaremare*, set against a backdrop of wholesome alternative activities like dressing up as Bible characters instead of monsters, bobbing for apples in place of trick-or-treating, and campfire games rather than ghost stories. Still in existence, *Scaremare* continues to rely upon (and recently, perhaps in response to the popularity of Hell Houses, has amplified) its graphic depictions of sin's consequences.

During the period of *Scaremare*'s inception, the wheels of evangelical youth culture were being greased by dissatisfaction with the perceived waywardness of the 1960s and the emptiness of the "counterculture." Other improvisations on the haunted house appeared on the evangelical landscape. Bill Bright's Campus Crusade for Christ, for example, regularly sponsored alternative haunted houses with less controversial themes whose primary purpose was the distribution of conversion literature at the event's conclusion. As evangelical popular culture continued to flower between the 1970s and 1980s, the proliferation of Halloween alternatives served as one sign among many of an oppositional stance present not only in evangelical political organizing but also in other spheres of public life, serving almost as nodes connecting the different arenas. However, it was with the emergence of, first, Judgement Houses and, later, Hell Houses—explicitly positioned against conventional celebrations of Halloween, rather than just modifications thereof—that such entertainments became more explicitly confrontational and controversial.

Founded in 1983 in Clearwater, Florida, by Tom Hudgins, Judgement House actually preceded Roberts in appropriating the example of *Scaremare*. From his conservative Calvary Baptist Church, Hudgins sought to construct vivid, dramatic narratives which would illustrate to children and adolescents the gory, demonic consequences of decisions they would soon face. The original Judgement House—now sponsored by Hudgins's New Creation Evangelism—has endured as a popular annual event, particularly in the South, and has been attended by nearly 70,000 people internationally.[14] A Judgement House is geared toward not only evangelization and conversion but also institutionalization. For example, part of the basic "outreach" of Judgement House includes regular conferences (which cost $30–45 to attend) and the invitation to become a "covenant church" (which costs $355 annually). Everything Judgement House touches is registered and trademarked, especially matters pertaining to covenant churches (whose benefits include use of the Judgement House logo and name, new copyrighted scripts annually, and one free conference admission for a "lay leader").[15] Judgement Houses generally run for five nights, with attendances of approximately 300–500 per night. The organization's Web site keeps statistics of the number of annual salvations and rededications and advertises fundraising events, such as annual golf tournaments.[16]

An additional variation, the Revelation Walk, emerged in the 1990s from Pell City, Alabama's Eden Westside Baptist Church. This thirteen-scene outdoor tour focuses on the awful fate awaiting those left behind after the Rapture. It claims to be rooted in the book of Revelation but is also clearly indebted to popular dispensationalism. This link has become especially pronounced in recent years, as audiences are now asked whether they want to accept the mark of the beast—in play, of course—a decision which will determine the rest of their experience of the production. There is also more attention recently to the Antichrist's plots (he amasses armies, shouting, "War on every continent!").[17] Similarly inclined is Stockbridge, Georgia's Metro Heights Baptist Church, which sponsors the Tribulation Trail, whose central scene is called "The Chilling Fields."[18] Just as I was completing work on this book, Garner Free Will Baptist Church changed its annual production to Rapture House, combining the scene-based structure of a Hell House with the dispensationalist narrative of a Rapture Walk or Tribulation Trail. One final source is the longstanding and popular production *Heaven's Gates, Hell's Flames*, which the Sunshine Evangelistic Association claims has been shown for over forty-five years (but which has only become nationally popular recently). The play is a comparably simple depiction of life-after-death scenarios.[19]

The leading figure in the popularization of Christian Halloween alternatives is Keenan Roberts, an Assemblies of God pastor active in the Southwest since 1990. In an association that would delight any conspiracy theorist, Roberts staged his first Hell House in 1992 in Roswell, New Mexico (the axis mundi of UFOlogy).[20] In 1995, he first packaged and sold his "Hell House

FIGURE 5.1 Hell House demons. Courtesy New Destiny Christian Center.

outreach" kit from suburban Denver's Abundant Life Christian Center.[21] That year, Roberts's local production was attended by about 5,000 people (by the following year, there were approximately 200 churches nationwide staging productions). By this point, Roberts had fine-tuned his seven-scene "morality play," whose purposes were broadly similar to those of *Scaremare*: to use representations of fear and dramatizations of sin as conversion devices. Yet the specific features of Roberts's improvisation soon became marked by their debt to genre horror and, in the terms of this book, by the erotics of fear and the demonology within. Roberts has since sold thousands of kits—each complete with a 263-page instructional manual, a DVD of a standard performance, a CD featuring recordings of God's voice, and various audio and visual special effects (such as the demons who whisper into the ears of teens contemplating suicide, peals of demonic laughter, and so forth)—and has achieved fame and notoriety as the "spiritually flammable" Hell Houses have become ever more popular in conservative evangelical cultures. Since Roberts began selling his kits, over 4,100 sites have sponsored Hell Houses nationwide. One may also purchase a tour production (to construct a stand-alone version of the entire housing) or a stage production (to be implemented in extant settings like sanctuaries or meeting rooms). Roberts also gives casting advice and prop recommendations. Since 1995, he has regularly appeared on high-profile television shows (the old *Donahue* show, *CNN Newsnight*, ABC and NBC nightly news), been covered by innumerable print media (including *Newsweek*, *Christianity Today*, the *New York Times*, the *Times* of London, and the *Wall Street Journal*), and had his script lampooned on *The Simpsons* and performed satirically by Hollywood actors in the popular *Hollywood Hell House*.[22] Roberts's script has even been purchased with the intention of turning it into a major studio film. Roberts believes that the dramas are both authentic and superior to "secular" entertainments. Indeed, he told me with disappointment that Scott Derrickson—the director of the well-received horror film *The Exorcism of Emily Rose*—had just dropped out of preproduction for the Hell House movie (though he laughed heartily when I consoled him by saying, "yeah, but just think what you'll be able to do with that kind of effects budget").[23]

Roberts—now senior pastor at Thornton, Colorado's New Destiny Christian Center—is clearly delighted with the notice his productions have received ("if you don't capture the controversy of both sides," he explained, "you don't have Hell House").[24] He believes that the scorn Hell House receives is confirmation of its success in challenging the norms of a fallen culture. The language of embattlement and militarism is ubiquitous in the promotional literature. Even though he has actively courted media attention from the outset—he told me that "part of the power of what God has created is that the element of controversy has driven this from the beginning"—this is a surprising degree of exposure for a religious creation so explicitly combative in its self-presentation.[25] As I argue below and in the book's conclusion, this popularity represents another important stage of development in the religion of fear's social criticism. The kit's promotional materials revel in this complexity, describing Hell House—in language that smacks of both the aspiring hipsterism endemic to youth pastors and the hellfire tradition of American preaching more generally—as "the most in-your-face, high-flyin', no denyin', death-defyin', Satan-be-cryin', keep-ya-from-fryin', theatrical stylin', no holds barred, cutting edge evangelism tool of the new millennium."[26]

It is significant that it was in 1995 that the first *Left Behind* novel and the first commercially packaged Hell House surfaced. The mid-1990s were a period of fascinating political (and religious) restructuring in the United States. Americans entered that decade buoyed by an optimistic belief that the major ideological and cultural conflict of the century—between Soviet communism and liberal democracy—was over. The book of history had been closed, in Francis Fukuyama's widely cited Hegelian formulation.[27] While not all Americans endorsed Fukuyama's particular brand of Straussianism, his text captured the prevailing mood of political triumphalism in the early 1990s: democracy and civility had triumphed over autocracy and corruption; any remaining conflicts could be resolved through increasingly efficient, highly technologized military operations; and politics would consist henceforth of technical adjustments to a basically sound system. How like the spirit of mid-1950s political theorists who exuded a similar confidence in what Robert Dahl once called the "polyarchy" of post–World War II America.[28] And yet everywhere this confidence was challenged: in postcommunist Eastern Europe's discourses of radical democracy and civil society, which seemed to mock American democracy's hollowness; in the disquieting spectacles of the 1992 Rodney King riots in Los Angeles and the ATF raid on the Branch Davidian compound in 1993; in the presence of survivalist and militia movements during the mid-1990s (many of which embraced the white supremacist creed "identity Christianity"); in the confluence of conservative forces—from the Christian Coalition to Newt Gingrich's "Contract with America"—in the Republican victories in the 1994 midterm congressional elections; in protracted ethnic conflicts in the former Yugoslavia and in Rwanda, among other places; in Timothy McVeigh's bombing of the Murrah Federal Building in Oklahoma City (which he claimed was a reprisal against the federal government for its actions at Waco); in the seemingly endless parade of bizarre or violent spectacles endlessly covered by twenty-four-hour news channels (Susan Smith, O. J. Simpson, Heaven's Gate, and the latest public monster); and in the shrill hectoring surrounding the Clinton administration, which many conservatives denounced with the kind of alarmist political rhetoric usually reserved for war criminals or terrorists.

This changed political sensibility—both the increase of conservative political power in the 1990s and a preoccupation with violent spectacle—is manifest in Hell Houses' improvisations on both conventional haunted houses and on their own evangelical predecessors. Their confrontational tone is born of the larger context of political fragility as well. Circulating in the political cultures of the 1990s are twins: the glare and bombast of public media, and a resurgence of deep ambivalence about (and, at times, hostility toward) the state. One sees in expressions as seemingly far-flung as the Christian Coalition's grassroots campaigns and the Michigan militia's Upper Peninsula target training a retreat from institutional confidence and a turn to the local. While Reagan conservatives might have hoped to use the language of antistatism only to assume control over the state's machinery, it is in the context of this chastening of Americans' attitudes toward government—a ubiquitous strain of political sentiment that erupted once more during this period—that we see a new sense of urgency or combative self-determination in religious constructions like Hell Houses. And here we see long-developing themes in the religion of fear engaging the political in the most explicit fashion thus far.

When Roberts and his "prayer warriors" scan American culture, they see two camps pitched for battle: those who adhere to firm standards of religiosity or "godliness," and those who collude, knowingly or not, with evil. Roberts believes that "Satan is winning" the battle for American culture, for American youths: he claims that "the Devil is orchestrating a play, a plot, a scheme to further keep people in bondage to the lie."[29] And so Roberts responds—along with similarly inclined religious critics—to these purported culture wars by raising hell. Literally. Following a period when public concerns about hell and the devil had markedly decreased, the emergence of the religion of fear in the wake of the 1960s represents a dramatic and combative turn in cultural politics.[30] Roberts's creations reflect but do not directly engage post–Cold War ideologies: they reveal that longtime conservative evangelical concerns about race, gender, community, national sovereignty, and economics can find expression in popular narrations of fear and evil as surely as they can be articulated in policy interventions. These narrations and confrontational theatrics are seen by Roberts as vehicles to alert the unsuspecting to a larger battle between the forces of good and evil, one in which cosmic forces manifest in social behaviors, political orientations, and consumer tastes. In his blunt formulation: "Hell House is cutting edge, it is shocking, it is offensive. But it is the Truth."[31] Hudgins echoes these concerns and told me that he feels that aggressive outreach is necessary because governments will not address important problems. He explained:

> Edmund Burke said "All that is required for evil to prevail is for good men to do nothing." We must be "roaring lambs." ...We need Christian

lawyers, doctors, school teachers, factory workers, movie producers, actors, athletes, public servants and politicians who are willing to be "salt and light." We have been silent too long.[32]

Hell House and Judgement House share with their predecessors in the religion of fear (specifically with anti-rock preachers) the sense that pop culture may lure young people unknowingly into evil: "There are things like the entertainment issues now—music influence and television and movies, along with drugs and alcohol and sex."[33] If these influences are left unchallenged, they risk indoctrinating evangelical children into what Roberts believes are "un-Christian" opinions on the crucial issues: homosexuality ("No one is born gay," according to Roberts), abortion (which "is not merely a surgical procedure"), teen suicide (which can be avoided if teens simply let "Jesus carry you through"), drunk driving (which exemplifies the "false highs and constant lows of alcohol"), and a general risk of damnation ("Hell is definitely not a party place" or, at one production I attended, "There's no parties in Hell, just one big BBQ").[34] Images of risk and defense suggest that unseen forces are at work, advancing an agenda that is hostile to religious citizens: the non-denominational Victory Hill Church of Scottsville, Kentucky, advertised its 1998 production with fliers proclaiming, "Homosexual Lies . . . Violent Rape . . . Medical Murder . . . Business is Booming in Southern Kentucky!"[35] Roberts echoes this sentiment, contending that Hell Houses must take on the "irresponsibility of the media," since "people are being fed misinformation and a bill of goods, stuff that's just not true."[36] This general disposition—expressed in conservative Christian culture everywhere from daytime radio to national conferences organized to address "religious bigotry"—is echoed throughout the world of Hell Houses. For example, the Northside Assembly of God's Hell House on Mississippi's Gulf Coast urges, "People need to hear and see that much of what the media and entertainment propagate in the areas of homosexuality and abortion, for instance, is lies."[37] Productions like this justify the willful offensiveness of Hell Houses by suggesting that it is necessary in order to trump worldly offenses that are "protected" by a liberal regime that tolerates amorality under the aegis of "neutrality" and "free speech": "Teenagers influenced by the poison they watch and listen to through concerts, television, and CD's, which tell them over and over again that suicide is the escape they are searching for, is offensive to the Christian. This is why Hell House must be bold. Hollywood is bold."[38]

In fear's declension narrative, it is not simply that immoral entertainments should be replaced with moral ones; rather, the proposed alternatives emerging from this sensibility reflect larger concerns about liberalism, national sovereignty, and the politics of the intimate and domestic spheres. Roberts told me that he was concerned that "the courts have attacked the

Bible" and that the government could not be relied on to protect religious interests.[39] Such sentiments point to a society that has lost its priorities, and they suggest that the gore-filled episodes of Hell House would not have been necessary in what was once a Christian America. By asserting that such gruesome ends could happen to any of us, at any time, the productions generate a framework or an interpretive template through which to view society: policy and personal decisions alike are now couched in a discourse of endangerment and soteriology, whose urgency is driven home through a use of the techniques and images of genre horror. These "ordinary" evils are frightening enough to participants in these productions: "We don't need Jason or Freddy to scare people," said Shawn Logan of Detroit World Outreach, in a rich meta-reference.[40]

Roberts has long insisted that these strategies are rooted in good, sound exegesis: "It's Romans 6:23 in contemporary packaging. 'The wages of sin is death.'"[41] From the beginning, he has sought to articulate such ideas in mainstream media outlets. But, as he explained on National Public Radio in 1999, "We're not doing this to win a popularity contest. We're saying look, sin is hurting our nation and Jesus Christ is the answer."[42] In order to avoid what New Creation Evangelism calls "the ultimate haunted house, which is where [people] will spend eternity if they do not accept Jesus Christ as their personal Savior," audiences are urged to accept the altar call that concludes each presentation.[43] Successful evangelization occurs when the productions can "bring participants face to face with their mortality and Creator."[44]

In this worldview, the largest obstacle to the Holy Spirit's successful work with young Americans is the "spiritual battle" raging in public culture, where the salacious and the seductive divert teens' attention from true happiness. Roberts told me emphatically that "you have to care about what's going on socially in the world," and "if doing what God has called us to do spiritually ultimately has some kind of political benefit, good!"[45] Hell Houses consciously embrace the tools of the "fallen culture," redeploying them in explicitly political fashion as part of a perceived "culture war." The rude awakenings of these productions are thought to be the only way to jar young minds free from the seductions of mass culture, even as the Hell House simultaneously offers them an equally thrilling entertainment. For Roberts, fulfilling the great commission (Jesus' instructions, in Matthew 28:16–20, to "go and make disciples of all the nations of the world") practically demands dealing with "very cutting edge issues in our community," and he believes that his prayer warriors must "brave the crossfire of criticism and misunderstanding" in the "battle against sin." For Roberts, a fighting ethos is consistent with Christ's love since opponents are, to Roberts, actively designing schemes which target good Christians unfairly. It is not enough merely to preach; one must aggressively challenge one's enemies (Roberts cannot understand those who act otherwise, "like we're supposed to be some little lamb, lying in a green field").[46] In a telling indicator of some of his larger sensibilities, replete with military imagery and Cold War patriotism, Roberts asked one interviewer:

> Consider the same analogy in light of, say, if our country went to war with Russia. Who truly loves America more? The young men that are willing to go and battle for our freedom? Or the young men that flee to Canada and hide, and don't want to be drafted? Well, it's the young men that put their neck[s] on the lines and are willing to risk their own safety for the freedom of others. And that's what this church does.[47]

As we see throughout the religion of fear, we learn much about the socio-political sensibilities of creators by attending to their representations of hell and the Antichrist. It is not only the spiritual world that is populated by angels, demons, and moral forces but the social and political realm as well. Evil is a reality both visible and unseen here, each of whose concrete manifestations— whether in sinning heart or wicked legislature—suggests that the world is pregnant with unseen foulness that could erupt in our lives at any moment, a sense of expectancy that these creations underscore. Evil's reality is as palpable as the divine goodness with which it is locked in combat. Evidence of this conflict is visible everywhere to conservatives of this orientation, not just in the inbreaking of the supernatural into the everyday but in evil's worldly effects. That abortion is not completely criminalized, that pornography is common-place, and that school prayer has been ruled unconstitutional—all examples that are central to the religion of fear's declension narrative—stand to these creators as evidence of evil's growing dominion and of America's precipitous slide as it turns away from its purported Christian heritage. The declarations of Biloxi, Mississippi's Northside Assembly of God—"Satan is very real and wants to destroy [you] with an everlasting destruction. . . . there is a spiritual battle raging each day"—are representative of this general sense of the soteriological drama written onto the sociopolitical.[48] The details, in other words, are in the devil.

THE TECHNE OF A HELL HOUSE

Of all the creations of the religion of fear, Hell Houses partake most liberally and most suggestively of the tropes and techniques of horror. The primary attribute of a Hell House is, of course, its brutal consequentialism: those who commit certain actions will meet with a grisly fate, in both a bodily and spiritual sense. The ghouls and frights creeping from the shadows of these walk-throughs signify that Hell Houses appropriate one of horror's most recognizable traits: the starker and more resolute the moral conviction, the deeper the detail and exuberance in the portrayal of gore and fear. The substance connecting Nosferatu with Freddy Kruger or George Romero's zombies is human flesh, at risk, in pleasure, and in decay in horror's "shared anxiety rituals."[49] As in cultures of fear more broadly, Hell Houses surround themselves with images of death and doom, hoping thereby to confirm that these are not the fates of the devout. These grim narratives serve simultaneously as denials, projections, and fantasies blurring the boundary between material (and political) reality and the instability of the Gothic imaginary. As Walter Kendrick aptly suggests, "scary entertainments can entertain only because even as they apparently violate the taboo against showing the aftereffects of death, they transform them into affirmations of the body's impregnability."[50] Hell Houses evince a similar strategy, vividly and gleefully representing sin and evil as a means to establish the security of conservative evangelical culture and belief.

A typical Hell House experience is structured as a narrative through which attendees are led and in which they ideally see themselves as participants. Those who sponsor the events do so largely out of a conviction that audiences may be at risk and can benefit from exposure to the productions. Thus, local pastors and organizers believe that Halloween is the appropriate occasion for the dramas, not simply because of the holiday's conventional associations but because there is something to the notion that Halloween is a time for the mingling of the supernatural and the mundane. The productions usually consist of several scenes designed to illustrate specific sins whose presence has grown during a "permissive" era of American history. The actors are primarily drawn from church youth groups (though they also include clergy and community members of all ages), and the scenes (each of which lasts for several minutes) are planned and rehearsed for up to six months out of the year. The aim is to generate an overall impression of the "hell and destruction that Satan and this world can bestow on those who choose not to serve Jesus Christ."[51] In a typical Hell House, groups ranging from twelve to forty visitors are led through the narrative by a personal demon who serves as a frightful tour guide, explaining to audiences the infernal origins of the moral conflicts an average teen might face. These episodes are charged with a soteriological urgency because, the visitor hears, they are defined by stark ethical choices with eternal consequences. As one student participant put it, "Part of life is death. It's an eternal death. It's hell. But the gift of God is life."[52] Hudgins echoed this stark sensibility, telling me he was inspired by the question, "what if we use the concept of a haunted house and tell a different story about life and death beyond the grave for the believer and the unbeliever?"[53]

A paradigmatic production concludes with two scenes that actually represent hell and heaven themselves. Most heaven scenes function as an altar call, and audience members get the opportunity to commit or recommit to Christ, or to speak with on-site counselors (Hudgins calls them "encouragers") if they are merely interested. In my experience, pastors usually ask audience members to close their eyes so that audiences do not know who has or has not answered the call. One young woman with whom I spoke recalled a Judgement House in Ayden, North Carolina, that concluded with characters finding out whether or not they were in Saint Peter's "book."[54] Satan generally appears throughout the productions and gets considerable time to make infernal declarations, boasts, and promises. Indeed, this is a coveted role: I was told by one young man who had acted in several productions: "I got to play Satan—it was sooooo fun."[55] God is occasionally heard from, but rarely appears (and then only in Michelangelo-esque portraits rather than via actor portrayals). Jesus is a ubiquitous presence at a Hell House's conclusion, although there is far less attention devoted to his presence than to Satan's (in the degree of "stage time" afforded to good and to evil forces, Hell Houses are analogous to Chick tracts). In many productions, a churchgoer portrays Jesus, but it is also common to rely on portraiture (often a reproduction or a loosely based imitation of Warner Sallman's 1941 *Head of Christ*). Most productions include an abortion scene, a teen suicide (often carried out under the influence of rock music of various sorts), a drunk-driving accident, and an AIDS death. It is also common to see a school shooting and a rave scene (which doubles as a cautionary tale about the dangers of both pop music and drugs). What links these scenes is not simply the risk of erroneous belief but the destruction of the body and its public display. Most Hell Houses, however, leave room for either the adaptation of existing scenes or the introduction of new scenes (Roberts's recent innovations include more focus on "the domestic tornado" of spousal abuse and a character named Cyberchick, who introduces audiences to "Firestorm Laboratories," the home base for the manufacturing of sin).[56] This serves to keep the productions contemporary, keeping pace with fast-moving youth cultures and appetites, and also to dramatize events or issues that are seen as having immediate political consequence. Roberts, for example, even went so far as to remove some of his central scenes in 1999 so that he could introduce a Monica Lewinsky and a Marilyn Manson scene.[57]

The sins and causes of damnation portrayed are clearly linked to the hot-button moral and political issues that have for over three decades been at the heart of NCR culture and activism. This is not to downplay the Hell Houses' and their sponsors' intentions to proselytize and save souls they believe are at risk. But it is crucial to understand that the risks envisioned and narrated are those that conservative evangelicals have long attributed to post–World War II American liberalism. Like Chick tracts transposed to the stage, Hell Houses are unabashed in proclaiming that audiences will spend an eternity being tormented in hell if they participate in or support abortions, homosexuality, adultery, or dabbling in the occult, for example. The effectiveness and persuasiveness of the message, however, depend upon the skill of the performance and the production.

Hell Houses are designed to be staged repeatedly during the weeks surrounding Halloween, usually with several performances a night. The dramas
usually last between thirty and forty-five minutes. The scale of the production
and the audience size vary depending on the location and size of the host
building, as well as the community's budget (while Hell Houses are ways for
churches to make money for their other activities, they also cost money to
produce; in addition to purchasing the basic materials, someone must make
the costumes, make the blood, and purchase the props, for example). The
now-renowned Trinity Church in Cedar Hill, Texas—the subject of Ratliff's
documentary—is a particularly long-standing and visible example of the
genre's success.[58] Its efficient production is geared toward crowds of approximately forty being led through the Hell House every half hour. Church
officials claim that, when given the opportunity at the production's end, one
in five visitors proclaims his or her conversion. Roberts's New Destiny Church
claims that 35 percent of its attendees convert.[59] Most Web pages—both the
home pages of sponsor churches and those which host "virtual" Hell
Houses—keep running tabs on the number of overall attendees, the number
of renewed commitments to Christ, and the number of first-time commitments. Other productions are geared toward smaller numbers—between
twelve and twenty people per tour—but the structural features remain fairly
consistent in their reliance on Roberts's template.

Between the mid-1990s and 2001, Hell House attendance grew markedly
each year, often growing by 500–1,000 visitors annually per site. While initially
a phenomenon particular to the South, Southwest, and Mountain West, its
popularity soon extended to the Northeast, Midwest, California, and even
Hawaii. There are also Hell House and Judgement House performances
outside the United States. The change in attendance coincided with the decision by many sponsors, in 2001 and 2002, to make reference to the attacks of
September 11, 2001. This was sometimes considered quite distasteful even to
sympathizers, many of whom refused to attend. Nixon suggests that during
this period—when Roberts actually took a year off for reflection in 2002—
some audiences saw Hell Houses as "too over the top" and thought they had
perhaps lost their original focus.[60]

Audiences consist largely of local evangelicals and Pentecostals (predomi-
nantly those who already have an affinity with the conservatism embodied in
the Hell Houses themselves), and it is common to see buses pulling in and out
of church parking lots during the season. But almost all productions attract
non-Christians (both sympathetic and derisive). The majority are adolescents
(who are, after all, the target audience)—some accompanied by parents, some
alone—but there are adults and, if the site in question permits it, children
under the age of twelve (some churches set the bar at age ten, but regardless of
the cutoff age, it is quite common to see children who appear younger). This

has been true in my visits to Hell House and Judgement House productions, and also in nearly every article or journal account I have read.

Much of the information conveyed in Roberts's "outreach kit" is delivered in the form of a sales pitch, focusing both on removing harm from society and also on his own product's superiority to those of his competitors and to do-it-yourself productions. He boasts, "This is absolutely a modern day parable.... It is using the tools that are attractive to this culture to help them understand spiritual principles of Christ."[61] Since employees are unpaid (coming from the congregations themselves) and the churches are tax exempt, Hell Houses can also be profitable. Some studies comparing individual church budgets with intake (number of entrants multiplied by admission price) suggest that an average Hell House may realize well over 50 percent in profit.[62] Some productions do not charge admission, while others realize profit in the form of charitable contributions inspired by the productions.

While this financial element may be somewhat unremarkable, what is more interesting is how this entertainment serves as an opportunity for fantasy and imagination for both producers and consumers. The productions' reliance on the techne of horror and shock theater yields settings that often vividly recall horror films, with eerie lighting, spectral presences, and computer-generated graphics designed to unsettle and startle. Hell Houses assault the senses: they are usually quite hot and often earplug-worthy in their volume; they frequently incorporate strobe lighting or other devices aimed to disorient participants; and they often even have an olfactory register (Roberts encourages productions to cook Limburger cheese in the hell throne room, and I have detected the smell of smoke in hell scenes). Roberts believes that the productions are most effective in soul saving if they can "grab the attention of the sight and sound generation. It's a rock-n-roll gospel."[63] In an interview with Focus on the Family, he proudly boasted that "Hell House is the most politically incorrect thing you've ever seen in your life."[64] Hudgins's Judgement House scripts are, like some other variations, somewhat less gory and confrontational than Roberts's splattery critical interventions.

Hell Houses have, of course, attracted a good deal of criticism from fellow Christians and other constituencies: some believe that the productions blur boundaries too much and actually encourage interest in "the occult" (Pastor Philip Wise of Second Baptist Church, Plainview, Texas), while others protest against what they see as unchecked bigotry (in 1998, citizens in Bowling Green, Kentucky, countered a Hell House's advertising campaign by posting signs with directions to "Bigotry House").[65] As a result, many churches are guarded about revealing information about participants: names on office doors are taped over, church volunteers double as security throughout performance sites, and—as one sees with airport or rock concert security—signs forbidding cameras, tape recorders, bags (including fanny packs), and cell phones are posted.[66] At many productions, there are warning signs about the disorienting effects of the smoke and lighting, such as one finds at amusement parks (I recall seeing one cast member whisper to a frail elderly woman that she might wish to avoid the stairs descending to the pitch-black hell scene); elsewhere, there are recorded announcements of regulations played near entrances. Occasionally, concerns about child safety arise: Nixon writes about an incident where, allegedly, a "young girl was thrown into a standing wooden coffin where upon [sic] immediately the lid was closed and fastened.... The young girl told her family that she kicked and pounded at the coffin lid, resulting in bloodied, scraped arms, hands, and knuckles, and some torn clothing."[67] It is also not uncommon to spot the church's own video cameras and monitors inside the church itself (though these may have been in place prior to the Hell House). Some writers have claimed that those who try to call Roberts's church with their number blocked will not have their call answered.[68] It may be, though, that Roberts delights in such criticism not just because it confirms his oppositional stance toward "the world" but also because it is free publicity. And indeed, I recall the impression that—despite the security measures—the environment surrounding the performances (unlike the performances themselves) is friendly and filled with the kind of jittery anticipation of a Friday night football game. Both this exuberance and a social-critical militancy are abundantly on display in the performances themselves.

"DEMONS, DRAG THE SMART GIRL TO HELL!": SCENES FROM HELL

Although it is in the individual scenes where the political religion of Hell Houses becomes most evident, most productions take great care in the construction of the overall narrative. Mood, pacing, tension and release, and other largely cinematic elements are managed so that, at the event's conclusion, an audience member feels that the stakes of a potential conversion are high. The desired result is an immersive experience, wherein all people walking through the production feel themselves to be part of the religious drama unfolding around them. There are three general narrative strategies, each pursued by a different theatrical model: the scene-based morality of Roberts's model (replicated to some degree in Revelation Walk, Rapture House, and Tribulation Trail); the Judgement House story line, which pursues the lives of several teenagers as they make fateful decisions; and the Heaven's Gates, Hell's Flames narrative, which depicts the moment when individuals learn whether or not they have earned a place in heaven. Though all of the strategies share a sociopolitical sensibility and a general aesthetic, Roberts's productions are by far the most aesthetically powerful of these creations in their liberal use of shock and gore; and Roberts's script also most clearly manifests the erotics of fear and the demonology within. I will describe Judgement House, Rapture House, and *Heaven's Gates, Hell's Flames* first before a detailed discussion of each scene in Roberts's creation.

At Durham, North Carolina's Bethel Christian Center, the Judgement House–derived "Halloween alternative" *Fate's Place* is first and foremost "scriptural based," but, according to a church volunteer, "he [the architect of this particular installation] will take you through some stuff.... It's mostly about life choices, dramatizations.... there is a Hell and then there is a Heaven."[69] Local productions are often referred to not as Hell Houses or Judgement Houses, but simply as "dramatizations." At many churches, the concluding scene actually occurs under a white tent outside (recalling old revival traditions) where people are asked if they want to "accept Jesus Christ as their savior." On the one hand, there is a clear sense just from these descriptive statements that the scenes depicted are real. Yet there is also, as is often the case in these grisly dramas, a clear sense of artifice and play at work.

The setting for this particular production—which ran in Durham for several years, until 2006—is typical of the Judgement House model: a night on which four carefree teenage women are out on the town, driving drunk, when they hit a young boy with their car, killing him instantly. Focusing on the illicit activities of young women, as do many contemporary horror films (in *Halloween*, for example, only the chaste Jamie Lee Curtis survives Jason Voorhees' slasher spree), the production follows the four lives as they unfold after this event, and the paths they took either toward or away from God. One young woman got pregnant, had an abortion, eventually accepted Jesus along with her mother (they later named the aborted child Hope), but died a year later (the narrative conveys a slight sense that her death was causally linked to early bad choices, or at least was not surprising in light of these choices, but the young woman went to heaven nevertheless). A second young woman also became involved in abortion and reproductive issues—again, we see the hot-button moral issues long central to the NCR—but followed the extreme path of Operation Rescue and ended up bombing abortion clinics. This woman was judged doubly: she went to prison and to hell. The path of the third teen was in some ways the most interesting: she ended up being a producer of horror movies in Hollywood. She went to hell, ostensibly because she was a horrible, selfish person; yet aside from the obvious assumption that Hollywood carries an evil taint, there is the fascinating—but, alas, unexplored—irony that the very genre whose tropes are so liberally pilfered by these productions should be seen as sinful. After all of the others died, the final participant in the original car crash accepted Jesus while kneeling by graves in a cemetery. Perhaps, an attendee might speculate, only a reckoning with gore, death, and tragedy can spare one from the fiery pit; maybe Christians only really know Jesus if they come to him through blood and fire.

From this graveside scene, the visitor then proceeded to hell ("Satan's Pad," as it was called here). It was dark, smoky, and filled with people whose faces and bodies were twisted and gnarled. Satan was dressed in a suit and, according to one observer, looked "kind of like a TV preacher to me," while his minions "looked like Marilyn Manson." Satan pontificated about his plans for world dominion, promised to defeat God, and boasted that his true name was Charles Manson. He also at one point identified himself with "the little boy next to the statue of Andy Griffith in Pullen Park."[70] This is a reference to a public monument in a Raleigh, North Carolina, park and presumably indicated that Ron Howard—who portrayed Opie Taylor, the character in question—had become damned by his longtime inhabitance in the sordid world of Hollywood.

The production concluded with a visit to heaven. Festooned with puffy clouds, garlanded by angels, and bathed in white, heaven was in the Bethel Christian Center's chapel, which now shook to the strains of generic Christian rock (at Garner Free Will Baptist, the music is smooth jazz). It was meant clearly to conform to standard representations of the heavenly afterlife but also to surround participants in familiar sights and sounds. The four young women reappeared at the gates to heaven, two of whom were claimed by Satan while the other two were allowed into heaven. Here, the dress of the women clearly marked them in moral and salvific terms. One "hell girl" was in a prison outfit, for example. The "heaven girls" were, though dressed in ostensibly chaste white and light blue, showing midriff and sporting tight clothes (many teen actors wear conventional clothes throughout). Before passing through the pearly gates, they had to verbalize that they accepted Jesus as Lord and Savior, that they had been ignoring him for too long, and that they would now live their life for him. This was a very emotional moment, with many participants noticeably crying and shaking. The young woman who had the abortion got to meet her child, Hope, in heaven. As Christianity is pitched in very general terms at the end of these productions, one presumes that the more specific work of theology and doctrine occurs later in one's postproduction religious narrative.

The narrative template of *Fate's Place* stems from the story line officially endorsed (and copyrighted in 1983) by Judgement House. Hudgins originally constructed an eight-scene narrative tracking the fates of three archetypal teenagers whose pivotal, life-defining moment occurs as they find themselves threatened by a sudden, all-consuming fire. The first teen, Darren, is a skeptic who has rejected Christ. He is killed instantly by the fire, and we learn that he has been damned. The second teen, Whitney, had made an unambiguous conversion and pledged herself to Christ. She is mortally wounded in the fire and is seen being spirited away after a valiant medical team cannot save her. Billy is initially undecided but ultimately accepts Jesus. He, too, is spared from the fire. The narrative then invests great energy in a representation of hell itself. The Judgement House kit advises that, during this scene, the hell room be quite dark and heated up to above 80 degrees (although some productions try to go far higher than this, with some even claiming to produce temperatures up to 140 degrees) as audiences are crammed into the small space, with recordings of human screams cranked through the loudspeakers. One young woman told me how terrified she was after being "taken into the boiler room of the church with the lights off."[71] The heaven room is brightly lit and pleasantly cool.

Variations from the template are encouraged as long as the basic structure remains intact; different articulations of the life-altering event may be necessary, promotional literature explains, to reach potential converts. For example, one scene focused on the gory spectacle left in the wake of natural disaster: Daytona Beach, Florida's First Baptist Church played up Floridians' perpetual hurricane-related anxiety by constructing a grisly street scene littered with bodies, fallen palm trees, and general wreckage, with one lonely, blood-strewn child wandering about asking, "Have you seen my Mom?" In each variation, the dominant impression is that death waits just at the edge of consciousness, the Grim Reaper peering just over our shoulders; indeed, Hudgins told me directly, "I believe that death is something [audiences] need to think about."[72] It has even been reported that, in some productions, attendees were actually placed in small closets adorned with coffin lids for doors; these served as passageways between the main scenes and the hell room. In some of these mock coffins, speakers played a prerecorded message warning audiences of the consequences of not accepting Christ.[73]

At Garner Free Will Baptist, the setup and feel of Rapture House was structurally similar to others in the general idiom. As I observed actors' preparations beforehand—as one man entered the building, a woman chided him, "Don't attack anybody!"; he responded, "Oh, I might . . ."—I wondered if only the name had changed. The first phase consisted of disappearance scenes. Audiences were led into a tiny room with several rows of mini-bleachers. The host described the importance of coming to Christ, lest cataclysm and despair befall us during the Tribulation. Her words were cut short, the room went black, and when the lights came on thirty seconds later, the host's clothes were lying limp on the floor and a woman dressed as an angel remained as our guide (in a twist on Roberts's demon guides). She led us through several scenes of stunned, post-Rapture discovery: a high school where students discover that their colleague—whom the teacher has just asked for an answer—is not at her desk; a bedroom where a husband wakes to discover his wife's disembodied lingerie next to him in the bed; a baby's nursery, where horrified parents find an empty crib while a music box plays "Jesus Loves Me, This I Know."

The group next walked from the main church building to a bungalow whose interior now resembled a church. At the conclusion of a service, a preacher told his parishioners that they had not been good enough Christians, despite regular church attendance and charitable acts. One woman proclaimed that the gospel truth "was like a free gift—all we had to do was reach out and take it." At this point, three beefy men in grey camouflage (with sewn patches that read "NWN," which stood for "New World Nation") burst into the church. The angel told us that Christianity would be outlawed during the Tribulation, and these emissaries of the New World Nation were meant to illustrate the repressive future that is central to many of the antiliberal arguments crafted by contemporary conservatives. The actors then dragged a resister outside, and two fake gunshots went off. Then, screeching in the churchgoers' faces, they herded the remaining Christians out of the church to be incarcerated.

Following this was the hell scene, in the church's basement. The audience walked through utter darkness, with a faint red glow in the distance. There were dangling fake spider webs that brushed one's face, and cloaked figures actually stood inches from one's shoulders, whispering and groaning in attendees' ears. The procession stopped in the devil's throne room, where Satan appeared with a cowled face and pasty green makeup. He verbally abused his demon lackeys and even punished one with blue electric jolts from his fingertips. The audience was told of its good luck at being in hell during "visiting hours" only. The demons pleaded, "Can't we keep just one?" The devil relented and paced before us, ultimately selecting a screaming girl (clearly, part of the church staff). As the audience filed out, the demon lackeys muttered things like "see you tonight on your computer—I'll be there." The heaven scene resembled those described above.

The long-standing stage play *Heaven's Gates, Hell's Flames* is comparably the mildest of these dramas. One version of the production spends a good deal of time focusing on the character Henry, a homeless African American man who travels through the entire production as narrator and uncomfortably conforms—in both comportment and speech—to long-outmoded minstrelsy era representations of African American behavior and religiosity (but whose Stepin Fetchit voice disappears after he is healed by the well-appointed Caucasian Jesus awaiting him at heaven's gates). The key scene in this drama shows various young people being led before a council of angels to determine whether or not their names are in the book of heaven. Skeptics, non-evangelicals, and even God-fearing backsliders are led screaming from the angels and dragged into hell as a demonic Satan cackles through the loudspeakers ("Demons, drag the smart girl to Hell! Show her something real. There's two gods, baby! There's Him. And all them other gods? That's me!").[74] In Niagara Falls, New York's Reality Outreach's lavish production, the devil closely resembles metal icon King Diamond, and there is some debt to Roberts's imagination, as various horrific accidents—car crashes, plane crashes (prior to which one victim says, "God? I'll show you God: M-O-N-E-Y!"), even a drink-caused forklift accident at a warehouse—lead the characters to their moment of judgment.

Across these productions, one encounters such a variety of horror—rendered in documentary detail—that one might reasonably conclude that few places of safe purchase exist in the world. Yet even in this frightful landscape, there is little mistaking a Roberts-style Hell House, whose brio and bloody aesthetic are distinct among these dramas. Hell House exteriors are instantly noticeable. When churches do not actually have billboards or signs advertising the event—Biloxi's Hell House sign announces, "It'll Scare the Hell Out of You" right next to the red-lettered number 396-HELL—it is common for church property to be strewn with red Christmas lights or for the lawn to be dotted with crosses memorializing aborted fetuses. As in other productions, audiences are generally intrigued about the performances but also about each other. Many of the skeptical attendees—college students especially—are outfitted in ways that are designed to attract attention (such as heavy metal T-shirts, Goth attire, died hair, and piercings). Immediately upon entry one is, as one young attendee described to me, "confronted with maniacal laughter and gallons of blood."[75] The tone is often set by playing music—frequently the very genres described in chapter 4—that is generally associated with hell's dark denizens. Significantly, it is common for young audience members to know all of the words to the songs contextualized as demonic. Secular pop culture may be seen as part of hell's designs, but it is nonetheless something with which producers and participants are quite familiar.

The demon guides are among Hell Houses' most recognizable characters and usually their most spirited actors. The opportunity to portray a demon is among a Hell House's more coveted roles. Usually played with considerable energy by a parishioner (Roberts himself generally plays the part at his own church), the demon leads audiences through the narrative and continually interprets the imagery and events for them. Roberts's script draws inferences from the larger culture of American conservatism and filters these into local communities via grisly scenes. As there is a considerable amount of darkness and doomy atmospherics in most productions, the demon's narration is crucial, providing a kind of anchor amid the rapid pace and frequently disorienting effects of the dramas. The demon guide also makes sure that audiences are led swiftly through the scenes (the purpose of this speed is not only to ensure that the evening proceeds efficiently but also to contribute to sensory overload and disorientation). Some of these actors are highly inventive and improvisational, cracking jokes and interacting with audience members exuberantly. Some attendees who have worn Goth or metal clothing or who have tattoos or body piercings have been told that they "look the part" or that they should "feel right at home." I have often been struck by the similarity between such exchanges and athletes talking trash to one another: demons lean over the crouching bodies of the damned, taunting them like a safety who has just leveled a wideout, as when one demon said to a recent suicide surprised to be in hell, "There's no peace here, stupid!"[76]

The abortion scene is one of every Hell House's centerpieces (Roberts contends that this topic and homosexuality cannot be omitted from the production). Soaked with blood and declamatory in their politics, these scenes offer one of the surest examples of the religion of fear's link between combative conservatism, genre horror, and piety. Productions vary greatly in their actual representations of the procedure itself. The message is consistent with anti-*Roe* politics in general, contending that life begins at conception, that a fetus is a human being with a soul, and that abortion is murder. These themes are articulated in a flexible manner. More reserved productions concentrate on "the future that would have been," a canonical cinematic gesture where a young woman who has had an abortion experiences deep remorse (usually involving an acceptance of Christ) and is shown by an angel the various stages of life with her child that she is forever denied. The angel guide is generally very encouraging as the woman—witnessing herself on life's path, enjoying a happiness she seems currently to lack—experiences loss and regret. Elsewhere, an actress portrays the child who was aborted (who is almost always female) at various stages of the life she would have led: the child who asks "why did you kill me, Mommy?"; the teenager who berates her mother for missing her sweet sixteen party; the contented wife and mother; the aged maternal figure who touched so many people throughout her life. Even these productions, which avoid actual depictions of the procedure, often lead audiences through a darkened room that is supposed to be an empty womb and is filled with the sound of what is purportedly a fetus's heartbeat (in the darkness, a girl's voice cries, "Mommy, can you see me?").[77]

Roberts's original script, however, is considerably more intense and confrontational, vividly portraying the procedure it condemns (along with references to RU-486, for example).[78] Chrissy is the name of the "abortion girl," a role which, along with the "rape girl," is highly coveted by female performers. (The DVD of Ratliff's documentary has a fascinating extra: a clip of Trinity Baptist's Hell House Awards ceremony, where the lucky winner of the award for "best rape girl" squeals euphorically.) Chrissy's script directions indicate that she is to cry, scream, and spasm violently, as a cold-hearted medical staff performs the abortion. Roberts's script instructs that green or blue gossamer be used to simulate hospital settings, that actors wear medical attire ("greenies"), and that an examination table be used. More revealingly, the kit instructs sponsors to use "[p]ieces of meat placed in a glass bowl to look like pieces of a baby," in addition to vast amounts of theatrical blood (stored in a location known as "Blood Central"), and a vacuum (used to suck the baby out of Chrissy, with the hope that the abrupt sound will repulse viewers).[79] Props for hospital scenes are often donated by congregants in the medical professions.

The scene opens as mute technicians operate on a wailing Chrissy, as a CD plays "hospital sound effects" (of the wet, squishy, very organic variety) in the background. Trays stuffed with surgical instruments flank the patient's bed, and bloodied towels are clearly visible. Some productions include, in the background, a television showing "videotaped footage of a real fetus inside a womb, until the last moment when doll parts are discarded into a metal bowl (an emphatic plopping sound) and the screen goes black."[80] The demon quips to the audience, "You're about to witness the product of young love, compliments of the back seat of a '94 Camaro" (the Camaro is one of Roberts's favorite devices). As Chrissy continues to cry, squirm, and protest, the doctor and his assistant coldly tell her to "be still. This was your *choice!*" and "SHUT UP! You pay the money! I do the work AND the talking!"

The demon guide emerges here as an emissary of the plot against decency, his presence a confirmation of what might otherwise be shrouded in conspiracy as he describes the "lies" fed to the public by the "liberal media." One such lie has people "convinced that a child is only tissue. But the truth is that that tissue has a brain and a heartbeat—and can feel his little arm being RIPPED off his body." At this moment, it is common to hear the sound of a heartbeat played as part of this scene's soundtrack. Roberts's script also instructs actors to respond to the demon's utterance of the word "ripped," upon which the doctor makes a dramatic yanking motion while Chrissy howls in agony. Over her continued sobs and protests, the surgical staff claims, "it's only a medical procedure"—perhaps meant to dramatize the way in which such cold proceduralism is out of step with morality—as they scoop the bits of meat (which the instructional kit explains should be those that most closely resemble an aborted fetus) from beneath the blood-soaked white sheets, plopping them casually in a bowl or jar. When Chrissy finally screams, "I want my baby!" the doctor's assistant snorts without compassion, "You should have thought of that a long time ago." Ironically, the medical staff display the kind of cold judgmentalism of which Hell Houses themselves are often accused. Roberts has the demon guide provide commentary here, explaining to audiences, "Killing babies is a wonderful *choice*. It's so-o-o-o convenient."[81] And at the conclusion of this scene, the demon is also instructed to point out a young woman in the audience and sneer, "It's just too bad I didn't get YOU!"

The Victorious Life Church of Waco, Texas, once combined its abortion scene with post-9/11 reflections on terrorism and God's wrath. Echoing Jerry Falwell's and Pat Robertson's infamous September 13, 2001, statements that the attacks of September 11 represented God's judgment against "the liberals, the abortionists, the homosexuals," the script positions a young woman in this moral framework by having her show up early for her "abortion appointment" on the morning of the attacks "because I start a new job today and I need to get to work in the Twin Towers."[82] Upon revealing the abortion procedure itself, the ubiquitous demon guide points out a small basin containing a doll supposed to be the recently dispatched fetus. The demon dips a pointy finger into the container and proclaims, "This one tastes like boy!" The scene then returns to Ground Zero, where a sort of Rapture is taking place as angels lead the righteous souls from the wreckage of the World Trade Center, framed in the backdrop by a video montage of news broadcasts and footage of representations of Jesus.[83] In this worldview, even the smallest or most seemingly mundane thoughts and actions can be magnified, literally exploded into horror. Roberts's recent innovations include a "post-birth abortion" scene, "where mothers can bring their children to the International Center of Post-Birth Abortions to be aborted (shot execution style)."[84] Roberts, who once called legalized abortion "the American Holocaust," defends his representations—frequently denounced as "offensive" by his detractors—by saying, "What Satan and his entourage of demons inflict on people through the killing of innocent unborn babies is offensive to the Christian."[85]

Consistent with Hell Houses' concern with the politics of the body, one of the production's most long-lasting and energetically performed scenes is the gay wedding. The location of the wedding is often rendered as a conventional church crossed with a set from a Hammer horror film, complete with winding staircases, candelabras, and a sinister-looking altar, from which a demon preacher performs the ceremony. Two gay males are to be married. They are portrayed by a male and a female whose hair is tied back and who wears a fake beard (Roberts has said, "I'm just not going to have two guys kiss").[86] Both are dressed in formal wear and stand patiently as the demon guide interprets the event for audiences. The most forceful assertion of conservative evangelical attitudes toward homosexuality occurs when the demon confesses— again asserting that the liberal media and education have been eager pawns in his schemes—that he convinced the two men that they had been born gay. The notion that homosexuals are not born gay but choose instead to follow a sinful "lifestyle" is not normative for all conservatives, but it is quite prominent in conservative evangelical cultures and is bluntly reinforced in Hell House narratives. Roberts aims to reach those who are "buying into what they think is fact" because of what the media have told them about homosexuality: "no one's ever proven people are born gay," he told me.[87] The implication is that, if one is not born gay and instead chooses homosexuality, then one can use the same volition to "convert" to heterosexuality; anyone who willfully maintains a "sinful" lifestyle presumably deserves their damnation. The unsubtle subtext implies further that anyone maintaining a different understanding of homosexuality has similarly been duped by demonic forces. Roberts has asserted, "I don't hate homosexuals, I just hate homosexuality. We're not saying that if you have AIDS you will go to hell; many people like hemophiliacs get AIDS. But you have to face the fact that in this country 75% of the people that have AIDS are male homosexuals. Somebody's got to be willing to shine the light."[88] Nixon interviewed a young man named Landon, a participant in the dramas who once experimented with his sexuality and is convinced that Hell House is addressing the issue appropriately: "Like our lesbian suicide—I love that, man, because that just preaches it out there. . . . it's okay to have these thoughts, it's a temptation from Satan."[89]

The demon preacher then actually performs the marriage, reading lines from Roberts's script. One of the ersatz vows asks, "Do you agree that you can never spend your life with only one sexual partner?" This association between gay marriage and promiscuity in some sense represents a rehabilitation of long-standing conservative critiques of homosexuality. For several decades, following the politicization of the Stonewall riots and the emergence of gay rights politics in the late 1960s and early 1970s, conservative Christians in the United States denounced homosexuality as sinful outright, claiming that homosexuals were all wantonly promiscuous and despised the conventions of marriage.[90] As more homosexuals sought to marry and establish families, conservative Christians have adapted this erstwhile critique, fusing the two strains. The demon concludes the ceremony by pronouncing the couple husband and husband, cackling madly through the words as the newlyweds are urged to kiss each other ("kiss the groom"). The production's prurience is evident when the demon urges them to use "a little more tongue," which inevitably titillates the audiences, who react with a mixture of compulsion and revulsion (transfixed onlookers often exclaim "gross" or "yuck"). The guide then alludes, using coded language, to the acts awaiting the couple in their honeymoon suite, telling the audience, "I know you want to know all about it." But he demurs, leading the audience instead to the second part of this scene, the AIDS funeral (widely regarded in this worldview as a likely consequence of homosexuality).

The tone of Hell Houses' AIDS representations differs from other configurations of the sinning body: some show a bleak, lonely graveside scene (audiences are told that the dead teen's father did not even show up for the funeral and—in a narrative gesture linked to the world of Promise Keepers— that teens like these lack the strong paternal presence that might have prevented them from "choosing" homosexuality) while others focus on the dying patient himself in a hospital bed.[91] Great care is taken to present the patient's body in as severe a state of distress as possible, something that is common in these productions (although these scenes tend to focus only on the male body: I have never encountered a lesbian couple as the focus of a gay marriage scene,

FIGURE 5.2 Gay wedding. Courtesy New Destiny Christian Center.

nor a female dying of AIDS). Elaborate makeup shows a drawn, gaunt face; all manner of welts, lesions, and bruises are rendered on his body; and a forest of tubes, catheters, and monitoring devices envelops the doomed patient. As in the abortion scenes, the medical staff here are presented as coldly professional and largely uncaring (patients are just so much meat, presumably; hospital procedures are mere exercises in technical proficiency). The demon explains, as the patient wails in agony, that this grisly scene is the fate awaiting "homosexual sinners." In some productions, the "sinner" craves atonement, only to be brusquely denied by the demon; in some, he is hauled away by demonic hordes, dragged into offstage hell; elsewhere, he is simply left behind as the guide leads the audience to the next scene. Marietta, Georgia's Hell House features an online tour that includes a scene called "Unrepentant Sodomite," in which a Catholic priest experiences a crisis of theodicy from the bowels of hell. The scene opens with Gregorian chants and cathedral bells, and the doomed priest wonders, "If God really loved me, I wouldn't be here dying of AIDS. Why should God care about who I choose to love, and how, anyway? If God is a God of love, he wouldn't send anyone to Hell, especially a loving homosexual." The scene mocks such speculation as the priest suffers eternally.[92]

One Hell House articulates its message on homosexuality by exploring other tropes of conservative evangelical culture: the God-hating academic and the liberal media, here in collusion to promote the "radical homosexual agenda."[93] Blogger Bill Geerhart describes the scene, which to him recalled a black mass, wherein a "portly satanic professor" is teaching his "minions (played by black-hooded children)" the "lie" that gay people are "born gay." This falsehood is disseminated by militantly anti-Christian media, and at one point the professor shouts to the audience that they can learn more about being born gay by calling "1-800-666-HOMO."[94] Another Satan in another production shouts, "We've got your alternative lifestyle, all right—in Hell!" Such caustic rhetoric is a frequent accompaniment to Hell House depictions of homosexuality's consequences. It is common, for example, to encounter the use of the word "fag," which occasionally prompts laughter, especially in younger audience members.

Drunk-driving scenes provide an opportunity for Hell Houses to display their technical mastery quite vividly. Unlike some of the other topics the productions address, there is no larger theorization about human life or civic authority behind Hell Houses' admonition against drunk driving. These scenes are simple, blunt cautionary tales which are revealing insofar as they demonstrate Hell Houses' fascination with and affinity for scenes of graphic violence. The scenes do not recreate the actual crash but its aftermath. Injured bodies proliferate in these scenes, all dripping with the fake blood that runs throughout Hell Houses; in an effort to create a tableau of authenticity, many productions use cars wrecked in real accidents.[95] Some bodies lie motionless, with limbs akimbo, while other bloodied teens cry out for assistance. In Hell Houses, bodies in pleasure are encountered only as bodies led astray; the body destroyed is an object lesson both positive and negative.[96] Reynoldsburg, Ohio's *Hell Stop* required audience members—in order to get to the next scene in the production—to crawl through the wrecks themselves (Addie Kurtz told Nixon that "[b]lood and body parts were everywhere" amid the broken windshields).[97] Cedar Hill's Trinity Assembly of God has a gruesome electric chair scene that displays the inevitable fate of a drunk driver who injures others but survives himself. The chair is on a swivel with a live actor on one side. But when the chair flips around, one sees baggy prison clothes hanging over a stump of bloody flesh. Without fail, the first response to DUI crashes in these scenes comes not from EMTs but from demons who wait—laughing and taunting—to carry the victims into the lake of fire.

At the Park Ridge Chapel in Bothell, Washington, the drunk-driving scene begins at a sports bar where audiences are shown—by a demon guide, of course—the lonely beginnings of alcoholism. Frequently woven through such scenes are injunctions to parents, both direct and implicit, not to stray from watchfulness over their children. The scene proceeds from the bar—one sin to the next—to the car crash itself, where two corpses are splayed before the telephone pole their car struck. This prompts the demon to quip, "We love two-for-one happy hour: two deaths for one drunk." Audiences are next

FIGURE 5.3 Drunk-driving scene. Courtesy New Destiny Christian Center.

shown teenaged Josh's struggle with substance abuse and depression which, at the demon's urging, leads him to shoot himself in the head (whereupon the lights go out and the audience is splashed with water, as if this were Josh's blood and brain matter).[98] Many of the drunk-driving scenes seem to have been energized by the reimagined evangelical family and gender ideology of the Promise Keepers movement: the scenes' implication is that the wayward fathers and sons who find themselves impaled on a highway sign or wrapped around a tree could have avoided their grisly fates had they remained stead-fastly at home with their families. Hudgins in particular has explicitly linked his productions to such overarching concerns about family life in the United States. Indeed, one of his key motivations in starting his project was to counteract the "disintegration of the home," which he linked to processes begun in the 1960s. As he told me, "[W]ith Dad 'out of place,' mom becomes 'displaced' and...America needs godly men."[99]

A similar note is struck in the representation of adultery. During the period of Hell Houses' public ascendance, between the late 1990s and 2001, this theme was provocatively explored through a reconstruction of former presi-dent Bill Clinton's peccadilloes. In articulating their opposition to adultery, actors reveled in the opportunity to portray the philandering head of state, whose "depraved" actions inside the Oval Office gave the faux Clinton and

Monica Lewinsky the opportunity to make out with abandon (to the pulsating strains of various popular musics). Though the scene focused exclusively on Clinton's carnal appetites, the notion that even the office of the president is corruptible clearly opened up the possibility of broader meditations on Clinton's role in worldly or political evil. Aside from the fact that most conservative evangelicals regarded Clinton's character as falling somewhere between odious and damnable on the spectrum of moral integrity, the suggestion was that the larger evils that have all but overrun American society have now acquired such power that they are unapologetically displayed even in the highest political office. Together, such things show that, in Roberts's formulation, "moral decay will be our undoing" unless challenged.[100] With Clinton out of office, the Lewinsky affair lost its immediacy, and many adultery scenes now focus on the world of online affairs and chat rooms (Judgement House has a script called "Web of Lies" in production). Here, it is common to encounter not only a lonely wife furtively typing away in a darkened room lit by the blue glow of her computer screen but also a neglectful husband, whose chainsaw snoring on the couch signals his disinterest and abdication of patriarchal responsibility. These scenes frequently end in bloody carnage, with vengeful fathers awakening from beery slumber to pummel the adulterers to death. Another scene shows a cuckolded husband tracing his wife and her lover's actions through their online history; when he finds them, he clubs "Jimmy" to death and subsequently chokes his wife.[101]

Of all of the cautionary tales in Hell Houses, the warnings against premarital sex contain some of the most detailed enactments of what is forbidden (and, significantly, they often display some of the most vigorous acting by young parishioners). Roberts's script focuses on a couple who find themselves alone in a bedroom when the parents are out for the evening. The demons tell the audiences that the young couple, whom we see under the sheets, is completely nude. While the male is the sexual aggressor, the demons focus on the female, and they attempt to prey on what we are told are her weaknesses. Eventually, the couple dives entirely under the sheets as the demons discuss the merits of the various sexually transmitted diseases the young woman (but apparently not the young man) might receive. In most productions, they decide to give her AIDS.

What follows is among a Hell House's most alarming scenes, as the young actress watches a video of herself on one of the monitors in the scene. It is an interpretation of the sexual activity going on beneath the sheets. The woman is seen choking or drowning to death, which the demons describe as the moment when her chastity and purity are robbed from her in these very violent actions: the demons announce that they are going to "execute the pearl of her virginity," and Roberts's script calls for "underwater noises" to accompany this moment.[102] When the drama returns to the couple actually in the room, the sex is over and the young man is trying to get out as quickly as possible. As he dresses and prepares to leave, the demons begin to verbally assault the young woman, denouncing her as a slut and a tramp. Some Hell Houses transform such scenes into date rapes, where young actors struggle and spasm for minutes. One grim rendition shows "a teenaged girl punished for entertaining a single brief thought about meeting a guy on spring break—a thought that leads directly to her being viciously gang-raped."[103] Heather Hendershot has described similar phenomena in her interpretations of evangelical television programs that depict scenes of "unhinged desire" as cautionary tales that would fit in a Hell House: "what sounds like rape is here defined as the victim's fault because she has been so thoroughly instructed in biologically compulsory fornication." Edge TV works through sexual material (at times urging tempted teens to picture their parents' faces when they feel sexually aroused) by resorting to stock characters like "the antilust football player, the suffering masturbator, and the repentant homosexual."[104]

References to the occult saturate the religion of fear, and Hell Houses trade heavily therein. The productions peer in on Satanic rituals (almost always involving human sacrifice) or, in an almost nostalgic gesture, the harm of role-playing games like *Dungeons and Dragons* (once thought by some critics to be one of the most dangerous gateways into occult seduction, a status now generally accorded to either *Harry Potter, Lord of the Rings,* or Ouija boards). In some productions, the adolescents who dabble in role-playing games or *Harry Potter* novels become possessed. Exorcism and possession scenes can be quite vivid (it is worth noting that anti-rocker Bob Larson, now an exorcism specialist, has praised Hell Houses often), and some refer obviously to horror films: in one scene, a homunculus bursts through a possessed teen's stomach (in a nod to *Alien*), while elsewhere the possessed's head swivels (recalling *The Exorcist*).

Hell Houses' focus on the direct seductions of the occult mark the dramas' shift away from the politics of the body. Though most forms of fallenness are linked to the material presence of evil in America, a Hell House links specific sins to transformations that can be wrought through exposure to the wrong kinds of entertainments, specifically music. In one 1996 production, a teenage lesbian listens to Nirvana records just before killing herself (we also learn that her absentee parents could have spotted the warning signs, had they not placed work above family and God).[105] Playing on long-standing concerns about pop music's potential to oversexualize, corrupt, and brainwash adolescents, Hell Houses' date rape and teen suicide scenes are often linked explicitly to music regarded as demonic. One regular target is the once-popular phenomenon of raves. House music and raves have faded considerably from youth culture, but one gets the sense that, for the producers of Hell Houses, this scene is meant as a stand-in for any combination of teen gatherings, popular music, and drugs. The demon guide leads audiences into a dark room with strobe lighting, black-clad teens (many of whose faces are decorated with fluorescent paint) dancing to techno, and manifold references to sex and drugs. As usual, the scene focuses on the licentious activities of a young female, who here is urged to swallow a pill (presumably meant to be Ecstasy, the drug once de rigueur at raves). A worst-case scenario unfolds: sometimes, the girl is seduced into sexual misadventure, while elsewhere she experiences a violent reaction to the drug, choking to death on the dance floor as her peers stare impassively (or even laugh at the spectacle). Some drug scenes end in spectacular, albeit nonsexual violence. Shelly Hattan describes one scene wherein a drug deal goes wrong, leading to a female customer getting shot (by a real gun loaded with blanks) before the drug dealer is killed by his rival (who shoves his head into a mound of cocaine, thereby suffocating him).[106] Elsewhere, a drama "showed someone taking a hit off a joint, and then killing everyone in their fraternity."[107] Yet another scene concludes in a graveyard where the dead come back to warn the audience: " 'It's so hot, ' the heroin addict moans. 'It's too late for me, but it's not too late for you. ' "[108]

More visceral still is the Hell House focus on teen suicide, which has since 1999 been refracted almost exclusively in school violence sequences. Schools are often the sites of larger struggles—both cosmic and political—in the religion of fear. For a time, Roberts urged direct reenactment of the events at the Littleton, Colorado, Columbine High School shootings (following the shootings, Roberts organized protests that led to the cancellation of a Marilyn Manson appearance at the Ozzfest metal festival in Denver). One of the victims, Cassie Bernall, was said to have been asked by Eric Harris and Dylan Klebold—the perpetrators—if she believed in God and, replying in the affirmative, was assassinated on the spot. This is widely believed not to have happened, yet the possibility of Christians being targeted provided grist for the Hell Houses' mill. The Trinity Baptist Church profiled in Ratliff's documentary was once so intent on "authentic" reenactments of this scene that they used real firearms during their production (a judge subsequently ordered the church not to use real guns and to increase its security contingent).[109] Indeed, one of the most powerful tropes that evangelical political organizations employed during the 1990s—a notion that remains powerful in this culture—was that of the victimization of Christians. Though enjoying a period of unprecedented political influence, evangelicals since the 1994 midterm elections have successfully organized around claims, for example, that the "tolerance" advocated by "secular humanists" constitutes a formal bias against "people of faith" or that a "judicial war on faith" is under way.[110] Indeed, one local supporter—both despondent and irate in the wake of failed Bush Supreme Court nominee Harriet Miers—intoned "[p]ray for our nation" before calling on every community to sponsor a Hell House or Judgement House.[111]

The school violence scenes are soaked with the erotics of fear, as they blend together hellish music, violence, sexual obsession, and occult references. Even before their Columbine recreations, many Hell Houses sought to achieve authenticity by using real guns loaded with blanks. In some communities (such as Santa Fe, New Mexico), this has been a cause for concern, leading to judge's orders to use prop guns and to increase security. The focus is almost always on a teenaged male who has been going through difficult times (usually having recently been jilted by his girlfriend and become the subject of merciless cliquish gossip) and whose lack of familial or religious support has left him at the end of his rope. The young man begins to hear voices speaking to him through his beloved metal music (this is one of many places where the religion of fear's various manifestations overlap and harmonize with one another). He becomes convinced, as the music blares into the ears of the audience, that revenge against his peers is the solution to his problems. Talking to the demons peering over his shoulder, he finds himself unable to resist their prodding and produces a gun from his backpack or trench coat. What follows then is a very intense assassination scene (resulting in the deaths of several high schoolers) and concluding with the shooter standing in front of the blackboard, stuffing the gun barrel into his mouth, and a corona of gore materializing behind him. The young man is then hauled off to hell by the very demons who goaded him on.

Some school violence episodes (also used in several Tribulation Trail productions) reflect the eternally recurring concern about religious expression in public schools, made current once more owing largely to the recent emergence of groups like the Judeo-Christian Council for Constitutional Restoration (whose slogan is "Confronting the Judicial War on Faith"). In these variations, an inversion of the teacher-driven formula found in Chick tracts, a young black-clad student—who loudly protests that s/he is tired of hearing about Jesus and school prayer—produces a handgun and shoots a fellow student during a debate on the First Amendment.[112] Such classroom scenes have often become vehicles for the expression of concern about the overbearing influence of state-mandated curriculums, the "crowding out" of religious voices from the schoolhouse, and, occasionally, the possibility that the federal government may eventually (whether through "activist judges" or some other, more nefarious means) target "people of faith." In these parables of Christian victimology, one occasionally encounters scenes where a well-meaning science teacher—who has discussed creationism in class—has her classroom turned upside down as a secretive para-police group confiscates all religious materials before hauling the teacher herself outside and murdering her. Elsewhere, a small group of girls is at the center of a Chick-like nightmare—again, femininity is the focus of Hell Houses' attention, just as one sees in horror tales; chastity and virtue violated or defended are at the center of this moral/sexual universe—has their prayer session or Bible study disrupted as a similar organization bursts through a doorway to seize the girls and lead them to execution. Such scenarios may seem outlandish now, the scene suggests, but with each ACLU defense of gay marriage or court decision banning creation science from public schools, America moves further down a slippery slope which can only end in outright government tyranny over the religious.[113]

These larger concerns with government and political order are generally only implicit. Yet in 2004 at Lynchburg, Virginia's Heritage Baptist Church, a production entitled *Judgement House: Homeland Security* engaged these issues directly. The dominant theme was anxiety centering on terrorist attacks, and the production portrayed an America constantly besieged by unidentified terrorists. Focusing on a virtuous young schoolteacher who embodies respectable womanhood and whose steadfast faith sees Jesus as "the ultimate Homeland Security," the production tracks her schoolhouse ministry (with so much terrorism confronting American society, classroom confessionalism is apparently low on the list of public concerns) and the decisions of her students (who, much like the teenage women who populate most Hell Houses, make representative decisions with representative consequences).[114] The students who laughed off their teacher's entreaties to convert find themselves burning eternally.

The conclusion of every Hell House gives attendees the opportunity to repent and convert. Many productions conclude in what is known as a "decision room" or "response room," where one can fill out surveys and sign testimonials of various sorts. As noted above, the theology and doxology presented in these spaces is comparatively minimal. One knows that Jesus is represented as the antithesis of what one has encountered over the previous thirty minutes (although there is the occasional note of darkness, as when a woman begs forgiveness from Christ, who responds, "I never knew you," and opens a trap door, sending the woman to hell).[115] Whereas the multisensory experience of sin and demonology is loud, overwhelming, and fearful, the feelings most customarily described in the spaces of conversion are those of relief (although, in one production, this scene also featured scenes from the Mel Gibson film *Braveheart* projected onto a screen in the background).[116] For example, Yarelis Mora, seventeen, of Jacksonville, Florida, proclaimed, "As I said the salvation prayer, I felt so overwhelmed. I started to cry. I felt relieved. I came out . . . feeling like a new person."[117]

"THE MONEY SHOT": POLITICAL DRAMA AND RELIGIOUS DESIRE

What are the political registers of this "newness," and how might these experiences be understood in light of the religion of fear's larger sensibilities? The political direction of these productions is, both in the general sense and in terms of specific concerns, intimately linked with recent transformations in conservative evangelicalism. If it is the case that the high-water mark of post–World War II liberalism coincided with a period of increased secularism and "permissiveness," as the declension history suggests, then the restoration of a "Christian America" requires the inversion of liberal politics and culture. In Hell Houses, we see this kind of political challenge generated via an "objectification of evil as an unconscious 'negative transference' . . . onto a convenient 'snag.' "[118] The rituals and representations by which this is accomplished serve as pedagogies of the self or as fear templates with abundant political resonances. They recall the "staged crises" of what Bill Ellis calls "ostension," which in Hell Houses constitute "a hybrid of fictional narrative and reality show, which follows in the tradition of American didactic drama."[119] The anxiety latent in the religion of fear's work is "either hidden behind protective fictions of plenitude or horrifically erupts from behind such screens."[120] These, then, are horror tales, laden—like all horror—with psychosocial anxieties. Walter Kendrick claims that behind the innovations of the horror genre lie larger processes of "cultural conservatism."[121] The cemetery landscape of early horror may indeed have represented a kind of cultural longing for a religious past left behind, whose merely visible trappings found expression only in the literary or cinematic world of fright. But what of the sex and gore found in contemporary horror, the slicks of blood or the weapons of vigilante murderers or possessed household appliances that preoccupy contemporary creators? These elements are integral to Hell Houses and embody what director John Carpenter refers to as "right-wing horror," where the threats identified are located externally (as opposed to "left-wing horror," which is concerned with internal threats).[122] Horror's formulaic cycle of threat-safety-threat has certainly long subsisted on fears of contact and contagion. In Hell Houses, the religion of fear's explicit conservatism blends elements of internal and external anxieties, both precisely defined and inchoate, ripe for narration and symbolic/cultural work. Its horrors become reality when culture craves a mask.

There is little evidence in these representations of a finely wrought understanding of the philosophical foundations of political liberalism. Yet, clearly enacted throughout are long-standing conservative criticisms—of hostility toward religion, indifference to the survival of the family, a hypocritical acceptance of free expression found unacceptable by conservatives while denying conservatives their own freedom of expression—projected onto liberalism, which together have proven resilient in conservative activism. These rallying points, successfully disseminated by the NCR since the 1970s, have, over time, found expression in conservative evangelical popular culture as well, where they are redirected toward audiences and recast as horrors.

Popular creations like Hell Houses not only narrate the "sins" whose existence is at least partly attributable to political liberalism's naïve "tolerance";

they also participate in an alternate culture for those seeking to construct antiliberal communities or identities. Cultural architects like Roberts insist that their creations are aimed mostly at personal salvation rather than ideological interventions, yet evident throughout the dramas are specific targets that are engaged in the political spheres along with criticism that harmonizes with the NCR's projects. For the most part, these concerns articulate a politics of the body that is distinct from (and, in some cases, opposed to) conventional forms of identity politics while also being filtered through antiliberal and antistate concerns.

Hell Houses infrequently engage conservative anxieties about race and ethnicity (other than the occasional note of panic struck in response to rap music) in the way that is evident in, for example, conservative contestations of multicultural curriculums (although Roberts did tell me that he was designing some scenes focused on gang violence).[123] But in other respects, the body is the locus of the politics of Hell Houses. Teen chastity and renunciation of secular culture's taints are advocated not simply because they help one to avoid infernal punishment; this advocacy also represents conservative evangelicalism's belief that a hostile, overbearing state has illegitimately wrested control of sex education from parents and local communities, where it is properly located. While, in Hell Houses, one does not encounter an antifeminism that is quite as overt as in the *Left Behind* series, the tone is nonetheless present. In addition to the ways in which young women are made instrumental to the ends of the morality plays, the centrality of abortion (long seen by commentators from Phyllis Schlafly to Pat Robertson as an effect of feminism's success) as a key horror exemplifies, along with narrations of the purported "decline of the family," Hell Houses' position in gender politics. While the denunciations of "the homosexual lifestyle" are not as venomous as those of Topeka, Kansas's Fred Phelps (infamous for his bilious "God Hates Fags"), the prominence of sexual orientation in Hell Houses is another parallel to the contemporary NCR (which is steadily doing for the issue of gay marriage what its 1970s ancestor did for abortion).[124]

Outside of the occasional 9/11 reference, there is usually no overt connection made between geopolitics and apocalypticism in Hell Houses. The moral panics instead usually center on the temptations of youth. While the dangers of drugs, sex, rock music, and the occult are treated singly, they are also understood to be windows onto a larger cultural-political sensibility. Liberalism's pursuit of chimerical rationality and neutrality has, either through ignorance or conspiratorial machination, stripped the public sphere of the religio-moral traditions necessary to combat political and cosmological evil. But the sense is that, as with school violence, the root problems require not so much legislation as proselytization; government, after all, has failed and hopes are best placed elsewhere. Roberts noted that "when people begin to change what the word of God says, good things never happen."[125] Hell Houses dramatize the bad things and situate them in a narrative of religio-political decline.

Rather than embracing particular policy arguments, Roberts's and Hudgins's creations enact what George Lakoff calls "strict father morality" in their advocacy of combative interventions.[126] So their narrations and dramatizations can be seen on one level as simply exhortations, instances of the old tradition of the jeremiad, where the religious social critic warns a backsliding nation of its impending judgment and doom.[127] Yet the specifically religious grounds of these performances and their political sensibilities are rooted firmly in conservative evangelicalism's identity work. Of their effectiveness in this regard, one attendee—whose church has regularly sponsored such events—told me, "They know exactly what to do to back you in a corner... to make you feel constraint and confusion."[128]

Certainly, Hell Houses' articulations of fear and vivid representations of the demonic are some of the religion of fear's most aesthetically powerful frames, instrumental in commending specific types of behavior that map onto political programs. Yet the anxieties fueling these narrations—called "the dramatic equivalent of Jack Chick–style religious tracts"[129]—are also indices of the erotics of fear and the demonology within, which Hell Houses articulate in multiple ways. They inhere most obviously in the emotional tone of the productions and, sometimes, of the participants and audience members themselves, whose reactions often fuse reverence with terror. Nixon writes that "[s]pectators weep, faint, and become physically ill."[130] Adam Butler, a visitor to Westwood Baptist Church's Judgement House in Birmingham, Alabama, describes the sight of "two children praying through tears at the end of a performance.... The mentality of churches to produce such an atrocity is simple—scare children early in their lives and they'll fear it until they die."[131] One group of panicked girls attending *Scaremare* held hands as they moved through the dark set, intoning in unison, "I like Jesus, I like Jesus, I like Jesus."[132] Roberts has said of such responses among small children, "How do you know that just because you see tears, that's an adverse effect?"[133] These are not the only affective responses to Hell Houses—one sees joy, relief, and confidence too—but it is clear that the fear regime constructed in these representations intends to encourage such dramatic choices and such a stark sense of one's position in an ethical universe.

The erotics of fear are quite vividly displayed in Hell Houses' tendency to incorporate elements of precisely those elements of secular culture deemed to be forbidden. Rock music, Hollywood, and the occult may indeed be deemed carriers of evil's contagions, but Hell Houses certainly do not deprive their audiences of the opportunity to learn about these evils up close and in great detail. Consider a 2006 commercial for the Hell House at the Victory Christian

Center in Azle, Texas. The piece juxtaposes reenactments of Roman centurions flogging Christ (the screen is tinted red) with excerpts from the local production (a leather-jacketed teen with a gun to his head, another being dragged by demons from a drunk-driving wreck) while quotes from scripture scroll across the screen and an Evanescence song plays in the background. The commercial shifts abruptly as a voice intones, "But if that doesn't convince them," before a fast-flickering montage of blood-covered youths staring into the camera (one with a simulated bullet hole in his forehead), which then fades out to the sound of a beating heart and simulated Tibetan monastic chanting.[134] Note again that the moral drama of the Hell Houses—where teenagers drinking and fornicating in cars always die in a grisly crash—draws on the same tropes and retributive episodes that one finds in horror films. The liberal use of blood and meat reveal a kinship with what Jack Morgan calls "the biology of horror" and a fascination with the body's destruction.[135] The sets of a Hell House are littered with broken bodies, blood, weapons, and debris, with demons and malevolent spirits flitting between worlds to torment the waking, who suffer through graphic portrayals of late-term abortions, murders, risen corpses, and sexual trauma. The promotional literature is often zealous and can even be taunting: Marietta, Georgia's Hell House penned a memorable advertisement which boasted, "[L]et's just see how many of those Rebel flags we see tearing out of Hell House parking lot this year . . . with their wet diapers on and crying for their momma's. . . . Better bring a clean pair of undees with you."[136] And, as noted above, many productions use loud, violent metal of the sort they denounce: a Laredo, Texas, Hell House advertised itself with grainy photos of teen parties—beer bongs and one-hitter pipes were visible—in a video clip that rocked to Metallica's "For Whom the Bell Tolls."[137]

Part of what is at work here is the desire to produce entertainments which can compete with those of the "fallen" world. This necessitates the construction of vivid, authentic dramatizations that capture audiences: in one of Ratliff's scenes, for example, the director reminds his crew, "Make sure the people in the occult scene have a knife for the slitting of the bride's throat"; another production boasts of its "exact replica of a rave hall"; and Roberts directs potential customers to a business selling what are, in his estimation, the most lifelike gun replicas around.[138] It also requires generating thrills that can hold the attention of young audiences. For example, at a Waco Hell House, fourteen-year-old Jeremy Duhr was standing in line when the actor portraying Satan charged directly at him. Afterward, in the kind of tones usually reserved for those leaving a summer blockbuster film, Duhr breathlessly announced, "It was awesome."[139] Another audience member, Stacy Holbrook, said, "It freaked me out, it's so real."[140] But what is more palpable in these liberal pilferings from the culture of the damned is conservative evangelicalism's preoccupation with—and orientation to—the desires it condemns.

A general rule of thumb when reading Hell Houses is that the greater the cultural anxiety surrounding the moral concern being depicted, the more vivid the prurient imagination and fantasy scenes. For example, an Oklahoma Hell House made one of its primary settings a college keg party (setting the stage for the inevitable drunk-driving scene). Considerable energy was spent detailing the sinful scene: rampant beverage consumption and "tasteful" necking on couches.[141] A 2004 Tribulation Trail displayed a huge blown-up photograph of Madonna and Britney Spears kissing onstage, which was displayed "as one example of the decline of family values."[142] It is difficult to imagine these productions maintaining their popularity without their aggressive tactics or the opportunity to experience vicariously those things forbidden in customary social circumstances. Roberts says, "[W]e paint the black part as black and as dark and as ugly as we can" so that the concluding scene seems all the more attractive to audiences. Fear, then, can be seen as an expression of care, according to Roberts. And it directs audiences toward a representation of hope and forgiveness, which he described to me quite suggestively as "the money shot."[143]

Equally powerful in articulating the two instabilities is the centrality of performance. As Ann Pellegrini notes, role playing has become one of Hell Houses' most memorable features (especially for participants involved in the productions themselves).[144] Clearly, one dimension of the performative element involves the enactment of evil for civic purposes, however narrowly such purposes might be defined. As Ingebretsen reminds us, "The theater of fear . . . is pedagogical, teaching by preemptive example."[145] Yet the prominence of play and performance, the emphasis on inhabiting identities or enacting behaviors usually written off as sinful, is of greater significance. Adolescents from whom sex, drugs, and rock 'n' roll are screened off can, under ritualistic circumstances, engage in licentiousness and illicitness. It is not necessarily the case that sexual pleasure or narcotic intoxication are actually experienced on a physiological level. But performances are nonetheless marked with an obvious exuberance, as in the Salinas, California, Sanctuary Christian Fellowship production, which featured a scene with corpse-painted teens trapped inside a chain-link fence, screaming and mewling almost sexually.[146] There may additionally be a great desire among teen actors to perform *as if* these acts and feelings were real and to do so for the benefit of the community under accepted conditions, as established by these productions. For example, as noted above, there is often fierce competition among young women to play the "abortion girl" or "rape girl" ("they're the biggest chick parts").[147] And one actress told Nixon that, "despite knowing she was only *playing* the victim of sexual abuse, an act of violence which was simulated as many as two dozen times per night and repeated nightly over the course of the production, she eventually felt ' . . . personally violated . . . , ' ' . . . sad, like an outcast..., ' and '...unclean. ' "[148] Roberts says, "[W]e're having a great time," and "people's lives are being changed."[149]

In this conservative evangelical theatrics of fear, the demonology within is manifest not only in the struggle to define and maintain boundaries through the performances themselves, but also in the proximity of the damned to the devout. Audiences get to watch the public dramatization of fallenness and participate in the satisfactions of shaming those who lapse into lewd behavior, with the safe reassurance that these "mere" entertainments are not the real thing. In this, it is possible to view Hell Houses as embodying what David Chidester and Edward T. Linenthal identify as the three related features of sacred space: "ritual space, a location for formalized, repeatable public performances"; "significant space, a site, orientation, or set of relations subject to interpretation because it focuses crucial questions about what it means to be a human being in a meaningful world"; and "contested space, a site of negotiated contests over the legitimate ownership of sacred symbols."[150] The dramas also manifest what Gregory S. Jackson calls the "aesthetics of immediacy" generated by moving through space.[151]

Hell Houses routinely blur the line between the sacred and the profane, the sinful and the pure, the supernatural and the mundane. Even in the spaces surrounding the performances, it is not uncommon to encounter bodily eruptions into normally reserved environs: ebullient prayers, the laying on of hands, and speaking in tongues frequently bubble up from the crowds. The enthusiasm for this theater of fear, and for its promised respite from evil, is one sign of the ways in which conservative evangelicals are working to enact and maintain their identities in postliberal America. By the time the religion of fear came to express itself in Hell Houses in the 1990s, something had happened. American political sensibilities had become ever more chastened and become refracted through ever-denser webs of commerce and entertainment, signifying matrices that are now ubiquitous in establishing identities and in which trust in government and liberalism seem to have floated away like spirits released from torment. Picking up on themes that resound in Chick tracts and in the stentorian preaching of the anti-rockers, Hell Houses' criticism seems somehow to have struck a chord among a wide range of American audiences, its alternate story of national hardship and restoration tapping into some shared experience of and appetite for violence, titillation, and visions of the end. Though heaven may seem relatively boring when compared to the lurid, fantastic spectacles of torture and sin so lavishly rendered in the religion of fear, it is in the exchange between apparent opposites that these identities come to life. The idea in projecting a litany of post-1960s sins in this fashion, narrating them in this way, is to horrify and revolt audiences; yet this revulsion depends on a kind of carnality that also fuels desire.

6

"Already Decided and Carrying a Weapon!"

The Political Terrors of Being *Left Behind*

Like My Father, with whom I am one, I have no pleasure in the death of the wicked, but that is justice, and that is your sentence. —Jesus, in *Glorious Appearing: The End of Days*

This know also, that in the last days perilous times shall come. —2 Timothy 3:1

Yessss!...Yes! Yes! Yes! Yes! —Nicolae Carpathia, in *Desecration*

When the planes failed to fall from the sky, when computer networks did not unravel around the world, when hordes did not take to the streets, pitchforks and torches raised, to battle over canned goods, many Americans breathed sighs of disinterest.[1] Now firmly on the other side of a particularly public episode in the history of catastrophism, one might wonder if American speculation about the end of the world (or, at the very least, of society as we know it) was merely a passing fancy of the late twentieth-century imagination, some crisis of confidence in technology and infrastructure that, once addressed, was safely sublimated. And yet, of course, there were planes that did come careening down from the clouds, into buildings and onto a field. To many Americans, such as Jerry Falwell and Pat Robertson, the two episodes— one imagined, one brutally real—were linked through a conservative evangelical imaginary whereby unpredictable and apparently unrelated events are understood as evidence of an apocalyptic plot.[2]

American Christian apocalypticism is both a highly resilient tradition and also quite fluid and improvisatory in its way. While many Americans regard these traditions and some of their more flamboyant representatives with snickering disdain, the apocalyptic has shaped American public life from its inception to the present. Since World War II in particular, the tradition has become more urgent and more public. This stems in part from the growth of evangelical media during this period; but its urgency represents a response to geopolitical trends like the proliferation of nuclear weapons, protracted conflicts in the Middle East (the locus of at least one apocalyptic narrative), and the advent of a global economy, which seems to many interpreters to fulfill central portions of prophecy. Indeed, prominent representatives of this tradition—from Hal Lindsey to Tim LaHaye—have invoked such transformations as signs of humanity's decline and the imminence of the end times. The vigor of apocalyptic criticism has also consistently benefited from an active writing culture, extending from commentaries and annotated scripture to heated letters to public officials and to novels. Apocalyptic pulp fiction has had a long life in the United States and is currently quite vigorous. Long before the sleek black editions of Tim LaHaye and Jerry B. Jenkins's *Left Behind* series began appearing in 1995, conservative evangelicals in particular have held forth about the degradations of modern American life. Not just in political tracts, theological primers, and self-help manuals, a culturally and politically conservative evangelical voice has been crafted in genre fiction of all sorts: science fiction, crime or mystery (including works by the dean of the subgenre, Frank Peretti), and even romance novels (some by Tim LaHaye's wife, Beverly, co-founder of Concerned Women for America).[3] But the *Left Behind* series has pursued turn-of-the-millennium evangelical conservatism with rare vigor and unprecedented (if considerably complicated) popularity.

These novels are unique among the religion of fear's creations insofar as they are not only quite well recognized (I am still shocked when, on very rare occasions, I meet somebody who has not heard of them) but have received widespread public commentary.[4] These books represent the religion of fear's widest audience, its move from the cramped offices of Chick Publications, through the seminars and radio broadcasts of the anti-rockers, through the public spectacles of Hell Houses, all the way to the *New York Times* bestseller list. The series has sold over 63 million volumes, a figure that clearly indicates it is a phenomenon that has long since moved beyond evangelical communities alone; and it is estimated that 9 percent of the population of the United States has read at least one of these books (including at least 3 million readers who are not evangelicals).[5] Hundreds of articles and editorials have appeared in mainstream magazines and in newspapers; talk shows and news programs have discussed the novels' success; and even academics (notably Amy Johnson Frykholm, Melani McAlister, and Glenn W. Shuck) have entered the conversation. And of all the religion of fear's creations, these novels—while they certainly are not reducible to their politics—represent the clearest and most enduring link to figures, organizations, and ideas with tangible influences in the political sphere. Of course, most people know that these novels embody both a conservative religiosity and conservative politics. Both Frykholm and Shuck treat such matters, yet—while each offers insights into the series—they have not addressed the origins, specific shapes, and implications of the series' political vision robustly enough. McAlister's essay is an excellent guide to the series' global sensibility, specifically its resonance with what she calls "the revitalization of Christian Zionism," but it is not directed toward the themes of declension and criticism central to the religion of fear.[6] I will show specifically how the series constitutes its politics and how the authors seek to commend it to readers. I read these novels and their creators, focusing specifically on fear's declension narrative and its hostility to liberalism, while also unpacking the two instabilities. My intent is not to isolate an audience or a movement but to identify a creative impulse with clear political overtones. As political narrative, *Left Behind* is a suggestive object of study when read against the aspirations and contexts of LaHaye and Jenkins. The horrors portrayed in these twelve novels— and in their myriad product spin-offs—are articulated in the future tense, positioned chronologically and historically as consequences of worldly behavior now. Thus, the greater the detail in which these frights are rendered, the more vivid the possibility that the reader might act to avoid them. As both entertainment and education, the books provoke.

"ALL THIS WILL COME UPON THIS GENERATION"

Central to the appeal and the power of the *Left Behind* novels and their politics is LaHaye's particular theological orientation, dispensational premillennialism. Most of the series' readership is roughly aware that the authors' Christianity is evangelical and that they are preoccupied with the Rapture, the end times, and apocalyptic scenarios; indeed, it would be difficult to read more than a few pages without discerning this. More specifically, LaHaye's beliefs are shaped by the prophetic tradition represented in the books of Amos, Joel, Ezekiel, Isaiah, and Jeremiah. These prophets were social critics, reminding audiences of their covenant with God and warning them that failure to honor the covenant was the reason for current hardship. Prophetic writing thus focuses its interpretive gaze on worsening circumstance. Apocalyptic literature goes beyond the prophetic in depicting revelations, couched in symbol and allusion, of another reality articulated in visions of the eschaton, future judgment, and the supernatural consequences of worldly actions. Most apocalyptic works were also written in a social context where the groups being addressed faced misery or direct threats to their existence.[7] The apocalyptic genre is thus not only historically specific but, in its responsiveness to crisis, is aimed at theodicy and the recuperation of identity. It is marked by what Stephen D. O'Leary calls a "specifically argumentative dimension" that aims to secure audiences through "proofs" or correlations of contemporary events with the symbolic codes of the texts themselves.[8] The discourse promises not simply the end of time but, what is more socially and politically significant, the end of evil, thereby acting to justify the authors' descriptions and injunctions.

The complex imagery and chronology of Ezekiel and Daniel still preoccupy contemporary interpreters, as does the notion that the end times, with its eventual restoration or purification, are linked to moral degeneration. But no source is more rich and graphic than the book of Revelation. Written in a time of persecution (John's exile to the Isle of Patmos), this text was directed against the tyrannical power of the Roman Empire. It is meant to reassure believers that, no matter what suffering they currently endure, God's justice and mercy will eventually triumph over temporal powers; as Boyer puts it, "John is radically hostile to the secular power of the state."[9] This text is filled with beasts, visions, numbers, warnings, and apocalyptic portents: the lamb who is slain; opening the seven seals; the Four Horsemen of the Apocalypse; angels blowing trumpets; the 144,000 elect; a woman clothed with the sun; and finally, the 1,000-year reign of the saints.

Christians have interpreted this text in a wide variety of ways: some read it as a caution against political power, some as a suggestion that Christians live in a figurative state of exile, while others interpret it quite literally as a codebook for reading the signs of the times. LaHaye and Jenkins fall clearly into the latter category, convinced by both the texts and their world that the end is nigh. Prophecy believers have historically been convinced of this for several reasons. The first is that, in Matthew 25:31–46, Jesus refers to the "kingdom of heaven" and predicts a great judgment: here, "The Son of Man comes in all His glory, and all the angels with Him and He will sit on his glorious throne and before Him will be gathered all the nations and He will separate them one from another just like a shepherd separates the sheep from the goats." The sheep are the righteous, to be invited into the kingdom, while the goats are the wicked, destined to dwell in everlasting fire. In addition to Jesus' words, early Christians believed that Jesus would come back during their lifetimes, and so experienced urgency about evangelism and conversion. Since early Christians were persecuted, ridiculed, and at times barred from mainstream life, their apocalyptic sensibility can be seen in part as an expectation of coming vindication. Later generations of Christians had to adjust their sensibilities and contend with the fact that the world had not ended. Many ceased reading texts literally, and attempted in various ways to live on earth as if the kingdom had been established (an idea which itself has spawned a multitude of meanings).

As Christianity developed, some believers followed the texts literally and invoked them during times of strife, while others read them symbolically or allegorically. Among the former, prophets of doom appeared fairly regularly in the Middle Ages, the Reformation, and Civil War England. But it was in the modern era, particularly in the United States, that the apocalyptic resurfaced with vigor. Following a resurgence of this genre during the revolutionary period, many of the nineteenth century's architects of the contemporary idiom responded to two developments: secular humanism (the perceived drying up of religious energy and the ubiquity of nonreligious thought) and modernity (a series of intellectual, cultural, and political developments that, many believed,

FIGURE 6.1 McKendree Robbins Long Sr., *Vision from the Book of Revelation*. Courtesy Smithsonian American Art Museum, museum purchase.

were ultimately hostile to "traditional religion"). In this period, the apocalyptic often took one of the following forms: some preachers (like William
Miller and Charles Taze Russell) predicted actual dates for the end of the
world; some connected the end of the world with the return of Jews to Pa-
lestine; and some began to look for signs of an apocalyptic plot (an often
heavily political engagement linked to current events).[10]

One view which emerged was premillennialism, which stipulated that
Christ would return prior to the millennium, a scenario guided by the belief
that the world is becoming progressively more wretched.[11] Following this
event comes the Tribulation, seven years of turmoil when the Antichrist will
take over the earth, only to be defeated by Christ and the host of saints at the
battle of Armageddon. Since premillennialists believe that these events are
imminent, they write with a sense of urgency to save as many souls as possible
before it is too late. The specific variant of millennialist thought encountered
in *Left Behind* has nineteenth-century roots. John Nelson Darby (1800–1882),
of the English sect the Plymouth Brethren, was one of this theology's primary
architects and first articulated the idea of a secret Rapture in 1827. Basing his
reflections on 1 Thessalonians 4:16 ("we who are still alive and left will be
caught up together with them in the clouds to meet the Lord in the air"),
Darby believed that, instead of one second coming, there would be two: a
secret one in which the faithful are "Raptured" and a subsequent public one.

From this basic adjustment in the periodization of salvation history, Darby
went on to elaborate an interpretive framework known as dispensationalism,
which parcels history into periods called dispensations (during each of which
God has made a special dispensation of grace, or is revealed differently to
God's followers). The first five dispensations cover the time recorded in the
Hebrew Bible, from the Creation to the Roman occupation of Judea; the sixth
dispensation is the "church age," or the era of the Christian tradition; and the
final dispensation will consist of the unfolding of the apocalyptic plot and the
coming of the kingdom of God.[12]

Darby and his followers insisted that Christians should expect the second
coming soon and that worldly events confirmed the nearness of these transformations. Darby's idiom was partly critical, condemning other Christians
while praising the faithful remnant whom he believed would stand alone. These
doom-struck pronouncements had a powerful allure since, as Frykholm notes,
they confirmed for Darby's followers that their distance from conventional
cultures was a sign of the strength of their convictions.[13] In the United States,
dispensationalists have been shaped by the work of Cyrus I. Scofield (1843–
1921), the founder of Dallas Theological Seminary, whose *Scofield Reference
Bible* is heavily annotated with dispensationalist keys to interpreting scripture.
His notes to the King James Version of the Bible are filled with suggestions that
contemporary events should be read according to his understanding of human

history. In his notes to Revelation 13:8, for example, Scofield invoked the term "world-system" (a rhetorical commonplace among dispensationalist interpreters), and he suggested that the applicability of his code work would grow as humanity approaches the end times: "[d]oubtless much which is designedly obscure to us will be clear to those for whom it was written as the time approaches."[14] He argued in effect that the Bible can—with some extrapolations— provide the answer to any question. This template was embraced by, among others, Lyman and Milton Stewart (1840–1923 and 1838–1923, respectively; they were responsible for commissioning the influential series of pamphlets *The Fundamentals of the Faith* from 1910 to 1915) and John F. Walvoord (1910– 2002; for decades, the president of Dallas Theological Seminary, the doctrine's institutional home, where hundreds of prominent preachers, theologians, and authors have been trained). As dispensationalism developed, there existed a parallel fictional tradition expounding on the theology, positing interpretive links between the world and "the Book," and enabling readers to empathize with characters sharing their sensibilities.

The influence and presence of apocalyptic Christianity is certainly widespread in contemporary America. As noted in the introduction, Paul Boyer describes the world of prophecy belief as one of concentric circles. At the center is a core group of believers like LaHaye, who devote themselves to interpreting the Bible's apocalyptic readings and attempting to correlate them with current events. This inner sphere is extraordinarily productive, and one can sense its presence throughout the world of evangelical media and even more broadly in American life. In addition to the many communities shaped by dispensational premillennialism, there are television shows (like Robertson's *700 Club* and *Jack Van Impe Presents*, among many programs airing on the Trinity Broadcasting Network and Robertson's Christian Broadcasting Network); huge swaths of prophecy books, newsletters, and magazines (such as the Web site www.RaptureReady.com, James McKeever's *End-Times News Digest*, Pete Lalonde's *Omega Letter*, and Salem Kirban's *Rapture Alert Newsletter*); and apocalyptic films like *Thief in the Night* (and its sequels like *A Distant Thunder*, *Image of the Beast*, and *The Prodigal Planet*), *Gone: The Film*, and *The Omega Code*.[15] But perhaps the single biggest influence on LaHaye's prophecy writings has been Hal Lindsey's *The Late Great Planet Earth*. The 1970 book, since reprinted dozens of times, is premised on the assumption that Matthew 23:36 ("All this will come upon this generation") applies to our time, when signs of Christ's return are visible everywhere. The most important sign to Lindsey was the 1948 restoration of Israel, whose presence grew more significant during the Cold War. Lindsey estimated that, by "generation," Matthew meant a biblical generation of approximately forty years, reasoning from this that "within forty years or so of 1948, all these things could take place."[16] He enumerated several signs that he (and other prophecy figures) thought made this clear: in Revelation 13, he saw the ten horns of the beast as a symbol for the ten-member Common Market; he believed that the Antichrist was the ecumenical movement; he believed that the battle of Armageddon would be precipitated by conflict in the Middle East; and from Revelation 9:3–11, he interpreted the plague of locusts as a symbol for the Cobra helicopters used in the Six-Day War of 1967.

For Lindsey, the Tribulation would focus mostly on Israel. So for Lindsey, Walvoord, and other thinkers in this mold, Jews occupy a precarious position. On the one hand, because Jews made covenants with God that have not yet been broken, most apocalyptic Christians support Israel and Zionism. On the other hand, some apocalyptic Christians also suspect that Jews have in fact failed many of God's tests (including recognition of Jesus).[17] Lindsey, in short, popularized the notion that the end times would occur in the Middle East. As is well known, Lindsey achieved direct political influence in Ronald Reagan's administration and was permitted to discuss with Pentagon officials the possibility of nuclear war.[18] Ultimately, the Lindsey tradition does not necessarily believe that the United States will play a direct role in the end times; but the tradition is adamant that the United States must continue to support Israel and other Middle Eastern allies and must maintain strength against aggressor nations. Lindsey has continued to engage such materials actively. He and Walvoord have helped to popularize many of the standard contemporary representations of the Antichrist: as a Gentile dictator, the European Common Market, or the "super church," among many others.[19] And perhaps unexpectedly, such ideas have filtered into popular fiction.

GOOD BOOKS AND THE GOOD BOOK

One way to understand the shapes of evangelical fiction is to situate them within long-standing struggles with the notion of "worldliness." While evangelicals have always been alike in their concern to redeem individual souls—and, for many believers, the world as well—there have always been disputes concerning the degree to which one should maintain contact with a fallen world in these pursuits. Historically, many have tended to describe this world in an idiom of warnings, of indictments, of the tortured conscience. Among the temptations, the lures, and the dangers the regenerate face are the trappings of the world, the market, and materiality in general. In a pluralistic, changing, and increasingly immoral culture, so the narrative goes, the sexual, financial, and ideological temptations to the believer are manifold, and often craftily concealed. While some evangelicals have advocated strict separatism, others have sought to engage the fallen culture and transform it from within by establishing evangelical alternatives to popular entertainments. These alternatives—regardless of how closely they approximate their secular counterparts or how fully they appropriate certain secular media—are charged with a keen sense of boundaries: between the sacred and the profane, the saved and the damned, the illicit and the permitted. So, while evangelicals orient themselves to popular cultures in multiple fashions, their cultural creations almost always are marked by an awareness of their own Otherness relative to what is seen as a fallen society.

In terms of evangelical fiction in particular, there are multiple genres—notably romance and morality tales—whose roots lie in the nineteenth century. And, as Peter Gardella notes, there exists an old fictional tradition—including works by C. S. Lewis, John Bunyan, and John Milton, among others—of depicting angels and humans and demons in conflict, a popular theme in contemporary evangelical fiction.[20] Yet contemporary fiction truly began to take shape when, in the decades after World War Two, the evangelical Christian culture industry was built. Among the more significant components of this vast and complicated entertainment culture, and its print culture specifically, is the Christian Booksellers Association (CBA), the largest and most influential religious publishing association in the United States (with 2,500 member stores).[21] Formed in 1950, the CBA was an institutional response to the proliferation of Christian bookstores after World War Two, following a period when door-to-door sales were the norm.[22] The considerable success of Christian publishing and its recent extension into many areas of genre fiction would be unthinkable without the CBA's presence (and its huge, slick conventions).[23] While many of the motivations inspiring evangelical authors, and their symbolic range, are indebted to earlier eras, the mass mediation and marketing of Christian fiction are more contemporary phenomena.

The majority of Christian authors believe that their works—whether meant to entertain, inspire, convert, or frighten—are evangelistic tools, which partially fulfill the great commission. While nearly every genre of popular fiction has been appropriated by Christian authors, none has been quite as successful and enduring as those inflected with the apocalyptic idiom. Rapture fiction has been produced at least since the early twentieth century, when—as Crawford Gribben notes—Sydney Watson published several formative works, including *Scarlet and Purple, The Mark of the Beast*, and *In the Twinkling of an Eye*.[24] As the contemporary genre took shape in the 1970s—an important moment of coalescence, when conservative evangelicals began more explicitly to appropriate pop culture and to move into direct political engagement—it drew upon some of the tropes being explored in apocalyptic films. As Randall Balmer shows, many of the most successful evangelical films of the 1970s—such as Don Thompson's *Thief in the Night* and its sequels—wrought from this idiom both a sense of urgency and an affinity for the horrific that have influenced contemporary fiction writers.[25] These films, still shown to youth groups and Bible study groups, drip with the viscera of fear; they are "replete with radiation sickness, blood-curdling screams, increased repression...and stainless-steel guillotines."[26] Often shown at churches or at Bible camps (which often serve as testing grounds for evangelical media strategies), the films have also had a very open emphasis on conversion. As Thompson revealed, "I would rather have been scared into heaven than have to go through" the torments depicted in his films.[27]

The primary aim of apocalyptic fiction, as in the religion of fear generally, is to generate interpretive frames for readers: the narratives, often simple in construction and symbolism, convey to sympathetic consumers ideal, typical evangelical understandings of nationalism, gender, economics, sexuality, and politics more broadly. Central to the contemporary fiction boom is the work of Frank Peretti, whose writing "almost single-handedly expanded the field of Christian fiction beyond the romance novels of the 1970s."[28] Abetted by the growing number of evangelical bookstores and radio stations, Peretti's hit novel *This Present Darkness* suggested that, lurking beneath the seemingly innocent veneer of everyday life, minions of Satan were at work undermining institutions and morality. As we have seen in previous cases, the details are in the devil, and the identity of evil reveals a considerable amount about the politics and social circumstances of the author. Peretti's fiction has energetically identified tools of Satanic machinations, frequently naming long-standing sources of evangelical concern like international financial organizations, New Age practitioners, and feminists.[29] What is significant about Peretti's example, however, is not simply the politics of his genre fiction but the ways in which these are advanced through a medium of popular entertainment engaged in the kind of boundary negotiation central to the religion of fear.

Such narratives remap the world, rendering its once-familiar landscapes in the blood-red tones of spiritual battle. In Peretti's books, this is true in a literal sense as "Christians and demonic forces hold particular cities and territories."[30] The demonic lurks everywhere: in homosexual rights, in premarital sex, in the popularity of Eastern religions, for example. Shuck documents the presence of this sense of embattlement in other prophecy writers who have emerged since the 1970s. Authors like Carol Balizet and Salem Kirban acknowledge Hal Lindsey's *The Late Great Planet Earth* as an inspiration; they also write in a vivid populist style that incorporates abundant shock and horror tropes.[31] Following Peretti's example, Larry Burkett's *The Illuminati* articulated this sense of embattlement in a way that reflected the passage of the Cold War. After the Cold War, Burkett seemed to suggest, American overconfidence and inattention to God's law could place the nation in jeopardy: the Illuminati, his novel warned, could seize upon such waywardness to install an operative in the Oval Office, a scenario which Burkett then used to unpack several well-known dispensationalist fears (global financial control in the hands of an elite and an electronic identification system akin to the mark, for example).[32]

Most of these authors share not only a sense that fictional narratives can serve to articulate their sociopolitical anxieties but a willingness to appropriate the structure and style of successful "mainstream" fiction. One encounters familiar plot lines, page-turning styles, generally happy endings, and identifiable characters. What is distinct, of course, is the use of conversion strategies and the effort to reinforce religious norms. This literature is not technically religious instruction but rather, as Cordero points out, "mediates knowledge about the world indirectly."[33] And while many religious authors stop short of fully approximating secular fiction in their resistance to themes of overt sexuality and violence, the *Left Behind* series in particular exuberantly manifests the erotics of fear, discussing violence and moral backsliding in forensic detail. These themes, and this propensity, are consistent with the long and very public career of Tim LaHaye.

THE BATTLES OF TIM LAHAYE

Dr. Tim LaHaye (b. 1926) was well known for decades before *Left Behind* was spawned.[34] While writing novels is a relatively new pursuit for LaHaye, intense political activity is not. Long before his name appeared embossed on the glossy black covers of his bestsellers, LaHaye was an outspoken critic of the "secular humanism" that, as he saw it, had crept into government, education, and American culture more broadly. He has long urged Christians to purify this degraded culture by taking their values from the church into the public square. A graduate of Bob Jones University with a doctorate in divinity from Western Theological Seminary and a doctorate in literature from Jerry Falwell's Liberty University, LaHaye cut his teeth in the mid-1960s by helping to establish a Christian high school in the San Diego area. During this period, LaHaye was pastor of Scott Memorial Baptist Church and was also connected to the John Birch Society (an association that lasted well into the 1970s).[35] At a time when many conservative evangelicals were first considering abandoning public education (in part because of Supreme Court decisions, like *Engel v. Vitale* and *Abington v. Schempp*, which were seen as gutting schools of their moral content), LaHaye was among the more savvy activists in this area. His educational endeavors extended to a second high school, then to a miniature network of alternative Christian institutions which comprised something like a school system, and in 1970 to Christian Heritage College (which trained students to work in Christian schools themselves). During this same period, LaHaye's organization Californians for Biblical Morality supported Ronald Reagan's gubernatorial candidacy and subsequent administration. From the outset of his public life, then, electoral, governmental, and cultural politics were all part of LaHaye's purview.

LaHaye quickly became a well-connected figure in the NCR of the 1970s. Broadening his cultural critique and positing that children from "broken homes" could not resist the profligate sexuality surrounding them, LaHaye helped to found Family Life Seminars in 1971, with the hope that it could train families to defend themselves from liberalism and secularism by adopting "biblical principles for family living as a means of counteracting the harmful influence of humanistic education."[36] LaHaye is also the co-founder of Concerned Women for America (CWA), along with his wife, Beverly (who is also a prolific author of evangelical romance novels, such as the *Seasons* series); with Dr. Henry Morris, of the Institute for Creation Research; and with Tommy Ice, of the Pre-Trib Research Center of Arlington, Texas (which aims "to research, teach, and defend the pretribulational rapture and related Bible prophecy doctrines").[37]

LaHaye also has authored dozens of books on sociopolitical matters. In the 1980s, he issued an influential trilogy of critiques: *The Battle for the Family*, *The Battle for the Public Schools*, and *The Battle for the Mind* (the latter was updated in 2001, co-authored with anti-rocker David Noebel, in *Mind Siege: The Battle for Truth in the New Millennium*). His general assertion in these texts is that no dimension of American culture is free of the contest between secular liberalism and Christianity; behavior, commerce, sexuality and marriage, education, and politics are all key battlegrounds in a clash of worldviews.[38] In addition to such social critical works, LaHaye has published on a wide variety of topics ranging from personality tests, sex and marital counseling (including the curiously titled *How to Be Happy though Married*), anger and depression, and an interpretation of the religiosity of the American founders (where LaHaye challenges the legitimacy of church-state separation with an idiosyncratic reading of early American history).[39]

Throughout his career, LaHaye's writings and activism have vigorously engaged the political (though not always the electoral) process. Underlying these engagements is a consistent repudiation of the legacies of the 1960s. LaHaye has been a forceful advocate of NCR policies, a power broker whose name appears on the foundational documents of many NCR organizations, and a high-profile author whose ideas have kept the NCR's post-1960s declension narrative in public discourse. In his writings, one encounters assumptions central to the NCR more broadly: that the triumph of technocratic liberalism is manifest in the overbearing presence of an administrative state, which seizes decision-making power from everyday citizens and invests it in isolated groups of political elites who, among their other faults, ushered in an era of social permissiveness while also undermining the interests of religious citizens. Indeed, as he wrote in a 2004 support piece for George W. Bush's reelection campaign, "liberal ideology" in the judiciary is responsible for

> the removal of the Ten Commandments from our federal buildings; the attempted removal of "one nation under God" from the pledge of allegiance; the attempted removal of IN GOD WE TRUST from our currency; the ongoing practice of abortion, including partial-birth abortion; and the legalization of homosexual marriages.[40]

This political sensibility animates the *Left Behind* series too, and its vast popularity has given the religion of fear extremely widespread expression.

LaHaye participated in the first wave of NCR organizations which served to popularize this narrative and to galvanize disaffected citizens. In addition to his counsel and advice during the formation of famed groups like Moral Majority and Religious Roundtable, LaHaye was one of the early participants in Christian Voice (founded in the 1970s, once housed in the Heritage Foundation and originator of the now-ubiquitous congressional "report card"). He went on to found the influential groups American Coalition for Traditional Values and Coalition for Religious Freedom. These organizations were explicitly restorationist, promising a return to moral and political clarity in the wake of Vietnam and Watergate, while also reinserting messianic discourse into American political life. They cited legalized abortion, gay rights, feminism, and secular humanism not just as bad policy but as deviations from a historic path of national righteousness. LaHaye also served on the board of the Council for Revival, which vowed to "reinstate" "biblical law" in America.[41]

The success of the NCR during its first decade stemmed largely from its fusion of sentiment, policy, and historical narrative, all of which promised to alleviate discontent by rolling back liberalism. In 1981, LaHaye resigned his work as a pastor to devote himself full time to political endeavors. While some of his political projects have sought to evangelize institutions, he has arguably been more effective in crafting a specific rhetoric and discourse that reflect and support NCR projects. During the 1980s and early 1990s, CWA helped to fund and promote conservative candidates for office. This was perhaps most notable when LaHaye served as co-chair of Jack Kemp's 1988 presidential campaign (a position he resigned after fallout from anti-Catholic statements LaHaye made) and in CWA's support for Home School Legal Defense Association founder Michael Farris's 1993 campaign for lieutenant governor of Virginia. Following his ousting from the Kemp campaign, the Bush camp invited LaHaye to several events (one of which was the occasion when Jerry Falwell introduced LaHaye to future president George W. Bush), signaling the continuation of his long-standing GOP connections.[42] It was during this period that LaHaye decided to try writing some novels.

LaHaye enlisted the services of Jerry B. Jenkins, whose career had consisted of ghost-writing biographies of male hero exemplars like Nolan Ryan, Hank Aaron, Mike Singletary, Orel Hershiser, and Billy Graham. Jenkins does most of the writing, while LaHaye checks the books for "prophetic accuracy." The first volume was published in 1995, at the hottest point of a cultural moment preoccupied with Gingrich's Contract with America, the Oklahoma City bombing, and ethnic conflicts abroad. The books—*Left Behind, Tribulation Force, Nicolae, Soul Harvest, Apollyon, Assassins, The Indwelling, The Mark, Desecration, The Remnant, Armageddon,* and *Glorious Appearing* (the only volume with a white cover)—narrate events central to the dispensationalist worldview. Each book has been a hit, often jockeying for position with *Harry Potter* on bestseller lists. Aside from the *Left Behind* books (and their innumerable offshoots), LaHaye's writing energy has focused mostly on issues relating to prophetic interpretation. For the most part co-authored with Ice, LaHaye's commentary on apocalyptic events—all of which filters into the series—encompasses a variety of genres: there is the *Pre-Trib Newsletter* (intended to document "exciting world events"—keeping "a watchful eye on Israel," in particular—in their relation to LaHaye and Ice's prophecy), large hardcovers containing multiple color charts and diagrams (of sacred geography, prophetic time lines, and the like), annotated Bibles, study guides, readings of contemporary political events (*Are We Living in the End Times?*), and several works of theology and apologetics.

In an overcrowded market, LaHaye and his team of associates have carved out for themselves a dominant position in the literature linking dispensationalism and political critique. From the *Left Behind* series itself has developed a miniature industry, many of whose products are highly visible in churches, bookstores, and airport departure lounges. Since the publication of the twelfth and so-called final novel in 2004 (although yet another sequel—*Kingdom Come: The Final Victory*—appeared in April 2007), LaHaye and Jenkins have continued to satisfy audience demands for more books. Directly related to the original series is the *Countdown* series, consisting of several prequels (*The Rising, The Regime,* and *The Rapture*) intended to shadow more closely the events of the present. LaHaye and co-authors Greg Dinallo and Bob Phillips write the *Babylon Rising* series (*Babylon Rising, The Secret on Ararat, The Europa Conspiracy,* and *The Edge of Darkness*). Appropriating themes similar to those in Dan Brown's *The Da Vinci Code* and the myriad potboilers in that genre, these books follow Michael Murphy, an action-ready scholar of biblical prophecy. Focusing on prophecies not covered in the *Left Behind* books, Murphy discovers artifacts authenticating biblical history and challenges global conspiracies to suppress this knowledge. There is also the *Political* series by Nessa Hart (including *End of State, Impeachable Offense,* and *Necessary Evils*), which focuses on the travails of White House chief of staff Brad Benton.

Mel Odom's *Military* series (*Apocalypse Dawn*, *Apocalypse Crucible*, and *Apocalypse Burning*) follows First Sergeant Samuel Adams "Goose" Gander and other members of the armed forces (as well as the activities of Goose's wife, Megan, whose work at home in Fort Benning, Georgia, includes fighting bureaucratic red tape in order to help teens orphaned by the Rapture) as the battles of the apocalypse unfold. Set in the near future, Joel C. Rosenberg's *The Ezekiel Option* narrates the way in which the Hebrew Bible's prophetic writings are unfolding in current events. The protagonist, Dr. Eliezer Mordechai, is ex-Mossad and a recent Christian convert who responds to Russian hostility and attacks on Israel by penning the military brief that gives the novel its title, a blend of war strategy and Bible prophecy. Rosenberg has also written post-9/11 techno-thrillers *The Last Jihad* and *The Last Days*, which use fiction to assert the tangible connections between Saddam Hussein and the September 11 attacks. And Jenkins's *Soon* series (*Soon*, *Silenced*, and *Shadowed*) explores the consequences of "the world government's prohibition on religion." The ominously named National Peacekeeping Organization seeks to expose and root out "underground religion" in these fictionalized expressions of the sense of embattlement central to much NCR activism and to the religion of fear's narrative of decline.

There is also a line of youth fiction, including graphic novel adaptations of the primary series and a *Left Behind: The Kids* series (*The Vanishings*, *Second Chance*, *Through the Flames*, *Facing the Future*, *Nicolae High*, and *The Underground*) that addresses the Rapture and the Tribulation through concerns about raves, cyber-stalkers, and MTV, among other topics. Since 2002, the series has been accessible as a syndicated radio program on nearly 400 stations.[43] Interested consumers can also purchase boxed sets of the books, leather-bound and embossed anniversary editions, worship CDs (such as *People Get Ready*), handbooks and reference guides, theological apologetics (denouncing the dozens of books which, in a growing counterindustry, denounce the series), daily calendars, greeting cards, CD-ROMs, DVDs, *Left Behind* "mobile prophecies" (or screen savers, or ring tones) for cell phones and other mobile devices, and the *Left Behind: Eternal Consequences* video game (the strategy-based play involves battling "Global Community peacekeepers" or demons with the power of prayer and searching for "Tribulation clues," which unlock different areas of the game). The publisher also sponsors seminars, Bible tours, and a *Left Behind* prophecy club (effectively a newsletter interpreting current events through the lens of the series and its theology). Despite such market saturation, I was refused permission to use *Left Behind* imagery for this book. Responses to my inquiries were both evasive and litigious.

The plot of the series seems, from one perspective, simply like a commercial fictionalization of biblical narrative. But these texts are also unmistakably political. To say this is, of course, in some sense to state the obvious. Yet while the observation is common in journalistic circles (and often made stridently and dismissively), it is often either played down (in the name of cautioning against reductionism) or only partly explored by academics (as is the case with Shuck's theorization of LaHaye's ambivalence about "network culture"). It is impossible, however, to understand the books' sensibility without understanding LaHaye's career-long antiliberalism. Aside from his decades-old religious social criticism, LaHaye's participation in the organizations noted above reveals the extent to which he has sought directly to influence or, in some cases, generate political programs. The organization most directly relevant to LaHaye's role in the *Left Behind* series is the Council for National Policy (CNP), which LaHaye founded in 1981. On one level, the CNP is an organization of political elites like many others: it is extremely well funded, its membership is highly selective (by invitation from the board), its meetings are closed, and it is run like a think tank. From its inception, the CNP was designed to serve as an umbrella group providing a home for leading conservatives—political and/or religious—to meet and strategize. Its members have included John Ashcroft, Gary Bauer, Bill Bright, Tom DeLay, Richard DeVos, James Dobson, Jerry Falwell, Michael Farris, Jesse Helms, Trent Lott, Edwin Meese, Grover Norquist, Oliver North, Ralph Reed, Pat Robertson, R. J. Rushdoony, Phyllis Schlafly, Kenneth Starr, Richard Viguerie, and Paul Weyrich. This list is obviously composed of conservative powerhouses, including all of the leading figures of the NCR since the 1970s. Though its foundational documents describe the institution as an "educational foundation" which is not directly involved in the political process, the CNP has often boasted of its influence at the highest levels of government (particularly in George W. Bush's administration).[44] Authors like Hugh Urban, Michelle Goldberg, and Kevin Phillips have suggested with some reason that LaHaye's apocalypticism has, through the CNP, influenced broader Bush administration and neoconservative strategies in U.S. Middle East policy. CNP members have boasted frequently of their frequent access to Republican administrations, which has been particularly pronounced in George W. Bush's presidency. LaHaye is also linked to the smaller, even more secretive, and apparently more influential Arlington Group, which claims to have once been in daily communication with Karl Rove.[45]

Far from simply articulating social concerns, LaHaye has actively pursued his criticism of American liberalism through an extended chain of organizations well connected to conservative political power. And he has continually linked these endeavors to apocalyptic thought, which he claims makes believers "more conscious of holy living in their unholy age."[46] The overarching concern for the enhancement of belief—though not necessarily for the improvement of the world, which is understood to be doomed—links living as if on the brink of the end with the necessity of robust religiosity. While LaHaye cautions against actually fixing dates for the end (as interpreters from William Miller to Hal Lindsey have done), he nonetheless sets his sights on a general time frame and supports his readings by turning to events in the political sphere. "The truth is," he and Jenkins write, "that the death of Rabin or any other world leader signifies only the anarchy predicted by the Bible for the end of the age."[47] Citing also the proliferation of "false" religions (including not only flamboyant new religious movements like Heaven's Gate, the People's Temple, and the Branch Davidians but also the rising popularity of Asian religions in the West), LaHaye and Jenkins write that they "expect deception to increase" as the world moves closer to the end.[48] LaHaye still anticipates geopolitical shifts (involving the Middle East, Russia, and China) which will move incrementally toward the Tribulation, but now concentrates on what he calls "the rise of commercial Babylon," where international financial elites will vacate old centers of commerce and relocate to the heart of the end-times narrative.[49] LaHaye sees in the ubiquity of bar codes, checkout scanners, and debit cards a recipe for the centralization of sociopolitical control. He exclaims, "Mark-of-the-Beast technology is already here!"[50]

That the *Left Behind* series can be—indeed, should be—read politically is no surprise. Frykholm, McAlister, and Shuck have all acknowledged the books' politics. While each writes insightfully about the way in which the series engages its contexts, my account of *Left Behind*'s politics supplements this literature by paying greater attention to particular issues and broader political sensibilities, reading them not only individually but as links in the larger declension narrative and critical antiliberalism which the religion of fear popularizes. I also house these findings in a different analytic structure, focusing on the two instabilities in detail. It is time, then, to tease out the meanings of *Left Behind*'s ensemble cast and post-Rapture escapades.

"GOD HAS SEEMED TO STREAMLINE EVERYTHING NOW"

While much could be made, for example, about commodity fetishes and identity or about the establishment of a paraculture through consumption, the primary source of the series' appeal is its cast of characters and its vivid imagining of the terrifying moment when one realizes one has been left behind. The basic narrative and its characters are now familiar to many. High over the Atlantic, en route to London, Captain Rayford Steele is piloting his 747 while thinking about a woman other than his wife. Suddenly, the object of his fantasy, flight attendant Hattie Durham, bursts into the cockpit screaming. She tells Steele that dozens of passengers have disappeared from the cabin, leaving behind clothes, glasses, pocketbooks, tooth fillings, hearing aids, and portable listening devices. A befuddled Steele returns the plane to Chicago and discovers, upon returning home, that his wife, Irene, and son, Raymie (both born-again Christians), are gone. Steele is left alone with his daughter, Chloe (a Stanford student who, like him, is agnostic). Seeking answers, they visit New Hope Church, where Pastor Bruce Barnes (left behind because his faith was not strong enough) helps them to understand that they have witnessed the Rapture, where Jesus returns for his "true family," leaving the rest of humanity behind.

Out of the ensuing chaos, a charismatic Romanian politician named Nicolae Carpathia (who was previously secretary general of the United Nations) emerges to capture the world's attention. His name resonates obviously not only with the political instability in the Balkans during the mid-1990s (the series quickly moved its focus to the Middle East) but with the lore of Dracula, whose famed haunt was in the Carpathian mountains, and with a vernacular name for the devil, Old Nick. Carpathia calls for disarmament, support for the United Nations, the adoption of a single global unit of currency, and efforts to unite the nations in a single global village (that mid-1990s neologism loathed by conservatives). He is named the "sexiest man alive" by *People* (a fact repeated frequently in the books) and names a new pope. Cameron "Buck" Williams, a reporter assigned to cover Carpathia (and whose story lines in the series are the most adventure-like), meets Rayford and Chloe (who have, by this point, converted) and, though Buck has a tough time swallowing the Rapture theory, he too converts. At the end of the first novel, this small band of believers discovers that Carpathia is the Antichrist.

The next several books follow standard dispensationalist chronology and document an ever-changing cast of characters and the growing power of the Antichrist, the establishment of one world government (Carpathia's "Global Community"), the implementation of the mark, the pouring out of the bowl judgments, and the inevitable culmination of the Tribulation in the battle of Armageddon. Early in the narrative, the main characters form an organization called the Tribulation Force, whose purpose is to combat Carpathia and convert those left behind. The plot then begins to assume soap operatic dimensions and appeal. Rayford and Buck infiltrate Global Community (GC), waiting for a sign from God that they should kill Carpathia. Rayford remarries, Buck and Chloe wed, and Hattie becomes pregnant with Carpathia's illegitimate child. As the Tribulation reaches its midpoint, there are earthquakes, meteor strikes, plagues, and an invasion of 200 million demonic horsemen who slaughter one-third of the world's population. Carpathia convenes a "global gala" in Jerusalem (where people pray to a "one-gender deity"), where things come to a violent head. In the middle of the series, the texts focus on the world's polarization between GC supporters and Christians, the latter now working to establish an increasingly elaborate counterculture, a theme of great resonance in the series. The Tribulation Force establishes outposts across the world to prepare for the "soul harvest," which "concerns the 144,000 witnesses, their winning many millions to Christ, the visible seal, and what we can expect in the way of judgments."[51] In *Apollyon*, two witnesses appear at the Wailing Wall, Tsion Ben-Judah emerges as the Tribulation Force's spiritual leader, and the trumpet judgments prophesied in Revelation continue. Amid fictionalized accounts of dispensationalist theology, readers also encounter longtime LaHaye themes and conspiracies. In *Assassins*, more Tribulation Force members infiltrate GC (and its religious outgrowth, Enigma Babylon One World Faith) while Carpathia lashes out against resisters. Members of the Tribulation Force prepare to fulfill the prophecy where the Antichrist receives a lethal head wound. Carpathia is killed, but rises from the dead and orders a hunt for all fugitives from his rule. To ensure loyalty, Carpathia imprints the mark on his subjects (refusal of which results in execution). In *Desecration*, Carpathia declares himself to be God and occupies the Temple in Jerusalem. In the series' final volumes, the remaining members of the Tribulation Force hide out in the Negev desert to await the battle of Armageddon and Christ's return.

Believers, Enemies, and the Undecided

One of the surest ways to understand the overall sociopolitical sensibility of the authors is to attend to the characters' conversion scenes. These sequences are located mostly in the early volumes (for a time, characters were listed at the beginning of every book as belonging to "The Believers," "The Enemies," or "The Undecided"; the latter category disappeared as the series went on). While the first novel's scenes of discarded clothing and driverless cars are compelling, even more significant are the many dialogues where characters explain their motivations, draw distinctions between good and bad arguments supporting conversion, and elaborate on the obligations that the Christian has in the world, even the Raptured world.

Rayford's early monologue reveals his erstwhile ambivalence about the existence of a "higher power." Prior to the Rapture, when Rayford was distracted by adulterous thoughts, he had seen vague appeal in something like rational theism or liberal Protestantism.[52] These beliefs, however, are revealed as insufficient to guarantee one's salvation; indeed, before his death, Pastor Bruce Barnes elaborates frequently on the watered-down belief systems that pass for Christianity. While the truly devout—such as Rayford's wife and those at a "Christian high school" in Indonesia—were Raptured, even many who believed themselves to be God fearing were left behind.[53] Steele comes to realize that every action's "consequences are eternal."[54] Sensing that he cannot rely exclusively on himself (something LaHaye frequently attributes to secular humanism), he begins to wonder if his wife's beliefs were correct, musing, "If heaven is real, if the Rapture was a fact, what does that say about hell and judgment? Is that our fate? We go through this hell of regret and remorse, and then we literally go to hell, too?" Fearfully, he wonders, "Had everyone who denied the truth pushed God to his limit?"[55]

LaHaye and Jenkins are clearly aware of standard arguments against religion, as when Buck recalls that it was the gap between church going and virtuous practice in the everyday which caused him to stop attending in the first place.[56] LaHaye's long-standing critiques of secular humanism enable the authors to flesh out these polemical sections, which contain traces of Hume, Freud, and Marx. They use this awareness to invest great detail in Rayford's arguments with skeptical, Stanford-educated Chloe. She counters her father's statements by cycling through classic arguments against theism: she notes the implausibility of an anthropomorphic deity, lamenting, "He never answered *my* prayers," and she says derisively that Rayford has only "latched onto this heaven thing because it makes you feel better."[57] Yet, in the end, Chloe relents, seeing not only the merit of Rayford's arguments but that he, too, railed against "phony" Christians and that conversion took one out of hollow individualism and into a "group or family thing."[58] The authors also clearly draw on and narrate fear as a motivating force as well. While, on the one hand, a character might insist that "[n]o one can be badgered into" conversion, there usually follows a response like "I hope there's no aftershock or attack that might get you killed before you are assured of heaven."[59] Some characters explicitly acknowledge the role of fear and thoughts of security in their conversion: "this wrath of the Lamb and the moon turning to blood, man, if nothing else convinced me, that sure did."[60]

Once one is saved, the authors suggest, it is "time to move beyond being a critic, an analyst never satisfied with the evidence," as if such criticism were a merely adolescent indulgence.[61] Clearly aware that many of their readers will share the characters' initial doubts, the authors make sure to give at least some sense of the reasoning process. Rayford had once "considered the 'born-again' label akin to 'ultraright-winger' or 'fundamentalist,'" yet even he could not overlook the evidence before him.[62] Whereas he had once "run everything through that maddening intellectual grid, ... [now] the supernatural came crashing through his academic pretense."[63] Throughout, the authors use the trope of evidence to underwrite their—and their characters'—readings of scripture. Indeed, it is often by crafting detailed exegeses and locating "evidence" in surrounding events that the Tribulation Force mounts its resistance. In a clear parallel with LaHaye's own activities, the novels assert that "world conditions" are "the key to understanding" the scriptures.[64] We see this in Tsion Ben-Judah's interpretation of Revelation, where he shifts between literal and allegorical models of reading, and in his technical exegeses, when he explains that it is possible to *have* both the mark of the beast and that of a believer but it is not possible to *take* both.[65] Exegesis can even be instrumental in planning battles. Ben-Judah reads the sixth bowl judgment, for example, as part of a military strategy: this event "makes it possible for the kings of the East to bring their armaments of war directly into the plain of Megiddo."[66] Assessing the particulars of experience in light of scripture, Carpathia cannot see how "a thinking person" would believe, while Ben-Judah counters that "a thinking person" cannot avoid doing so.[67] Those who choose not to believe in spite of clear evidence are described as "self-possessed, narcissistic, vain, proud. In a word, evil."[68] They fail to realize their complicity in "the tragedy that resulted from having missed the truth in the first place."[69]

This approach to reading the world at times shades into polemics against alternate methods of understanding scripture, both those of secular elites and those of liberal Christians. Pastor Barnes insists, capturing the larger themes of the religion of fear, "We don't want to simply survive" but also to combat what is regarded as evil. All that is needed for this is the word and a confessing community. When Chloe regrets not being able to continue her studies, Barnes explains that she "can go to college right here."[70] Barnes rails against those who see the biblical texts as "mere symbolism" or as "poetic and metaphoric."[71] In one of their nonfiction works tied to the series, LaHaye and Jenkins lay the blame for such errant readings at the feet of "seminary professors educated in secular graduate schools," who "were often humiliated by their humanist professors for believing 'the fundamentalist approach' to Scripture."[72] They challenge the authority of pastors who do not foreground apocalyptic materials. To rectify this situation, LaHaye and Jenkins provide their readers with several guidelines for reading scripture: "avoid the temptation to spiritualize anything that at first seems complex"; "[w]hen the plain sense of Scripture makes common sense, seek no other sense, but take every word at its primary, literal meaning unless the facts of the immediate context clearly indicate otherwise."[73] And, consistent with these issues, the series ultimately addresses—just once, in the final volume—Darwinian theory, which is often in the background of debates about biblical interpretation. In their final battle, Jesus rebukes Satan by saying, "For all your lies about having evolved, you are a created being."[74]

"A Very Offensive Message"

This concern with apologetics and argumentation is reflected in the series' engagements with and representations of other religions. Frequently included in these representations are characterizations of various racial Others, who are identified with these other faiths. There are Jews, Buddhists, and Muslims who convert, eventually joining the Tribulation Force; and there are others, often nameless, who adhere to their own traditions and eventually meet their doom. In a 2004 interview with *Fresh Air*'s Terry Gross, LaHaye responded to the question "Will non-converters go to Hell?" by stating bluntly, "That's a good summary."[75] A few years later, Jenkins said, "[W]e realize in an age of pluralism, in an age of tolerance, that this can be a very offensive message," but it "breaks my heart" that "I might not see [believers from other traditions] in eternity."[76] Although LaHaye has often been critical of specific areas of Supreme Court jurisprudence and has complained bitterly that Christians are often the victims of "bigotry" in secular liberal political regimes, he has never denounced the value of the First Amendment nor of religious toleration across the board. Yet, in the series' representations of religious pluralism under GC rule, one senses LaHaye's deep ambivalence about the relation between such pluralism and his understandings of America's religio-national destiny.

In many of Carpathia's public addresses as potentate (a title redolent with disdain for Roman Catholic culture), he gives voice to what the authors see as conventional pluralist understandings of the free exercise of religion. He announces, for example, that "every citizen of the Global Community is free to believe as he or she wants and to exercise that faith in any way that does not infringe upon the same freedom for others," balancing such claims with expressions of contempt for Christians: "I plead for common sense. I do not begrudge anyone the right to believe in a personal god. However, I do not understand how a god they describe as just and loving would capriciously decide who is or is not worthy of heaven and effect that decision in what they refer to as 'the twinkling of an eye.' "[77] Such speeches capture the hypocrisy that LaHaye and his sympathizers believe underlies arguments about freedom of religion; whereas political institutions may promise "the openness of the Global Community to diverse opinion and belief," they intend that this openness be selectively applied (and, according to the conservative declension narrative, usually to the disadvantage of Christians).[78]

Indeed, Carpathia's violence and persecutions are depicted as being masked by this same rhetoric of tolerance and religious pluralism. The authors seem to turn a critical eye on celebrations of religious diversity when they describe—often invoking quasi-colonialist stereotypes—Enigma Babylon's functions: "[e]ach potentate was greeted by music from his region and wild demonstrations from his people."[79] Indeed, descriptions of many of Carpathia's orderlies frequently signify the authors' understandings of "false" religions: "[p]otentate Rehoboth's palace housed his several wives."[80] And as "unbelievers are being slain" on his orders, Carpathia paints his detractors in ways suggestive of some of LaHaye's (and the NCR's) own demons: he accuses Christians of seeking to implement terrorism such as "germ warfare" (a cult-busting echo of Aum Shinrikyo, perhaps crossed with Saddam Hussein), and he denounces them using the loaded rhetoric often attributed to liberal, secular elites: the "Ben Judah-ites cannot persuade us with their exclusivistic, intolerant, hateful diatribes, so they choose to kill us!" Christians, he claims, do this in the name of "a myth no thinking man or woman can be expected to swallow."[81]

Perhaps the most complicated representation concerns Judaism. While most of the series' representations of Others are appended with statements emphasizing the clarity of the decisions that must be made ("God has seemed to streamline everything now"),[82] there is more complexity in the position of Jews after the Rapture. While it is clear that there remain Jews who do not accept that Jesus is the prophesied messiah, the novels never waver in their insistence on adhering to the prophetic/apocalyptic plot, which focuses on Israel's role in the end times. This focus is consistent not only with dispensationalist discourse but has had a widely remarked influence on both Ronald Reagan's and George W. Bush's foreign policy.[83] In the early novels, the tension between accepting and skeptical Jews is played out in the contrast between Tsion Ben-Judah (the blogging exegete who ultimately serves as the Tribulation Force's spiritual leader) and Chaim Rosenzweig (who first mocks biblical literalism but later accepts the authors' version of Christianity). Ben-Judah understands the pivotal role played by Jews and stipulates that one of the faithful remnant's most pressing goals is the conversion of Jews (as part of the gathering of the 144,000 witnesses prophesied in Revelation).[84]

Often in these books, the authors rely on the notion that sensible people will simply consult the evidence around them and will decide that conversion is the most prudent response to their circumstances. According to such thinking, it would be perverse to ignore the coalescence of one world government, the appearance of the two witnesses at the Wailing Wall, or the outpouring of the bowl judgments. There is, therefore, no fault in condemning those who persist as if the truth were not clear. Regarding those Jews who do not embrace Tribulation Force religiosity, we are told that Jews in Israel had struck a covenant with Carpathia: "God's chosen people, who planned to rebuild the temple and reinstitute the system of sacrifices until the coming of their Messiah, had signed a deal with the devil."[85] Ben-Judah himself claims that he is "astounded that the Jews still refused to believe that Jesus was who the Bible claimed He was."[86] And later, as the Tribulation draws to its bloody conclusion, Buck rationalizes to struggling Jewish practitioners, "When Jewish people such as yourselves come to see that Jesus is your long-sought Messiah ... you are not converting from one religion to another, no matter what anyone tells you. You have found your Messiah, that is all."[87]

While such representations may seem from one perspective to constitute blatant anti-Semitism, it is important to understand the reverence for Jews and Jewish history that is common in dispensationalist circles. As Yaakov Ariel points out, such representations of Jews are stereotypical but for the most part depict Jews as "errant but not evil."[88] There is real zeal for aspects of identity and history which connect to the original times and places of the Christian narrative. For example, in addition to this complicated evangelization of the Jews, the series uses Pastor Demetrius Demeter, an almost ethereally holy Greek Christian, to articulate a fetishization of texts in their original languages. Demeter speaks reverently of reading the New Testament in the Greek (though all supernatural figures in the series speak King James English).[89]

Though LaHaye has not engaged in anti-Catholicism to the degree that Jack Chick has, the series' descriptions of Global Community and especially of Carpathia's inner circle are replete with allusions to "popish" demagoguery and shadowy cabals. The names of "the Enemies"—"Supreme Potentate Nicolae Carpathia" (often referred to as "Eminence" by his flunkies), "Pontifex Maximus, Peter II," or "Regional Potentates" Rehoboth and Leon Fortunato—all ascribe to Carpathia and his legions both the kind of self-divinization of the late Roman Empire and the purportedly bloated ceremonialism of the Catholic church. Carpathia's Enigma Babylon One World Faith—used to consolidate power, administer the mark, and inspire blind allegiance—uses the Vatican as its headquarters. Beyond such associations between Rome and the Antichrist, many believers look back from the Tribulation to reflect upon false faiths, recalling that "[a] lot of Catholics were confused" prior to the Rapture.[90] And one character, who notices that the two witnesses now have crosses marked on their foreheads, proclaims—significantly using the past tense—that these marks are "like Catholics used to get on Ash Wednesday."[91]

The texts also regularly represent and interpret Islam. During their time in the Middle East, Tribulation Force characters often encounter Muslims in and around New Babylon. Most of these Muslims—like Albie ("Al B." from "Al Basrah," described as a "small, dark, former black marketer") and Abdullah Smith from Jordan (whose improbable name was assumed after his conversion, and about whose early life Buck muses, "Maybe he'd been a terrorist")—are familiar with Christian soteriological narratives.[92] The early books often make mention of Islam's failure to recognize not only Jesus' messianic status but the centrality of Israel and the Jews to God's salvific plan, as when a crazed Muslim with a machine gun charges the Wailing Wall claiming that "he's on a mission from Allah."[93] Later, Muslim converts become important figures in Tribulation Force espionage and evangelism, acting as double agents. In seeking to penetrate a highly guarded GC stronghold, Rayford asks Abdullah Smith to undertake a mission in disguise: "Do you have a turban?"[94] And the Tribulation Force also seeks to witness to errant Muslims who, clinging to their faith, line up at GC centers "to be processed."[95] Practicing, nonconverted Muslims also agree to one of Carpathia's directives to relocate the Dome of the Rock to the Antichrist's base of operations in New Babylon. Many of these scenes occur in *The Remnant*, the first volume to be published after the terrorist attacks of September 11, 2001. Rayford and his colleagues also invade

Islamic prayer in order to witness, suggesting to stunned Muslims that only conversion can save them from certain death and damnation.[96]

Hinduism and Buddhism are given only infrequent attention. There is an occasional dismissive generality about Asian religions, as when George Sebastian (a Tribulation Force army veteran) recalls that "[h]is superiors had trained the men in basic transcendental meditation, which most of them passed off as something for weirdoes, druggies, and holy men from the East."[97] LaHaye has revealed that, on one of his many trips to Jerusalem (where he frequently leads biblical history tours), he crossed paths with the Dalai Lama, whom he did not initially recognize. Asked by LaHaye if he "knew the truth about Jesus," the Dalai Lama replied that he was a practicing Buddhist. LaHaye recalled that he believed that the Dalai Lama was sincere but was sad because he "didn't know the truth."[98] Asian characters, however, play large roles late in the series and are often described in somewhat stereotypical terms. Their names are Chang (who "had been the fastest keyboarder in high school"), Ming Toy, and Ree Woo.[99] Each speaks with "an Asian accent."[100] Indeed, the authors seem to have a fascination with "ethnically" coded speech, invoking it as a way of demonstrating that while Carpathia's pluralism exists in the service of evil, the Tribulation Force is able to unite people of disparate backgrounds in a legitimate way. Early in the series, Tsion Ben-Judah begins his first phone call to Buck by asking, "Ees dis Chamerown Weeleeums?"[101] In the final book in the series, we encounter Carmela—"a fiftyish, heavyset Latina"—who explains her preconversion background in heavily clichéd dialogue: "[m]en tryin' to love me all day!" She proudly describes that her life has changed since conversion and reports arguing with her friend Shaniqua about not accepting Jesus.[102] McAlister notes that it is possible to see the inclusion of nonwhite characters in the series as a parallel to the NCR's grudging entry into post-1960s conversations about race.[103] This is accurate as far as it goes, yet does not capture fully the depth of alterity in these books. Through naming (conferring stereotypical or whitened names on Tribulation Force members, whereas nonconverts are often referred to as "the African" or "the Asian"), speech (both racialized dialogue and expressions of deference to the Tribulation Force's white male leaders), and representations of "false" faiths, the series often equates Otherness with ignorance.[104]

Family Values

One of the most successful and enduring components of the conservative evangelical declension narrative posits that post-1960s political culture, in pursuing legislation that addresses needs articulated by feminist activists, has become hostile toward the interests of "traditional" families modeled on "traditional" gender roles. These themes have proved to be amazingly resilient.

What is more, the narrative alleges that such disruptions to the order of things have created a "permissive" social climate that has facilitated the legalization of abortion and the toleration of sexual "deviance." The early volumes—which document the multiple reasons one can be left behind after the Rapture—focus heavily on gender, family, and sexuality in ways that reflect the LaHayes' long-held criticisms in this area. As both Sara Diamond and Linda Kintz demonstrate, Beverly LaHaye's CWA activism was defined in many ways by its refusal to restrict itself to "merely" domestic engagements. In texts like 1984's *Who but a Woman?* LaHaye made the argument that elected officials were not to be trusted and that the surest way of combating social ills was to work in both the private and public spheres.[105] LaHaye had women's activism in mind, but sought to encourage women to support traditional gender roles—using "feminine" power in the pursuit of legitimate political ends—rather than to support feminist achievements.

Frykholm points out that dozens of volumes in the Rapture fiction genre begin with the rapture of one pure female character, who embodies Victorian norms regarding proper feminine virtue.[106] That role is embodied in *Left Behind* by Rayford Steele's wife, Irene, whose name conveys the peace one finds in Christ and whose earthly work with Amway (whose founder, Richard De-Vos, is a longtime supporter of NCR organizations) is seen as exemplifying Irene's charitable spirit.[107] Throughout, there are also references to "essential" differences between males and females. In *Tribulation Force*, for example, Rayford's new love interest, Amanda, winks, "Don't doubt my intuition," while later going on to explain that, although she had never met somebody as evil as Carpathia, in her experience as a woman, she had run across "a few garment wholesalers who might fit the bill."[108] Rayford's daughter, Chloe, does not so completely embody women's knowledge or experience—Frykholm rightly describes her as an updating of the feminine ideal—although she does somewhat quickly embrace a version of male headship.[109] Another central figure in the Tribulation Force—former nurse Leah Rose—is described as being "too strident and opinionated" prior to her conversion.[110]

Women who fail to approximate these virtues or whose activities challenge traditional women's roles likely risk being left behind or being associated with evil. Hattie Durham is set up in the early novels not merely as a doubter but as someone whose arguments in the face of possible conversion dangerously mirror those of Carpathia ("[t]he irony was lost on her").[111] As Hattie ultimately makes the wrong decision, her personality erodes; she later describes herself as "a scared, angry, shaken young woman who has been used and abandoned by many in her life."[112] The treatment of businesswomen Verna Zee (a "militant" newspaper editor who makes Buck Williams's reporter job a long-suffering one) and Viv Ivins (Carpathia's cousin, who is employed by GC and whose name, as Shuck points out, begins with VI VI VI, the roman numerals for 666) is far more withering.[113] Zee is introduced with feminist-baiting rhetoric: "[a]ren't you afraid *Ms. Zee* sounds too much like *Missy?*"[114] There is later an exuberant passage detailing Zee's toadying response, and implied hypocrisy, when she is "put in her place" by her superior.[115] Following several hints that Zee is a lesbian, she confronts the converted Buck and Chloe (whom Zee found to be "all wacky").[116] As the text prepares to confront Verna's sexuality, she is described alternately as "a pretty cynical and miserable person" who gave Chloe "the willies" and as a stereotypical feminist bitch who delights in telling Buck that she "holds all the cards."[117] One reads echoes of the long-standing claim that the "choice" to be gay makes one miserable because it alienates you from God's order. In these exchanges, Zee defends her feminism and her atheism before Buck and Chloe.

There is also, as Frykholm and Shuck acknowledge, a tentative reevaluation of evangelical models of masculinity. Though each book celebrates male heroism, adventure, and technological/military prowess—which together help to establish some crossover appeal among audiences—there is also an interesting reclamation of male emotionalism. Part of Rayford's adjustment to the Tribulation—and to the religious truths he had forsaken previously—is his embrace of a specific type of masculine emotion. As Frykholm notes, his emotional changes lead him to embody the kind of masculinity promoted by Bill McCartney's Promise Keepers.[118] Indeed, Rayford's internal musings make it difficult to miss this point. "What a failure he had been as a husband and father!" we hear, in an echo of one of the organization's famed Seven Promises. Rayford "had always considered emotion weak and unmanly. But since the disappearances, he had seen many men weep."[119] (In another possible allusion to this group, we hear that Ben-Judah's followers now "swell to fill the largest stadiums on the globe.") This captures the kind of reformation and expansion of gender roles encouraged by Promise Keepers, even as basic conservative gender norms are preserved throughout the series. Part traditional evangelical and part Promise Keepers new man, Rayford's emotional experience is registered here as countercultural (even as it reinscribes conservative cultural politics).

Sexual issues are engaged with slightly less fluidity than gender. Whereas both Chloe and Rayford preserve traditional roles with expanded room for self-expression, sexual morality remains firmly unchanged. Even in the earliest moments of the series, the reader is urged to consider the links between sexual behavior and salvation. An airplane passenger complains that her husband has wandered off without his clothes, explaining that "[h]e's a religious person and he'll be terribly embarrassed," as if the link between piety and being ashamed of nudity were self-evident.[120] During Chloe's and Buck's courtship, there is considerable discussion of the virtues of premarital abstinence. The authors again present "traditional values" as daring, even countercultural.

Even at hedonistic Stanford, Chloe never had sex. When Buck admits that he'd rather marry a virgin than a sexually experienced woman, Chloe congratulates him: "[t]hat's something to be proud of these days."[121] Indeed, the Tribulation Force quickly arrives at a consensus on matters of sexual purity, agreeing that no further reflection on the subject is needed.[122] By contrast, Carpathia boasts proudly of his promiscuity, claiming that he would never commit himself to just one woman.[123] Indeed, readers learn that he has impregnated Hattie Durham with no intention of wedding her.[124]

Homosexuality is addressed infrequently, but the authors make clear their positions on the matter. In 1978, LaHaye published *The Unhappy Gays*, where he apparently mulled over the death penalty for homosexuals: "[w]ho is really being cruel and inhuman—those whose leniency allows homosexuality to spread to millions of victims . . . or those who practiced Old Testament capital punishment?"[125] While the *Left Behind* series does not endorse anything close to such harsh treatment, it does clearly situate active homosexuality alongside the narrative's other evils. In *The Rising*, it is revealed that Carpathia is the product of "evil seeds": he was fathered by two gay men, as the brainchild of international monetarists.[126] There is one gay male in the series, Guy Blod. In a scene with Tribulation Force member David Hasid (who has infiltrated GC at a high level), the authors indulge in some pointedly stereotypical characterizations of Blod as a "huffy and put-out"—and impeccably dressed—artist who was commissioned to sculpt a statue of Carpathia. Blod's dialogue is heavily coded with stereotypical language ("anyhoo" and "dear boy," for example), and he rebukes Hasid for his discomfort with the idea of a nude sculpture ("[y]ou obviously have some hang-up about the human form and can't appreciate the beauty"). The flamboyant Blod frequently gestures "with a flourish," summons green-fingernailed assistants to his side, and proclaims theatrically, "I love new clothes." Temperamental, audacious, arty, and swishy, Blod's stereotype is difficult to mistake in the hands of the zealous authors.[127]

Verna Zee's sexuality is treated somewhat more discreetly, if no less emphatically. Initially shocked and outraged that Chloe and Buck are aware of her sexual orientation, Zee is partially won over by the couple's sincere attempts to convert her from both atheism and homosexuality. They explain to Verna that they are acting from a position of love and tolerance, that they hate the sinful behavior but not the sinner (however, Chloe at one point explains that this confrontation was necessary because of Verna's hostile interactions with Buck; in Chloe's words, Zee "rattled the wrong cage").[128] Verna begins to accept what she is being told, though she worries about potential violations of her privacy. Assuring her of their discretion, Buck and Chloe lead Verna through an exegesis of the Bible's teachings on homosexuality, concluding with the consolation: "[m]y Bible . . . may call practicing homosexuals sinners, but it also calls heterosexual sex outside of marriage sinful."[129]

Abortion, for many years the central rallying issue for the NCR, receives minimal direct treatment, but the themes and references are consistently blunt. Readers learn in the first volume that, after the Rapture, there was no business for abortion clinics, as the innocent unborn had been spirited away.[130] After learning she is pregnant, Hattie confesses to Rayford that Nicolae would "probably tell me to have an abortion."[131] Carpathia later does just this, and Hattie finds herself in a clinic where zealous doctors urge her, at Carpathia's behest, to undergo the procedure. The link between evil and abortion is further illustrated when Carpathia exercises his power as GC's "potentate" to guarantee the funding of abortions "for women in underprivileged countries," an obvious reference to the United Nations Population Fund and similar efforts.[132] The series' positions are occasionally defended with arguments grounded in the sanctity of life; this is exemplified in a scene where Rayford confronts Carpathia's decision about Hattie's abortion by asking, "[Y]ou will pay for the murder of the child?"[133] There is, however, no universal commitment to the sanctity of life, for there are several occasions in the series when Tribulation Force members debate the ethics of killing evil persons in the name of God.

One World Government

LaHaye has long been an unambiguous supporter of free market capitalism, specifically advocating minimal regulation, "family-friendly" tax codes, and a trickle-down theory of distribution.[134] His basic contention, reflected throughout conservative cultures, is that largely unregulated free market capitalism is a way to channel human self-interest in positive ways. Excessive governmental regulation, on this account, constrains human volition and talent while also cutting off avenues for charitable activity. These general economic convictions are reflected in concerns, displayed in many dispensationalist narratives, that the establishment of one world government will include—along with its false religion, the implementation of the mark, and the cult of personality—both a unified media organization and one world currency. Indeed, in many of his nonfiction texts—specifically in his *Battle* series—LaHaye includes elaborate diagrams detailing the worldly conspiracies which would eventuate in the unfolding of end-times scenarios. Economics and media loom large in these scenarios, also reflecting concerns about national autonomy and sovereignty, as they do in the *Left Behind* series.

Anxieties about international economic institutions and global capital are articulated virtually as soon as Carpathia assumes political power. In an address before the United Nations, an institution that the Antichrist praises effusively, Carpathia constructs a historical narrative of institution building and social progress which culminates in the birth of GC, which will ensure peace, harmony, and prosperity for all humans. Among the institutions named as central to this progress are the International Monetary Fund and the World Bank.[135] As Shuck explains, these longtime dispensationalist concerns grew during the early 1990s, as many interpreters believed that the passage of the North American Free Trade Agreement (NAFTA) and the General Agreement on Tariffs and Trade (GATT) represented a substantive push toward the new world order.[136] The circulation of global capital and the triumph of information economies is of special import to dispensationalists owing to the long-standing beliefs that the mark is central to the methods of exchange and commerce during the Tribulation and that the shift to one world currency facilitates the consolidation of power that will occur under the Antichrist.[137] Thus, we learn that GC quickly moves "close to a cashless society" and that the GC administration will heavily tax all electronic transactions and each barrel of oil.[138] As Carpathia puts it, "Ownership is not the issue. Control is."[139]

To facilitate this economic consolidation, Carpathia quickly suspends democratic activities and establishes a media empire to disseminate pro-GC propaganda. The issue of economic autonomy is therefore linked to concerns about media power, which have long served—in warnings about the power of "liberal" or "secularist" media—as a rallying point for NCR activists and organizations. When questioned about these designs, a flustered Carpathia asks, "[W]hat is wrong with controlling global news when we are headed toward peace and harmony and unity?"[140] He ultimately acquires extant media—including bastions of the "liberal media" like the *New York Times*, the *Washington Post*, and the *Boston Globe* as well as the Trinity Broadcasting Network and the Christian Broadcasting Network—and absorbs them into his communications empire, whose crown jewel is the familiarly named Global Community News Network (GCNN).[141] (At one point, while on his personal Learjet, Carpathia mentions his new cell phone/solar power corporation entitled Cell-Sol, a homonym for "sell soul.")[142] Throughout the series, the reader is told of the GCNN's efforts to spin reality, to exert totalizing influence over its audience, and—like those reluctant or unwilling to convert—to ignore all clear evidence of religious truth. So overwhelming is Carpathia's hostility toward the Christian remnant that GCNN refuses to report on the deaths of assassinated resisters or even on the final, undeniable apocalyptic events: "the [GCNN] ignored the nature show."[143]

These concerns relate to larger fears about the dissolution of American sovereignty and autonomy in the world. One index of these fears is located in the series' accounts of specific nations following the Rapture. The first novel contains numerous references to Russian power, a standard of dispensationalist interpretation during the Cold War. In *Left Behind*, "Russia had become a great brooding giant with a devastated economy and regressed technology."[144]

As the Rapture occurs, there are, significantly, no losses reported in Israel. Russia makes a "secret alliance with Middle Eastern nations, primarily Ethiopia and Libya," and proceeds to attack Israel.[145] These themes are addressed less frequently as the series comes to focus more rigorously on Global Community, New Babylon, and events in the Middle East that are central to the apocalyptic plot.

The authors' discourse about state sovereignty and national autonomy is also expressed in the language of conspiracy theory, long a part of LaHaye's writing. As the narrative establishes links among Carpathia, global finance, unified religious communities, and disarmament, the authors weave these disparate subjects together into a singular causal force. They do so with references to "that internationalist monetarist confab" which, with the guidance of the United Nations, will eventually seek one world currency; news reports of the Vatican's role in "the installation of a new leader in Europe"; the sponsorship of an "ecumenical religious convention"; and the emergence of both "Jewish Nationalist leaders interested in one world government" and "Orthodox Jews from all over the world looking at rebuilding the temple."[146] Carpathia, in other words, becomes the mouthpiece for widely familiar dispensationalist tropes linking the end times unfolding in Israel, international monetarists, ecumenism, the power of the United Nations, and a single currency.[147]

In *Tribulation Force*, the United Nations is moved to Babylon (where GC will eventually be based) in a way that harmonizes with prophetic descriptions found abundantly in LaHaye's other writings.[148] In an effort to curtail growing international hostilities, Carpathia facilitates "an understanding" between the United States and the United Nations—which effectively cedes American military and political autonomy to the United Nations—and brokers a seven-year treaty between Israel and outside aggressors. This, as Barnes points out, signals the beginning of the Tribulation: "the clock starts ticking."[149] The conspiracies unfold fully in *Nicolae*, much of which reads like a narration of one of LaHaye's elaborate diagrams. And, in what may be a quite rich meta-reference or unintended irony, the authors have one character complain that "[p]eople make a hobby of ascribing all manner of evil to the Tri-Lateral Commission, the Illuminati, even the Freemasons, for goodness sake."[150] GC's "peacekeeping forces" monitor both Christians and Americans, embodying concerns about mortgaging American sovereignty to international bureaucracies, whose rhetoric and practice of officialdom are hostile to domestic (not to mention religious) interests. The authors even, perhaps unpredictably, invoke George Orwell to buttress their denunciations.[151] The series, then, is ambivalent about nationalism. On the one hand, the authors embrace a standard apocalyptic sensibility that sees nationalism as temporal and limited, of little concern when measured against God's power and purview. Yet the specific brand of eschatology espoused by the authors is one that, following from the

Lindsey tradition, sees U.S. foreign policy as absolutely central to the imminence of the end times. The evils of the one world government are therefore positioned against the sovereignty and providential role of the United States, whose rugged individualism and isolationism are reflected in the go-it-alone militarism of the Tribulation Force itself.[152]

Embattled Majority

This relates to one of the most revealing themes in the series, that of the embattled Christian. This notion, reflected in the series' identification of Carpathia's anti-Christian "bigotry," has long been a successful trope around which to build political motivation and organization. It also represents the most powerful public expression of fear's declension narrative—where the divine purposes that once steered the United States were attacked in the mid-twentieth century by hostile elites—as well as a politics of social resentment, themes exemplified in the series' portrayals of the Tribulation Force as holy fugitives, pious resisters, and post-Rapture adventurers. Capturing the spirit and the jargon of the techno-thriller, this characterization is also one of the most fascinating markers of these books' politics.

In their discussions of the validity and necessity of the series, LaHaye and Jenkins have explained that "God's wonderful plan" is also fearful and, because it is "countercultural" in a sense, has also led to the persecution of Christians because the culture is so thoroughly headed in a non-Christian direction.[153] As I discuss in the conclusion, it has become increasingly common for NCR activists to describe the longtime political discontent and antiliberalism of this complicated culture by using the language of bigotry and persecution. Indeed, LaHaye and Jenkins effectively summarize many of the most frequent charges, quoting generously from many influential sources. Citing missionaries who report with alarm that it is forbidden to preach publicly in, for example, China, LaHaye and Jenkins note that several features of American culture may constitute a slippery slope toward exactly this kind of society (a slide which mirrors the coming of the end times as well). American religious freedom, they write, has been compromised, and thousands of believers have been "tricked by seminary professors into thinking [the second coming] is 'confusing' or 'not relevant for today.'"[154] As we see elsewhere in their work, the authors' interpretive frame folds together intra-Christian polemics with conspiracy theory, combative rhetoric, and Reagan era conservatism into a fearful *kulturkritik*. The Christian thus adopts a kind of resistance position by default: simply living faithfully places one in a political position, since political hostility toward faith is now ubiquitous.

The natural outcome of such political hostility is seen in the Carpathia regime and its persecution of the Tribulation Force. Out of Carpathia's mouth comes the kind of epithets and mockeries attributed by NCR activists to their opponents. Carpathia variously refers to the Tribulation Force (and, by extension, Christians in general) as "religious zealots," "radical fanatic fundamentalist[s]," "traitor[s]," and "an intolerant, close-minded cult that excludes everyone who disagrees."[155] Fortunato often announces his contempt for "the Judah-ites! Espousing such exclusivistic, close-minded doctrines as there being but a single path to God!"[156] Readers are left to conclude that those who denounce Christians in like manner risk allying themselves with evil. In a regime that brands the faithful as outlaws, embracing fugitive status is a mark of piety. When confronted with the old theological trope announcing two competing systems of laws, the Tribulation Force chooses to reject—and is rejected by—the temporal order.

As is often the case in the series, Tsion Ben-Judah announces the authors' view of reality: "[o]nce he had clearly stated his belief, he became a marked man."[157] In living out this fugitive existence—filled with civil disobedience and risk—the Tribulation Force must grow more combative as the Tribulation marches on. The authors take great care to describe the believers' safe houses (in what is surely meant as a parallel with the status of early Christians in the Roman Empire), bases of operation where the characters hold clandestine meetings to plan their divine disobedience. As these portraits of fugitive life become more detailed in each volume, the authors pay more attention to the Tribulation Force's defiance of arbitrary or anti-Christian authority. Ben-Judah blogs, "For all the trumpeting by the Global Community that freedom of expression has arrived, the same has been denied those of us who know and believe the truth of God"; and "[t]hose who pride themselves on tolerance and call us exclusivists, judgmental, unloving, and shrill are illogical to the point of absurdity."[158] This reflects the keen sense of embattlement that is so often articulated in the so-called culture wars in the United States.

As the believers grow more confident in the historical narrative unfolding around them, and in their own righteousness, they more frequently confront GC flunkies and orderlies ("Sorry, GC, but we're on a mission from the real risen Lord, and we have both human and edible cargo we don't wish to surrender").[159] The authors clearly delight in showing how an intrepid minority can survive even under pressure from the GC's "Peacekeepers and Morale Monitors," its "loyalty mark application sites and enforcement facilitators," and other expressions of its bureaucratic oppression.[160] When there are casualties, as with the central character Chloe, these are described in the idiom of martyrdom literature. After having her faith tested in her jail cell, in an imprisonment narrative meant (like many of Saint Paul's letters) to confirm Christians' status as an oppressed minority, she is martyred under a GC guillotine: "Chloe heard only the pull of the cord and the drop of the sharpened edge of death that led to life eternal."[161]

The tone used to describe such conflicts between systems of law and authority is a revealing one. The themes themselves clearly reveal a sense of antistatism and a self-understanding as the subject of bigotry, which work together to situate the authors as participants in contemporary struggles around issues that often parallel those central to the NCR. The Tribulation Force's enemies are meant to exemplify—in both words and actions—some anti-Christian critics in the present moment. Yet the tone, interestingly, is not merely one of exegesis, declamation, litany; it is the tone of the techno-thriller. McAlister also calls attention to the "science-fiction address of the series."[162] The world of the Tribulation is one not just of secret hideouts and pious resistance, but one wherein a fetish for technology and consumption accompanies Christian militancy. The Tribulation Force is defined by, and owes its resilience to, its technological and military savvy. With all of the trappings of a Tom Clancy or Stephen Hunter potboiler, characters enumerate the weapons, gadgets, and technologies at their disposal. In the heat of mission planning, Albie asks, "You need everything? Wet suit, mask, snorkel, tanks, fins?"[163] David Hasid disguises the ISP of Tribulation Force bulletin boards so that communications remain untraceable. And even as they hide out in "the Pueblo bunker" or "Quonset-hut style" shelters, members like Buck Williams drive from place to place in brand new Hummers.[164] This is a complex religious identity being crafted in these novels, one where the exuberant violence is situated against not only identity's necessary demons but a sense of cultural Otherness that is simultaneously displaced and absorbed.

"OUR GENERAL IS BETTER THAN YOUR GENERAL"

It is well known that the word *apocalypse* means "uncovering." In exploring the two instabilities in the *Left Behind* series, one sees precisely what kind of religio-political identity is uncovered in these books. In *Desecration*, as the Tribulation begins to move into its endgame, the authors deliver an unforgettable characterization of Tribulation Force member George Sebastian: "[i]t had done his soul good to see what happened to anyone who thumbed his nose at God. *Our general is better than your general*, he thought, *so game over*."[165] In many ways, this statement crisply captures the manifestation of the two instabilities in *Left Behind*. The in-your-face violence exemplifies the erotics of fear, which here take the form of gore and violence. It also, however, limns the shape of *Left Behind*'s demonology within: the narration of evil is necessary for the delineation of the specific form of identity the authors commend to readers; yet the juxtaposition of demonic and pure is paralleled here by the juxtaposition of countercultural and accommodationist tendencies. The authors establish the boundary between self and demonic Other through a discourse of consumption and "worldly things."

The series maps this boundary by establishing the limits of moral, religious, and political acceptability within the framework of fear's self-understandings. Technology fetishes and resistance fantasies mark the authors' complicated relationship with culture as well as with evil. The first book takes pains to associate *People* magazine's "sexiest man alive" with commercial culture and technology.[166] As the series goes on, however, it is the members of the Tribulation Force who begin to craft a religious identity through the appropriate use of technology and an acceptable reliance on the things of this world. As Rayford and others become aware of themselves as experiencing a new life through Christ, they insist often that only the word is necessary. They look upon Carpathia's sympathizers with contempt: when Buck sees that his former editor has joined Carpathia's staff, he notes derisively that he "looked like a clone of Carpathia... [with a] thick, black-leather portfolio... razor-cut, blow-dried, styled, and moussed [hair]... and designer-frame glasses," among other features of fashionista comportment.[167] Soon, however, this simultaneous contempt for and fascination with worldliness blooms not into neo-Luddism but into a different strategy of technological and cultural appropriation.

The Tribulation Force begins to establish its relationship with its demons through a fetishization of particular forms of culture combined with a larger criticism ("[t]hat is not a popular message, not a warm fuzzy you can cling to").[168] The things of the world are to be rejected, but an exception is now granted if these things are seen as necessary for evangelization or for outwitting the forces of evil. "You should see the technology, Chlo'," Rayford exults.[169] Buck marvels at the "rig" on his brand-new Range Rover: "[i]t has everything. It will go anywhere. It's indestructible. It comes with a phone. It comes with a citizen's band radio. It comes with a fire extinguisher, a survival kit, flares, you name it."[170] And the Tribulation Force soon finds itself in a world of cell phones, Hummers, Uzis, and blogs. Following an initial contrast between Carpathia's invisible web of communications technology and the invisible realm of the spirit, the Christians begin to amass technologies as religious goods. They bug GC intercoms and phone banks (using something called a "hidden reverse intercom button"), they download scripture onto zip drives, and they explore the convergence between biblical numerology and code programming.[171] Speaking for the Tribulation Force as a whole, Rayford "cast his lot with God and the miracle of technology."[172]

Technology breeds liberation, as good-guy hackers match wits with gearhead demons; technology, initially the devil's tool, is now appropriated as a means of evangelization itself. The Ben-Judah blog begins in the fourth novel and is the central means of disseminating his teachings to the underground (he intends the blog to be biblically significant as well, since he hopes it will be visible to many of the 144,000 witnesses).[173] "Technology has allowed me a congregation," Ben-Judah enthuses.[174] So, while the series maintains its early ambivalence about plenitude and technology to some degree, the dominant tone—as salvation history moves inexorably forward—becomes not simply fascination with technology but near reverence of it. Indeed, in what could almost be a meta-reference to LaHaye's own media engagements, Ben-Judah exclaims, "I envision thousands of technological experts creating a network of resources for believers, informing them of safe havens, putting them in touch with each other."[175]

The development of this identity—where the appropriation of culture is a key area in which protagonists wrestle with their demons—extends notably to a familiarity with military technology. The group's increasing tendency toward violence reveals not just the Tribulation Force's fugitive status but *Left Behind*'s erotics of fear. In early volumes, the authors' erotics could be discerned in their detailed accounts of the sins for which one was left behind. In successive books, however, there is a far clearer exuberance in the engagement with the world's destruction, the almost forensic detail with which violence and gore are described, and a rapt accounting of the terrors of judgment itself.

Though one could argue that the entire premise of the series is rooted in a kind of ontological violence, it is with a specific plot line in *Soul Harvest* that the Tribulation Force begins to consider the legitimate use of militarism, which is described with zeal. Between this book and the next, Rayford considers assassinating Carpathia. He assumes that God will forgive any words he utters to Carpathia and wonders then if God would forgive his actions.[176] Over the course of several chilling scenes, Rayford thinks to himself, "Your day is coming . . . and I hope God lets me pull the trigger."[177] He tries to convince himself to "[b]e God's weapon, the instrument of death" in the murder of Carpathia.[178] In a partial and probably unintentional echo of the kind of rationales articulated by antiabortion renegades like Paul Hill and the Army of God's Michael Bray, Steele and Ben-Judah discuss whether sacred murder can be legitimized if it is done in alignment with God's purposes, when one acts as a divine avenger. Since it is prophesied that Carpathia will rise from the dead, and hence that his "death wound is only temporary," the Tribulation Force eventually agrees with Ben-Judah that "we are at war. In the heat of battle, killing the enemy has never been considered murder."[179] Ultimately, it is not the devout Christian Rayford but Chaim Rosenzweig who undertakes the assassination. And in an incredible scene, the tone of the series shifts from fairly sober reflection to hyperviolence, "as Carpathia's body met the blade, and the sword slipped into his neck and straight through the top of his head as easily as a bayonet would slice a watermelon."[180]

This shift in tone parallels the events unfolding in the Tribulation, specifically the outpouring of various judgments and their awful consequences. The world begins to erupt with violent natural phenomena and becomes populated by supernatural figures of the sort often encountered in horror fiction. In the wake of these cataclysms, Buck looks upon a field of the dead and imagines the "millions of corpses all over the world."[181] Rayford follows "a river of blood" and must "cross paths with a zombied and bleeding queue of fortunates who staggered out of a crater."[182] The spectacle of gore is supplemented with occasionally Lovecraftian prose ("the wailing and moaning he knew he would never be able to forget") or garlanded with stock horror imagery ("a full moon...turned to blood" or "the wisp of black vapor").[183]

Carpathia himself is depicted as a horror figure. After Rosenzweig assassinates him, Carpathia rises again in a scene that combines fears of vampirism (bloodless bodies becoming animate) with *Frankenstein*'s horrors in the face of artificial life ("Carpathia's left finger lifted an inch off his wrist for an instant, then fell again").[184] Having imbued his underlings with demonic power prior to his assassination, Carpathia is given new life via dark spells and incantations. (His rebirth inspires among his followers an even deeper servitude and confers upon him even greater control: he is worshipped on "monstrous monitors," and all clocks are henceforth set to "Carpathia Time.")[185]

Yet the identity constructed and offered as the alternative to Carpathia's is, while not described as evil, an equally violent one. LaHaye and Jenkins would certainly note that, during the Tribulation, special circumstances and end-times urgency can rationalize actions that might be completely forbidden in earlier biblical dispensations. Yet the sensibility is nonetheless one that encourages readers to think about biblical history as violent (as an ineluctable part of the tradition) and is distinguished by its incredibly vivid imaginings of sin and the destruction of opponents. In addition to fairly conventional narrative elements—violent visions of the angel Michael, for example, or reports of multiple judgments unleashed on the wicked—there are fantastical portraits of ruined landscapes (multi-helicopter crashes, bombed skyscrapers, and endlessly blackened skies) and ominous articulations of God's vengeance.[186] Responding to the mass deaths occurring around him, Ben-Judah speculates, "God may be winnowing from the evil forces the incorrigibles whom he, in his omniscience, knows would never have turned to him regardless."[187] And Mac McCullum, jogging from bunker to bunker, thinks, "[M]ay God have mercy—or not—on anyone who dared stand between them and freedom."[188]

More than in theological meditation, this worldview is manifested in the techne of the horror genre and in its images of gory death. We see here the religion of fear's customarily exacting detail in depictions of the viscera of fearful events and the technical details of horrifying circumstances. The most grisly fates are rendered with cinematic clarity. Dead characters are described with forensic scrutiny, as narrative becomes coroner's report. GCNN reporters ask questions—"Which is more dangerous, the black smoke or the yellow?"—which seem to anticipate cable news "terror alert" color codes.[189] These gory passages are enhanced by the details-driven style of the techno-thriller, whose audiences delight in knowing precisely what equipment the protagonists use in their bloody endeavors. We learn, then, that the Tribulation Force quickly masters the military arts. Characters, particularly those with experience in the armed services, speak frequently in the clipped military dialogue that is a genre staple: "[c]oldcock the girl!" or "show Socrates what a twelve-gauge does to the front door," for example.[190] There are lengthy passages describing weaponry and tactics, from mob-style executions to the details of bomb construction ("[e]ighty percent of their weight is made up of a gel consisting of polystyrene, ammonium nitrate, and powdered aluminum") to characters' shocked recognition of GC brutality ("[b]ecause [Rayford] knew warheads... [his] heart sank when he saw the black pole attached to the nose of each bomb").[191]

The novels' vision of the last days, and perhaps their vision of ultimate redemption, emerges in splattery images of bodily destruction and sci-fi-inspired violence. The authors spend considerable time constructing horrified descriptions of the powers of evil. The Carpathia regime employs implements of evil both supernatural—as when Leon Fortunato destroys his opponents with "[g]reat beams of fire [which] burst from the cloudless skies and incinerated" them—and conventional, from the oft-used guillotines (an iconic horror reference given new life in this series) to a techno-thriller "directed energy weapon... [which] can shoot a concentrated beam of waves that penetrates clothing and heats any moisture on the skin to 130 degrees in a couple of seconds."[192] Vivid, almost languorous discussions of violence come from the mouths of GC characters, as when Carpathia opines on the best methods for shooting someone:

> As they lie howling and others abandon them in fear, you still have five rounds do you not?... Both knees, each shoulder. Particularly painful. Make them change their mind, Hut. Make them say they love me and that they are sorry they opposed me. And you know what to do with the final round... Heart?... A cliché! No creativity!... You put the hot muzzle of the weapon to their forehead, right where the mark should be. And you ask if they are prepared to pledge their loyalty. And even if they scream to the heavens that they have seen the light, you give them their own mark. It will be the only round they do not hear or feel.[193]

Carpathia then goes on to insist that the corpse must still be guillotined.

The final volumes contain multiple gruesome torture and interrogation scenes. Several central figures—from Chang to Chloe—are tortured and beheaded in scenes that suggest a preoccupation with death and the destruction of the body. Even Tribulation Force members, however, display knowledge of the mechanics of torture, as Mac opines about a secret location that "[i]t's where I would terrorize a hostage."[194] They describe scenes of intense gore in indifferent tones: "Shot. Marcel in the face. Back of his head gone. We had to work to pull him from under the dashboard. K took one in the neck from behind. Probably cut his spinal cord. Laslos in the forehead."[195] They allow readers to feel firsthand the intensity of the struggle between good and evil, as George Sebastian resists Elena, a GC assassin: their tussle involves the "sensation of skin on skin" and, with his "massive quads and hamstrings" he "slammed into her so fast and hard" that Elena "projectile regurgitated over him."[196] And they embody heroic militarism with their exhortations to battle, which range from Ben-Judah's teachings on the ease of using an Uzi to barked war cries like "Let's kill us some One World Army!"[197]

The more violent the Tribulation becomes—with its brutal implementation of the mark, its "blood and ooze," and its countless beheadings in "the bloodiest season in the history of the world"—the more sacred it becomes, as its degradations and slaughter confirm that ours is a cosmos of vengeful retribution in which good ultimately prevails.[198] Yet, perhaps even more common than such portraits of the destructive enemies are those episodes of violence written into the series' larger sense of justice. This violence is not simply inverted glory; it is also itself a divine vehicle. Divine judgment pours out into the world with violent intensity, with "ten thousand wails and moans and shrieks... orange and red and black... the stench of fire and metal and oil and rock... [a] sea of raging flames... [and] roiling mushroom clouds."[199] The authors' enumeration of the bowl and trumpet judgments allows them to convey a sense of God's righteousness and retributive justice written in gore. As the inevitable final battle draws near, Carpathia's supporters are infected by sores; their bodies decay.[200] And Nicolae himself begins to falter, the vampiric imagery often used to describe him now painting him not just as bloodless but as lifeless, with his "bluish lips" and "the mouth of a dead man."[201]

The most extraordinary carnage, however, occurs not simply at the time of Jesus' appearing but through Christ's own actions. The epicenter of the final battle "was worse than any war zone. Hundreds of horses and even more men and women lay dead in hideous repose, broken, trampled, torn to pieces. The stench of stables was nothing compared to the hideous entrails of human and beast."[202] Into this scene strides Christ. His most powerful weapon is the Word itself, which comes to bloody life and which the authors refer to as "that sword from His mouth."[203] When Christ begins to speak, "tens of thousands of United Army soldiers fell dead, simply dropping where they stood, their bodies ripped open, blood pooling in great masses."[204] Jesus' voice alone flays GC bodies, rending them in half and creating miles and miles of the "splayed and filleted bodies of men and women and horses."[205] It is no interpretive stretch to call these very long, very detailed battle scenes blood-soaked, for the authors make such points repeatedly. The "very words of the Lord had superheated their [the United Army's] blood, causing it to burst through their skin and veins."[206] The enemies, whom Christ had been willing to forgive until the last, "writhed as they were invisibly sliced asunder.... [their] innards and entrails gushed to the desert floor."[207] Some soldiers killed themselves before Christ could, while others "looked like cartoon characters on speed, using any implement they could find to dig holes and bury themselves, trying to hide from the piercing light and convicting words of Christ."[208] For almost 100 pages, God's enemies have "their flesh dissolved in their sockets, and their tongues dissolved in their mouths."[209] Nearly each sentence finds GC soldiers "screaming in terror and pain and dying... [as] blood poured from them in great waves, combining to make a river that quickly became a swamp."[210]

It is an extraordinary conclusion to the series, yielding a vision of the world defined by love and compassion and forgiveness (the scenes in *Glorious Appearing* when Jesus speaks to the survivors and reunites them with their loved ones can be affecting) but also by terror and bloody vengeance. The intense boundary work from which this distinction takes shape, and the cultural ambivalence that is the occasion for this work, reveals the intimacy of sacred and infernal, the demonology within. The erotics of fear is visible in the forensically detailed and energetically portrayed gore. Jenkins, who is partially aware of the complexity of this fascination, described his strategy in writing such scenes as "just think[ing] of the worst thing I can imagine."[211] To his critics who are uncomfortable with such scenes, Jenkins replies curtly, "These are people who haven't read the series or haven't read the Bible. I mean, we didn't make that stuff up."[212]

It may be possible, then, to see such scenes simply as effective writing, to some extent rooted in the authors' understanding of the Bible. Yet this would ignore some fairly obvious and suggestive dimensions of these texts. My suggestion that these scenes embody the erotics of fear does not mean that this dimension of these creations is neatly distinguished from others, but rather that this interpretive category helps to capture a dimension of this political religion which might be overlooked in other orientations to this literature. So the erotics are both a discernible feature of *Left Behind* and also a way of unpacking the meanings of the writing style. There is clearly something to be said about how much gore there is in these books and about the sociocultural spaces of tension where the two instabilities go to work. On my account, these relate clearly to fears of retribution for believing and doing wrong things. While authors like Stephen King use gore in the name of effective writing, LaHaye and Jenkins are distinct insofar as their devices are combined with religious sensibilities and political concern. And it is in many ways a very successful style: as one fifteen-year-old fan said, "The best thing about the *Left Behind* books is the way the non-Christians get their guts pulled out by God."[213]

The books shift between a kind of fuzzy domesticity (where commodity consumption underscores the brightly optimistic vision of the confessing community) and a world of fugitive existence, hostile organizations, and ceaseless carnage. The two instabilities develop in the space between these impulses. That these elements are visible in this pop apocalypse reveals much about the way LaHaye and Jenkins contemplate politics and their own cultural critique and about the kind of evangelical identity they craft through their representations. On the one hand, the series presents itself as a scathing critique of contemporary society and morality; yet, on the other hand, it presents no alternative vision of the way things should be. The authors' goal is certainly that more people come to accept Christ. Toward this end, they have continued to publish—through the Pre-Trib Research Center, which LaHaye co-founded with Tommy Ice—a number of defenses of the series' scriptural accuracy and biblical authenticity.[214] Indeed, the novels are filled with meta-references and allusions underscoring this goal: believers in the Tribulation refer continually to the necessity of spreading the gospel, which is precisely the function that LaHaye and Jenkins envision for their novels.[215] In *Assassins*, there is a rich scene where several characters stumble upon numerous tracts and pamphlets (one of which is entitled "Don't Be Left Behind").[216] And Ben-Judah continually instructs his flock, and the books' readers, on what is necessary for conversion and why the time to convert is now: "[i]f you agree that God is using the period we now live in to get people ready for the millennial kingdom and for eternity, what will you do with your life?"[217]

But what do such questions require practically? If the books constitute the authors' final warning to a doomed culture, what should people do following conversion? In their readings and projections of what is sinful and damnable, the novels obviously establish a script or a template for living as one saved. When fictional characters announce that "[t]he self is the center of this manmade religion, and devoting one's life to the glory of God stands in stark relief. . . . Join a team. . . . We cannot both be right," it is evident that LaHaye's antihumanist arguments have survived the 1980s and assumed a different, more powerful form.[218] As Ariel points out, by constructing a speculative future, the novels help to resolve present-day tensions.[219] These books represent what Gershom Gorenberg describes as a world without the dissonance felt by many conservative practitioners.[220] Yet both the enemies and the conflicts are politicized in ways that can reasonably be seen as contributing to such dissonance, a quality that bodes ill for American politics, considering that these novels represent the fullest and most publicized stage of the religion of fear, a discourse now as thoroughly a part of public culture—perhaps even "mainstream"—as one can imagine.

The authors borrow from genre fiction in order to demonstrate vividly, in fine-grained detail, what acts are forbidden and which fates lead to grisly doom. And they wrestle with what Shuck suggestively identifies as "network culture" because they believe that technology enables a greater readiness to read the signs of the imminent end. Indeed, as I suggested above, these signs and the narrative responses the authors fashion are not just politically coded, they represent a substantive political engagement themselves. Yet if the world is simultaneously doomed and its redemption by Christ is inevitable, why bother with politics at all? Buck even admits, "Scripture didn't seem to indicate that even Christ's followers would be able to do more than simply bear up against" the Antichrist.[221]

The fashioning of this critical discourse, however, supports contemporary political engagements while also allowing for their symbolic resolution. The authors' projections of and solutions to sociopolitical crises reveal the texture of their social criticism and also the fluid nature of the identity they craft. The discourse, though fictional, presents itself as authoritative in its projection of an end (and thereby, as Kenneth Burke noted, of an essence).[222] LaHaye and Jenkins use the temporal discourse of the apocalyptic to undermine the kind of political authority they believe is embodied in contemporary American (especially liberal) politics and the sinning lifestyles they believe such a politics enables. They supplement this with the legitimation of an alternate political sensibility. The demons of the *Left Behind* series are clearly identifiable and stand in the way of just authority. In time, the authors insist, "We will live in righteousness. We will have plenty."[223] And, unlike most authors in the tradition of apocalyptic writing, LaHaye and Jenkins believe that these are political (and, of course, spiritual) goals to be pursued now.

The apocalyptic is a politically useful genre insofar as the continually delayed end it posits keeps attention focused on what its authors identify as this end's most likely causes. This endlessly protracted present, always poised on the edge of ruin, is clearly more than just a framework within which to understand history and the problem of evil. In this series, it constitutes a refracted argument, as the causes isolated by the authors in this fictional scenario overlap clearly with those whose presence in American society are lamented in NCR criticism and activism. In this discursive world, the urgency of the last days is linked to a politics of spectacle, consumption, and critical engagement with a culture seen as overrun with evil.

The series offers its readers a set of political goggles. Though the idiom that the authors favor may suggest a kind of pessimism about society's eventual fate, it is optimistic about evangelization and about sociopolitical engagement. Whereas interpreters like Shuck find it "ironic" that LaHaye and Jenkins seek to intervene and transform their culture, these impulses are wholly consistent with conservative evangelical activism broadly and with LaHaye's activism specifically.[224] In tracing the connections among this popular literature, a specific kind of political pedagogy, and the two instabilities at work in the religion of fear, I am not suggesting that the series has had a univocal effect on American society. Indeed, considering how very public this particular instantiation of the religion of fear has been, it is difficult to avoid the contentious debates that have surrounded it: consternated liberals have bemoaned the "tremendous boost" that the Bush administration has received from the books; others have snarled that the series embodies "the Theocon culture of death"; and one occasionally encounters in cyberspace comparisons of the authors to the "American Taliban" or a likening of their books to "Pretrib porno."[225] While it is certainly true, as Forbes suggests, that the books are embraced owing partly to their appropriation of "well-established themes already pervasive in American popular culture," I have sought instead to examine the interplay of fear and politics in the construction of these representations.[226] Readers may not be uniformly convinced of the world's imminent demise, or of the politics appropriate to live out such a sensibility, but the authors certainly are.

Their fearful dreams and messianic optimism promise certitude but yield an erotics and a demonology that pull against, or at least defer, this promise. The authors do not fear social change as such but desire a different kind of change, one seen as a restoration of past glories. The novels thus provide a revealing angle of insight into evangelical America. As Michelle Goldberg writes of *Left Behind*, "[T]his is the story that's captivating America."[227] In order to truly understand these stories, and the political culture from which they emerge, we must look to their monsters. As LaHaye said—quoting Churchill—to journalist David Gates, "Writing a book is an adventure.... It becomes a mistress. Then it becomes a master ... [until] you kill the monster and fling it to the public."[228] Yet the monster—a different one, perhaps one invisible to its authors—springs to life at precisely this moment, to announce its centrality to the life of these books.

7

"Like Beating the Dog"

Fear, Religion, and American Democracy

When an objection cannot be made formidable, there is some policy in trying to make it frightful; and to substitute the yell and the war-whoop, in the place of reason, argument, and the good order. —Thomas Paine, as quoted by Joseph Lewis in *Inspiration and Wisdom from the Writings of Thomas Paine*

So we turn to the news, which provides an unremitting mood of catastrophe. This is where we find emotional experience not available elsewhere. —Don DeLillo, *Mao II*

Just 'cause you feel it, doesn't mean it's there. —Radiohead, "There There"

Martin Amis writes in *The War against Cliché*, "[D]esensitisation is precisely the quality that empowers the violent.... in the moments leading up to violence, the nonviolent enter a world drenched with unfamiliar revulsions."[1] American culture is now replete with "unfamiliar revulsions," as well as with those we have come to tolerate as familiar. Dependent on high-speed Internet, digital cable channels, and podcasts, we lap up the bad news, which keeps coming, recoiling in shock at small doses (a mother killed her baby, a white girl went missing) while being ground down by and numbed to the big picture, the slow-moving outrages that appear so clear in retrospect.

So too does political culture slouch forward in America. Whatever our individual or collective outrages, all political discourse seems to narrow its focus to the election cycle, twisting away so as to avoid overmuch any reckoning with politics beyond this spectacle, whose white noise filters through to every place and every moment like the background radiation from the Big Bang. It numbs us, captivates us, lulls us. It is no surprise, then, that scholars of American religions are not immune to its effects.

My department's phones began to ring more frequently in late 2004. As any academic reading this surely knows, interest in religion scholarship can be quite ephemeral. This is not to say that such interest—from newspapers, civic groups, or radio stations—is superficial, but that it most frequently responds to a "hot" idea circulating in nonacademic media. And academics love such interest, almost as passionately as they deny that they love it. Following the presidential elections of November 2004, it became common to receive inquiries about the supposed correlation between evangelical faith and Republican politics, the likelihood of an American theocracy, the distinction between "red states" and "blue states," and, as November ceded to December, something called "the war on Christmas." I gladly accepted these calls, as did many hundreds of my colleagues, and did my best to do justice to these occasions, patiently explaining that evangelicalism is a tradition of great complexity and that the generalizations of a nasty political season cannot always serve as guides for further inquiry.

Yet, while such cautions are legitimate and deserve heeding, they have not seemed to deter the frenzy of media interest in all things religious. Indeed, since that time, there have been unceasing—and often unenlightening—discussions of the role of "values" in electoral politics. Despite the occasional journalistic spasm that informs readers that yes, Virginia, there really are moderate and progressive evangelicals, there remains an enduring feeling of bitterness and disbelief among not only cultural leftists but academics too (again, much as they may deny it) that the United States is becoming "Jesusland" (to note only one of the less crude terms in circulation).[2]

And yet nothing is more common in American history, particularly recently, than for political religions to surface in public life. Evangelicals are deeply divided about the merits of political engagements as these are commonly understood, and Americans continue to wrestle with one another over the "proper role" of religion in the political sphere. Despite these complexities and ambivalences, however, evangelicals are overdetermined in the media, repeatedly discussed but seldom understood. Indeed, it is impossible to understand "evangelicals" or "evangelicalism" *tout court*; the mere attempt is a fool's game. One can only hope to generate a useful or suggestive interpretation of some evangelicals, some beliefs, some practices, a reading that stimulates thought about the whole without presuming to stand for it. So what is lost in such fomenting interest in all things evangelical is that evangelicalisms are continually wrestling with their own identities through, among other spaces, media entertainments and cultural politics.

The religion of fear is part of these processes, emerging from the complicated cultures of evangelical conservatism as both product of and contributor to political engagements. While these popular entertainments cannot be reduced to politics alone, if I have demonstrated anything in the preceding pages, it is that they are no mere diversions: they are born of sociopolitical concern and reliant on a narrative of religio-political declension; they aim to disseminate a highly politicized worldview; and their widely distributed and accessible efforts to do so are often well funded by or even institutionally linked to the New Christian Right. These cultural portraits not only reflect the religio-political agenda of their creators, they also serve as templates for inhabiting a political world. As such, they reveal much about the changing shapes both of conservatism and of political religions broadly speaking. But if we examine the religion of fear as a measure of the health of American democracy, what does it tell us? If fear's portraits of social chaos reveal an understanding of American social decline, what can these tales tell us about fear's ideal society?

As I engage these issues below, I do not take up questions about how or under what circumstances religions should be "allowed" to participate in public and political life. Not only are such questions of limited use in analyzing the religion of fear, but American religions have always participated in political life. While there are important goods in keeping religious influences from government, something politically important is lost when Americans debate endlessly about *whether* religions should participate in politics rather than focusing on *how* they should do so or what the meanings of political religions are. What, then, does the religion of fear mean politically? Instead of laughing these tales off as kitschy pleasures or ignoring them as the ramblings of fringe figures with no influence on public life, they should be confronted as important documents of a steadily growing critical voice in America, angles of insight into a particular dimension of American evangelicalism, and as symptoms of a larger political crisis since the 1960s. These representations generate an orientation to political culture that is worrisome. I say this not because of their religiosity but because their vision of public life reveals signs of distress in American democracy.

Everyone knows that religions use fear, of course. I have strived to elaborate this commonly voiced theme from vernacular culture and to read the development of the religion of fear with an eye to its political qualities—as well as its cultural and religious anxieties—so as to generate an interpretive language that will enable more meaningful and less simplistic talk about political religions. I hope my approach will prove useful more broadly: for thinking about American conservatism as a whole, about political religions, and about religions and fear generally. Where and under what circumstances have religious identities been driven by or manifested the demonology within? Where do we see the erotics of fear? How might we tell stories about American religions differently by using these categories? And how might we think and name more clearly those still-developing forms of American political religion that are defined by bellicosity, a preoccupation with violent imagery, exclusivism, and entertainment value? It bears repeating that I am not claiming that all evangelicals identify with the religion of fear, nor that it reflects the majority will. But it is vital not to overlook its power as a rhetorical, political force by equivocating and making so many qualifications that scholarly writing is neutered, friendly, and safe. My own critical engagement in this book has sought a middle path between those who fear that every evangelical craves theocracy and wants women to wear chastity belts, and those who worry that the critical engagement of political religions ineluctably leads to such mis-representations. I explore these interpretive impulses below, as I situate the religion of fear's development alongside the growing influence of the NCR and against the backdrop of a crisis in America's democracy.

DECLINE AND FALL

In the preceding chapters, I have told a story about the development of con-servative evangelicalism since the 1960s. We see in the religion of fear the growth and the hardening of a social criticism and political sensibility that have moved from the margins of public life to its center. Paralleling this journey have been the explosion of evangelical media and an increased politicization in American religions. The religion of fear is not, of course, a monolithic force that is unchanging and undifferentiated. While its entertainments are similar in structure, tone, sentiment, and critical sensibility, there are also important differences among them. The specific cultural aspirations of creators differ, with Chick remaining doggedly focused on tract ministry as a self-contained activity, while Roberts and LaHaye explicitly seek to shape and participate in larger conversations about society. They vary in the degree to which they foreground the apocalyptic tone, and as to which particular issues they name as most central. There is also a clear range of marketing power, institutional links to the NCR, sophistication of aesthetics, and exposure in the mainstream. Yet the religion of fear consistently builds on old themes and concerns, shaping them into a potent and highly public idiom of discontent. These texts and their contexts feed off each other. We can account for the emergence, proliferation, and meanings of fear by examining how its heavy emphasis on specific themes and narratives harmonizes with those of the NCR in the resonance chambers of American public life.

The religion of fear is a product of, and thrives in, a conservative subculture shaped by the emergence of the NCR in the 1970s. The sense of cultural crisis found so widely in conservative evangelical communities has been publicized for decades by NCR figureheads and organizations, yielding both a broad sensibility about political morality and specific points of advocacy that are reflected in the religion of fear. It is widely known that, following World War Two, Christian conservatives in the United States were rarely directly involved in political life. While it was common to avow anticommunism and to issue sharp moral rebukes in certain specific areas like entertainment, there was little explicit politicization among conservatives. While a conservative evangelical subculture was energetically organizing in the areas of media, education, and communication, it was only toward the end of the 1960s that a sharp sense of political urgency began to emerge in public commentaries by evangelicals.[3]

Significantly, the NCR emerged not during the period it regards as a golden age of American culture (the mid-1940s to the mid-1960s) but in the 1970s, when American democracy began to experience a legitimation crisis. Following a period of relative abundance and stability, questions arose about bureaucracy and statism, about the ethics of war and free market capitalism, and about the place of rights- and identity-based social movements in American society.[4] Aside from social conflicts emerging around specific areas of law and public policy, there surfaced profound questions—normative and practical—about the legitimacy of postwar liberalism. In a moment of fascinating convergence between the American Left and Right, new social movements—from student groups like Students for a Democratic Society and Young Americans for Freedom to the feminist or environmental movements and newly resurgent Christian activists—began to assert their moral and political vitality against what they believed was the federal government's excessive size, intrusiveness, and lack of moral direction. Both sides championed a return to "genuine" democracy, celebrating the virtues of localism, self-determination, and identities that could not be captured by party or economic affiliation.[5]

Conservative critiques in particular had first coalesced earlier in the 1960s, initially in response to Supreme Court decisions declaring school prayer (*Engel v. Vitale*, 1962) and Bible reading (*Abington v. Schempp*, 1963) to be unconstitutional, to urban riots in 1965–1968 that triggered anxieties regarding the Civil Rights movement's successes, and to protests that seemed to fray society's edges. Self-styled populists from Barry Goldwater to George Wallace ran campaigns against the legislative initiatives of the New Frontier and the Great Society. Against the backdrop of hope and optimism still extant, Goldwater and Wallace warned that the rise of protests and social discontent would weaken America's image in the eyes of other nations and that the rapid restructuring of social life could be adduced to the machinations of liberal elites. Following the tumultuous 1968 and the erosion of support for the Vietnam War and for the Johnson administration, political acrimony and discontent increased. As the 1970s began, New Left constituencies began to fracture as the galvanizing movements of Civil Rights and anti-Vietnam dissipated; frustration with movement-based politics on the Left fed into the growth of identity politics, communitarian experimentation, and sheer apathy. This was compounded by economic malaise—stemming from "stagflation" (which marked the end of the post–World War II growth economy), Nixon's removal of the United States from the gold standard, and the OPEC oil embargo—and by Watergate. In many ways, these trends opened the door for the emergence of the New Right.[6] Spearheaded by figures like Richard Viguerie and Paul Weyrich, the New Right copied New Left organizing strategies, supplemented them with tactics like direct mailing, and promoted hot-button moral issues as a way of driving a wedge between unions (economically progressive but culturally more conservative) and more Left-leaning Democrats.

These political shifts helped to facilitate the emergence of the NCR in the late 1970s, closing the door on the era of one important political religion—the Civil Rights movement—and opening the door to another. As conservative evangelicals became ever more active in the public sphere—initially in response to the Supreme Court's *Roe v. Wade* decision and to the proposal of the Equal Rights Amendment—many of these figures believed that the disruptions of the 1960s required a restoration of the purported golden age of the mid-twentieth century, a born-again experience writ nationally. Toward this end, many began at the end of the 1970s to establish their own national political organizations. Under the leadership of figures like Ed McAteer, Jerry Falwell, and Tim LaHaye, NCR organizations like Moral Majority and Religious Roundtable used the rich language of Christian discontent to capture what they believed was the moral, religious, and political decline precipitated by the "permissive" 1960s. These critics linked the rise of libidinous entertainments with economic hardship, compromised political sovereignty, an activist judiciary, and a state too vast to take the moral pulse of its citizens. The first organizations identified specific issues—abortion, feminism, and public school curriculums, for example—as emblematic of America's cultural waywardness. Claims against the authority of the state were sometimes made using the language of policy, but resounded more clearly with the emotional languages of evangelicalism (even though Catholics would become part of the NCR coalition to some degree) and the critical idiom of the jeremiad.[7]

During its initial ascendancy, roughly from the formation of Moral Majority in 1979 until the Bush inauguration in 1989 (when a second wave began in a meeting between Pat Robertson and Ralph Reed, which eventuated in the mid-1990s power of the Christian Coalition), the NCR blended these kinds of "moral campaigns" with direct involvement in lobbying efforts, electoral campaign support, and nationally distributed voter guides. From these collective endeavors, there emerged a narrative explaining America's decline and promised return to glory, an account which harmonized with and indeed paralleled that of the religion of fear. Focusing anxieties both symbolically and pragmatically on the idea of restoration, the NCR named its Others—liberalism, statism, permissive or licentious entertainments, activist judges—and challenged them in the name of protecting unknowing citizens from manipulation by such forces. Underlying such claims is the belief that twentieth-century liberalism represents not only a threat to well-meaning citizens and "people of faith" but also a perversion of the vision of America's founders.[8]

This marks a change, from a language emphasizing shared institutions and mutual investment in the democratic process to a language of radical scorn, shifting between persecution and triumphalism; it is a shift between what

Michael Walzer identifies as the modes of connected criticism to criticism in exile.[9] This sensibility is also manifest in the religion of fear. These two enduring modes of conservative discourse share themes, imagery, concerns, and a general sense of embattlement. These expressions stem in part from an ardent patriotism, staunch support of free market capitalism, and commitment to America's role as a beacon to other nations.[10] Just as evident as its convictions, however, are the discourse's panics: anxieties about feminism and gender roles, about multiculturalism, about religious pluralism and cults, and about American economic and political autonomy are all central to this discourse. While the religion of fear has not always found direct expression in the NCR's national politics, nor has it been explicitly driven by participation in or sponsorship by any major NCR organizations, it partakes of a cultural ethos that has been kept vital by the NCR. In particular, the NCR's post-1960s declension narrative is partly indebted to what George Lakoff calls a "strict father morality," which is advocated as a form of disciplinarian correction of moral/political deficiencies.[11] It also refracts this ethos, authorizing it in entertainments that focus on the self and on society. The impulse to restore a lost order both contextualizes the sense of isolation and marginalization frequently expressed by evangelicals, while also reinscribing evangelical identity through a vigorous articulation of antiliberalism.[12]

There are clearly ambiguities and differences in evangelical attitudes about key social and political questions, yet it is important to note nonetheless that the success of conservative evangelicalism has come in part through its ability to convey certitude, conviction, and uniformity. Faced with concerns about the growth and moral valence of a bureaucratic state, a political ethic of personal responsibility is espoused. When considering disparities of wealth and economic justice, minimally regulated free market capitalism is advocated as a just court of economic appeals. Angered by what they perceive to be an activist judiciary seeking to enforce a hostile version of secularism, evangelical cultural critics seek "the reconstruction of U.S. culture so that it is in tune with the natural law of the Ten Commandments and Judeo-Christian values."[13] This narrative had coalesced firmly (along with Hell Houses and the *Left Behind* series) by the mid-1990s, when—as James Morone points out—"conservatives were screaming about the meltdown of the American family: broken homes, unwed mothers, a divorce pandemic, abortions, homosexuality, teenage predators, welfare queens, an underclass."[14] Challenging these legacies of the 1960s, which necessitates engaging in nostalgia, is seen as a social panacea.

This declension narrative suggests additionally that the 1960s marked the beginning of an unwarranted assault on heterosexual privilege, on traditional gender roles, and on the status of the conventional family as the crucible of morality.[15] America's divinely appointed status as beacon to the nations, these observations suggest, was compromised by introducing pluralism and ambiguity into the national narrative. Both the conservative evangelical critique of post-1960s politics and the ideal state it postulates once existed (and must be restored) trade heavily in "a symbolic discourse of nationalism...[that] circles around a relatively narrow and deceptively simple range of terms: 'life,' 'mother,' 'family,' 'nation,' 'free market,' 'God.'"[16] In the face of these "outrages," the religion of fear promises restoration. Yet it is not just a narrative of religio-political decline and a specific range of targets that the NCR and the religion of fear share. The deep resonance between the rhetoric of fear and the imagery of violence reveals not only the kinship of these two expressions of conservative evangelicalism but symptoms afflicting American culture more broadly.

POLITICAL DEMONOLOGY

The religion of fear not only reminds audiences of religious commitments, it also seeks to create (or reinforce) specific political commitments. Each panel drawn, lyric parsed, sin portrayed, and page written delineates the contours of hell, beckoning audiences to peer in deeply before pronouncing their rejection. These representations promise to serve as a bulwark against the steadily mounting forces of evil, staving off corruption, demonic influence, and sinful temptation. Yet these promises, and the representations that sustain them, reveal an identity that is tellingly unstable in places. Consider the details of a Bob Larson screed, a sweat-soaked Chick tract, or a Hell House: their Others are not merely announced but evoked in symbols, narratives, and sociopolitical sources of justification. Thoroughly American in its demonology, the religion of fear constructs its politics amid a bestiary of monsters.[17] These efforts—whose purpose is, in the words of Tom De Luca and John Buell, "to thoroughly stigmatize individuals, types of persons, or groups whether for political or other advantage, righteous belief, or both"—are responses to external opportunities and threats.[18]

By naming and narrating the feared—whether indwelling or external—and squeezing it into conventional forms, the religion of fear constructs symbolic resolutions to sociopolitical concerns. These representations and narrations can achieve a clarity often lacking in the messiness of the everyday. The common thread underlying such stories of political fright is their propensity—whether they mean to soothe or alarm—to warn us of the consequences of bad behavior or bad beliefs. Yet in fear's complicated dance with its enemies, there is the possibility that the categories of self and Other will bleed together. As Morone notes by way of example, "What was most terrifying about the natives was not anything they actually did but the possibility that, deep in the American wilderness...the saints might morph into pagans."[19] As Mechal Sobel observes, enemy Others have their identities built of "rejected inner characteristics" but remain "an important part of the self as well, an inner alien that could be reaffirmed" in dramatic or expressive settings.[20] The "inner alien" has its existence confirmed whenever outer aliens are singled out for damnation. So, fear's boundary work and its engagement of its Others seeks to establish a self, yet ironically the result is never secure, never finished.[21]

The two instabilities I have traced throughout this book, then, are registers of category or identity crisis, spaces where fear's architects consort with the forbidden in a (perhaps unintended) confirmation that the very demons and desires so fervently denounced are necessary for the establishment of an orthodox self. These constructions—arising from the complicated exchanges among religion, politics, and culture—highlight the importance of exactly what they seek to erase; on these craggy, uneven boundaries, the saintly and demonic coexist.[22] This criticism takes shape in the intermingling of desires and repudiations, of compulsion and scorn. Its combative stance toward what it sees as a fallen culture belies its own complicated position therein. The religion of fear's strategies of alterity constitute a politics of inclusion and exclusion, constructed in its own dissent and through its taxonomies of identity. Yet the religion of fear also exudes a fetishization of the flesh—in sex and in violence—that parallels horror's own.

This is not, however, a discourse of mere cruelty or barbarism; it is also encoded with immense symbolic detail and weighted with a specific history: of martyrs, demonism, and punishments that display the bodies of the wicked for the benefit of those yet to be judged. As Giorgio Agamben says of *homo sacer*, and as Kristeva says of the effect of horror on the psyche, the representation of the punished or tortured body is a simultaneous articulation and containment of the abject.[23] In its willing adoption of the status of marginality, the religion of fear aims to construct a kind of religio-political authenticity. It denounces policy and fallen culture in part by gesturing to a history of pious outsiders—early Christians persecuted under Roman rule or holy fugitives from law—even as it promises normalcy. There is, then, something strangely subversive about the religion of fear: it aims to reassert an ordered domestic tranquility yet seeks to accomplish this through bloody representations of the monstrous, of violations, of perversity and addiction. The stability and normalcy it craves are defined and justified through embattlement and demonology. And its ever-wagging finger not only signals disapproval of the salacious and forbidden but beckons audiences to a closer examination thereof. While its moral emphasis seeks to overshadow or overpower the two instabilities, it seldom succeeds. For where political fear seeks to banish its frights and monsters, the religion of fear depends upon its. Through images of torture, death, horror, and judgment, a specific conception of moral obligation and political authority emerges, understood both as ontological truth and as rhetoric with which to denounce a political culture thought to be hostile. In these tales of gore and violence, the religion of fear frightens audiences not simply with the specter of ultimate judgment but with the possibility of loss: of history, of power, of primacy. These horrors work, as Bernard McGinn suggests, as consolation, theodicy, and fearful motivation alike.[24]

What politics comes of the religion of fear's images of pain and bodies tormented? If political authority establishes or imposes its imagination of collective life—whether in Mather's New England or LaHaye's raptured America—by reading its citizens' pain, sex, and death, then what do the religion of fear's abiding preoccupations with pain, sex, and death reveal about its politics? Such reckonings with pain and pleasure can be used as foundations for a politics of human rights or protection under the rule of law. But fear's politics of sin and redemption is, in Slavoj Žižek's words, "haunted by the ambiguous attitude of horror/envy with regard to the unspeakable pleasures in which sinners engage."[25] There is no comfort in fear's politics, articulated in a discourse of unshakeable piety but continually raging not just at a sinful world but against its own position therein. It pronounces its own contentment and certitude, achieved via its distance from Babylon, yet seeks normalcy within this very world and craves power according to this fallen world's own standards. This embattlement expresses itself in the two instabilities, generating the distinctive horror politics of the religion of fear. And, like all horror, it constitutes a kind of revenge fantasy, a displacement and symbolic resolution of conflicts opened up by a fallen world.[26] These tales of fright enable the tellers, and perhaps their audiences, to imagine the destruction of enemies in God's judgment. Such criticism is also, it should not be forgotten, extremely violent in its simultaneous censorship and firsthand experience of dark desires.

Through blood and fire, then, we see the flickering shadows of a power that Michel Foucault once described as an assemblage of opposites by which cultures map the acceptable and unacceptable and distinguish those granted access to public life from those excluded. This mapping generates religio-political authority through denunciation of what is deemed to be unacceptable. If one goes looking in the halls of government or political campaigns, one may find little direct evidence of the religion of fear's impact on American politics. For unlike other conservative political discourses, the religion of fear does not primarily produce a theory of state power, strategic mobilization, or distributive rights; it generates a political ethos sustained by images of fright. Studies of politics oriented only to statecraft, systems of law, or elections overlook the ways in which power circulates and passes through local spaces— resonance chambers—where the work of power is done (later reflected in political institutions). The religion of fear's social criticism exercises disciplinary power, in the spaces that government cannot reach. Its cautionary tales form part of an extended network of power relations, which Foucault called "techniques of power present at every level of the social body and utilised by very diverse institutions."[27] These projects confirm the complexity of conservatism's position in American politics, but also signal a kind of political exhaustion, a blank space in which the frenetic, overdriven aggression of the religion of fear offers a surrogate. This virulent social criticism is part of a resurgence of preoccupations with the demonic in a period of intense political antagonism. The politics of these popular entertainments are anything but innocuous. More than simply registers of the horrific or of religious anxiety, they are signs of a political culture in a state of severe distress.

FEAR AND SOCIAL CRITICISM

The popularity of these creations at this moment reveals connections between these "mere" entertainments and the political, as well as the instabilities of the kind of religio-political identities that the authors trumpet. The ascendance of this discourse reveals troubling signs about our culture. Why, then, do scholars of religion so seldom engage such matters? While some scholars reflect broadly on these issues in the context of religious ethics, those who write about American culture and history usually locate the political in the range of sub-specializations noted in the introduction. More recently, the focus has shifted to the recrudescent "culture wars" or the impact of "values voters." These orientations often privilege the state in their formulations, by examining the rule of law or looking at groups seeking recognition from the state. For example, David Leege et al.'s *The Politics of Cultural Differences* tracks changes in voter mobilization, and Geoffrey Layman's *The Great Divide* focuses on religion in American party politics. Elsewhere, this literature trades heavily in rhetorical constructions that are either blunt or outmoded. For example, older texts like Richard Neuhaus's *The Naked Public Square* and James Davison Hunter's *Culture Wars* are still cited routinely as explanatory models, while texts like David Gutterman's *Prophetic Politics* adhere to older theoretical models that, while admirably comparative in scope, seem only to suggest *that* religions sometimes criticize politics rather than why or how they do so.[28] These entries also come, significantly, from outside religious studies.

I do not want to frustrate readers who have made it this far with a literature review. I bring up these examples, which I regard as representative, to suggest that conventional paths, while valuable, cannot reliably capture the complex interactions of religions and politics in the United States. A position of real theoretical breadth—sensitive to exchanges between these enduring modes of American public expression—is necessary to map the cultural politics of creations like the religion of fear.[29] So, scholars of American religions have appropriated, unconsciously or not, a kind of political myopia. At a time when the study of religions is beginning (somewhat belatedly in terms of other conversations across the humanities) to understand its own "political" location, there seems to be a disciplinary tentativeness in engaging American political religions. This is amplified in studies of contemporary religions, since it is in some ways safer to study the religious worlds of dead people than of the living: the living, after all, can talk back; and our fellow citizens are more likely to have heated opinions about contemporary political religions (what, then, distinguishes scholarship from editorializing in print or in conversation?). It is also a challenge to think and write reasonably about political religions when public discourse seems too often to consist of denunciations of secular liberalism and fervent complaints about "red state America" or "fundamentalists in flyover country." Randall Balmer, Tanya Erzen, Melani McAlister, Jeffrey Stout, Winnifred Sullivan, and Hugh Urban have made important contributions to the growing literature on American religions and democracy.[30] Yet, aside from these happy counterexamples, the languages available to us have not proven adequate to capture the multiple registers of presences like the religion of fear, which merits documentation and interpretation but also demands to be engaged critically.

Religious studies has customarily avoided such critical (as opposed to merely documentary) engagements. For several decades, scholars in the humanities have been beset by the historical and sociological predicaments of their own changing position in American society. The cottage industry devoted to studies of public intellectualism, which seemed to explode during the Clinton administration, remains vigorous, as academics continue to wonder why there are no longer any Dwight Macdonalds or write meta-discourses about what public intellectuals would do were there any public intellectuals (this is the scholar's own declension narrative).[31] Yet, in efforts to connect to a wider audience, to get some toehold in a larger reading culture, academics have written in the thick of ironies. We wring our hands and bite our nails at the very thought of writing critically about those we study, and we often do so for good reasons, primarily because we seek to avoid misrepresentation. We also cling to visions of times gone by, when public intellectuals graced the covers of *Time* and *Life.* Yet the very age of public intellectualism longed for in these narratives of loss celebrated precisely the kind of work that makes contemporary academics uneasy; the synthetic, interpretive works of great social critics were anything but nervous about methodological transgressions against the cultures they stared down. The contemporary humanities professor's pulse quickens with delight and inspiration when reading C. Wright Mills's description of "cheerful robots," yet keeps this sentiment concealed like a forbidden desire, as if giving vent to this urge would emblazon a virtual scarlet "A" on a conference name tag.

Over the last several decades, religious studies' methodological awakening— particularly in American religious studies, which has slowly shaken off the cobwebs of "church history"—has generated an often laudable attention to the dangers of misrepresenting those about whom we write. Religious studies has pursued an enormously beneficial scholarly path, an orientation toward lived social history, toward ethnography, toward an engaged but noncritical situatedness in relation to the cultures we study. Slowly, a theoretical sensibility—almost a tacit normative boundary, possibly constructed unintentionally—has emerged to warn us that critical activity invites reductionism and misrepresentation. Taking a cue from theoretical work done in postcolonial studies, literary criticism, and poststructuralist philosophy (much of it now several decades past, it should be noted), religious studies has embraced with the zeal of the newly converted the notion that making normative statements risks violating the self-understandings of our "subjects," or risks committing epistemic violence against them. Because we mean to do no representational harm to those we study, scholars of religion have gone about simply documenting and describing, in ever more scrupulous detail and after ever-lengthier participant observation.

I cannot document precisely why religious studies has not engaged political matters more fully, nor why the available literature conforms mostly to standard analytical patterns. My sense is that this may be partly explained by these methodological trends, which may be seen as yielding a kind of disciplinary tentativeness or a fear that to enter these conversations in a different way risks muddying the methodological waters. There is perhaps an unconscious impulse to step back from engaging public and political matters in a truly critical fashion, as if simply to study political religions beyond certain established parameters constituted a disruption of those methodologies now taken for granted in the field.[32] This approach to the study of religion preserves certain vital scholarly ideals like fairness, judiciousness, reflective listening, and a resistance to self-aggrandizing. I worry, however, that in the name of preserving these laudable principles, other competing principles are given short shrift, namely, the obligation to recognize the scholar's responsibility to interact with a broader public on issues of common concern and the obligation to speak more broadly about democratic values. It is past time for religious studies to renew and remake its engagements with the political, for failure to do so risks political irresponsibility precisely *because* this discipline is uniquely qualified to embolden this discourse, to deliver it from stale dualisms, and to ask people to think about the nuances. There is not only an intellectual good in this, but a democratic one, because these descriptions dovetail with democracy's provisionalism and commitment to conversation, and they demand an attentiveness that translates well into the messy work of dialogue and procedure. But this does not mean that scholars should refrain from criticism, for this too is part of our responsibility.

Reservations are certainly understandable, and caution is certainly warranted in some respects. In the absence of rigorous engagement from the academy, the void is filled by pundits and commentators who focus on the "spectacle" of political religions. Sociologist Adolph Reed, Jr., recalls the moment when he realized—after the 2004 elections—that his colleagues were backing away from such issues in their proclamations that there were so many people out there who were "just not like us."[33] And so readers are left too often with public commentary that can be shrill and superficial. Widely discussed authors like Michelle Goldberg, Christopher Hedges, and Lauren Sandler peer into American religions and find omens of "Christian nationalism" and "American theocracy" amid the revivals of Acquire the Fire or the newly opened Creation Museum in Petersburg, Kentucky.[34] While I admire some dimensions of this writing, and share some of its political concerns, I find that it too often presses the panic button in a way that is no more satisfying an intellectual response to political religions than stepping cautiously away into the familiar climes of constitutional debates and voter analyses. Each body of literature, then, has profound limits. Religious studies could improve and refocus this discourse by becoming more engaged and responsible, not just in documentary work but in criticism. Scholars of American religions must supplement the extant literature while also clarifying, participating in public debates, and defending democratic norms; these things do happen on occasion, of course, but in general the conversation about such matters is arid.

My concerns about the political meanings of the religion of fear are not grounded in the fearfulness of public chest thumping about theocracy or Jesusland, which I believe often masks what is truly of political concern. Nor is it the religiousness of the religion of fear that troubles me, since preoccupation with whether or not religions should be "allowed" in politics not only essentializes "religion," it also leaves us floating away from history since religions always have been and always will be involved in politics (though not necessarily in government). This approach to political religions leaves us with more ironies, as we often talk ourselves into corners where we are forced to make the very normative judgments that many in religious studies seek to avoid, constructing the categories of "good" religion (like Martin Luther King, Jr.'s, whose politics happen to mirror our own and who is thereby seen as an acceptable participant in public life) and of "bad" religion (like Jerry Falwell's, whose politics we do not share and who is therefore seen as a danger in public life).[35]

I find the evasion of normative and critical discourse in religious studies to be deeply conservative. It flies in the face of those who ostensibly seek a return to public intellectual discourse, and its yearning for scholarly impassivity also conflicts with the embrace of theoretical concerns that every scholarly intervention (including impassivity itself) inevitably acts on and transforms its subjects. More important, I find the reflexive desire to avoid "truth claims" or critical evaluations to be an untenable evasion of political responsibility. Strangely, in the looking-glass world of American public discourse, even the staunchest conservatives have appropriated the lessons of theory, effectively arguing that there is little to prohibit public confessionalism or challenges to various kinds of rationalism if all truth claims are equally discursive constructions.[36] As these theoretical languages have come unmoored, their conventions have been challenged and expanded by theorists like Christopher Norris and Terry Eagleton, who write in the spirit of George Orwell and warn against the political obfuscation that such conventions can invite.[37] Yet these exchanges seem not to have reached all corners of the American academy. Both the tender remove of scholars and the studied disdain of pundits are wrapped in the rhetoric of populism and civic concern: academics often embrace a cheerful populism that celebrates the accomplishments of the "everyday" even as it embodies the culture of therapy (where observers can "feel your pain" and rename it empowerment), while nonacademics sidestep charges of elitism by claiming that their cries of "theocracy!" are only intended to defend the *real* American middle. But I worry that, in following these well-worn paths, scholars of religion somehow manage to establish in the field the very kind of normative boundary they decry at a general theoretical level, constituting a "respectable" religion against detractors. As Robert Orsi writes, "[T]he discipline was literally constructed by means of exclusion...of these and other ways of living between heaven and earth, which were relegated to the world of sects, cults, fundamentalisms, popular piety, ritualism, magic, primitive religion, millennialism, anything but 'religion.'"[38] Surely, scholars might say of the religion of fear, nothing this base, this seemingly one-dimensional, and this linked to unsavory political contests can be "real religion," worthy of study. Nonacademics too generate a normative model of political life, where citizens found to be too alien are—through the smirking disdain of "snarkenfreude" or by crying wolf—described as unfit for politics.

All the ready-to-hand explanations of something like the religion of fear—though they may be partly illustrative—reflect what Frank Furedi calls the "politics of denial." The constitutional response (should religion be allowed?) denies the reality of religions' enduring presence in political life, with all of the messiness that entails; the pundit's response (religions are dangerous and can therefore be dismissed collectively, or American Christians crave theocracy and therefore should be barred from political life) denies the same reality, while also avoiding a real reckoning not just with the complexity of American religions but with their own (that is, the pundits') political position (since there is inevitably the assumption that they are right and must band together to "stop the Christians"); the standard academic response (sober and nonjudgmental, in a desire to avoid committing epistemic violence or imposing some normative truth claim that subjects might not accept) denies both the conservatism of its methodological stance and its accountability to and responsibility for political problems.

Such responses are also ahistorical, for there is nothing more recognizably American than this darkness, this simultaneous challenge to and desire for political power. We as citizens deny this history if we thunder that the religion of fear should itself be feared. We as scholars deny it when we acknowledge fear regimes past, but look away from those present. Democratic culture, however, requires not such conversation-ending denials but conversation-starting provocations. Simply positing the religion of fear as an Other or deciding that critical engagement constitutes methodological sin absolves us of the kind of responsibility I regard as central to intellectual life: the responsibility to de-scribe, to clarify, and to draw connections. Fear must be named clearly and countered not with hand wringing or back turning but with sober political vision. To engage and critique the religion of fear's politics, then, is neither reductionism nor misrepresentation. It is, rather, a different kind of respon-sible engagement with religious discourses and cultures. The distinctions be-tween intimacy with one's subjects and impartial remove, or between the critical and the documentary mode, are not necessarily moral ones that sep-arate "proper" analysis from "debased." Criticism must simply acknowledge the grounds on which it is made. Mine is a social and political interpretation of a powerful discourse of evil. In focusing on these issues, I am not concerned with psychologists' or philosophers' aims to assess intentions, the sincerity of be-lievers, or the validity of truth claims. Rather, I am interested in fear's political "cash value." And I raise these concerns not to counter fear with fear, to create another "bad" religion, but with respect for—and an invitation to—the very democratic processes I worry the religion of fear may evade or even harm.

Americans need different stories about ourselves, and different languages for discussing political religions. Conventional language sometimes works. But the ways in which political religions are evolving suggest that the lan-guages of "red state/blue state" or of "culture wars" are deficient. This du-alistic language resembles fear's own, and reveals more about those who use it than about what it claims to describe. I write this not because I favor privileging class talk over culture talk, as critics like Adolph Reed, Walter Benn Michaels, Thomas Frank, and Eric Lott suggest.[39] My sense is that loose talk about culture and values does not so much shield us from an appreciation of economic reality as direct our attention away from the sense of political exhaustion and breakdown that continues to grow in American life. These standard tales do not adequately address our anomie and detachment from politics; whether in the service of smug disdain or carefully manicured scholarly distance, they only confirm what we tell ourselves is true: that what we think and write and do cannot make a difference.

"LIKE BEATING THE DOG"

The task, then, is to accept the burden of practically, substantively articulating political problems. If new interpretive languages do not themselves constitute challenges to political vision, they at least call attention to the limits of what is taken for granted and help us to think about alternatives. How, then, should a person committed to democratic politics think about the politics preached by the religion of fear? Is this politics radical, restorationist, antidemocratic, antistatist? Fear's politics is less of the procedural, institutional, or ideological sort than a kind of jeremiad, emerging from a recognizable "culture of complaint."[40] The cases teach ways of seeing and thinking, establishing a kind of political code that exemplifies the overdriven rhetoric of conflict, a mood of unrelenting panic, and a palpable sense of political exhaustion, which all define our political moment.[41] The religion of fear wears these features like armor, representing a cultural refusal of the politics of postwar liberalism, a catalog of discontent with the managerial politics of the welfare state, a denunciation of political reason and mutual accountability in favor of a discourse of narrow triumphalism and combativeness. The costs of ignoring this political vision are high. These themes resonate sympathetically with the religion of fear and—when read against the contextual backdrop and the social world we know exists around its creators—they trace a progression both chronological and cultural. Each case exists as a significant part of American evangelical cultures; but when considered chronologically—Chick tracts emerged in the 1960s, anti-rock in the 1970s, Hell/Judgement Houses in the mid-1980s, and *Left Behind* in the mid-1990s—their significance increases. For this progression—a long move from the margins with Chick tracts to the center with the *Left Behind* series—reveals the normalization of the religion of fear's politics.

While the responses noted above might register surprise that conservative Christians are so numerous and influential in political matters (a surprise similar to that registered in the 1970s, it is worth noting), the conditions for this influence were sown long ago, in an all-American blend of flamboyant pop, symbolic violence, and religious antistatism. These themes took shape as early as Chick's 1960s tracts, and their audience has grown steadily, reaching not only more people but becoming, if not "cool," then certainly standard fare in American life. The religion of fear has highlighted these themes and kept them in circulation, and these pop entertainments have thus played a significant role in legitimating and normalizing these sociopolitical sentiments over decades. This transition also reveals how fear's brand of religious doom has paralleled the exhaustion of political energy and the evacuation of meaning in political discourse. This emerges first in the harmonization between the religion of fear's violent, conflict-laden visions of the world and the larger preponderance of conflict rhetoric in public life, so often a surrogate for reasoned democratic dialogue. Politicians, religious activists, and commentators alike resort to military rhetoric and to images of oppression or coercion. Blogs like *The Revealer* sponsor links to an Easter weekend of "blogging against theocracy"; Christopher Hedges denounces the entire Christian Right as antidemocratic and even "fascist"; Senator John Ashcroft (echoing earlier claims—by James Watt and Tom DeLay in the 1980s—that government agencies like the Environmental Protection Agency were "gestapos") denounces the "wall of religious oppression"; and, since the 1990s, innumerable expressions of these themes have emerged from conservative evangelical cultures: the War on Christians Conference, the Judeo-Christian Committee for Constitutional Restoration, the House of Worship Free Speech Restoration Act, the First Amendment Restoration Act, David Barton's Wallbuilders, Rick Scarborough's Vision America and Enough Is Enough! rallies, the Constitution Restoration Act, and Alan Sears's claim, via his Alliance Defense Fund, that a homosexual "agenda" threatens "the American family and the American way of life," among many other examples.[42] Differences over religio-national destiny are issued as challenges, not to conversation partners in the work of democracy, but to the opposing team, whose utter defeat offers the only true consolation, the surest sign of victory. In the echo chamber of American politics, this rhetoric gets a pass in the absence of passionate defenders of democratic norms and procedures.

These interventions into discourses about pluralism, participation, and the nature of public life reveal a curious lack of depth. Outside of isolated specific instances—such as Judge Roy Moore's Ten Commandments Action Center or the 1995 *Rosenberger v. University of Virginia*—the terms of this discourse are symbolically central but left strangely unfleshed, abstracted from real specificity, as if their sole purpose were to galvanize emotions and to provoke. Specific details are certainly invoked in these claims, which often cite instances of controversy surrounding public school curriculums (perhaps most famously in 1987's *Mozert v. Hawkins* case) or the public expression of non-Christian religious symbolism as if they were self-evident, or they occasionally extend comparisons of the political status of American Christians with oppressed minorities around the globe.[43] For example, John W. Whitehead's 1994 *Religious Apartheid: The Separation of Religion from American Public Life* compares the "discrimination" suffered by American Christians with the oppression suffered by black South Africans under apartheid: "[f]rom the removal of crosses and nativity scenes in public places to the prohibition of individual prayer in the schools, examples of this apartheid are occurring daily (sometimes hourly) throughout the country."[44] Despite the circulation of such claims, the key terms of the discourse itself—"bigotry" and "secular"—function as abstractly as do terms like "Christian"; they are meant to be singular and self-evident in their meanings. Who, after all, would be callous enough to support "bigotry" or to reject "family values"? What kind of politics could stomach the willful disadvantaging of a Christian majority (albeit one that is increasingly likely to paint itself as an embattled minority)? The religion of fear draws these themes together, gives them shape and context, and sends them back into the world; taken together, they work, in William E. Connolly's perceptive formulation, "to place a series of defiled doctrines, institutions, and constituencies under daily suspicion . . . to foment a collective will to revenge."[45]

Another mode of shared resonance is found in the religion of fear's embrace and narration of a politics of nostalgia, a common reflex whereby declension narratives come to serve as palliatives. Fear is always narrated, of course, its content imbued with a sense of urgency and expectancy by a sternly wagging finger. These narratives name political causes (an intrusive state, an activist judiciary) or religious ones (demons at work in unseen places). Yet these tales locate their solutions outside the political and outside of any shared notions of rationality, communication, or community. Though it hardly needs to be said that these narratives of historical nostalgia (including fear's entertainments) involve a kind of forgetting, they are also arguments whose structure, presentation, and occasion are all strategic. Remembrance of a placid historical past is a narrative strategy which functions to remove the source of anxiety, to change vision and redirect the interpretive gaze, to place audiences in a position where they simply do not have to reckon with and live with that which is their Other. A symbolic and narrative purity is achieved by purging the political imaginary of mystery and ambiguity, and of terrors.

There is clearly a politics of consumption at work here as well. Just as the immediate aftermath of Y2K and 9/11 involved a wave of purchases of items (like gas masks and duct tape) thought to aid in creating safety, so too do fear's representations promote a kind of safety through consumption.[46] The pleasurable demonology in these religious worlds promises closure (and justice) to its audience, achieved through naming, containing, and displacing its Others. Yet it is in fear's detachment from, and rejection of, the politics of common purpose that its impact—in both its own effects and its embodiment of a tired moment—is of greatest concern. Its demons call into question some deeply held political fundamentals—pluralism, a commitment to procedure (including dialogue and mutual accountability or responsibility), the role of the state as guarantor of liberties and distributor of entitlements—and suggest to audiences that politics is dead, reason is a zombie, and at least there is life, both bloody and redemptive, in fear. While in some expressions of Christian apocalypticism, particularly the Johannine, there is a demand that one reject the world in order to remain pure, the religion of fear delivers—even amid its many combats—a kind of worldliness. It is a position defined by a fear not only of losing autonomy but of disconnection. And so it is a worldliness of creature comforts, as well as tests of faith, which critically engages political problems, only then to defer and deflect them. Even as NCR activists criticize the state, the courts, the laws, and other citizens—even as they engage resolutely with political matters—there is an overriding conviction that no human effort can fix what evil has broken. Individual hearts can be turned, but history is proceeding inevitably toward its holy doom. So, despite fear's extremely combative political demonology, its response is in many ways quietist. This resignation is unsettlingly apposite for our moment in American culture. Fear as politics challenges liberal pieties regarding rationalism, but substitutes for it an eternal judgment and watchfulness, the perfect political discourse for the PATRIOT Act era.

Commonly generalized fears (about food or airplanes or stalkers) are internalized and, occasionally, institutionalized. Yet the religion of fear represents an externalized fear as well, one which captures some long-standing developments in American politics. These discourses of safety and risk, comfort and fear, mark a detachment from the political process in some sense, a shift into criticism in exile. The distrust of politicians and a prevailing antistatism are prolonging American democracy's legitimation crisis by keeping reformist or progressive impulses in check. The religion of fear is a sign not only of the recrudescence of religious antistatism—part of these broader political processes—but also a contributor to the fear talk that is part of our political stasis. It is a rejection of New Deal statism but also in some way of democratic localism (other than small-scale "moral campaigns"). Ironically, then, fear's move from the margins to the mainstream has eventuated in the acquisition of some kind of representational or discursive power, but one that is achieved at the expense of the "genuinely" political.

As Furedi writes in his important *Politics of Fear*, "the exhaustion of public life is paralleled by the decline of the Enlightenment ideal of personhood," and "the interaction of the two provides the dynamic for the politics of fear."[47] When we read Chick's brimstone-laden denunciations of pluralism or LaHaye's deflection of change onto millennial hopes, or when we hear Larson's contention that purging our record collections serves as change enough or Roberts's demon guides claiming that political activism and governmental reform are tricks of the devil, we become part of an American public life where responses to insecurity and crippled politics consist of a rejection of reason, an abandonment of faith in reform, and a recourse to discourses of anger and panic. When judgment and renunciation replace empathy and pluralism, democratic culture cannot survive; conversations end, and the ongoing process of democratic argumentation is snipped off. Jeffrey Stout writes, "Given the fact that liberty and justice are constantly being threatened . . . the expression of anger, grief, and disappointment is essential to democratic politics."[48] Yet when the target of this anger is the democratic process itself, something is awry. As Stout continues, "[T]he sadistic desire, expressed in much apocalyptic, to imagine one's enemies cast into hellfire" is at odds with the mutual accountability required for a healthy political culture.[49]

Such responses are, according to Furedi, symptoms not only of ideological disputes but of "the absence of a clear alternative."[50] They effectively tell us "to become reconciled to life as it is" and consequently convey "a diminished sense of human potential."[51] Disconnected from institutions in which we have no trust, detached from political visions we are told have been exhausted, and continually encouraged (in everything from overt antipolitics to the triumph of "ironic" humor) to think of ourselves as disempowered, Americans encounter the religion of fear as a discourse that asserts authority, that promises the resolution of conflict and anxiety, that delivers one system of causality in the wake of reason's demise. Fear's apocalyptic judgment is summoned in these circumstances, its power nurtured in this climate of political exhaustion: the end of history comes not with a well-ordered society but with ash and thunderbolts.

I realize that this normative moment may have lost me the sympathy of some readers while gaining me the sympathy of others. For some academics, terms like "reason" might solicit disapproving clucks at my apparent lapse, since it is of course still de rigueur (after many tedious decades) to intone yet again that "reason" is simply a myth undergirding "Western hegemony." Such an observation has theoretical merit. But what does it yield politically? Standard academic strategies can obscure political life more than they clarify it. Academics write endlessly about the play of signifiers, the subtle counter-hegemonic practices of the subaltern, and the ways in which all discourses are mere effects of the social construction of "truth"—important arguments that have contributed to a supple and suspicious critical sensibility in the last half-century. And yet *homo academicus*—to use Pierre Bourdieu's term—continues to wonder why political life has become seemingly inoculated against reasoned argument and why core features of liberal democratic life have suffered such disrepute so rapidly. The lingua franca used by academics is in some ways the mirror of the Right's denunciation of reason and respect, a discourse that gives comfort to those we would challenge politically while also robbing us of our critical voice. So, by invoking these terms, I signal my awareness of these long debates but also my intention to defend these categories as political practices and norms, even as a hermeneutic of suspicion must be maintained. In dark times like these, this is the real radicalism and the real challenge.

This demonology sits uncomfortably with the fluid, interactive, dialogic politics at the heart of democracy: the religion of fear asks us to see not only political life but human existence as fixed and settled; it contends that a single, irrevocable choice (us or them, in or out, identity or a self adrift) can serve as a surrogate for the messy indeterminacy of public life; it pitches an explanatory canopy, a representational screen onto which all potential sources of distress can be projected. The vision of political life and history emerging from the religion of fear represents in some sense a rejection of the political in favor of the narrowly particularist. Political life, as represented in these creations, has little place for the contest of ideas, for reasoned dialogue, or for the messy, halting steps of democratic procedure. Instead, it proposes jeremiads as a surrogate for a politics of common purpose or shared dialogic or institutional principles. More than simply the articulation of difference within a common political framework, fear's politics presents its audiences with a false choice, insisting that public life will be guided by either values or amoral technocracy, by Christian virtue or heterodoxy and hedonism. It replaces, in political theorist Wendy Brown's apt distinction, "a galvanizing moral vision" with "a reproachful moralizing sensibility."[52] If academics and citizens alike will not name and criticize this demonology with the clarity that is our moral and political responsibility, then we have failed to respond not only to fear's challenge but to the crisis of legitimation in American political life.

The religion of fear has slowly constructed a frame through which public life is seen in terms of conflict rather than cooperation and dialogue, supplementing this with the conviction that basic structural features of political life are crippled. It is one thing to suggest that certain features of American democratic culture require renewed legitimation, or that extant understandings of political speech and participation can be insufficiently hospitable to religions. Yet to articulate grievances using the language of war, religious bigotry, and victimization marks a rejection of common purpose.[53] The growing power of such claims—articulated first in the sweaty exhortations of Chick tracts and now festooned throughout American megastores in LaHaye's books—is mirrored in the widespread detachment and apathy described above, something to which academic discourse may have unwittingly contributed. Nowhere in the religion of fear do we see suasion and reason, only ramparts manned and fingers pointed.

It is stating the obvious to acknowledge that political life involves struggles for power, but fear seeks its cultural power by denouncing the merits of the political. Unlike the projects of neo-Straussians like Norman Podhoretz, fear positions its demonology above the political, superseding the merely human, no longer in need of the compromises or long view of democracy, but only seeking contest and reward. The historical narrative that fear advances suggests that political concerns and debates can be addressed through habits of consumption, a shift in emotional valence, or participation in shared representations. These religio-political texts approach the shared space of American politics, in the apt words of a student of mine, "like beating the dog" to make it behave.[54] A politics articulated through visions of destruction, vengeance, punishment, and gore is one that, to put it mildly, signals that American public life is troubled. This approach to questions of democratic legitimacy, pluralism, public speech, and the role of religion in politics is no substitute for genuine political conversation and participation. Fear's representations advance a form of power that seeks to raise questions in order to confer legitimacy upon authors and sympathizers, while also suspending constructive political engagement to the authors' advantage as well. I am concerned, then, about the way this representational power mirrors and contributes to an already advanced state of degeneracy in American political cultures. This conception of powers should be challenged, but not in the name of supplanting it with some alternative, but equally narrow, conception of public life. Rather, fear calls attention to the need for alternate narratives of religion in public life, of pluralism and conversation. As part of public life, fear's political vision should be contested in the name of politics itself, with the goal of a reaffirmation of a democratic process allowing for the pursuit of reasonable compromises of principled differences. Americans have too often failed to see that these are the real issues in the culture wars.

The religion of fear's exemplars are public creations, representations meant for the entire sinning world, and I have interpreted them as combative interventions into a political process about which I have deep concerns and passions. Slowly, since the 1960s, the seeming outlandishness of its many claims has been reframed. The discourse now normalizes and naturalizes ideas that are antithetical to the kind of pluralism on which democracies thrive.[55] In criticizing them, I am not suggesting that fear's creators have no political right to articulate these ideas, that such representations should be banned from democratic society, that they constitute exceptions to the very pluralism I defend. Yet these entertainments, so clearly politicized and public, cannot expect to be insulated from the political process and hence from criticism.

Strangely, unavoidably, fear's creators are acting out of care and concern. Despite the richness of the fear and the combativeness of the politics, the religion of fear is concerned for the welfare of souls and seeks to champion "God's supervening grace against any human attempts to merit (earn) that grace."[56] What is so provocative about these creations is the coupling of sincere concern and violent imaginations. And this admixture stems, too, from the desire for power. This discourse may seem hyperbolic and improbable, but its architects are convinced that they are locked into a battle of absolutes, where those unaware that it rages on are its most likely victims; the stakes are pitched at this level of ultimacy, and the punishments too are eternal. As both nostalgic lament and angry rebuke, the religion of fear promises precisely that which it never delivers: a cause that can be contained, an end to the violence. The entertainments serve as templates for living in an unstable world. They represent a species of evangelicalism which, in the words of Christian Smith, "thrives on distinction, engagement, tension, conflict, and threat."[57] They articulate a specific set of religio-political convictions and self-imaginings, presenting them as true through the emotional resonances made possible in stories of hell and pain and evil. Such resonances reinforce identity, even as they provide audiences with the means to contest this very identity.

I fear that, in the endless echo chamber of American politics, these ideas resound too loudly. It is no surprise that what Michael Rogin calls our "national dream-life" is still overrun with demons, given the Gothic dispositions of our culture and our historic love affair with symbolic and real violence.[58] But what will we make of or do with these particular demons, whose increased presence in public life and commerce marks the triumph of a kind of political will that is hostile to certain basic features of democracy? Will audiences turn away in indifference? Will they appropriate and reinterpret these entertainments, undercutting the intentions of their authors? Or does the religion of fear simply confirm something about American life that is already true rather than representing some dangerous new turn?

The flat space of politics is given life in this fearful discourse, which excoriates and condemns the present in order to achieve a kind of symbolic power and authority. It draws energy away from reform, even as it perfectly captures American political ennui. Yet the religion of fear's messianic/demonic visions do not so much promise a new birth in the political sphere as they represent a continuation of a different kind of political order. Here, political reformers and those with faith in (or at least, like me, with a chastened hope for) the process are told that they have placed their moorings in a doomed culture, a doomed world. Peace and equality are not projects to be achieved through the messiness of political work but primarily through Christ's future return. The political exists merely as an arena in which to maintain control over discourse and through which to enjoy freedoms from illegitimate coercion by those deemed to be outsiders. In this narrative, America's providential history is a holding pattern which finds the righteous waiting at a distance for their redemption. Each warning, each call to conversion, each stentorian challenge to the demonic perpetuates rather than changes the discourse. This perpetuation promises that it engages political problems, by linking salvific joy with safety, justice with hegemony. But it requires nothing of us, other than to declare which side we are on. These tidings bode ill for American public life. And if it is not yet time to abandon all hope, it is past time to wonder whether we get the politics that we deserve.

Notes

Chapter 1

1. This term is commonly used in literature on religion and politics. It refers to a specific cluster of evangelical organizations that emerged in public life beginning in the 1970s. As Leo Ribuffo notes, the term "Christian Right" is misleading since there have been many periods of conservative Christian activism. Likewise, the term "religious Right" does not capture specifically Protestant sensibilities. So, while I occasionally use the term "Christian Right" for its felicity of phrasing, my focus is mostly on the period between the 1970s and the present, when both conservative Christian politics and evangelical popular culture have been ascendant.

2. I sometimes refer to this—for purposes of style—simply as *fear*. Some readers may wonder briefly about the discrepancy between the book's title and my focus in the text on *the* religion of fear. Simply put, while my argument and observations focus on a specific expression of religion of fear, it is my hope (as I write in this chapter and the conclusion) that my observations may prove fruitful in the broader context suggested by the title.

3. I use the term *representations* throughout, since it seems to capture the symbolic constructions of these entertainments in both their verbal and visual forms.

4. Lynn Schofield Clark, *From Angels to Aliens: Teenagers, the Media, and the Supernatural* (New York: Oxford University Press, 2003), very briefly discusses Keenan Roberts's Hell Houses. Amy Johnson Frykholm, *Rapture Culture: Left Behind in Evangelical America* (New York: Oxford University Press, 2004); Melani McAlister, "Prophecy, Politics, and the Popular: The *Left Behind* Series and Christian Fundamentalism's New World Order," *South Atlantic Quarterly* 102:4 (Fall 2003); and Glenn W. Shuck, *Marks of the Beast: The* Left Behind *Novels and the Struggle for Evangelical Identity* (New York: New York University Press, 2005), are fine studies of the *Left Behind* phenomenon, even if they—as I argue below—do not adequately capture the political resonances of the books.

5. See, among many others, Walter Capps, *The New Religious Right: Piety, Patriotism, and Politics* (Columbia: University of South Carolina Press, 1990); John Green, Mark Rozell, and Clyde Wilcox, eds., *The Christian Right in American Politics: Marching to the Millennium* (Washington, DC: Georgetown University Press, 2003); David S. Gutterman, *Prophetic Politics: Christian Social Movements and American Democracy* (Ithaca, NY: Cornell University Press, 2005); James Davison Hunter, *Culture Wars: The Struggle to Define America* (New York: Basic, 1992); Isaac Kramnick and R. Laurence Moore, *The Godless Constitution: A Moral Defense of the Secular State* (New York: Norton, 2005); William Martin, *With God on Our Side: The Rise of the Religious Right in America* (New York: Broadway, 1995); Matthew C. Moen, *The Transformation of the Christian Right* (Tuscaloosa: University of Alabama Press, 1992); Leo P. Ribuffo, *The Old Christian Right: The Protestant Far Right from the Great Depression to the Cold War* (Philadelphia: Temple

University Press, 1983); and Clyde Wilcox, *Onward Christian Soldiers: The Religious Right in American Politics* (Boulder, CO: Westview, 2006).

6. We see this interest in blogs like *The Revealer* (www.therevealer.org); in popular texts like Kevin Phillips, *American Theocracy: The Perils and Politics of Radical Religion, Oil, and Borrowed Money in the 21st Century* (New York: Viking, 2006); Michelle Goldberg, *Kingdom Coming: The Rise of Christian Nationalism* (New York: Norton, 2006); and in academic works like Randall Balmer, *Thy Kingdom Come: How the Religious Right Distorts the Faith and Threatens America: An Evangelical's Lament* (New York: Basic, 2006). See also Daniel Radosh's fine *Rapture Ready: Adventures in the Parallel Universe of Christian Pop Culture* (New York: Scribner's, 2008).

7. Edwin S. Gaustad, *Dissent in American Religion* (Chicago: University of Chicago Press, 1973), remains a benchmark study. See also Robert Bellah, *Varieties of Civil Religion* (New York: Harper & Row, 1980); Grace Kao and Jerome Copulsky, "The Pledge of Allegiance and the Meanings and Limits of Civil Religion," *Journal of the American Academy of Religion* 75:1 (2007): 121–149; and Andrew Sharks, *Civil Society, Civil Religion* (Oxford: Blackwell, 1995).

8. See, among many examples, David Chappell, *Stone of Hope: Prophetic Religion and the Death of Jim Crow* (Chapel Hill: University of North Carolina Press, 2004); Andrew Kohut et al., *The Diminishing Divide: The Changing Role of Religion in American Politics* (Washington, DC: Brookings Institution Press, 2000); Geoffrey Layman, *The Great Divide: Religious and Cultural Conflict in Party Politics* (New York: Columbia University Press, 2001); David C. Leege et al., *The Politics of Cultural Differences: Social Change and Voter Mobilization Strategies in the Post–New Deal Period* (Princeton, NJ: Princeton University Press, 2002); and Winnifred F. Sullivan, *The Impossibility of Religious Freedom* (Princeton, NJ: Princeton University Press, 2005).

9. See, for example, Richard King, *Orientalism and Religion: Postcolonial Theory, India, and "the Mystic East"* (New York: Routledge, 1999); and Russell McCutcheon, *Manufacturing Religion: The Discourse on Sui Generis Religion and the Politics of Nostalgia* (New York: Oxford University Press, 2003).

10. For insight into these transformations, consult Alan Brinkley, *The End of Reform: New Deal Liberalism in Recession and War* (New York: Vintage, 1995); José Casanova, *Public Religions and the Modern World* (Chicago: University of Chicago Press, 1994); E. J. Dionne, *Why Americans Hate Politics* (New York: Touchstone, 1991); William Greider, *Who Will Tell the People?* (New York: Touchstone, 1992); Paul Lyons, *New Left, New Right, and the Legacy of the Sixties* (Philadelphia: Temple University Press, 1996); and James Morone, *The Democratic Wish: Popular Participation and the Limits of American Government* (New Haven, CT: Yale University Press, 1990).

11. In addition to literature cited elsewhere, see D. G. Hart, *That Old-Time Religion in Modern America: Evangelical Protestantism in the Twentieth Century* (Chicago: Dee, 2002); Kenneth J. Heineman, *God Is a Conservative: Religion, Politics, and Morality in Contemporary America* (New York: New York University Press, 1998); and R. Laurence Moore, *Touchdown Jesus: The Mixing of the Sacred and the Secular in American History* (Louisville, KY: Westminster John Knox, 2007).

12. Sean McCloud notes that such languages of impurity and contagion can be located in nineteenth-century nativism and twentieth-century conflicts surrounding eugenics.

See McCloud, *Divine Hierarchies: Class in American Religion and Religious Studies* (Chapel Hill: University of North Carolina Press, 2007).

13. James Morone, *Hellfire Nation: The Politics of Sin in American History* (New Haven, CT: Yale University Press, 2003), p. x. As Morone points out, discourses of fear have not been exclusively repressive: abolitionists, among others, pounded pulpits righteously in describing the hell that awaited supporters of slavery.

14. Colleen McDannell, *Material Christianity: Religion and Popular Culture in America* (New Haven, CT: Yale University Press, 1995).

15. Personal communication, August 2006.

16. Paul Boyer, *When Time Shall Be No More: Prophecy Belief in Modern American Culture* (Cambridge, MA: Belknap, 1992).

17. See Brenda E. Brasher, *Give Me That Online Religion* (New Brunswick, NJ: Rutgers University Press, 2004); and Lorne L. Dawson and Douglas E. Cowan, eds., *Religion Online: Finding Faith on the Internet* (New York: Routledge, 2004).

18. See George Marsden, *Fundamentalism and American Culture: The Shaping of Twentieth Century Evangelicalism, 1870–1925* (New York: Oxford University Press, 1980).

19. It is worth noting that, in general, the religion of fear is a discourse wherein African Americans do not figure overmuch.

20. Andrew Greeley and Michael Hout, *The Truth about Conservative Christians: What They Think and Believe* (Chicago: University of Chicago Press, 2006), p. 1.

21. See, for example, David Bennett, *The Party of Fear: From Nativist Movements to the New Right in American History* (New York: Vintage, 1995); and John Mickelthwait and Adrian Woolridge, *The Right Nation: Why America Is Different* (New York: Penguin, 2005).

22. See Thomas A. Tweed, *Crossing and Dwelling: A Theory of Religion* (Cambridge, MA: Harvard University Press, 2006), p. 62.

23. See William E. Connolly, "The Evangelical-Capitalist Resonance Machine," *Political Theory* 33:6 (December 2005); and Gilles Deleuze and Felix Guattari, *A Thousand Plateaus: Capitalism and Schizophrenia* (Minneapolis: University of Minnesota Press, 1993).

24. William Reddy, *The Navigation of Feeling: A Framework for the History of Emotions* (Cambridge: Cambridge University Press, 2001), p. 129. See Michel Foucault, *The Order of Things: An Archaeology of the Human Sciences* (New York: Vintage, 1994); and Talal Asad, *Formations of the Secular: Christianity, Islam, and Modernity* (Palo Alto, CA: Stanford University Press, 2003).

25. Asad, *Formations of the Secular*, p. 25.

26. John Corrigan, "Introduction," in Corrigan, ed., *Religion and Emotion: Approaches and Interpretations* (New York: Oxford University Press, 2004). What Corrigan calls the universalist path is grounded in Charles Darwin's 1872 *The Expression of the Emotions in Man and Animals*. Structuralists rely on the universalist contention that structural similarities in social performance or moral codes enable comparisons of emotional depth and variety. More recently, there has been interest in the resources of biology and neuroscience, as in Pascal Boyer, *Religion Explained: The Evolutionary Origins of Religious Thought* (New York: Basic, 2001). Culturally oriented authors disagree about the extent to which selves are social constructs, but most agree that emotions—like human self-understandings, feelings, patterns of social interaction, and beliefs—are strongly influenced by culture and history.

27. See Arlie Russell Hochschild, *The Managed Heart: Commercialization of Human Feeling*, 2nd ed. (Berkeley: University of California Press, 2003); and Robert Fuller, *Wonder: From Emotion to Spirituality* (Chapel Hill: University of North Carolina Press, 2006).

28. Robert C. Roberts distinguishes between dispositional fears (linked to specific situations) and object-related fears (where "the object must be construed as aversive"). Fear is thus not one of Hume's "passions" but instead construes possibilities and probabilities in situations understood as risky. On this basis, Roberts distinguishes fear from anxiety (which is less tied to specific objects and possibilities), fright (which involves a more "dramatic aversive possibility"), dread (which "sees the aversive object not as present, but as inevitably approaching"), terror ("more or less paralyzing"), panic (specific spontaneous actions resulting from perceptions of aversion), horror (where aversion figures into one's perception in a way that is not tied into the situation's probability, e.g., one's horror upon seeing corpses), and being spooked (reacting to "the strange, the mysterious, the unknown"). Roberts, *Emotions: An Essay in Aid of Moral Psychology* (Cambridge: Cambridge University Press, 2003), pp. 193–202.

29. Christian Smith, *American Evangelicalism: Embattled and Thriving* (Chicago: University of Chicago Press, 1998), p. 95.

30. Quoted in Eric Lott, *Love and Theft: Blackface Minstrelsy and the American Working Class* (New York: Oxford University Press, 1995), p. 3.

31. Ibid., p. 6.

32. Julia Kristeva, *Powers of Horror: An Essay on Abjection* (New York: Columbia University Press, 1982). See also Bill Ellis's important *Raising the Devil: Satanism, New Religions, and the Media* (Lexington: University of Kentucky Press, 2000); and David Frankfurter, *Evil Incarnate: Rumors of Demonic Conspiracy and Satanic Abuse in History* (Princeton, NJ: Princeton University Press, 2006).

33. See David Chidester, *Authentic Fakes: Religion and American Popular Culture* (Berkeley: University of California Press, 2005); McDannell, *Material Christianity*; and David Morgan, *The Sacred Gaze: Religious Visual Culture in Theory and Practice* (Berkeley: University of California Press, 2005).

34. See David D. Hall, "What Is the Place of 'Experience' in Religious History?" *Religion and American Culture: A Journal of Interpretation* 13:2: 241–250. Exceptions include Sean McCloud, *Making the Religious Fringe: Exotics, Subversives, and Journalists, 1955–1993* (Chapel Hill: University of North Carolina Press, 2003); and Lynn Neal, *Romancing God: Evangelical Women and Inspirational Fiction* (Chapel Hill: University of North Carolina Press, 2006).

35. Lawrence W. Levine, *Highbrow Lowbrow: The Emergence of Cultural Hierarchy in America* (Cambridge, MA: Harvard University Press, 1988), p. 31.

36. Clark, *From Angels to Aliens*; Frykholm, *Rapture Culture*; and Heather Hendershot, *Shaking the World for Jesus: Media in Conservative Evangelical Culture* (Chicago: University of Chicago Press, 2004).

37. Quote is from www.chick.com/information/authors/chick.asp (accessed April 7, 2008).

38. Jeffrey Stout, *Democracy and Tradition* (Princeton, NJ: Princeton University Press, 2003).

Chapter 2

1. See, in particular, David L. Holmes, *The Faiths of the Founding Fathers* (New York: Oxford University Press, 2006); and Frank Lambert, *The Founding Fathers and the Place of Religion in America* (Princeton, NJ: Princeton University Press, 2006).

2. Quoted in John M. Murrin, "Religion and Politics in America from the First Settlements to the Civil War," in Mark Noll, ed., *Religion and American Politics* (New York: Oxford University Press, 1990).

3. See Timothy K. Beal, *Religion and Its Monsters* (New York: Routledge, 2002), p. 7. Similarly, Edward Ingebretsen shows how "[f]ear and dread . . . are traditional markers of divinity." Edward J. Ingebretsen, *At Stake: Monsters and the Rhetoric of Fear in Public Culture* (Chicago: University of Chicago Press, 2001), p. xiii.

4. See Corey Robin, *Fear: The History of a Political Idea* (New York: Oxford University Press, 2004).

5. John Hollander, "Fear Itself," *Social Research* 71:4 (Winter 2004): 874.

6. Beal, *Religion and Its Monsters*, p. 82.

7. David Hume, *Dialogues and Natural History of Religion*, ed. J. C. A. Gaskin (New York: Oxford University Press, 1998).

8. See Sigmund Freud, *The Future of an Illusion* (New York: Norton, 1989).

9. Rudolf Otto, from *The Idea of the Holy*, quoted in Carl Olson, ed., *Theory and Method in the Study of Religion: A Selection of Critical Readings* (Belmont, CA: Wadsworth, 2002), p. 109.

10. Harvey Whitehouse, "Rites of Terror: Emotion, Metaphor, and Memory in Melanese Initiation Cults," in John Corrigan, ed., *Religion and Emotion: Approaches and Interpretations* (New York: Oxford University Press, 2004), p. 133.

11. Henry James, *The Aspern Papers and the Turn of the Screw* (New York: Penguin, 1984), p. 148.

12. Barry Glassner, *The Culture of Fear: Why Americans Are Afraid of the Wrong Things* (New York: Basic, 1999), p. xi. Glassner shows how fear narratives direct attention away from facts through repetition, through rendering isolated incidents as trends, and through misdirection. See also Debbie Nathan and Michael Snedeker, *Satan's Silence: Ritual Abuse and the Making of a Modern American Witch Hunt* (New York: Basic, 1995); and Elaine Showalter, *Hystories: Hysterical Epidemics and Modern Media* (New York: Columbia University Press, 1998).

13. Ulrich Beck, *Risk Society: Towards a New Modernity* (London: Sage, 1992), p. 183.

14. Mary Douglas and Aaron Wildavsky, *Risk and Culture*, quoted in Glassner, *The Culture of Fear*, p. xxvi.

15. See David H. Bennett, *The Party of Fear: From Nativist Movements to the New Right in American History* (New York: Vintage, 1995); Morone, *Hellfire Nation*; Corey Robin, *Fear: The History of a Political Idea* (New York: Oxford University Press, 2004); and Michael Rogin, *Ronald Reagan: The Movie, and Other Essays in Political Demonology* (Berkeley: University of California Press, 1988).

16. On American conspiracy theory, see Michael Barkun, *A Culture of Conspiracy: Apocalyptic Visions in Contemporary America* (Berkeley: University of California Press, 2003); Gregory S. Camp, *Selling Fear: Conspiracy Theories and End-Times Paranoia* (Grand

Rapids, MI: Baker Book House, 1997); and Robert Goldberg, *Enemies Within: The Culture of Conspiracy in Modern America* (New Haven, CT: Yale University Press, 2001). René Girard, *The Scapegoat* (Baltimore, MD: Johns Hopkins University Press, 1989), remains a valuable resource.

17. Biological or epidemiological fears have proven to be remarkably resilient in American media, which suggests that a bevy of epidemics—from the bird flu to various super-viruses soon to awake from dormancy—is growing and intensifying. Not only do many fear discourses trade in biologized language (purity and contamination, or moral "decay" and "illnesses"), the focus on bio-dangers amplifies our sense of personal vulnerability. See Judith Walzer Leavitt and Lewis A. Leavitt, "After SARS: Fear and Its Uses," *Dissent* (Fall 2003): 54–58.

18. See Frank Furedi, *Politics of Fear: Beyond Left and Right* (New York: Continuum, 2005); Erich Goode and Nachman Ben-Yehuda, *Moral Panics: The Social Construction of Deviance* (Oxford: Blackwell, 1994); Brian Massumi, ed., *The Politics of Everyday Fear* (Minneapolis: University of Minnesota Press, 1993); Robin, *Fear;* and a special issue of the *Hedgehog Review* 5:3 (Fall 2003), entitled *Fear Itself.*

19. Robin, *Fear,* p. 162.

20. Leonie Huddy, "Fear and How It Works: Science and the Social Sciences," *Social Research* 71:4 (Winter 2004): 802.

21. Furedi, *Politics of Fear,* p. 3.

22. Randall Balmer, *Blessed Assurance: A History of Evangelicalism in America* (Boston: Beacon, 1999). See also Mark Noll, *A History of Christianity in the United States and Canada* (Grand Rapids, MI: Eerdmans, 1992).

23. See F. Ernest Stoeffler, *The Rise of Evangelical Pietism* (Leiden: Brill, 1971).

24. Balmer, *Blessed Assurance,* p. 27. See also Sydney E. Ahlstrom, *A Religious History of the American People* (New Haven, CT: Yale University Press, 1973); Jon Butler, *Awash in a Sea of Faith: Christianizing the American People* (Cambridge, MA: Harvard University Press, 1990); Nathan Hatch, *The Democratization of American Christianity* (New Haven, CT: Yale University Press, 1989); William G. McLoughlin, *Revivals, Awakenings, and Reform: An Essay on Religion and Social Change in America, 1607–1977* (Chicago: University of Chicago Press, 1980); and Harry Stout, *The Divine Dramatist: George Whitefield and the Rise of Modern Evangelicalism* (Grand Rapids, MI: Eerdmans, 1991).

25. See Richard J. Carwadine, *Evangelicals and Politics in Antebellum America* (New Haven, CT: Yale University Press, 1993); and Whitney Cross, *The Burned-Over District: The Social and Intellectual History of Enthusiastic Religion in Western New York, 1800–1850* (Ithaca, NY: Cornell University Press, 2006).

26. See Jack S. Blocker, *American Temperance Movements: Cycles of Reform* (Woodbridge, CT: Twayne, 1989); Bruce J. Evensen, *God's Man for the Gilded Age: Dwight L. Moody and the Rise of Modern Mass Evangelism* (New York: Oxford University Press, 2003); and Clifford Putney, *Muscular Christianity: Manhood and Sports in Protestant America, 1880–1920* (Cambridge, MA: Harvard University Press, 2003).

27. See Martin E. Marty, *Modern American Religion,* vol. 1: *The Irony of It All, 1893–1919* (Chicago: University of Chicago Press, 1997).

28. Andrew Greeley and Michael Hout, *The Truth about Conservative Christians: What They Think and Believe* (Chicago: University of Chicago Press, 2006), p. 22.

29. See Michael Kazin, *A Godly Hero: The Life of William Jennings Bryan* (New York: Knopf, 2006).

30. See George Marsden, *Fundamentalism and American Culture: The Shaping of Twentieth-Century Evangelicalism, 1870–1925* (New York: Oxford University Press, 1980); and Ernest Robert Sandeen, *The Roots of Fundamentalism: British and American Millenarianism, 1800–1930* (Grand Rapids, MI: Baker Book House, 1978).

31. This historiography is widely documented. See, among other sources, Joel A. Carpenter, *Revive Us Again: The Reawakening of American Fundamentalism* (New York: Oxford University Press, 1997).

32. See Robert Booth Fowler, *A New Engagement: Evangelical Political Thought, 1966–1976* (Grand Rapids, MI: Eerdmans, 1982); and Jon R. Stone, *On the Boundaries of Evangelicalism: The Postwar Evangelical Coalition* (New York: Palgrave Macmillan, 1997).

33. See Randall Balmer, *Mine Eyes Have Seen the Glory: A Journey into the Evangelical Subculture in America*, 3rd ed. (New York: Oxford University Press, 1989).

34. See Yvonne Chireau, "Supernaturalism," in Philip Goff and Paul Harvey, eds., *Themes in Religion and American Culture* (Chapel Hill: University of North Carolina Press, 2004); and Kenneth P. Minkema, "Possession, Witchcraft, and the Demonic in Puritan Religious Culture," in Colleen McDannell, ed., *Religions of the United States in Practice*, vol. 1 (Princeton, NJ: Princeton University Press, 2001), pp. 366–401. On European religion and demonology, Keith Thomas, *Religion and the Decline of Magic: Studies in Popular Beliefs in Sixteenth and Seventeenth Century England* (New York: Oxford University Press, 1997), remains authoritative.

35. Joyce Carol Oates, "Introduction," in Oates, ed., *American Gothic Tales* (New York: Plume, 1996), pp. 1–2.

36. Quoted in Jack Morgan, *The Biology of Horror: Gothic Literature and Film* (Carbondale: Southern Illinois University Press, 2002), p. 118.

37. Julius Rubin, *Religious Melancholy and Protestant Experience in America* (New York: Oxford University Press, 1994), p. 54. See Sacvan Bercovitch, *The Puritan Origins of the American Self* (New Haven, CT: Yale University Press, 1975); and Perry Miller, *The New England Mind: From Colony to Province* (Cambridge, MA: Belknap, 1983).

38. Cited in Edward J. Ingebretsen, *Maps of Heaven, Maps of Hell: Religious Terror as Memory from the Puritans to Stephen King* (New York: Sharpe, 1996), p. 16. See also Victor Sage, *Horror Fiction in the Protestant Tradition* (New York: Palgrave Macmillan, 1988).

39. Lynn Schofield Clark describes an evangelical "dark side" that drives interest in specific kinds of non-evangelical pop culture. *From Angels to Aliens*, pp. 13–14.

40. See Ann Taves, *Fits, Trances, and Visions: Experiencing Religion and Explaining Experience from Wesley to James* (Princeton, NJ: Princeton University Press, 1999). See also Butler, *Awash in a Sea of Faith*; Timothy D. Hall, *Contested Boundaries: Itinerancy and the Reshaping of the Colonial American Religious World* (Durham, NC: Duke University Press, 1994); and Leigh Eric Schmidt, *Hearing Things: Religion, Illusion, and the American Enlightenment* (Cambridge, MA: Harvard University Press, 2002).

41. See Mechal Sobel, *Teach Me Dreams: The Search for Self in the Revolutionary Era* (Princeton, NJ: Princeton University Press, 2000).

42. Quoted in ibid., p. 22.

43. This tendency of Edwards's is most remarkable in his image, from "Sinners in the Hands of Angry God," of the lone sinner—undeserving of God's love—being held over the pits of hell much as one might hold a "loathsome insect." See Frank Lambert, *Inventing the "Great Awakening"* (Princeton, NJ: Princeton University Press, 2001).

44. Elisabeth Bronfen, *The Knotted Subject: Hysteria and Its Discontents* (Princeton, NJ: Princeton University Press, 1998), p. 139.

45. See John Putnam Demos, *Entertaining Satan: Witchcraft and the Culture of Early New England* (New York: Oxford University Press, 1982).

46. Christine Leigh Heyrman, *Southern Cross: The Beginnings of the Bible Belt* (Chapel Hill: University of North Carolina Press, 1997), is a superb study of the evangelical southern Gothic.

47. See Butler, *Awash in a Sea of Faith*; Hatch, *The Democratization of American Christianity*; and McLoughlin, *Revivals, Awakenings, and Reform*.

48. See Heyrman, *Southern Cross*, p. 65.

49. Marina Warner, *No Go the Bogeyman: Scaring, Lulling, and Making Mock* (New York: Farrar, Straus and Giroux, 1998), p. 3.

50. Ibid., p. 161.

51. Bernard McGinn, *Antichrist: Two Thousand Years of the Human Fascination with Evil* (New York: Columbia University Press, 2000), p. 2. See also Robert Fuller, *Naming the Antichrist: The History of an American Obsession* (New York: Oxford University Press, 1995).

52. See Paul Boyer, *When Time Shall Be No More: Prophecy Belief in Modern American Culture* (Cambridge, MA: Belknap, 1992); Arthur Lyons, *Satan Wants You* (New York: Mysterious, 1989); and Eugen Weber, *Apocalypses: Prophecies, Cults, and Millennial Beliefs through the Ages* (Cambridge, MA: Harvard University Press, 1999).

53. See Mitchell B. Merback, *The Thief, the Cross, and the Wheel: Pain and the Spectacle of Punishment in Medieval and Renaissance Europe* (Chicago: University of Chicago Press, 1999). My thanks to Winnifred Sullivan for this reference.

54. Fuller, *Naming the Antichrist*, p. 52.

55. See Walter Kendrick, *The Thrill of Fear: 250 Years of Scary Entertainment* (New York: Grove Weidenfeld, 1991), p. 79. Also see Noel Carroll, *The Philosophy of Horror; or, The Paradoxes of the Heart* (New York: Routledge, 1990).

56. Edward J. Ingebretsen, S.J. *Maps of Heaven, Maps of Hell: Religious Terror as Memory from the Puritans to Stephen King* (Armonk, NY: Sharpe, 1996), p. 79.

57. See David J. Skal, *The Monster Show: A Cultural History of Horror*, rev. ed. (New York: Faber & Faber, 2001); and Terry Heller, *The Delights of Terror: An Aesthetics of the Tale of Terror* (Urbana: University of Illinois Press, 1987).

58. The narrative roots of monsters are, as interpreters like Beal and Ingebretsen show, somewhat surprising: the *monstrum* was originally understood as a divine messenger of sorts, as befits its derivation from the Latin *monstrare*, meaning "to show" or "to warn." See Beal, *Religion and Its Monsters*; and Ingebretsen, *At Stake*.

59. Ingebretsen, *At Stake*, p. 43.

60. Quoted in ibid., p. 29.

61. See Skal, *The Monster Show*, pp. 248–250.

62. See Peter Gardella and Colleen McDannell, "Catholic Horror: *The Exorcist* (1973)," in Colleen McDannell, ed., *Catholics in the Movies* (New York: Oxford University

Press, 2007); and Judith Halberstam, *Skin Shows: Gothic Horror and the Technology of Monsters* (Durham, NC: Duke University Press, 1995).

63. Warner, *No Go the Bogeyman*, p. 4.

64. Sissela Bok, *Mayhem: Violence as Public Entertainment* (Reading, MA: Perseus, 1998), provides an interesting account of such contemporary fascinations.

65. See Philip Greven, *The Protestant Temperament: Patterns of Child-Rearing, Religious Experience, and the Self in Early America* (New York: New American Library, 1979); and Marjorie Heins, *Not in Front of the Children: "Indecency," Censorship, and the Innocence of Youth* (New York: Hill & Wang, 2001).

66. Prominent NCR figure James Dobson, founder of Focus on the Family, has engaged these issues (most famously in his 1970 *Dare to Discipline*) as a means to combat what he perceives as the United States' long slide into cultural permissiveness. See Colleen McDannell, "Beyond Dr. Dobson: Women, Girls, and Focus on the Family," in Margaret Lamberts Bendroth and Virginia Lieson Brereton, eds., *Women and Twentieth-Century Protestantism* (Champaign-Urbana: University of Illinois Press, 2002), pp. 112–131.

67. Hart, *That Old-Time Religion*, pp. 172–174.

68. For example, R. Laurence Moore describes—in *Selling God: American Religion in the Marketplace of Culture* (New York: Oxford University Press, 1994)—debates about the use of "entertainments" in sermons, the use of advertising in evangelization, and whether or not popular literary techniques should be appropriated in pastoral literature.

69. Evangelical radio culture, which first emerged in the 1920s, remains quite vital today, thriving not only in a milieu dominated by conservative broadcasting (which, despite well-known protestations, constitutes some 75 percent of the radio market) but also serving as a key means by which evangelicals connect with one another (through listening, through call-in programs, and through the dissemination of key ideas and information). See Paul Apostolidis, *Stations of the Cross: Adorno and Christian Right Radio* (Durham, NC: Duke University Press, 2000).

70. Heather Hendershot, *Shaking the World for Jesus: Media and Conservative Evangelical Culture* (Chicago: University of Chicago Press, 2004), p. 8.

71. My thanks to Joe Yandle for describing this to me. Personal conversation, December 2006.

72. Hendershot, *Shaking the World for Jesus*, p. 10. See also Joel Carpenter, "Youth for Christ and the New Evangelicals," in D. G. Hart, ed., *Reckoning with the Past* (Grand Rapids, MI: Baker, 1995), pp. 354–375; and Alan Cooperman, "Coming Soon to a Church Near You," *Washington Post* (October 21, 2005), p. A01.

73. John Mickelthwait and Adrian Woolridge, *The Right Nation: Conservative Power in America* (New York: Penguin, 2004), p. 12.

74. Quoted in Stewart M. Hoover, "Introduction," in Stewart M. Hoover and Lynn Schofield Clark, eds., *Practicing Religion in the Age of Media: Explorations in Media, Religion, and Culture* (New York: Columbia University Press, 2002), p. 3.

75. See Pierre Bourdieu, *Distinction: A Social Critique of the Judgement of Taste* (Cambridge, MA: Harvard University Press, 2002).

76. Wade Clark Roof, *Spiritual Marketplace: Baby Boomers and the Remaking of American Religion* (Princeton, NJ: Princeton University Press, 1999), p. 49.

77. See Henri Lefebvre, *Critique of Everyday Life*, vols. 1–3 (New York: Verso, 2002); Theodor W. Adorno, *The Culture Industry* (New York: Brunner-Routledge, 2001); Guy

Debord, *The Society of the Spectacle* (New York: Zone, 1995); and Jean Baudrillard, *Simulacra and Simulacrum* (Ann Arbor: University of Michigan Press, 1995). See also Anne Norton, *Republic of Signs: Liberal Theory and Popular Culture* (Chicago: University of Chicago Press, 1993).

78. See Roof, *Spiritual Marketplace*, p. 79.

79. I borrow the term *mediascape* from Arjun Appadurai, *Modernity at Large: Cultural Dimensions of Globalization* (Minneapolis: University of Minnesota Press, 1996).

80. Roof, *Spiritual Marketplace*, p. 87.

81. Vincent J. Miller, *Consuming Religion: Christian Faith and Practice in a Consumer Culture* (New York: Continuum, 2003), p. 156.

82. See John Fiske, *Understanding Popular Culture* (New York: Routledge, 1989).

83. Lynn Schofield Clark, *From Angels to Aliens: Teenagers, the Media, and the Supernatural* (New York: Oxford University Press, 2003), p. 13.

Chapter 3

1. Throughout this chapter, all tract and comic quotations are—unless otherwise indicated—from the work directly under discussion. All tracts still in print are available for viewing online at www.chick.com.

2. The organization's Web site, www.godspeaks.org, claims that the group was inspired following the September 11, 2001, terrorist attacks, and one of its initial 9/11 memorials is available for viewing at www.wuzupgod.com/sept11/sept11_memorial_worldwide.html.

3. I learned during my research for this chapter that many of Chick's most ardent fans—whether they are religious supporters and fellow travelers or simply lovers of American kitsch—are extremely well versed in comics and fantasy literature of all sorts. Consider, for example, that Chick's name even surfaced in a September 2002 usenet discussion devoted to the old Gothic horror TV program *Dark Shadows* (alt.tv.dark_shadows). One poster in this discussion, David Windhorst, noted that Chick's tracts "look a lot like the nudie and erotica booklets that preceded Hefner as adolescent male rites-of-passage."

4. See "Christian Comic Books Hope to Soar," *Christianity Today* 37:8 (July 19, 1993): 48.

5. Recent writings on visual culture and religion—most notably by David Morgan, Sally Promey, and Stewart Hoover—are the obvious exceptions. Even here, however, there is surprisingly little discussion of comic art (even though Chick's tracts are actually preserved in the Smithsonian). Elsewhere in the humanities, attention to the visual is seen in Roland Barthes, *The Responsibility of Forms: Critical Essays on Music, Art, and Representation* (Berkeley: University of California Press, 1991); Martin Jay, *Downcast Eyes: The Denigration of Vision in Twentieth Century French Thought* (Berkeley: University of California Press, 1994); and W. J. T. Mitchell, *Picture Theory: Essays on Verbal and Visual Representation* (Chicago: University of Chicago Press, 1995). I have found particularly useful Larry J. Reynolds, "American Cultural Iconography," in Larry J. Reynolds and Gordon Hunter, eds., *National Imaginaries, American Identities: The Cultural Work of American Iconography* (Princeton, NJ: Princeton University Press, 2000), pp. 3–28.

6. The incredible, Hieronymus Bosch–like paintings of McKendree Robbins Long (the "picture painter of the apocalypse") deserve mention here. Long, a native of States-

ville, North Carolina, painted grisly scenes of hell populated by anonymous fornicators and renowned skeptics like Marx, Freud, and Nietzsche. I thank North Carolina Museum of Art director Lawrence Wheeler and curator David Steel for their invitation to the Long exhibit in October 2002 and also for the gracious gift of a book of Long's works. On illustrated Bibles, see Paul Gutjahr, *An American Bible: A History of the Good Book in the United States, 1777–1880* (Palo Alto, CA: Stanford University Press, 2001); Colleen McDannell, *The Christian Home in Victorian America, 1840–1900* (Bloomington: Indiana University Press, 1994); and Peter Wosh, *Spreading the Word: The Bible Business in Nineteenth Century America* (Ithaca, NY: Cornell University Press, 1994).

7. See Bernhard Lang, *Sacred Games: A History of Christian Worship* (New Haven, CT: Yale University Press, 1997); and Mark Noll, *A History of Christianity in the United States and Canada* (Grand Rapids, MI: Eerdmans, 1992).

8. Quoted in R. Laurence Moore, *Selling God: American Religion in the Marketplace of Culture* (New York: Oxford University Press, 1994), p. 21.

9. Mark Dery, "Fear and Loathing: The Gospel According to Jack," *Village Voice Literary Supplement* (April–May 1999), p. 2. See also Pagan Kennedy, "All about Evil: Jack Chick's Ire and Brimstone," *Village Voice Literary Supplement* (April 1992).

10. Moore, *Selling God*, p. 27.

11. See Michael Kammen, *American Culture, American Tastes: Social Change in the Twentieth Century* (New York: Knopf, 1999).

12. See, among other sources, Stewart M. Hoover, "Visual Religion in Media Culture," in David Morgan and Sally M. Promey, eds., *The Visual Culture of American Religions* (Berkeley: University of California Press, 2001), pp. 146–159; David Morgan, *Visual Piety: A History and Theory of Popular Religious Images* (Berkeley: University of California Press, 1998); Morgan, *Protestants and Pictures: Religion, Visual Culture, and the Age of American Mass Production* (New York: Oxford University Press, 1999); Sally M. Promey, "Religion in Plain View: The Public Display of Religion in the United States," *AAR Religious Studies News* (October 2005): 22; and Promey, "Taste Matters: The Visual Practice of Liberal Protestantism, 1940–1965," in Laurie Maffly-Kipp, Leigh E. Schmidt, and Mark Valeri, eds., *Practicing Protestants: Histories of Christian Life in America, 1630–1965* (Baltimore, MD: Johns Hopkins University Press, 2006).

13. Morgan, *History and Theory of Popular Religious Images*, p. 3.

14. Ibid., p. 17.

15. My thanks to Sarah L. Burns for these helpful illustrations and examples. Burns, *Painting the Dark Side: Art and the Gothic Imagination in Nineteenth Century America* (Berkeley: University of California Press, 2004), is a wonderful study of the Gothic impulse in nineteenth-century American art.

16. See Hoover, "Visual Religion in Media Culture."

17. He is often described as resembling the late actor Slim Pickens. Those who have met Chick insist that his associates and fans love him, in the words of Richard Lee, as they would "a Grandpa, a curmudgeon...but in this case Grandpa has sophisticated computers with a potential audience of 400 million!" Personal conversation, May 2007. See Raeburn's *The Imp*, no. 2 (self-published, Chicago, 1997); Michael Colton, "Cartooning for Christ: Jack Chick's Religious Comics," *Brill's Content* 2:9 (November 1999); and Richard von Busack, "Comic Book Theology: Unearthing Famed Christian Artist Jack Chick," *Metroactive Weekly* (San Jose, CA) (April 2, 1998). Finally, there are a few small

sound files—whose authenticity cannot be verified—of Chick's voice at http://member .newsguy.com/~sjames/chick/chick.htm.

18. Several fake obituaries have occurred over the years. See, for example, alt.-freemasonry, June 27, 2001.

19. Chicago cultural critic Dan Raeburn's zine *The Imp* has an issue devoted to Chick, where he speculates that Chick's firsthand observation of wartime carnage shaped his aptitude for cartoon gore.

20. See Robert Ito's article "Fear Factor," *L.A. Magazine* (May 2003), among the very few substantive sources.

21. Richard Lee, personal conversation, May 2007. Lee speculated that Chick would have few, if any, problems with the messages underwriting LaHaye's novels. Lee also noted that, despite his disinclination to associate with an institution, Chick has regarded several individual preachers favorably: John Hagee of TBN, Adrian Rogers, and Jimmy Swaggart ("other than the sexual immorality").

22. "Jack Chick," in Randall Balmer, ed., *Encyclopedia of Evangelicalism*, rev. ed. (Waco, TX: Baylor University Press, 2004), p. 152.

23. Raeburn explains that, according to Chick's recollection, "Chinese spies . . . had observed American children engrossed by comic books with titles like *Scream* and *Evil*" and learned thereby of comics' power. Raeburn, *The Imp*, no. 2, p. 5.

24. Conservative preacher Billy James Hargis—founder of Christian Crusade in the 1950s—was similarly inspired to conduct counter-flyovers from which Bibles would be rained upon the Chinese countryside.

25. See Dery, "Fear and Loathing."

26. The Reverend Richard Lee, a gracious man and serious comics historian, contrasted Chick's style with that of his associate Fred T. Carter, whose style Lee perceptively likened to that of *Prince Valiant* creator Hal Foster.

27. Lee, personal conversation, May 2007.

28. Raeburn suggests that one way to read Chick's work is as a compendium of portraits showing the slaughter of the innocents, from Herod to the present.

29. Quoted in Ito, "Fear Factor."

30. Raeburn, *The Imp*, no. 2, p. 27.

31. Ibid., p. 6.

32. Ito, "Fear Factor." "Devil Doll," an early issue of Clowes's well-regarded comic *Eightball*, was a Chick parody.

33. Post by "ronnie" on rec.arts.comics.strips, May 16, 2003. Second recollection from "kcaj" on alt.christnet, August 3, 2002.

34. The tracts have also been translated into more than 100 languages.

35. Interestingly, one of the only commercial outlets for purchasing Chick's tracts other than Chick Publications itself and certain Christian retail stores is Relapse Records, a heavy metal specialty store in Philadelphia.

36. Kurt Kuersteiner, *The Unofficial Guide to the Art of Jack T. Chick: Chick Tracts, Crusader Comics, and Battle Cry Newspapers* (Atglen, PA: Schiffer, 2004), p. 7. Kuersteiner also claims that Peace Corps workers have unexpectedly stumbled across Chick tracts in the remotest of villages.

37. Carter is also known as a painter of Afrocentric Christian images. See Morgan, *History and Theory of Popular Religious Images*, pp. 37–38.

38. See Ito, "Fear Factor." Raeburn calls Chick's work "hardcore Protestant por-nography." Raeburn, *The Imp*, no. 2, p. 9.

39. Ito, "Fear Factor." See Mark Noll, *The Eclipse of Old Hostilities between and the Potential for New Strife among Catholics and Protestants since Vatican II* (South Bend, IN: Cushwa Center, 1985), p. 94.

40. These examples are documented in Ito, "Fear Factor." On Todd's allegations in particular, see "The Legend(s) of John Todd," *Christianity Today* (February 2, 1979); and Darryl E. Hicks and David A. Lewis, *The Todd Phenomenon* (Harrison, AR: New Leaf, 1979), which documents many of the conspiracies alleged by Todd, including an "Illu-minati plan for world takeover" and a plan to destroy America from within by making every citizen "totally dependent on the Rothschilds."

41. Kuersteiner, *Art of Jack T. Chick*, p. 8. Chick also publishes full-length books by many of his consultants and associates. Lee briefly met Brown, whom he recalls as "flaky" and possibly suffering from a "chemical imbalance." Personal conversation, May 2007.

42. Rockney defends Chick's aversion to interviews by claiming that they "take him away from what he needs to do." Another Chick assistant, Amy, explained, "Mr. Chick doesn't really have time for interviews." See Colin Berry, "The Mystery of Chick Comics," *Wired* 5:2 (February 1997): 76.

43. Jimmy Akin of *Defensor Fidei* (an online blog focused on Catholicism and culture) was invited to the premiere of Chick's *Light of the World* (http://members.cox.net/jim-myakin/x-meet-jack-chick.htm) in Ontario, California, in 2003. Chick's official Web site has several illustrative clips of the film.

44. See John Kendall, "Lurid Comic Books Attack Beliefs of Most Religions," *Los Angeles Times* (January 25, 1981); and Kate DeSmet, "Comic Book Series Gets No Laugh from Christian Groups," *Detroit News* (April 8, 1989), p. 17A. Chick's tracts were a necessary part of Frank Stromberg's compendium, *The Comics Go to Hell: A Visual History of the Devil in Comics* (Seattle, WA: Fantagraphics, 2005).

45. Open letter from Chick, May 15, 1997. Quoted in Kuersteiner, *Art of Jack T. Chick*, p. 17.

46. Raeburn, *The Imp*, no. 2, p. 8.

47. Open letter from Chick, 1983. Quoted in Kuersteiner, *Art of Jack T. Chick*, p. 157.

48. Neopagan blogger Kerr Culuhain is an eager reader and critic of Chick's. See www.witchvox.com.

49. *Battle Cry*'s inception was in 1983, when the scandals surrounding Chick sym-pathizer Alberto Rivera began to peak.

50. The most frequently cited of these texts includes Raymond Williams, *The Country and the City* (New York: Oxford University Press, 1975); Lawrence Grossberg, *Bringing It All Back Home: Essays on Cultural Studies* (Durham, NC: Duke University Press, 1997); and Dick Hebdige, *Subculture: The Meaning of Style* (New York: Routledge, 1981). One notable study of comics is Scott Bukatman, *Matters of Gravity: Special Effects and Su-permen in the 20th Century* (Durham, NC: Duke University Press, 2003).

51. See Rebecca Edwards, *New Spirits: Americans in the Gilded Age, 1865–1905* (New York: Oxford University Press, 2005).

52. Michael Chabon, *The Adventures of Kavalier and Klay* (New York: Picador, 2000), is an extraordinary fictional meditation on this period and this medium. See also Gerard

Jones, *Men of Tomorrow: Geeks, Gangsters and the Birth of the Comic Book* (New York: Basic, 2004).

53. Bradford Wright, *Comic Book Nation: The Transformation of Youth Culture in America* (Baltimore, MD: Johns Hopkins University Press, 2001), pp. 9–11.

54. Ibid., p. 24.

55. Ibid., p. 37.

56. For a reading of similar impulses elsewhere in post–World War II popular culture, see Melani McAlister, *Epic Encounters: Culture, Media, and U.S. Interests in the Middle East since 1945* (Berkeley: University of California Press, 2005).

57. Quoted in Wright, *Comic Book Nation*, p. 27.

58. Ibid., pp. 89–90.

59. Quoted in ibid., pp. 94–95.

60. See Ron Mann's documentary *Comic Book Confidential* (Homevision, 1988).

61. David J. Skal, *The Monster Show: A Cultural History of Horror*, rev. ed. (New York: Faber & Faber, 2001), p. 230.

62. See Charles Hatfield, *Alternative Comics: An Emerging Literature* (Jackson: University of Mississippi Press, 2005).

63. The two most informative studies of the aesthetic particulars of the medium are the late Will Eisner's *Comics and Sequential Art: Principles and Practice of the World's Most Popular Art Form* (Tamarac, FL: Poorhouse, 1985); and Scott McCloud, *Understanding Comics: The Invisible Art* (New York: HarperCollins, 1993).

64. Wright, *Comic Book Nation*, p. xv. Wright's formulation is indebted to John G. Cawelti.

65. See Matthew P. McAllister, Edward H. Sewell, Jr., and Ian Gordon, "Introduction," in McAllister, Sewell, and Gordon, eds., *Comics and Ideology*, vol. 2 (New York: Peter Lang, 2001), p. 3. See also Matthew J. Pustz, *Comic Book Culture: Fanboys and True Believers* (Jackson: University of Mississippi Press, 1999).

66. See, for example, Douglas Kellner, *Media Culture: Cultural Studies, Identity and Politics between the Modern and the Postmodern* (New York: Routledge, 1995).

67. Robert B. Fowler, in his *The World of Jack T. Chick* (San Francisco, CA: Last Gasp, 2001), describes Chick's work as underground because of the control Chick exercises over his creations, the tight-knit distribution channels that Chick uses, and the extremely personal vision reflected in his works. Fowler claims to have consulted artist Robert Crumb, who purportedly agrees. Raeburn says, more succinctly, that "Chick is punk as fuck." Raeburn, *The Imp*, no. 2, p. 19.

68. Nearly all of Chick's tracts are viewable on www.chick.com, an invaluable resource for anyone interested in reading back issues of *Battle Cry* or *The Crusaders*. My account of his tract work is indebted to the painstaking work of Kuersteiner, Raeburn, and Fowler. See also the online "Jack Chick Museum of Fine Art," a sometimes ironic and sometimes sincere forum for discussing Chick sightings, interviews, memories of first exposure to tracts, and so forth (www.chickcomics.com).

69. See, for example, "Religious Leaflets Stir Anger at Schools," *San Diego Union-Tribune* (November 18, 2000).

70. See Bennett, *The Party of Fear*, p. 346; Mark S. Massa, S.J., "The New and Old Anti-Catholicism and the Analogical Imagination," *Theological Studies* 62 (2001): 549–570; and Mark Weitzman, "The Inverted Image: Antisemitism and Anti-Catholicism on

the Internet," paper delivered October 18–19, 1998, at the Fifth Biennial Conference on Christianity and the Holocaust, Rider University. Reprinted at www.bc.edu/research/cjl/meta-elements/texts/cjrelations/resources/articles/weitzman.htm. See William Shea, *The Lion and the Lamb: Evangelicals and Catholics in America* (New York: Oxford University Press, 2004).

71. Chick, *Smokescreens*, p. 5. See also William A. Donohue, "A Survey of Chick Publications," *Catalyst* (October 1996).

72. Amy Kuebelbeck, "Under Fire? Is Anti-Catholic Sentiment Increasing? Some Say Yes and Declare They're Not Going to Take It Anymore," *Los Angeles Times* (September 9, 1991), p. E1.

73. See Ted Anthony, "Where Comics and Christianity Meet," *Associated Press* (July 19, 1998).

74. See http://personal.bellsouth.net/w/p/wputnam3/Chick%20Tract.htm.

75. See the posts of "Tim" on alt.religion.christian.roman-catholic, April 19, 2000.

76. There was a rancorous argument on alt.religion.christian.baptist (August 23–24, 2001), concerning the legitimacy of Chick's anti-Catholic historiography. The debate was rekindled during May 2003, when a Chick defender ("John W") referred to the accuracy of Chick's history of Constantine's creation of the "Roman Catholic cult" and specifically his founding of the Jesuits, whose aim he claims was to rid the earth of "true Christians."

77. Post by "Elaine" on alt.christnet, August 19, 2002. See, among many other examples, Mike Cuellar's claims (on bit.listserv.christia, May 15, 1995) that "just because Chick said things in a wrong manner that [doesn't mean that] what he said was wrong." See also Roger Pearse's defense of Chick on alt.talk.creationism, January 8–9, 2004.

78. Chick's thoughts on Bible translations may be read at www.chick.com/information/bibleversions.

79. Kuersteiner's Web site (http://members.aol.com/monsterwax/chick.html) contains brief video clips of Rivera preaching.

80. Gary Metz, "Jack Chick's Anti-Catholic Alberto Comic Book Is Exposed as a Fraud," *Christianity Today* (March 13, 1981). See also "Booksellers' Group May Expel Chick," *Christianity Today* (October 23, 1981).

81. See also www.catholic.com/library/sr_chick_tracts.asp.

82. See Yaakov Ariel, *Evangelizing the Chosen People: Missions to the Jews in America, 1880–2000* (Chapel Hill: University of North Carolina Press, 2000); and Timothy P. Weber, *On the Road to Armageddon: How Evangelicals Became Israel's Best Friend* (Grand Rapids, MI: Baker Academic, 2005).

83. Fowler, *The World of Jack T. Chick*, pp. 2–37.

84. Regular tracts, however, are often translated for distribution in Asian countries and usually feature slightly altered drawings, including characters redrawn with slanted eyes.

85. See Akin, *Defensor Fidei* (http://members.cox.net/jimmyakin/x-meet-jack-chick.htm); and www.chick.com.

86. See Philip Jenkins, *Mystics and Messiahs: Cults and New Religions in American History* (New York: Oxford University Press, 2000).

87. In the March–April 1987 issue of *Battle Cry*, Larry Roundtree's editorial, "Rise of the Cults and Demise of America," articulated this kind of broad-brush social criticism and called for the restoration of a Christian social order.

88. The November 1997 Blessed Be and Meet Me in DC neopagan march in Washington, DC, generated several counterprotests. Activist Tammy Ritchie sought to mobilize "concerned Christian" responses to the march and, it was alleged, Ritchie got much of her information on Wiccans from Chick tracts. See an exchange on alt.religion.christian, September 26, 1997.

89. Open letter from Jack Chick, December 23, 1996. Quoted in Kuersteiner, *Art of Jack T. Chick*, p. 160.

90. Thanks to Sean McCloud for this anecdote.

91. *Battle Cry* has published many pieces attacking the *Harry Potter* phenomenon; see "Good Ol' Harry's at It Again" (July–August 2003), "Here Comes Harry" (March–April 2001), "Harry Potter: 'Making Evil Look Innocent'" (November–December 2001), and "Soul Winners Spook Satan on Halloween" (September–October 2003).

92. Open letter from Jack Chick, November 1, 2001. Quoted in Kuersteiner, *Art of Jack T. Chick*, p. 161.

93. See alt.fan.harry-potter (May 10, 2002).

94. Quoted in Kuersteiner, *Art of Jack T. Chick*, p. 210.

95. On Muscular Christianity, see David S. Gutterman, *Prophetic Politics: Christian Social Movements and American Democracy* (Ithaca, NY: Cornell University Press, 2005); and Clifford Putney, *Muscular Christianity: Manhood and Sports in Protestant America, 1880–1920* (Cambridge, MA: Harvard University Press, 2003). On Promise Keepers, see John P. Bartkowski, *The Promise Keepers: Servants, Soldiers, and Godly Men* (New Brunswick, NJ: Rutgers University Press, 2004).

96. An army veteran, posting under the name Dweezil Dwarftosser (on www.triangle.general.com, October 2005), recalls seeing Chick tracts while stationed in Germany in 1975. Tracts would frequently be left in barracks, and some personnel apparently began carrying tracts with them when they traveled, for purposes of dissemination.

97. Debates about the merits of rock music continue to cite Chick. See, for example, a February 1995 exchange on rec.music.christian.

98. This, as Kuersteiner points out, is the fate of many Chick characters who convert from lives of sin. See Kuersteiner, *Art of Jack T. Chick*, p. 113.

99. See "New England News Briefs," *Boston Globe* (April 7, 1999), p. C8; and Chris Bull and John Gallagher, *Perfect Enemies: The Religious Right, the Gay Movement, and the Politics of the 1990s* (New York: Crown, 1997).

100. Kuersteiner, *Art of Jack T. Chick*, p. 64.

101. Douglas Nicholson on alt.religion.christian.calvary-chapel, June 13, 1997.

102. See http://members.tripod.com/monsterwax/chickmemories5.html.

103. See Michael Lienesch, *In the Beginning: Fundamentalism, the Scopes Trial, and the Making of the Antievolution Movement* (Chapel Hill: University of North Carolina Press, 2007).

104. Jay Hosler, a cartoonist who defends evolutionary science against detractors, was inspired by Chick. See www.npr.org/templates/story/story.php?storyId=4495248.

105. Personal conversation, May 2007.

106. See Ralph Reed, "What Do Religious Conservatives Really Want?" in Michael Cromartie, ed., *Disciples and Democracy: Religious Conservatives and the Future of American Politics* (Washington, DC: Ethics and Public Policy Center, 1994), pp. 1–15.

107. See Lefebvre, *Critique of Everyday Life*, vol. 2 (New York: Verso, 2002); and Andy Merrifield, *Henry Lefebvre: A Critical Introduction* (New York: Routledge, 2006). Lefebvre's initial approach was primarily anthropological, since he sought to break from conventional Marxist approaches to social life that were disproportionately oriented to systems. Lefebvre influenced de Certeau, and his focus on the urban-rural axis of modernism would also preoccupy Raymond Williams and other theorists of the Birmingham school.

108. Michel de Certeau, *The Practice of Everyday Life* (Berkeley: University of California Press, 2002), p. 2.

109. Jennifer Davis, personal conversation, April 2007.

110. David Dagenhart, personal conversation, October 2006.

111. Michel de Certeau, "Reading as Poaching," in A. Bennet, ed., *Readers and Reading* (New York: Longman, 1995), pp. 150–163, 151.

112. Personal conversation, May 2007.

113. See John Fiske, *Understanding Popular Culture* (New York: Routledge, 1989).

114. Ernie DiMicco, Jr., reported this anecdote on alt.atheism, February 14, 2001. Several loving and lurid adaptations and visualizations of Chick tracts can be viewed on YouTube. There have also been several Web sites featuring parodies of Chick tracts, most of which have been shut down over the years under pressure from Chick's lawyers. In 1995, San Francisco's Hypnodrome featured a dramatic production entitled *Chick Habit*, a kind of Grand Guignol tribute to Chick. See www.suck.com, December 18, 1995.

115. Talal Asad, *Formations of the Secular: Christianity, Islam, and Modernity* (Palo Alto, CA: Stanford University Press, 2003).

116. Richard Lee, personal conversation, May 2007.

117. See Skal, *The Monster Show*, pp. 230–231.

118. Personal conversation, May 2007.

119. Ibid.

120. Raeburn, *The Imp*, no. 2, p. 9.

121. Richard Lee, personal conversation, May 2007.

122. Raeburn, *The Imp*, no. 2, p. 27.

123. Ibid., p. 29.

124. Ibid., p. 6.

125. Akin, *Defensor Fidei* (http://members.cox.net/jimmyakin/x-meet-jack-chick.htm).

126. See the exchange on alt.comics.jack-chick, June 1999. Self-described conservative evangelical Rob Henzel, who converted partly under Chick's influence, announced this criticism. Chick was defended by Carol Ragle and "tonyg."

127. "Is This Hate?" *Battle Cry* (May–June 1996).

128. Personal conversation, May 2007.

Chapter 4

1. See R. Laurence Moore, *Selling God: American Religion in the Marketplace of Culture* (New York: Oxford University Press, 1994); and Moore, *Touchdown Jesus: The Mixing of the Sacred and the Secular in American History* (Louisville, KY: Westminster John Knox, 2007).

2. Quoted in Michael Moynihan and Didrik Søderlind, *Lords of Chaos: The Bloody Rise of the Satanic Metal Underground* (Los Angeles: Feral House, 2003), p. 2.

3. See Martin Cloonan and Reebee Garofolo, eds., *Policing Pop* (Philadelphia: Temple University Press, 2003); Maria Korpe, ed., *Shoot the Singer! Music Censorship Today* (London: Zed, 2004); and David Trend, *The Myth of Media Violence: A Critical Introduction* (Oxford: Blackwell, 2006).

4. Quoted in Peter Blecha, *Taboo Tunes: A History of Banned Bands and Censored Songs* (San Francisco, CA: Backbeat, 2004), p. 1.

5. Efforts to censor music used for commercial ends are increasingly common. For example, the American Family Association lobbied to have Pepsi ads featuring Madonna's "Like a Prayer" removed from television; the beef industry boycotted singer k. d. lang after the musician spoke out against factory farming and slaughterhouse practices; and Ford Motors withdrew ads from the *New Yorker* after the magazine printed apparently offensive Nine Inch Nails lyrics.

6. Blecha, *Taboo Tunes*, pp. 39–41. One Christian anti-rock tome purports to cover much of this history. See David Cloud, *Rock Music vs. the God of the Bible* (Port Huron, MI: Way of Life Literature, 2000).

7. See Mark Anthony Neal, *What the Music Said: Black Popular Music and Black Public Culture* (New York: Routledge, 1998).

8. Blecha, *Taboo Tunes*, p. 45.

9. Quoted in Linda Martin and Kerry Segrave, *Anti-Rock: The Opposition to Rock 'n' Roll* (New York: Da Capo, 1993), p. 183.

10. Cited in ibid., p. 46.

11. Ibid., p. 46.

12. David Noebel, *Rhythm, Riots, and Revolution*, quoted in Johnny Marr, "Christ, Communists, and Rock 'n' Roll: Anti-Rock 'n' Roll Books," available at www.wfmu.org/LCD/18/antirock.html.

13. Ian Christe, personal communication, July 2007.

14. Bob Larson, *Rock & Roll: The Devil's Diversion* (McCook, NB: Larson, 1970). Also see Jon Trott's whistle-blowing piece "Bob Larson's Ministry under Scrutiny," *Cornerstone* 21:100 (1993).

15. Larson, *Rock & Roll*, p. 115.

16. Blecha, *Taboo Tunes*, p. 51. The song played backward is reputed to say "source of the devil."

17. Eric Nuzum, *Parental Advisory: Music Censorship in America* (New York: Perennial, 2001), p. 15.

18. See an illustrative exchange on rec.music.christian, October 1998.

19. Jacob Aranza, *Backward Masking Unmasked: Backward Satanic Messages of Rock and Roll Exposed* (Shreveport, LA: Huntington House, 1983), p. 43.

20. Ibid., p. 1.

21. Ibid., p. 2.

22. Comment by Mike S. Medintz on misc.activism.militia, February 2, 1996.

23. Steve Bonta, "Is It 'Only Rock 'n' Roll'?" *New American* 18:7 (April 8, 2002), online at www.newamerican.com (accessed March 17, 2007).

24. Quoted in David Konow, *Bang Your Head: The Rise and Fall of Heavy Metal Music* (New York: Three Rivers, 2002), p. 218.

25. Christe told me that he is convinced of an economic subtext to both the PMRC hearings and the RIAA hearings in the 1990s: "[t]he PMRC in particular represented congressional outrage during a time that the entertainment industry desperately needed government support for various taxes and levies on emerging technology—VCRs and cassette tapes. The RIAA agreed to warning labels, and got what it wanted from Congress." Personal communication, July 2007.

26. Zappa later arranged recordings of the proceedings into pieces on his record *Frank Zappa vs. the Mothers of Prevention.*

27. Quoted in Nuzum, *Parental Advisory,* p. 19. Ling's recollections of these events can be found at www.revjeff.typepad.com.

28. Quoted in Nuzum, *Parental Advisory,* p. 23.

29. Quoted in ibid., p. 11.

30. Both quotes from Blecha, *Taboo Tunes,* p. 54.

31. Jeff Godwin, *Dancing with Demons: The Music's Real Master* (Chino, CA: Chick, 1988), p. 19.

32. Ibid., pp. 30–31.

33. See Ian Christe, *Sound of the Beast: The Complete Headbanging History of Heavy Metal* (New York: HarperCollins, 2003), p. 294. On homosexual "conversions," see Tanya Erzen, *Straight to Jesus: Sexual and Christian Conversions in the Ex-Gay Movement* (Berkeley: University of California Press, 2006). A useful Web site chronicling many music censorship initiatives is www.roc.org.

34. See Mathieu Deflem, "Rap, Rock, and Censorship: Popular Culture and the Technologies of Justice," paper presented at the Law and Society Association annual meeting, Chicago, May 1993 (rev. March 2001), available at www.cas.sc.edu/socy/faculty/deflem/zzcens97.htm. See also www.talk2action.org/story/2006/5/10/112924/148.

35. Aranza, *Backward Masking Unmasked,* p. 25.

36. Ibid., p. 26.

37. Bob Larson, *Rock: For Those Who Listen to the Words and Don't Like What They Hear* (Wheaton, IL: Tyndale House, 1983), p. 8.

38. Ibid., p. 14.

39. Ibid., p. 15.

40. Aranza, *Backward Masking Unmasked,* p. 45.

41. Larson, *Rock,* p. 19.

42. Ibid., p. 21.

43. On bit.listserv.christia, June 3, 2000, "Samuele Bacchiocchi" advances such claims.

44. Godwin, *Dancing with Demons,* pp. 14–15.

45. Ibid., p. 25.

46. Ibid., pp. 37–39.

47. Jeff Godwin, *Devil's Disciples: The Truth about Rock Music* (Chino, CA: Chick, 1986), p. 204.

48. Ibid., p. 159.

49. Bob Larson, *Hippies, Hindus and Rock & Roll* (Carol Stream, IL: Creation House, 1972), p. 9. See also *Larson's Book of Cults* (Wheaton, IL: Tyndale House, 1989).

50. Larson, *Hippies,* pp. 13–16.

51. Ibid., p. 63.

52. Ibid., p. 31.

53. Ibid., pp. 51, 68, and 52.

54. Larson, *Rock*, p. 71.

55. Rebecca Brown, one of Jack Chick's primary resources for a time, has also written about the dangers of rock. She sees her demonological exploration as an extension of investigations into rock. Since his anti-rock criticisms resounded loudly with allegations about Satanic ritual abuse (advanced by other critics like Mike Warnke, Lauren Stratford, and Greg Reid) in the 1980s, Larson has come to focus heavily on exorcisms in his ministry, performing them publicly (he claims to have performed over 6,000 in ninety countries since the 1980s) at his Spiritual Freedom Conferences. See David Yonke, "Pastor Feels Called to Fight Demons," *Toledo Blade* (February 11, 2006).

56. Larson, *Rock*, p. 44.

57. Ibid., pp. 32–42. Aranza focuses specifically on the inside cover of Earth, Wind & Fire's *All 'n All*, which he denounces for its portrayal of "different occultic beings on the same level as the cross of Christ." Aranza, *Backward Masking Unmasked*, p. 57.

58. Larson, *Talk Back* radio (May 17, 2006).

59. *Talk Back* radio (February 16–March 22, 2006).

60. Aranza, *Backward Masking Unmasked*, p. 12.

61. Godwin, *Dancing with Demons*, pp. 1, 8.

62. Ibid., p. 16.

63. Ibid., p. 12.

64. Ibid., p. 189.

65. Ibid., pp. 89, 186.

66. See Michael K. Haynes, *The God of Rock: A Christian Perspective of Rock Music* (Lindale, TX: Haynes, 1982); D. L. Michelson, *Rock Music: Careful or Carnal* (Orlando, FL: Christ for the World, 1975); and William J. Schaefer, *Rock Music: Where It's Been, What It Means, Where It's Going* (Minneapolis, MN: Augsbury, 1972).

67. The myriad threads on rec.music.christian are replete with reminiscences of seminars given between the 1970s and the present at evangelical and Pentecostal churches. Younger posters frequently aver that this discourse is still thriving. For example, "na-mirillon" writes, "I quit attending Del City (OK) 1st Assembly of God because they condoned record/CD/tape/poster/whatever burning." April 2000, rec.music.christian. A useful overview and illustrative counterpoint is David Naugle's talk "Christianity and Rock & Roll," delivered in the spring of 2004 at Dallas Baptist University. Naugle enumerates a number of contemporary ministries, including Gainesville, Florida's Real 2 Real Ministries and Brunswick, Ohio's Chalmers Music Seminars, both of which are active in publishing and lecturing. The text is available online at www.dbu.edu/naugle/symposium_sp04.htm.

68. The term was apparently first used in a music review by Lester Bangs, reporting on a concert by Detroit's MC5.

69. Robert Walser, *Running with the Devil: Power, Gender, and Madness in Heavy Metal Music* (Hanover, NH: Wesleyan University Press/University Press of New England, 1993), p. 8.

70. Ibid., p. 3.

71. Examples include the shoeless Paul McCartney on the cover of *Abbey Road*, Jim Morrison's famous quip "You're drinking with Number 3," and the supposition that

Courtney Love had Kurt Cobain "whacked" (according to Il Duce, lead singer of the "rape rock" band the Mentors, in the documentary *Kurt and Courtney*). See Dale Sherman, *Urban Legends of Rock & Roll* (New York: Collector's Guide, 2003).

72. See http://www2.memlane.com/jmilner/stairwaybackwards.htm.

73. Black Sabbath has actually been called "the first Catholic rock band." Lester Bangs, "Bring Your Mother to the Gas Chamber," *Creem* (June 1972).

74. Osbourne recalls, "We were living in Birmingham. Drizzly rain, no shoes on my feet. And I thought 'This shit is for the rest of my life. ' And I put the radio on and there's some guy singing, 'If you want to go to San Francisco, be sure to wear a flower in your hair.' I thought, 'This is bollocks, the only flower I am likely to wear is on my fucking grave.' " See *Blabbermouth*: www.roadrunnerrecords.com/blabbermouth.net/news.aspx?mode=Article&newsitemID=73358.

75. One potent rumor had it that the band's special one-shot Marvel Comics publication had been printed with a portion of band members' blood in the printing ink itself.

76. The NWOBHM broadly included Judas Priest, Iron Maiden, Saxon, Motörhead, and Angel Witch (along with Australian act AC/DC), which aimed to return metal to its loud and decadent roots. In so doing, many of the bands were highly influenced by punk rock. Hair metal was inspired by the partying ethos of West Coast bands like Van Halen, and this genre became commercially dominant between the early 1980s and mid-1990s. Its primary representatives included Poison, Winger, Great White, Dokken, Cinderella, Skid Row, and Bon Jovi.

77. Fusing the instrumental virtuosity of the NWOBHM with the speed and aggression of hardcore punk, thrash metal bands like Metallica, Megadeth, Slayer, and New York's Anthrax followed the examples of Motörhead and Iron Maiden, while also taking inspiration from American post-punk bands like Black Flag, the Dead Kennedys, and especially the horror-obsessed Misfits.

78. Black metal emphasized technical virtuosity, a sense of Gothic melodrama, and a virulently anti-Christian streak. Early black metal bands like Mercyful Fate produced concept albums focusing on demons, hauntings, and Satanic rituals, establishing a tradition embraced by later groups such as Celtic Frost, Kreator, Mayhem, Cradle of Filth, Enslaved, and others. Less overtly associated with Satanism were death metal and grindcore, both of which were more directly inspired by the speed and energy of hardcore. Death and grind put virtuosity into the service of creating impossibly fast songs. Some bands, like England's Napalm Death and Carcass, often focused on sociopolitical matters, where others—such as Death, Deicide, and Obituary—penned songs about disembodied corpses, serial murders, and revenge fantasies.

79. Variations can be as seemingly esoteric as the Egyptological death metal championed by South Carolina's Nile. Math bands like Botch, the Dillinger Escape Plan, and Mastodon play music whose technical complexity recalls King Crimson or Frank Zappa more than Black Sabbath. Its counterpart, doom, ranges from the loping heaviness of St. Vitus and Electric Wizard to the hour-long feedback drones of Sunn0))), Earth, Boris, and Corrupted.

80. Jeffrey Jensen Arnett, *Metal Heads: Heavy Metal Music and Adolescent Alienation* (Boulder, CO: Westview, 1996), p. 4.

81. Ibid., p. 25.

82. Ibid., p. 69.

83. Walser, *Running with the Devil*, p. x.

84. Moynihan and Søderlind, *Lords of Chaos*, p. 6.

85. Quoted in Christopher M. Moreman, "Devil Music and the Great Beast: Ozzy Osbourne, Aleister Crowley, and the Christian Right," *Journal of Religion and Popular Culture* 5 (Fall 2003): 1–17, 4.

86. Quoted in Konow, *Bang Your Head*, p. 10.

87. Quoted in Deena Weinstein, *Heavy Metal: The Music and Its Culture* (New York: Da Capo, 2000), p. 1.

88. Walser, *Running with the Devil*, p. 142.

89. Christe, *Sound of the Beast*, p. 292.

90. Good accounts of both cases can be found in Stan Soocher, *They Fought the Law: Rock Music Goes to Court* (New York: Schirmer, 1998); and in Christe, *Sound of the Beast*. Anthropologist Sam Dunn's documentary *Metal: A Headbanger's Journey* (Warner Video, 2006) elaborates on the links between moral/religious criticism and metal's resurgent popularity. See also David Van Taylor, *Dream Deceivers* (PBS, 1992), a documentary covering the second of these two court cases, and a Christian investigative report entitled "Youth Suicide Fantasy—Does Their Music Make Them Do It?" (www.avgeeks.com/pivot/entry.php?id=106).

91. Bob Larson, *Satanism: The Seduction of America's Youth* (Nashville, TN: Thomas Nelson, 1989), pp. 9, 72.

92. Ibid., p. 10.

93. Ibid., p. 12.

94. Personal communication, July 2007.

95. Larson, *Satanism*, pp. 13, 17.

96. Ibid., pp. 14–15.

97. Ibid., p. 73.

98. Ibid., p. 29.

99. Ibid., p. 81.

100. Poster "DubleUD40" wrote about these recordings on alt.fan.bob-larson, December 15, 1998. "Ranger57" wrote about the Dallas event on rec.music.christian, July 3, 1998.

101. Ian Christe, personal communication, July 2007.

102. Swick post on rec.music.christian, June 23, 1998.

103. "My Dinner with Bob Larson: Interview with Boyd Rice," by Brother Randall, in *Snake Oil*, no. 2 (self-published zine, 1994). Photographs of the two together are available at www.boydrice.com/gallery/friends_gallery/pages/boyd_larson_gillmore.html.

104. Larson, *Satanism*, p. 77.

105. Quoted in Blecha, *Taboo Tunes*, p. 48.

106. Ibid., p. 57.

107. Nuzum, *Parental Advisory*, p. 127.

108. Blecha, *Taboo Tunes*, p. 57.

109. Joe Berlinger and Bruce Sinofsky, dirs., *Paradise Lost: The Child Murders at Robin Hood Hills* (HBO, 1996).

110. Many of my students over the years have described similar tales from their own experiences, in one case even reporting that a high school outside of Louisville, Kentucky,

insisted on see-through or mesh backpacks in order to facilitate security checks. My thanks to Colin Hiltner and Elizabeth Tamer in particular.

111. Albert Mudrian, personal communication, July 2007. Mudrian also noted that Wal-Mart, for reasons he cannot determine, will not stock his magazine.

112. Raffi Khatchadourian, "Azzam the American: The Making of an Al Qaeda Homegrown," *New Yorker* (January 22, 2007). In early 2007, it was revealed that, among the many methods of torture and coercion used at Guantanamo Bay's military prison, some interrogators had forced prisoners to listen to black metal for hours at a time. See Dan Eggen, "FBI Reports Duct-Taping, 'Baptizing' at Guantanamo," *Washington Post* (January 3, 2007).

113. Sarah Pike's provocative paper "After Columbine: Demonic Teens on the Internet, God's Martyrs in the Headlines" (presented at the annual meeting of the American Academy of Religion, November 2001) has been very helpful to my thinking here.

114. Nuzum, *Parental Advisory*, p. 48. Presumably, Waliszewski had in mind a 1998 Jonesboro, Arkansas, case where a student who purportedly liked rap went on a shooting spree. Similar claims arose in 2004 after a nightclub fire in Warwick, Rhode Island, during a Great White concert and following the Columbus, Ohio, shooting of guitarist "Dimebag" Darrell Abbott, which generated renewed concern about the dangers and violence associated with heavy metal. Dimebag's shooting was also the occasion for William Grim's editorial "Aesthetics of Hate" (on www.iconoclast.ca), which described metal fans as "ignorant, semi-human barbarians." He wrote, "The squalor, inhumanity, filth (both in the metaphorical and hygienic senses), depravity, ugliness and ignorance of everything that heavy metal represents ([l]ike rap, I cannot use the noble term music in a description of heavy metal) creates a mindset among its devotees in which Mr. Abbott's assassination was an event that was all but waiting to happen."

115. Nuzum, *Parental Advisory*, p. 126.

116. Ibid., p. 199.

117. Ibid., p. 200.

118. Quoted in Christe, *Sound of the Beast*, p. 293. Interestingly, such claims have recently spread to the world of video games. I am indebted to my former student Alex King for directing me to a Columbine video game that was (briefly) available for online play. See http://games.slashdot.org/article.pl?sid=06/05/16/1847229 and www .columbinegame.com. The 2007 Virginia Tech shooting also spawned an online video game. See www.news.com.au/dailytelegraph/story/0,22049,21743188–5001021,00.html.

119. The suggestive statement that I have used for this section's heading was made by my former student Brian Hagen Collins. I am indebted to Brian not only for this phrase but also for much excellent musical advice.

120. See Greg Tate, *Flyboy in the Buttermilk: Essays on Contemporary America* (New York: Simon & Schuster, 1992).

121. There are important terminological distinctions between rap and hip-hop. Throughout, I use the term *rap* as a category denoting both relevant stylistic distinctions and the larger cultural impact of hip-hop music.

122. Nelson George, *Hip Hop America* (New York: Penguin, 1998), p. 35. See also Jeff Chang, *Can't Stop, Won't Stop: A History of the Hip-Hop Generation* (New York: Picador, 2005).

123. See S. H. Fernando, Jr., "Back in the Day: 1975–1979," in Alan Light, ed., *The Vibe History of Hip Hop* (New York: Three Rivers, 1999).

124. John Szwed, "The Real Old School," in ibid., p. 4.

125. Ibid. See also Samuel Floyd's outstanding *The Power of Black Music: Interpreting Its History from Africa to the United States* (New York: Oxford University Press, 1996).

126. George, *Hip Hop America*, p. vii.

127. Ibid., p. xi.

128. Labels like Sugar Hill and Tommy Boy Records were central to the music's advancement, as were club meeting places like Danceteria.

129. George, *Hip Hop America*, p. 5. See also Tricia Rose, *Black Noise: Rap Music and Black Culture in Contemporary America* (Hanover, NH: Wesleyan University Press/ University Press of New England, 1994), p. 22.

130. The second wave of rap included established artists like Kurtis Blow and Run DMC (whose "Sucker MCs" was a popular early single) but also Cold Crush Brothers, Whodini, and Fatback.

131. The Def Jam label facilitated the commercial crossover that garnered significant nationwide attention for the first time. Along with the emergence of superstars LL Cool J and Eric B. & Rakim, Run DMC's rendition of Aerosmith's "Walk This Way" and the Beastie Boys' *License to Ill* were embraced by white suburbanites.

132. See Bakari Kitwana, *Why White Kids Love Hip Hop: Wangstas, Wiggers, Wannabes, and the New Reality of Race in America* (New York: Basic Civitas, 2005).

133. *Freebasing* refers to cocaine that has been boiled and then dropped into cold water, where it congeals into the material known as "freebase." *Crack* refers to small pieces that are broken off of freebase (named for the crackling sound made when it is put to flame). See George, *Hip Hop America*, p. 40.

134. Ibid., p. 42.

135. See George Lipsitz, *Time Passages: Collective Memory and American Popular Culture* (Minneapolis: University of Minnesota Press, 2001); and Richard Slotkin, *Gunfighter Nation: The Myth of the Frontier in Twentieth Century America*, new ed. (Norman: University of Oklahoma Press, 1998).

136. See Robert George, "Spirits in the Material World: The Soul in Rap Music," at www.beliefnet.com/story/41/story_4151_1.html; and Anthony B. Pinn, *Noise and Spirit: The Religious and Spiritual Sensibilities of Rap Music* (New York: New York University Press, 2003).

137. See, for example, James William Gibson, *Warrior Dreams: Violence and Manhood in Post-Vietnam America* (New York: Hill & Wang, 1994).

138. Both "Pac" and "Biggie," as they are referred to by fans, were killed in gunplay. They are both regarded as martyr figures by rap fans and artists alike.

139. George calls Campbell "hip hop's Willie Horton" (*Hip Hop America*, p. 183). Interestingly, Henry Louis Gates testified for the defense at Campbell's trial, effectively inverting standard modes of criticism by valorizing rap's form (with its link to historical forms of oral culture) over its content.

140. Griff's numerous anti-Semitic comments first came to public attention in 1988 and 1989. See Robert Christgau, "The Shit Storm," at www.robertchristgau.com/xg/ music/pe-law.php. On the controversial Body Count episode, see Christopher Sieving,

"Cop Out? The Media, 'Cop Killer, ' and the De-racialization of Black Rage," *Journal of Communication Studies* 22:4 (October 1998): 334–353.

141. Eithne Quinn, *Nuthin' but a "G" Thang: The Culture and Commerce of Gangsta Rap* (New York: Columbia University Press, 2005), p. 3. Tricia Rose also explores these dimensions of rap's critical impulse quite effectively.

142. Ibid., p. 12.

143. NWA, "Niggaz 4 Life," *Efil4zaggin* (Ruthless Records, 1991); Wu-Tang Clan, "Protect Ya Neck," *Enter the Wu-Tang (36 Chambers)* (BMG, 1993); Notorious B.I.G., "Ready to Die," *Ready to Die* (Bad Boy, 1994); and Ice Cube, "Now I Gotta Wet'Cha," *The Predator* (Priority Records, 1992).

144. Adam Krims, *Rap Music and the Poetics of Identity* (Cambridge: Cambridge University Press, 2000), p. 39.

145. Ibid., p. 81.

146. Nuzum, *Parental Advisory*, p. 8.

147. Quoted in Szwed, "The Real Old School," p. 6.

148. Blecha, *Taboo Tunes*, p. 126.

149. Rose, *Black Noise*, p. 131.

150. Quoted in ibid., p. 137. Panic has accrued to rock concerts dating back to the 1950s. See Martin and Segrave, *Anti-Rock.*

151. Quoted in Alan Light, "Public Enemy," in Light, ed., *The Vibe History of Hip Hop*, p. 168.

152. Glassner, *The Culture of Fear*, p. 122.

153. Positive rap like De La Soul and Arrested Development flourished briefly in the early 1990s, in contrast with the gangsta norm. While this moment passed quickly, independent and experimental rap has flourished since then, in bands both popular (The Roots, Jurassic 5, and Blackalicious) and marginal (cLOUDDEAD, Cannibal Ox, El-P, Mike Ladd, and Dälek).

154. Nuzum, *Parental Advisory*, p. 113.

155. See Blecha, *Taboo Tunes*, p. 128; and Christe, *Sound of the Beast*, p. 301.

156. See, for example, "In Your Face," *Focus on the Family Magazine* (September 1996), p. 11.

157. Nuzum, *Parental Advisory*, p. 110. See Blecha, *Taboo Tunes*, pp. 173–174.

158. Blecha, *Taboo Tunes*, p. 173.

159. See Hazel Trice Edney, "Imus Aftermath: Black Leaders Vow Protest of Rap Industry," *Black Press USA* (June 18, 2007). See also Matt Taibbi's caustic "The Low Post: The Imus Sanction," *Rolling Stone* (April 18, 2007); and a provocative roundtable discussion "Is Rap Racist?" *Salon* (April 18, 2007).

160. Godwin, *Dancing with Demons*, pp. 117–118.

161. Ibid., p. 119.

162. Ibid., p. 121.

163. Ibid., p. 124.

164. Ibid., p. 130.

165. Post by "forevernitefan" on alt.fan.bob-larson, March 11, 2006.

166. Quoted in Nuzum, *Parental Advisory*, p. 198.

167. For a telling survey of these events, see Glassner, *The Culture of Fear*, pp. 121–127 and 240–242.

168. Rose, *Black Noise*, p. 5.

169. Ibid., p. 12. This point is made in Amy Binder, "Constructing Racial Rhetoric: Media Depictions of Harm in Heavy Metal and Rap Music," *American Sociological Review* 58:6 (1993): 753–768. See also Michael O. Emerson and Christian Smith, *Divided by Faith: Evangelical Religion and the Problem of Race in America* (New York: Oxford University Press, 2001), p. 15.

170. The words used as the heading for this section are emblazoned on the back cover of Fletcher A. Brothers, *The Rock Report* (Lancaster, PA: Starburst, 1987).

171. *Larson's Book of Rock* (Wheaton, IL: Tyndale House, 1987), pp. 55–56.

172. Post by "don" on wpg.politics, April 2000.

173. Tom Beaujour, personal conversation, July 2007.

174. Albert Mudrian, personal communication, July 2007.

175. See a discussion of this possibility on alt.religion.christian, July 2003.

176. See Watkins's essay "Christian Rock: Blessing or Blasphemy" at www .av1611.org/crock.html.

177. Jennifer Davis, personal conversation, April 2007. There is, so far, little scholarship on these musical genres. I recommend Eileen Luhr's excellent "Metal Missionaries to the Nation: Christian Heavy Metal Music, 'Family Values,' and Youth Culture, 1984– 1994," *American Quarterly* (March 2005). On CCM, see Andrew Beaujon, *Body Piercing Saved My Life: Inside the Phenomenon of Christian Rock* (New York: Da Capo, 2006); Judith Bosman, "Christian Message, Secular Messengers," *New York Times* (April 26, 2006); Mark Joseph, *Faith, God and Rock & Roll* (London: Sanctuary, 2003); and Kelefa Sanneh, "Christian Rock and Mainstream Music Move Closer Together," *New York Times* (April 27, 2006).

178. See this piece at www.freedomministries.org.uk/godwin/hippies.shtml. This Web site is a rich general resource for Christian anti-rock writings, audio and video files, and so forth.

179. Godwin, *Devil's Disciples*, p. 343.

180. Post by "Scholar and Fool" on rec.music.christian, January 17, 1997. "Scholar and Fool" also boasted (on the same forum, October 18, 1995) that "Jeff cuts right to the chase."

181. Among many examples, see how these debates played out on rec.music.christian during April 1994, January 1997 (with a subdebate about Christian metal in particular), and January 2000.

182. See Arnett, *Metal Heads*, p. 31.

183. In addition to Peters, consult these two contemporary expressions: www.jesus-is-savior.com/Evils%20in%20America/devils_music_no_effect.htm and http://64.233.179 .104/search?q=cache:OQ_cLOMpr6UJ:english.sdaglobal.org/dnl/bacchi/books/rockroll .pdf.

184. Binder, "Constructing Racial Rhetoric," p. 754.

185. Ibid., p. 755.

186. For example, Brothers insists that Bruce Springsteen's "I'm on Fire"—whose opening line asks "Hey little girl, is your Daddy home?"—is about "Pedo molestation." See Brothers, *The Rock Report*, p. 82. Brothers is perhaps the only person in the United States willing to publish lengthy excerpts of the lyrics to Mentors songs like "Golden

Showers." One wonders about the pedagogic effect of exposing readers to lines like "on your face I build a shit tower," which he cites directly.

187. Ingebretsen, *At Stake*, p. 9.

Chapter 5

1. Some churches—like the Montclair Tabernacle Church of God in Dumfries, Virginia—have begun sponsoring Hallelujah House, a less gruesome Halloween alternative. See Karin Brulliard, "Faith through Fright: Shows Aim to Save by Depicting Hell," *Washington Post* (October 30, 2004).

2. Leigh Eric Schmidt, *Consumer Rites: The Buying and Selling of American Holidays* (Princeton, NJ: Princeton University Press, 1995).

3. Father Augustine Thompson, O.P., "Surprise: Halloween's Not a Pagan Festival after All" (October 19, 2000), available at www.belief.net/story/47/story_4771_1.html; and Father Augustine Thompson, "Should Our Kids Celebrate Halloween?" *Catholic Parent Magazine* (Huntington, IN) (September–October 1995). See also David J. Skal, *Death Makes a Holiday: A Cultural History of Halloween* (New York: Bloomsbury, 2002).

4. Elisabeth Ann Nixon, "Playing Devil's Advocate on the Path to Heaven: Evangelical Hell Houses and the Play of Politics, Fear, and Faith" (Ph.D. diss., Ohio State University, 2006), p. 22.

5. See Arthur Lyons, *Satan Wants You: The Cult of Devil Worship in America* (New York: Mysterious, 1988), a sound text despite its sensationalist title.

6. See Skal, *Death Makes a Holiday*; and also "Faith Facts: All Hallow's [*sic*] Eve" from Catholics United for the Faith (www.cuf.org).

7. Schmidt, *Consumer Rites*, p. 4; and Nixon, "Playing Devil's Advocate," p. 15. See also Jack Santino, ed., *Halloween and Other Festivals of Death and Life* (Knoxville: University of Tennessee Press, 1994); Jack Kugelmass, *Masked Culture: The Greenwich Village Halloween Parade* (New York: Columbia University Press, 1994); and Bill Ellis's study of Satanic panics, *Lucifer Ascending: The Occult in Folklore and Popular Culture* (Lexington: University of Kentucky Press, 2004).

8. Keenan Roberts, personal conversation, July 2007.

9. Throughout this chapter, I occasionally—specifically in comparative and contextual discussions—use the term "Hell House" to stand in for all productions.

10. See Nixon, "Playing Devil's Advocate," pp. 193–198.

11. The Liberty University administration sponsors Web-based Q&A pages devoted to topics relevant to students' lives. The page on Halloween (www.liberty.edu/wwwadmin/includes/search/QandA/QandA_Results_elmertowns.cfm?Searched=&AID=241&DisplayResults=1) is composed of Falwell-endorsed excerpts from texts like *Fundamentalist Journal* and *Psychology for Living*.

12. Ibid.

13. Sanford, North Carolina, youth minister Sylvia Dickens, quoted in Brulliard, "Faith through Fright." See also Gwen Florio, "Giving Them Hell," *Philadelphia Enquirer* (October 23, 1997).

14. Hudgins's creation has a decidedly international focus. He told me that he employs a full-time missionary in Brazil, who is responsible for training fifty-six churches to

sponsor Judgement Houses. He also has strong ties with the Vida Nueva Baptist Church in San Salvador, El Salvador, and notes that there is strong interest in Japan, South Korea, Thailand, and Ukraine. Closer to home, Hudgins noted, "We also have a 45 ft trailer in Alabama where we can take Judgement House to churches that can't afford to do one." Personal communication, June 2007.

15. By 2007, New Creation had begun offering a new line of Judgement House accessories, including a line of T-shirts designating specific members of the production staff (runner, door-knocker, kitchen crew, and security) and "covenant partner kits" (essentially day-planners in handsome red and black, embossed with the Judgement House logo). Personal e-mail, June 2007.

16. See www.judgmenthouse.org.

17. Nixon, "Playing Devil's Advocate," pp. 217, 220.

18. See www.edenwestside.org/revwalk.htm and www.tribulationtrail.org.

19. See http://mze.com/heavensgates.

20. Nixon claims that Roberts's initial production was modeled on an extant version at Cedar Hill, Texas' Trinity Baptist Church (later the subject of Ratliff's documentary). Nixon, "Playing Devil's Advocate," p. 24. She also notes the existence of a production called Hell House from 1983, which was sponsored by an organization called Northwest Evangelical Outreach. Nixon, "Playing Devil's Advocate," p. 219. There is also a very popular nonreligious haunted house—in Ellicott City, Maryland—that calls itself Hell House. I also wonder if Roberts intentionally adopted the moniker of the Richard Matheson book and film *The Legend of Hell House*, widely regarded by horror fans as one of the most frightening of all time.

21. As of this writing, July 2007, the Hell House outreach kit cost $299.

22. The *Hollywood Hell House* is both improvisatory and hyperbolic. Its sins include "Ate Hindu Food," "Sniffed My Sister's Bicycle Seat," and "Smoked Pot (2 Times)," and it concludes with a "Pin the Sin on Jesus" game. Nixon, "Playing Devil's Advocate," p. 316.

23. Roberts, personal conversation, July 2007.

24. Ibid. Even Richard Dawkins has shown up on Roberts's doorstep for an interview. See www.rationalresponders.com.

25. Roberts, personal conversation, July 2007.

26. See www.godestiny.org/ministries/hell-house/kit.php.

27. Francis Fukuyama, "The End of History?" *National Interest* (Summer 1989).

28. This term is from Robert Dahl, *A Preface to Democratic Theory* (New Haven, CT: Yale University Press, 1956).

29. Keenan Roberts, personal conversation, July 2007.

30. See Andrew Delbanco, *The Death of Satan: How Americans Have Lost the Sense of Evil* (New York: Noonday, 1996); and Mark Edmundson, *Nightmare on Main Street: Angels, Sadomasochism, and the Culture of the Gothic* (Cambridge, MA: Harvard University Press, 1997).

31. Quoted in Nixon, "Playing Devil's Advocate," p. 255.

32. Tom Hudgins, personal communication, June 2007.

33. Interview with Stacy Capps (1999), at www.du.edu/~scapps/documentary/index.html.

34. All quotations are from promotional literature advertising the Hell House touring kit.

35. Post by "BH2437" on alt.personals.hiv-positive (October 26, 1998).

36. Keenan Roberts, personal conversation, July 2007.

37. See www.hellhouse.ms.com.

38. Ibid. I also explore these themes in Jason Bivins, *The Fracture of Good Order: Christian Antiliberalism and the Challenge to American Politics* (Chapel Hill: University of North Carolina Press, 2003).

39. Keenan Roberts, personal conversation, July 2007.

40. "Christians Use Hell House to Help People Find God," available at www .ananova.com/news/story/sm_700705.html.

41. "'Hell House' Kits Selling Nationally," *Christianity Today* 40:2 (October 7, 1996).

42. Quoted at www.religioustolerance.org/hallo_he.htm.

43. See www.judgmenthouse.org.

44. All quotations are from www.judgmenthouse.org.

45. Keenan Roberts, personal conversation, July 2007.

46. Ibid.

47. Aside from the above two notes, all quotes in this paragraph are from Stacy Capps (see note 33 above). Roberts invoked the same analogy with me, though he referred only to "war" and did not name a specific enemy.

48. From the promotional materials at www.hellhouse.ms.com.

49. This phrase is from Skal, *The Monster Show*, p. 386.

50. Walter Kendrick, *The Thrill of Fear: 250 Years of Scary Entertainment* (New York: Grove Weidenfield, 1991), p. xviii.

51. From promotional materials at www.hellhouse.ms.com, a church known for its flamboyant evangelism. Gerald Benton recalls (on triangle.general, October 30, 2001) that members of this church attended Mardi Gras in New Orleans annually and could be seen "standing in the middle of the 600 block of Bourbon Street with their big wooden cross, handing out tracts."

52. Quoted in Brulliard, "Faith through Fright."

53. Personal communication, June 2007.

54. Jennifer Davis, personal conversation, April 2007.

55. Christopher Shreve, personal conversation, April 2007.

56. Virginia Culver, "Hell House Outlines Stages of Sin," *Denver Post* (October 6, 2000).

57. Roberts also omitted the school shooting scene in 1999, the year of the Columbine High School shootings in Littleton, Colorado.

58. See Ratliff's *Hell House* (Plexifilm, 2003). Ratliff's documentary is helpful for its coverage of the behind-the-scenes preparations and rehearsal that go into these productions.

59. See www.godestiny.org/ministries/hell-house/kit.php.

60. Nixon, "Playing Devil's Advocate," p. 28.

61. *CNN Newsnight* (October 31, 2005).

62. See Stacy Capps interview (note 33 above).

63. Quoted in www.ananova.com/news/story/sm_700705.html.

64. Greg Hartman, "Welcome to Hell," www.family.org.

65. *CNN Newsnight* (October 31, 2005), and first-person account of protest posted on alt.politics.homosexuality (October 24, 1999).

66. See, for example, www.postfun.com/pfp/features/98/nov/hellhouse.html.

67. Nixon, "Playing Devil's Advocate," p. 226. It is not uncommon on these listservs to encounter not only theological debates but exchanges about "proper methods and techniques for evangelism." See the illustrative dialogue (May–June 2000) on soc .religion.christian, for example, or the lengthy discussion on rec.music.christian (October 1997) under the heading "Truth no excuse for rudeness."

68. See Bill Geerhart's report at www.postfun.com/pfp/features/98/nov/hellhouse .html.

69. Interview with anonymous Bethel volunteer, November 2003. Bethel Christian Center, Durham, North Carolina. Most of the churches sponsoring Hell Houses in the Triangle, North Carolina, area report that approximately 5,000 people attend their performances each season.

70. The quotes in this paragraph are from Emily Linthicum, personal conversation, November 2003.

71. Amanda Comer, personal conversation, spring 2006.

72. Tom Hudgins, personal communication, June 2007. See also "Bible Belt Pastors Welcome Sinners to a Virtual House of Hell," *Times* (London) (November 1, 2002), p. 21.

73. Shelly Hattan, "Report from the Front Lines of Hell House!" available at www .atheists.org/flash.line/hallow4.htm.

74. Consult the video clips at http://mze.com/heavensgates and www.realityoutreach .org. My thanks to Lindsey Jones for her insights into these creations.

75. Jessica Headrick, personal conversation, December 19, 2005.

76. See www.sanctuarychristian.com.

77. *CNN Newsnight* (October 31, 2005).

78. All quotes throughout these sections are from Roberts's script.

79. This portion of the script is among the more readily available and was first published in "The Christian Fright," *Harper's Magazine* 295:1769 (October 1997): 20–22.

80. Ron Harris, "Some Churches Offer Sinful Scare," *Associated Press* (October 28, 1997).

81. Nixon, "Playing Devil's Advocate," p. 236. Italics mine.

82. See Tania Fuentez, "Church Uses Images of Sept. 11 Terrorist Attacks in Alternative Halloween Tour," *Associated Press* (October 30, 2001).

83. Terri Jo Ryan, "Church's Hell House Draws on Sept. 11 Tragedy," *Waco Tribune* (TX) (October 28, 2002).

84. Nixon, "Playing Devil's Advocate," p. 247.

85. Ibid., p. 255. Consider, for example, a nasty exchange (on bc.politics, September 24–25, 1997) about the abortion scene. Werner Knoll wrote about how distasteful he found the scene. "E. Gerk" responded, "Why, let's go visit an abortionmill where a doctor is about to perform a partial birth abortion. . . . you know the one where he/she delivers the baby feet first, then inserts some scissors at the back of the baby's head, then makes a hole and sucks out the baby's brain."

86. Interview with Richard Dawkins at www.rationalresponders.com.

87. Keenan Roberts, personal conversation, July 2007.

88. From "Denver's Sinners Form Queue for a Ticket to Hell," *Sunday Times* (London), "World" section (November 3, 1996).

89. Nixon, "Playing Devil's Advocate," p. 253.

90. See Chris Bull and John Gallagher, *Perfect Enemies: The Battle between the Religious Right and the Gay Movement* (New York: Crown, 1997).

91. See Nixon, "Playing Devil's Advocate," p. 231.

92. See www.hellhouse4t.com.

93. Such claims have been popularized by Alan Sears of the Alliance Defense Fund. Sears is also co-author, with Craig Osten, of the book *The Homosexual Agenda: Exposing the Principal Threat to Religious Freedom Today* (Nashville, TN: B&H, 2003).

94. See www.postfun.com/pfp/features/98/nov/hellhouse.html.

95. See Nixon, "Playing Devil's Advocate," p. 204.

96. See Robyn Ross, "The Scream Teams," *Austin American-Statesman* (October 7, 2004).

97. Nixon, "Playing Devil's Advocate," p. 212. See also Monica Maske, "Church Enacts Horrors of the End to Scare Unbelievers Out of Hell," *Star-Ledger* (Calvary, OH) (November 2, 1991).

98. This is a regular conclusion to teen suicide scenes. Jon Savelle, "Hell House Warns against Wayward Path," *King County Journal* (Bellevue and Kent, WA) (October 28, 2002).

99. Personal communication, June 2007.

100. Keenan Roberts, personal conversation, July 2007.

101. Shelly Hattan, "Metroplex Atheists Visit Hell House!" available at www.metroplexatheists.org/hell00.htm.

102. Nixon, "Playing Devil's Advocate," p. 247.

103. Post by Andrew Gumbel on alt.messianic (October 31, 2005).

104. Heather Hendershot, *Shaking the World for Jesus: Media in Conservative Evangelical Culture* (Chicago: University of Chicago Press, 2004), pp. 94–95.

105. Nixon, "Playing Devil's Advocate," p. 237.

106. See Hattan, "Metroplex Atheists Visit Hell House!"

107. Post by "Billie" on alt.gossip.celebrities (September 29, 1999).

108. Kristin Davenport, "Church Uses Scare Tactics on Halloween," *Santa Fe New Mexican* (October 27, 1999).

109. Marcus Kabel, "Texas Church Defends Columbine Scene in 'Hell House,'" *Reuters* (October 29, 1999).

110. Fine studies of NCR political rhetoric and activism include Susan Friend Harding, *The Book of Jerry Falwell: Fundamentalist Language and Politics* (Princeton, NJ: Princeton University Press, 2001); Linda Kintz, *Between Jesus and the Market: The Emotions That Matter in Right-Wing America* (Durham, NC: Duke University Press, 1997); and Michael Lienesch, *Redeeming America: Piety and Politics in the New Christian Right* (Chapel Hill: University of North Carolina Press, 1993).

111. Victor F. Antoine on alt.bible (October 9, 2005).

112. See www.atheists.org/flash.line/Hallow4.htm.

113. Sean Jamison, "Heaven and Hell," *North Texas Daily* (October 30, 2002).

114. See Ethan Blue, "National Trauma, Church Drama," available at http://bad.eserver.org/issues/2005/72/blue.html.

115. Nixon, "Playing Devil's Advocate," p. 220.

116. See Hattan, "Metroplex Atheists Visit Hell House!"

117. Quoted in Bob Allen, "Popular 'Hell Houses' Draw Praise, Criticism," *Associated Baptist Press* 00–95 (October 19, 2000).

118. James Aho, *This Thing of Darkness: A Sociology of the Enemy* (Seattle: University of Washington Press, 1994), p. 114.

119. Quoted in Nixon, "Playing Devil's Advocate," p. 187.

120. Elisabeth Bronfen, *The Knotted Subject: Hysteria and Its Discontents* (Princeton, NJ: Princeton University Press, 1998), p. xiii.

121. Walter Kendrick, *The Thrill of Fear: 250 Years of Scary Entertainment* (New York: Grove Weidenfield, 1991), p. 31.

122. Quoted in James B. Twitchell, *Dreadful Pleasures: An Anatomy of Modern Horror* (New York: Oxford University Press, 1987), p. 146.

123. Keenan Roberts, personal conversation, July 2007. Nixon also notes racial fears and concerns about the permeability of borders. Nixon, "Playing Devil's Advocate," p. 273.

124. See Bull and Gallagher, *Perfect Enemies*.

125. Keenan Roberts, personal conversation, July 2007.

126. George Lakoff, *Moral Politics: How Liberals and Conservatives Think*, 2nd ed. (Chicago: University of Chicago Press, 2001).

127. See Perry Miller, *The New England Mind: From Colony to Province* (Cambridge, MA: Belknap, 1983); and Sacvan Bercovitch, *The Rites of Assent: Transformations in the Symbolic Construction of America* (New York: Routledge, 1992).

128. Jessica Headrick, personal conversation, December 19, 2005.

129. See www.atheists.org/flash.line/Hallow3.htm.

130. Nixon, "Playing Devil's Advocate," p. 25.

131. Quoted in Allen, "Popular 'Hell Houses.' "

132. See Brulliard, "Faith through Fright."

133. *CNN Newsnight* (October 31, 2005).

134. See hellhouseazle.com.

135. Jack Morgan, *The Biology of Horror: Gothic Literature and Film* (Carbondale: Southern Illinois University Press, 2002).

136. See www.hellhouse.4t.com.

137. See the clip at www.youtube.com/watch?v=syEWR0ZIhwM.

138. Nixon, "Playing Devil's Advocate," p. 254.

139. Ryan, "Church's Hell House Draws on Sept. 11 Tragedy."

140. Kim Horner, "A Truly Haunting House," *Dallas Morning News* (October 21, 1999).

141. See www.aok.positiveatheist.com/archive/newsletters/html/2002-11.html.

142. Dahleen Glanton, "Halloween Bedevils Some U.S. Churches," *Chicago Tribune* (October 25, 2004).

143. Keenan Roberts, personal conversation, July 2007.

144. Ann Pellegrini, " 'Signaling through the Flames': Hell House Performance and the Structure of Religious Feeling," *American Quarterly* 59:3 (2007): 911–935. This piece appeared just as this manuscript was due at the press.

145. Ingebretsen, *At Stake*, p. 21.

146. See www.sanctuarychristian.com.

147. Adam Higginbotham, "One Hell of a Show," *Daily Telegraph* (November 18, 2002).

148. Nixon, "Playing Devil's Advocate," p. 26.

149. Keenan Roberts, personal conversation, July 2007.

150. From J. Shawn Landres, "Public Art as Sacred Space: Asian American Community Murals in Los Angeles," in Stewart M. Hoover and Lynn Schofield Clark, eds., *Practicing Religion in the Age of Media: Explorations in Media, Religion, and Culture* (New York: Columbia University Press, 2002), p. 95.

151. See Gregory Jackson, "Cultivating Spiritual Sight: Jacob Riis' Virtual-Tour Narrative and the Visual Modernization of Protestant Homiletics," *Representations* 83 (Summer 2003): 123–166.

Chapter 6

1. The title of the chapter comes from Tim LaHaye and Jerry B. Jenkins, *Armageddon: The Cosmic Battle of the Ages* (Wheaton, IL: Tyndale House, 2003), p. 345.

2. These remarks were made on the September 13, 2001, broadcast of Robertson's *700 Club*.

3. See Lynn Neal, *Romancing God: Evangelical Women and Inspirational Fiction* (Chapel Hill: University of North Carolina Press, 2006).

4. The *Slacktivist* blog (http://slacktivist.typepad.com), which is authored by an evangelical critical of LaHaye, is devoted to incremental readings of the books. Thanks to Gerry Canavan for this link.

5. Figures cited in Bruce David Forbes, "How Popular Are the Left Behind Books... and Why?" in Forbes and Jeanne Halgren Kilde, eds., *Rapture, Revelation, and the End Times: Exploring the* Left Behind *Series* (New York: Palgrave Macmillan, 2004), p. 9.

6. Melani McAlister, "Prophecy, Politics, and the Popular: The *Left Behind* Series and Christian Fundamentalism's New World Order," *South Atlantic Quarterly* 102:4 (Fall 2003): 773–798, 776.

7. My account is indebted primarily to Paul Boyer, *When Time Shall Be No More: Prophecy Belief in Modern American Culture* (Cambridge, MA: Belknap, 1992).

8. Stephen D. O'Leary, *Arguing the Apocalypse: A Theory of Millennial Rhetoric* (New York: Oxford University Press, 1994), p. 4.

9. Boyer, *When Time Shall Be No More*, p. 44. See also Eugen Weber, *Apocalypses: Prophecies, Cults, and Millennial Beliefs through the Ages* (Cambridge, MA: Harvard University Press, 1999).

10. See Paul Conkin, *American Originals: Homemade Varieties of Christianity* (Chapel Hill: University of North Carolina Press, 1997).

11. There are several other theories and versions of this chronology. Post-millennialism, for example, holds that only after steady progressive improvement will these events commence.

12. Stephen D. O'Leary contextualizes this periodization by noting the widespread sacred significance of the number seven among ancient Semitic peoples. O'Leary, *Arguing the Apocalypse*, p. 65.

13. Amy Johnson Frykholm, *Rapture Culture:* Left Behind *in Evangelical America* (New York: Oxford University Press, 2004), pp. 16–17.

14. The following Web site has a useful searchable version of Scofield's notes to the 1917 edition: http://bible.crosswalk.com/Commentaries/ScofieldReferenceNotes.

15. Many of these examples are from Boyer's work, which remains an indispensable resource in cataloging this culture's multitudes.

16. Hal Lindsey, *The Late Great Planet Earth* (Grand Rapids, MI: Zondervan, 1970), p. 54. See also Boyer, *When Time Shall Be No More*, pp. 189–190; and Hal Lindsey, *There's a New World Coming* (Santa Ana, CA: Vision House, 1973).

17. See Yaakov Ariel, *Evangelizing the Chosen People: Missions to the Jews in America, 1880–2000* (Chapel Hill: University of North Carolina Press, 2000).

18. See Andrew Austin, "Faith Matters: George Bush and Providence," Political Research Associates, *Public Eye* (March 18, 2003); and Michael Rogin, *Ronald Reagan: The Movie, and Other Episodes in Political Demonology* (Berkeley: University of California Press, 1988).

19. Bernard McGinn, *Antichrist: Two Thousand Years of the Human Fascination with Evil* (New York: Columbia University Press, 2000), p. 258.

20. Peter Gardella, "Spiritual Warfare in the Fiction of Frank Peretti," in Colleen McDannell, ed., *Religions of the United States in Practice*, vol. 2 (Princeton, NJ: Princeton University Press, 2001), pp. 328–345. Again, see Neal, *Romancing God*.

21. See Candy Gunther Brown, *The Word in the World: Evangelical Writing, Publishing, and Reading in America, 1789–1880* (Chapel Hill: University of North Carolina Press, 2004); Jonathan Cordero, "The Production of Christian Fiction," *Journal of Religion and Popular Culture* 6 (Spring 2004): 1–17; and David Paul Nord, *Faith in Reading: Religious Publishing and the Birth of Mass Media in America* (New York: Oxford University Press, 2004).

22. See Heather Hendershot, *Shaking the World for Jesus: Media in Conservative Evangelical Culture* (Chicago: University of Chicago Press, 2004), p. 21.

23. Randall Balmer, *Mine Eyes Have Seen the Glory: A Journey into the Evangelical Subculture in America*, 3rd ed. (New York: Oxford University Press, 2000), describes these conventions.

24. See Crawford Gribben, *Rapture Fiction and the Evangelical Crisis* (Darlington, England: Evangelical, 2006).

25. Balmer, *Mine Eyes Have Seen the Glory*, pp. 57–58.

26. Ibid., p. 62.

27. Quoted in ibid., p. 63.

28. Gardella, "Spiritual Warfare in the Fiction of Frank Peretti," p. 329. Richard Lee, who knows Peretti, speculates that Peretti was influenced by Chick; among other similarities, the two authors use similar themes and point to similar villains. Personal conversation, May 2007.

29. Pat Robertson, *The End of the Age: A Novel* (Dallas, TX: Word, 1995), projected into the Antichrist's inner circle a Jewish, Ivy League–educated scholar of Asian religions. Richard Jaffe brought this to my attention, with some trepidation. Personal e-mail, December 15, 2004.

30. Gardella, "Spiritual Warfare in the Fiction of Frank Peretti," p. 330.

31. Glenn W. Shuck, *Marks of the Beast: The* Left Behind *Novels and the Struggle for Evangelical Identity* (New York: New York University Press, 2005), p. 5.

32. Larry Burkett, *The Illuminati* (Nashville, TN: Thomas Nelson, 1996). Burkett's posthumously published *The Thor Conspiracy* (Nashville, TN: Thomas Nelson, 2005) narrates America's post-1960s decline by describing "an odd, yet frighteningly effective, alliance of international governments and inner-city gangs."

33. Cordero, "The Production of Christian Fiction," p. 9.

34. I was not successful in my requests to interview Dr. LaHaye. Most recently, in the summer of 2007, his gracious publicist, Beverly Rykert, noted that LaHaye was on an "extended vacation" to celebrate his and Beverly's sixtieth wedding anniversary.

35. See Rob Boston, "Left Behind," *Church and State* (January 2, 2002).

36. Tim LaHaye, *The Battle for the Public Schools* (Old Tappan, NJ: Revell, 1983), p. 10.

37. This wording is from the LaHaye ministries Web site: www.timlahaye.com.

38. I discuss LaHaye's critique of public education in detail in Bivins, *The Fracture of Good Order: Christian Antiliberalism and the Challenge to American Politics* (Chapel Hill: University of North Carolina Press, 2003).

39. See Tim LaHaye, *Faith of Our Founding Fathers* (Brentwood, TN: Wolgemuth & Hyatt, 1987).

40. LaHaye, "The Colossal Battle," *Esquire* (September 2004), p. 179.

41. See Boston, "Left Behind"; Michael Standaert, *Skipping towards Armageddon: The Politics and Propaganda of the* Left Behind *Novels and the LaHaye Empire* (Brooklyn, NY: Soft Skull, 2006); and Alan Jacobs, "Apocalyptic President?" *Boston Globe* (April 4, 2004). LaHaye has also had a long association with the Reverend Sun Myung Moon.

42. See Howard Fineman, "Ties That Bind: Bush and LaHaye Have a History, and Share a Sense of Mission," *Newsweek* (May 24, 2004).

43. Standaert, *Skipping towards Armageddon*, p. 20.

44. See David D. Kirkpatrick, "Club of the Most Powerful Gathers in Strictest Privacy," *New York Times* (August 28, 2004); Suzi Parker, "The Real Convention?" *U.S. News & World Report* (August 25, 2004); and Sarah Posner, "Secret Society: Just Who Is the Council for National Policy and Why Isn't It Paying Taxes?" posted at www.alternet.org/story/21372 (March 1, 2005). See also Hugh Urban, *Secrets of the Kingdom: Religion and Secrecy in the Bush Administration* (Lanham, MD: Rowman & Littlefield, 2007), and his "Bush, the Neocons, and Evangelical Fiction: America, 'Left Behind, '" *Counterpunch* (November 18, 2004).

45. See Kevin Phillips, *American Dynasty: Aristocracy, Fortune, and the Politics of Deceit in the House of Bush* (New York: Penguin, 2004); and Craig Unger, "American Rapture," *Vanity Fair* (December 2005), pp. 204–222.

46. Tim LaHaye and Jerry B. Jenkins, *Are We Living in the End Times? Current Events Foretold in Scripture . . . and What They Mean* (Wheaton, IL: Tyndale House, 1999), p. 22.

47. Ibid., p. 27.

48. Ibid., pp. 34–35.

49. Ibid., p. 195.

50. Ibid., p. 199.

51. Tim LaHaye and Jerry B. Jenkins, *Soul Harvest: The World Takes Sides* (Wheaton, IL: Tyndale House, 1998), p. 224.

52. Tim LaHaye and Jerry B. Jenkins, *Left Behind: A Novel of Earth's Last Days* (Wheaton, IL: Tyndale House, 1995), p. 5.

53. Ibid., p. 48.

54. Ibid., p. 104.

55. Ibid., p. 102.

56. Ibid., p. 109.

57. Ibid., pp. 164–166.

58. Ibid., p. 207.

59. LaHaye and Jenkins, *Soul Harvest*, p. 135.

60. Ibid., pp. 210, 235.

61. LaHaye and Jenkins, *Left Behind*, p. 214.

62. Ibid., p. 396.

63. Ibid., p. 237.

64. Tim LaHaye and Jerry B. Jenkins, *Tribulation Force: The Continuing Drama of Those Left Behind* (Wheaton, IL: Tyndale House, 1996), p. 70.

65. Tim LaHaye and Jerry B. Jenkins, *Desecration: Antichrist Takes the Throne* (Wheaton, IL: Tyndale House, 2001), p. 10.

66. LaHaye and Jenkins, *Armageddon*, p. 310.

67. LaHaye and Jenkins, *Soul Harvest*, p. 246.

68. Tim LaHaye and Jerry B. Jenkins, *Glorious Appearing: The End of Days* (Wheaton, IL: Tyndale House, 2004), p. 178.

69. Ibid., p. 194.

70. LaHaye and Jenkins, *Tribulation Force*, p. 31.

71. Ibid., pp. 65, 378. See also Tim LaHaye and Jerry B. Jenkins, *Assassins: Assignment: Jerusalem, Target: Antichrist* (Wheaton, IL: Tyndale House, 1999), p. 90.

72. LaHaye and Jenkins, *Are We Living in the End Times?* p. 4.

73. Ibid., p. 5.

74. LaHaye and Jenkins, *Glorious Appearing*, p. 318.

75. *Fresh Air* (March 12, 2004).

76. *On the Media* (April 6, 2007). Interview transcribed at www.onthemedia.org/transcripts/2007/04/06/04.

77. LaHaye and Jenkins, *Soul Harvest*, p. 213.

78. Tim LaHaye and Jerry B. Jenkins, *Apollyon: The Destroyer Is Unleashed* (Wheaton, IL: Tyndale House, 1999), p. 5.

79. Tim LaHaye and Jerry B. Jenkins, *The Indwelling: The Beast Takes Possession* (Wheaton, IL: Tyndale House, 2000), p. 343.

80. LaHaye and Jenkins, *Assassins*, p. 159.

81. Ibid., pp. 142 and 224.

82. LaHaye and Jenkins, *The Indwelling*, p. 108.

83. Unger, "American Rapture," p. 210. See also McAlister, "Prophecy, Politics, and the Popular," and Urban, *Secrets of the Kingdom*.

84. Tim LaHaye and Jerry B. Jenkins, *Nicolae: The Rise of Antichrist* (Wheaton, IL: Tyndale House, 1997), pp. 139 and 240; and LaHaye and Jenkins, *Assassins*, p. xi.

85. LaHaye and Jenkins, *Tribulation Force*, pp. 373–374.

86. LaHaye and Jenkins, *Nicolae*, p. 244.

87. LaHaye and Jenkins, *Armageddon*, p. 310.

88. Yaakov Ariel, "How Are Jews and Israel Portrayed in the Left Behind Series? A Historical Discussion of Jewish-Christian Relations," in Forbes and Kilde, eds., *Rapture, Revelation, and the End Times*, p. 132.

89. LaHaye and Jenkins, *The Indwelling*, p. 119.

90. LaHaye and Jenkins, *Tribulation Force*, p. 53. See also pp. 271 and 401.

91. LaHaye and Jenkins, *Soul Harvest*, p. 171.

92. LaHaye and Jenkins, *Desecration*, p. 3; and LaHaye and Jenkins, *Apollyon*, p. 364.

93. LaHaye and Jenkins, *Tribulation Force*, p. 323.

94. LaHaye and Jenkins, *Desecration*, p. 360.

95. Tim LaHaye and Jerry B. Jenkins, *The Remnant: On the Brink of Armageddon* (Wheaton, IL: Tyndale House, 2002), p. 293.

96. Ibid., pp. 292–297.

97. LaHaye and Jenkins, *Desecration*, pp. 372–373.

98. *Fresh Air* (March 12, 2004).

99. LaHaye and Jenkins, *Desecration*, p. 278.

100. LaHaye and Jenkins, *The Indwelling*, p. 6. The site www.leftbehind.com has sound files from the audio books. The racially and ethnically marked characters frequently speak in hackneyed and stereotypical accents.

101. LaHaye and Jenkins, *Tribulation Force*, p. 315.

102. LaHaye and Jenkins, *Glorious Appearing*, pp. 33–34.

103. McAlister, "Prophecy, Politics, and the Popular," p. 788.

104. Frykholm, "What Social and Political Messages Appear in the *Left Behind* Books," in Forbes and Kilde, eds., *Rapture, Revelation, and the End Times*, pp. 184–185.

105. See Sara Diamond, *Spiritual Warfare: The Politics of the Christian Right* (Boston: South End, 1989); Linda Kintz, *Between Jesus and the Market: The Emotions That Matter in Right-Wing America* (Durham, NC: Duke University Press, 1997); and Standaert, *Skipping towards Armageddon*.

106. Frykholm, *Rapture Culture*, pp. 30–31.

107. See Michael Lienesch, *Redeeming America: Piety and Politics in the New Christian Right* (Chapel Hill: University of North Carolina Press, 1993).

108. LaHaye and Jenkins, *Tribulation Force*, pp. 427, 433.

109. Frykholm, *Rapture Culture*, p. 33.

110. LaHaye and Jenkins, *Assassins*, p. 151.

111. LaHaye and Jenkins, *Left Behind*, p. 268.

112. LaHaye and Jenkins, *Assassins*, p. xiii.

113. LaHaye and Jenkins, *Tribulation Force*, p. 5; and Shuck, *Marks of the Beast*, p. 16.

114. LaHaye and Jenkins, *Tribulation Force*, p. 13.

115. Ibid., pp. 17–18.

116. LaHaye and Jenkins, *Nicolae*, p. 279.

117. Ibid., pp. 281, 341.

118. LaHaye and Jenkins, *Tribulation Force*, p. 401.

119. Ibid., pp. 22–23.

120. LaHaye and Jenkins, *Left Behind*, p. 22.

121. LaHaye and Jenkins, *Tribulation Force*, p. 200.

122. Ibid., p. 242.

123. LaHaye and Jenkins, *Nicolae*, p. 391.

124. LaHaye and Jenkins, *Soul Harvest*, p. 215.

125. Cited in Standaert, *Skipping towards Armageddon*, p. 45.

126. Ibid., p. 133.

127. LaHaye and Jenkins, *The Indwelling*, p. 66.

128. LaHaye and Jenkins, *Nicolae*, p. 350.

129. Ibid., p. 365.

130. LaHaye and Jenkins, *Left Behind*, p. 266.

131. LaHaye and Jenkins, *Nicolae*, p. 178.

132. Ibid., pp. 369–370.

133. LaHaye and Jenkins, *Soul Harvest*, p. 221.

134. Lienesch's *Redeeming America* is still one of the most rigorous analyses of NCR economics.

135. LaHaye and Jenkins, *Left Behind*, p. 243.

136. Shuck, *Marks of the Beast*, p. 51.

137. Apocalyptic author Mary Relfe "ties the advent of Antichrist to pocketbook issues more than political ones": "that Antichrist will mark his followers and that those without this mark will be forbidden to buy and sell casts fear into the heart of the stoutest Christian consumers.... the 666 system is already well advanced in computer programs, credit cards, production programs, and especially in the electronic bar codes." Quoted in McGinn, *Antichrist*, p. 261.

138. LaHaye and Jenkins, *Nicolae*, p. 125.

139. Ibid., p. 129.

140. LaHaye and Jenkins, *Tribulation Force*, p. 150.

141. Ibid., p. 338.

142. LaHaye and Jenkins, *Soul Harvest*, p. 153.

143. LaHaye and Jenkins, *The Remnant*, p. 260; and LaHaye and Jenkins, *Glorious Appearing*, p. 151.

144. LaHaye and Jenkins, *Left Behind*, p. 9.

145. Ibid., p. 14.

146. Ibid., pp. 57, 105, and 140.

147. See Michael Barkun, *A Culture of Conspiracy: Apocalyptic Visions in Contemporary America* (Berkeley: University of California Press, 2003); and Robert Goldberg, *Enemies Within: The Culture of Conspiracy in Modern America* (New Haven, CT: Yale University Press, 2001).

148. LaHaye and Jenkins, *Tribulation Force*, p. 26.

149. Ibid., p. 29.

150. LaHaye and Jenkins, *Nicolae*, p. 2.

151. Ibid., p. 243.

152. On isolationism, see Frykholm in Forbes and Kilde, eds., *Rapture, Revelation, and the End Times*, pp. 169–171.

153. LaHaye and Jenkins, *Are We Living in the End Times?* pp. 10–11.

154. Ibid., pp. 214–215.

155. LaHaye and Jenkins, *Nicolae*, pp. 61 and 248; LaHaye and Jenkins, *Assassins*, pp. 29 and 146.

156. LaHaye and Jenkins, *The Indwelling*, p. 344.

157. LaHaye and Jenkins, *Nicolae*, p. 144.

158. LaHaye and Jenkins, *Soul Harvest*, pp. 325 and 327.

159. LaHaye and Jenkins, *Desecration*, p. 240.

160. Ibid., pp. 79 and 368.

161. LaHaye and Jenkins, *Armageddon*, p. 260.

162. McAlister, "Prophecy, Politics, and the Popular," p. 786.

163. LaHaye and Jenkins, *Soul Harvest*, p. 109.

164. Tim LaHaye and Jerry B. Jenkins, *The Mark: The Beast Rules the World* (Wheaton, IL: Tyndale House, 2000), p. 62.

165. LaHaye and Jenkins, *Desecration*, p. 374. Italics in the original.

166. LaHaye and Jenkins, *Left Behind*, p. 270.

167. LaHaye and Jenkins, *Tribulation Force*, p. 110.

168. Ibid., p. 72.

169. Ibid., p. 376.

170. LaHaye and Jenkins, *Nicolae*, p. 24.

171. LaHaye and Jenkins, *Apollyon*, p. 1.

172. LaHaye and Jenkins, *Desecration*, p. 1.

173. LaHaye and Jenkins, *Soul Harvest*, p. 159.

174. LaHaye and Jenkins, *The Remnant*, p. 123.

175. Ibid., p. 119.

176. LaHaye and Jenkins, *Soul Harvest*, p. 4.

177. Ibid., p. 416.

178. LaHaye and Jenkins, *Assassins*, p. 2.

179. LaHaye and Jenkins, *The Indwelling*, pp. 89–90.

180. Ibid., p. 207.

181. LaHaye and Jenkins, *Soul Harvest*, p. 10.

182. Ibid., pp. 12 and 23.

183. Ibid., pp. 24 and 34; and LaHaye and Jenkins, *The Indwelling*, p. 345.

184. LaHaye and Jenkins, *The Indwelling*, p. 364.

185. LaHaye and Jenkins, *The Mark*, pp. 6 and 200.

186. Nicholas D. Kristof, in his controversial op-ed piece "Jesus and Jihad," likened such visions to "ethnic cleansing celebrated as the height of piety." *New York Times* (July 17, 2004).

187. LaHaye and Jenkins, *Assassins*, p. 174.

188. LaHaye and Jenkins, *The Remnant*, p. 155.

189. LaHaye and Jenkins, *Assassins*, p. 143.

190. LaHaye and Jenkins, *The Remnant*, pp. 139 and 103.

191. Ibid., pp. 3, 75, and 78.

192. LaHaye and Jenkins, *The Indwelling*, p. 350; and LaHaye and Jenkins, *Desecration*, p. 13.

193. LaHaye and Jenkins, *Desecration*, p. 32.

194. LaHaye and Jenkins, *The Remnant*, p. 129.

195. Ibid., p. 43.

196. Ibid., pp. 167–168.

197. LaHaye and Jenkins, *Armageddon*, pp. 310 and 357.

198. LaHaye and Jenkins, *The Mark*, pp. 42 and 146.

199. LaHaye and Jenkins, *The Remnant*, p. 9.

200. LaHaye and Jenkins, *Desecration*, p. 177.

201. LaHaye and Jenkins, *Glorious Appearing*, p. 81.

202. Ibid., pp. 93–94.

203. Ibid., p. 208.

204. Ibid., p. 204.

205. Ibid., p. 208.

206. Ibid., pp. 225–226.

207. Ibid., p. 226.

208. Ibid., p. 209.

209. Ibid., p. 276.

210. Ibid., p. 249.

211. "Jerry Jenkins on Violence in the Left Behind Series" (February 19, 2004), available at www.leftbehind.com/channelbooks.asp?pageid=933&channelID=198.

212. Quoted in *On the Media* (April 6, 2007).

213. Quoted in Joe Bageant, "What the 'Left Behind' Series Really Means," *Talk to Action* (February 8, 2007), available at www.talk2action.org/story/2007/2/8/04932/02745.

214. See Mark Hitchcock, Tommy Ice, and Tim LaHaye, *The Truth behind* Left Behind: *A Biblical View of the End Times* (Colorado Springs, CO: Multnomah, 2004). See Standaert, *Skipping towards Armageddon*, p. 180. There is of course a critical cottage industry that denounces the series as well.

215. See, among many examples, LaHaye and Jenkins, *Soul Harvest*, p. 249.

216. LaHaye and Jenkins, *Assassins*, p. 95.

217. LaHaye and Jenkins, *The Remnant*, p. 232.

218. LaHaye and Jenkins, *Soul Harvest*, p. 329.

219. Ariel, "How Are Jews and Israel Portrayed," p. 135.

220. See Gershom Gorenberg, *The End of Days: Fundamentalism and the Struggle for the Temple Mount* (New York: Oxford University Press, 2000). See also Gorenberg's excellent review of the series, "Intolerance: The Bestseller," *American Prospect* (September 23, 2002).

221. LaHaye and Jenkins, *Tribulation Force*, p. 365. See Chip Ward, "Left Behind: Bush's Holy War on Nature," *Nation* (September 16, 2005).

222. See O'Leary, *Arguing the Apocalypse*, for a suggestive application of Burkean thought to the apocalyptic genre.

223. LaHaye and Jenkins, *The Remnant*, p. 229.

224. Shuck, *Marks of the Beast*, p. 55.

225. See Joseph Cannon's comments on Bush on alt.politics.liberalism (June 16, 2004); a discussion of Frank Rich's *New York Times* editorial "A Culture of Death, Not Life" (April 10, 2005) on alt.society.liberalism (April 2005); and the comments of "Patriotboy" on talk.politics (October 19, 2003).

226. Forbes, "How Popular Are the Left Behind Books . . . and Why?" p. 25. See also Bruce Olin, "From Gentle Jesus to Macho Messiah," *New York Times* (April 9, 2004); and Nancy Gibbs, "The Bible and the Apocalypse," *Time* (June 23, 2002).

227. Michelle Goldberg, "Fundamentally Unsound," *Salon* (July 29, 2002).

228. David Gates, "The Pop Prophets," *Newsweek* (May 24, 2004).

Chapter 7

1. Quoted in Phil Baker, "The Hum of the Tuning Fork," *Hindu* (July 1, 2001). Portions of this chapter have appeared previously in Jason C. Bivins, "Religion in Bush's America," *Sofia* (May 2006).

2. See Laurie Goodstein, "Disowning Conservative Politics, Evangelical Pastor Rattles Flock," *New York Times* (July 30, 2006); E. J. Dionne, "A Shift among the Evangelicals," *Washington Post* (June 16, 2006); and Michelle Luo and Laurie Goodstein, "Emphasis Shifts for New Breed of Evangelicals," *New York Times* (May 21, 2007).

3. See Joel Carpenter, *Revive Us Again: The Reawakening of American Fundamentalism* (New York: Oxford University Press, 1997).

4. The story of political discontent during this period is far more complex than this suggests, of course. I invoke this moment in American political history simply to assert that the 1960s were a watershed. See John Patrick Diggins, *The Rise and Fall of the American Left* (New York: Norton, 1992); Todd Gitlin, *The Sixties: Years of Hope, Days of Rage* (New York: Bantam, 1993); Mark Kurlansky, *1968: The Year That Rocked the World* (New York: Random House, 2005); James Miller, *"Democracy Is in the Streets": From Port Huron to the Siege of Chicago* (Cambridge, MA: Harvard University Press, 1994); Doug Rossinow, *The Politics of Authenticity* (New York: Columbia University Press, 1998).

5. The literature on identity politics is vast, of course. I have found the following sources to be especially helpful and suggestive: Kwame Anthony Appiah, *The Ethics of Identity* (Princeton, NJ: Princeton University Press, 2007); Seyla Benhabib, ed., *Democracy and Difference: Contesting the Boundaries of the Political* (Princeton, NJ: Princeton University Press, 1996); Todd Gitlin, *The Twilight of Common Dreams* (New York: Metropolitan, 1995); Amy Gutmann, *Identity in Democracy* (Princeton, NJ: Princeton University Press, 2004); Amy Gutmann and Charles Taylor, eds., *Multiculturalism* (Princeton, NJ: Princeton University Press, 1994); Eric Lott, *The Disappearing Liberal Intellectual* (New York: Basic, 2006); and Walter Benn Michaels, *The Trouble with Diversity: How We Learned to Love Identity and Ignore Inequality* (New York: Metropolitan, 2006).

6. See Robert W. Whitaker, ed., *The New Right Papers* (New York: St. Martin's, 1982).

7. See Michael Cromartie, ed., *Religion and Radical Politics: The Religious New Right in American Politics* (Washington, DC: Ethics and Public Policy Center Press, 1993); William Martin, *With God on Our Side: The Rise of the Religious Right in America* (New York: Broadway, 1995); Matthew C. Moen, *The Transformation of the Christian Right* (Tuscaloosa: University of Alabama Press, 1992); and Clyde Wilcox, *Onward Christian Soldiers: The Religious Right in American Politics* (Boulder, CO: Westview, 2006).

8. See Christian Smith, *Christian America? What Evangelicals Really Want* (Berkeley: University of California Press, 2000), pp. 26–27, 35.

9. See Michael Walzer, *Interpretation and Social Criticism* (Cambridge, MA: Harvard University Press, 1987).

10. Greeley and Hout write, "Conservative Protestants are conspicuously patriotic. Their members are prominent in the military and at public events that have a patriotic flavor. They express more pride, especially in the military, than other Americans." Greeley and Hout, *The Truth about Conservative Christians*, p. 90.

11. George Lakoff, "Framing the Dems: How Conservatives Control Political Debate and How Progressives Can Take It Back," *American Prospect* (September 2003): 32–35.

12. Smith, *Christian America?* p. 4.

13. Linda Kintz, "Culture and the Religious Right," in Linda Kintz and Julia Lesage, eds., *Media, Culture, and the Religious Right* (Minneapolis: University of Minnesota Press, 1998), p. 7. See also Michael Lienesch, *Redeeming America: Piety and Politics in the New Christian Right* (Chapel Hill: University of North Carolina Press, 1993); and Daniel Marcus, *Happy Days and Wonder Years: The '50s and the '60s in Contemporary Cultural Politics* (New Brunswick, NJ: Rutgers University Press, 2004).

14. James Morone, "The Tropes of Wrath," *Dissent* (Spring 2005): 93–97.

15. See Philip Jenkins, *Decade of Nightmares: The End of the Sixties and the Making of Eighties America* (New York: Oxford University Press, 2006).

16. Kintz, "Culture and the Religious Right," p. 8. See Stephanie Coontz, *The Way We Never Were: American Families and the Nostalgia Trip* (New York: Basic, 2000).

17. David Frankfurter, *Evil Incarnate: Rumors of Demonic Conspiracy and Satanic Abuse in History* (Princeton, NJ: Princeton University Press, 2006), is a rich resource in this area.

18. Tom De Luca and John Buell, *Liars! Cheaters! Evildoers! Demonization and the End of Civil Debate in American Politics* (New York: New York University Press, 2005), p. 5.

19. Morone, *Hellfire Nation*, p. 74.

20. Sobel, *Teach Me Dreams*, p. 27.

21. See Richard Kearney, *Strangers, Gods and Monsters: Interpreting Otherness* (New York: Routledge, 2003).

22. Julia Kristeva, *Powers of Horror: An Essay on Abjection* (New York: Columbia University Press, 1982), p. 12. Kristeva's theory of abjection and horror captures what is at stake in the religion of fear. For Kristeva, abjection occurs during moments of crisis, when structures of meanings threaten to collapse; it emerges from those spaces where selves are in conflict, ultimately attempting to exclude the self's indwelling "foreign" substance: "I abject myself within the same motion through which 'I' claim to establish myself" (3). The success of the demonology within is achieved precisely to the extent that the proximity of self and Other, of saint and demon, is overlooked or forgotten. To acknowledge their proximity and mutual dependence would threaten the destruction of a world, the collapse of boundaries.

23. See Giorgio Agamben, *Homo Sacer: Sovereign Power and Bare Life* (Palo Alto, CA: Stanford University Press, 1998).

24. Bernard McGinn, *Antichrist: Two Thousand Years of the Human Fascination with Evil* (New York: Columbia University Press, 2000), p. 15.

25. Slavoj Žižek, *On Belief (Thinking in Action)* (New York: Routledge, 2001), p. 68.

26. Terrence Rafferty, "Bitter Spirits," *New York Times* (January 28, 2007).

27. Michel Foucault, *The History of Sexuality*, vol. 1: *An Introduction* (New York: Vintage, 1990), p. 141.

28. A special issue of the *American Quarterly*, which is devoted to religion and politics, appeared too late to discuss fully here. I hope it signals the beginning of new engagements with these matters. See David S. Gutterman, *Prophetic Politics: Christian Social Movements and American Democracy* (Ithaca, NY: Cornell University Press, 2005); James Davison Hunter, *Culture Wars: The Struggle to Define America* (New York: Basic, 1992); Geoffrey Layman, *The Great Divide: Religious and Cultural Conflict in Party Politics* (New York: Columbia University Press, 2001); David C. Leege et al., *The Politics of Cultural Differences: Social Change and Voter Mobilization Strategies in the Post–New Deal Period* (Princeton, NJ: Princeton University Press, 2002); and Richard Neuhaus, *The Naked Public Square: Religion and American Democracy* (Grand Rapids, MI: Eerdmans, 1986). See also Edith L. Blumhofer, ed., *Religion, Politics, and the American Experience: Reflections on Religion and American Public Life* (Tuscaloosa: University of Alabama Press, 2002); Paul Djupe and Laura Olson, eds., *Religious Interests in Community Conflict: Beyond the Culture Wars* (Waco, TX: Baylor University Press, 2007); Charles W. Dunn, *Faith, Freedom, and the Future: Religion in American Political Culture* (Lanham, MD:

Rowman & Littlefield, 2003); David S. Gutterman and Andrew R. Murphy, eds., *Religion, Politics, and American Identity: New Directions, New Controversies* (Lanham, MD: Lexington, 2006); Michael J. Perry, *Religion in Politics: Constitutional and Moral Perspectives* (New York: Oxford University Press, 1999); Alan Wolfe, *The Transformation of American Religion: How We Actually Live Our Faith* (Chicago: University of Chicago Press, 2005); and Nicolas Wolterstorff and Robert Audi, *Religion in the Public Square: The Place of Religious Convictions in Political Debate* (Lanham, MD: Rowman & Littlefield, 1996).

29. The *Journal for Cultural and Religious Theory* 8:2 (2007) discusses "Religion, Democracy, and the Politics of Fright." A version of this book's introduction appears therein, along with several provocative essays that mark happy exceptions to the trends I note here.

30. See, for example, Randall Balmer, *Thy Kingdom Come: How the Religious Right Distorts the Faith and Threatens America: An Evangelical's Lament* (New York: Basic, 2006); Tanya Erzen, "Warriors for Christ: The Electoral Politics of the Religious Right," *New Labor Forum* 14:3 (October 2005): 45–52; Jeffrey Stout, *Democracy and Tradition* (Princeton, NJ: Princeton University Press, 2003); Winnifred Sullivan, *The Impossibility of Religious Freedom* (Princeton, NJ: Princeton University Press, 2005); Melani McAlister, "Prophecy, Politics, and the Popular: The *Left Behind* Series and Christian Fundamentalism's New World Order," *South Atlantic Quarterly* 102:4 (Fall 2003); and Hugh Urban, *Secrets of the Kingdom: Religion and Secrecy in the Bush Administration* (Lanham, MD: Rowman & Littlefield, 2007).

31. See Russell Jacoby, *The Last Intellectuals: American Culture in the Age of Academe* (New York: Basic, 1996); John Michael, *Anxious Intellects: Academic Professionals, Public Intellectuals, and Enlightenment Values* (Durham, NC: Duke University Press, 2000); and Richard Posner, *Public Intellectuals: A Study of Decline* (Cambridge, MA: Harvard University Press, 2003).

32. Theorists in the field, such as Jeffrey Stout, engage in this kind of critical activity. Indeed, Stout's work is laudable in many ways. Yet it is far less common to find such a critical focus outside of theoretical literature.

33. Adolph Reed, Jr., "The 2004 Election in Perspective: The Myth of the 'Cultural Divide' and the Triumph of Neoliberal Ideology," *American Quarterly* 57:1 (2005): 12–13.

34. See Michelle Goldberg, *Kingdom Coming: The Rise of Christian Nationalism* (New York: Norton, 2006); Christopher Hedges, *American Fascists: The Christian Right and the War on America* (New York: Free Press, 2006); Christopher Hitchens, *God Is Not Great: How Religion Poisons Everything* (New York: Twelve, 2007); Esther Kaplan, *With God on Their Side: George W. Bush and the Christian Right* (New York: New Press, 2005); Damon Linker, *The Theocons: Secular America under Siege* (New York: Anchor, 2007); Kevin Phillips, *American Theocracy: The Perils and Politics of Radical Religion, Oil, and Borrowed Money in the 21st Century* (New York: Viking, 2006); Lauren Sandler, *Righteous: Dispatches from the Evangelical Youth Movement* (New York: Viking, 2006); Jeff Sharlet, "Through a Glass, Darkly: How the Christian Right Is Reimagining U.S. History," *Harper's* (December 2006); and Gordy Slack, "Inside the Creation Museum," *Salon* (May 31, 2007).

35. Isaac Kramnick and R. Laurence Moore, *The Godless Constitution: A Moral Defense of the Secular State* (New York: Norton, 2005), train their focus on the electoral process and public speech—the preoccupation with religious "arguments" is one of the more curious focuses in this literature—and continue to note their concern about the

"inappropriate" ways in which religious practitioners (like James Dobson) "endorse" political candidates.

36. Goldberg makes this point wittily and perceptively in *Kingdom Coming*, p. 102.

37. See Terry Eagleton, *After Theory* (New York: Basic, 2004); and Christopher Norris, *What's Wrong with Postmodernism? Critical Theory and the Ends of Philosophy* (Baltimore, MD: Johns Hopkins University Press, 1990).

38. Robert A. Orsi, *Between Heaven and Earth: The Religious Worlds People Make and the Scholars Who Study Them* (Princeton, NJ: Princeton University Press, 2005), p. 188. Orsi also speaks compellingly about the political dimensions of these considerations in "What Christian Nation? For a Reality-Based Religious History of the United States," paper delivered at North Carolina State University (December 4, 2006).

39. See, for example, Thomas Frank, *What's the Matter with Kansas? How Conservatives Won the Heart of America* (New York: Holt, 2005).

40. I borrow this term from Michael Walzer, whose *Interpretation and Social Criticism* has shaped my investigations into cultures of religious complaint in this book and other writings.

41. See James Squire and Jane Smiley, "Fear Factor," *American Prospect* (April 2004).

42. See Balmer, *Thy Kingdom Come*, pp. 196–197; Elizabeth A. Castelli, "Notes from the War Room," *Revealer* (April 5, 2006); Michelle Goldberg's interview with Hedges, "The Holy Blitz Rolls On," *Salon* (January 8, 2007); Phillips, *American Theocracy*, pp. 64, 216, 233; and Jeff Sharlet, "Preachers of Doom," *New Statesman* (July 19, 2007).

43. See Bivins, "Religious and Legal Others: Identity, Law, and Representation in American Christian Right and Neopagan Cultural Conflicts," *Culture and Religion* 6:1 (March 2005): 31–56. See also Hans J. Hacker, *The Culture of Conservative Christian Litigation* (Lanham, MD: Rowman & Littlefield, 2005).

44. Quoted in Bull and Gallagher, *Perfect Enemies* (1997 ed.), p. 211.

45. William E. Connolly, "The Evangelical-Capitalist Resonance Machine," *Political Theory* 33:6 (December 2005): 875.

46. I have recently been persuaded by Scott Sandage, *Born Losers: A History of Failure in America* (Cambridge, MA: Harvard University Press, 2005), to think about an additional valence of fear's commercial life. In addition to the explicit commodity dimension, there is a symbolic dimension. While it may not be the case that these mass-produced narratives create a single mold into which the righteous must fit themselves, it remains apparent that economic language is everywhere: the wages of sin, debt, the credit that is due to God.

47. Frank Furedi, *Politics of Fear: Beyond Left and Right* (New York: Continuum, 2005), pp. 3–4.

48. Jeffrey Stout, "The Spirit of Democracy and the Rhetoric of Excess," *Journal of Religious Ethics* 35:1 (March 2007): 3–21, 3.

49. Ibid., p. 5.

50. Furedi, *Politics of Fear*, p. 19.

51. Ibid., p. 22.

52. Wendy Brown, *Politics Out of History* (Princeton, NJ: Princeton University Press, 2001), p. 22.

53. See Noah Feldman, *Divided by God: America's Church-State Problem—and What We Should Do about It* (New York: Farrar, Straus and Giroux, 2005).

54. I thank Brooke Outland for this wonderful phrase and for permission to use it here.

55. See William R. Hutchison, *Religious Pluralism: The Contentious History of a Founding Ideal* (New Haven, CT: Yale University Press, 2004).

56. Greeley and Hout, *The Truth about Conservative Christians*, p. 12.

57. Christian Smith, *American Evangelicalism: Embattled and Thriving* (Chicago: University of Chicago Press, 1998), p. 89.

58. See Michael Rogin, *Ronald Reagan: The Movie, and Other Essays in Political Demonology* (Berkeley: University of California Press, 1988); Richard Slotkin, *Gunfighter Nation: The Myth of the Frontier in Twentieth Century America*, new ed. (Norman: University of Oklahoma Press, 1998); and Larry J. Reynolds, "American Cultural Iconography," in Larry J. Reynolds and Gordon Hunter, eds., *National Imaginaries, American Identities: The Cultural Work of American Iconography* (Princeton, NJ: Princeton University Press, 2000), p. 12.

Bibliography

Adorno, Theodor W. *The Culture Industry*. New York: Brunner-Routledge, 2001.

Agamben, Giorgio. *Homo Sacer: Sovereign Power and Bare Life*. Palo Alto, CA: Stanford University Press, 1998.

Ahlstrom, Sydney E. *A Religious History of the American People*. New Haven, CT: Yale University Press, 1973.

Aho, James. *This Thing of Darkness: A Sociology of the Enemy*. Seattle: University of Washington Press, 1994.

Allen, Bob. "Popular 'Hell Houses' Draw Praise, Criticism." *Associated Baptist Press* 00–95 (October 19, 2000).

Anthony, Ted. "Where Comics and Christianity Meet." *Associated Press* (July 19, 1998).

Apostolidis, Paul. *Stations of the Cross: Adorno and Christian Right Radio*. Durham, NC: Duke University Press, 2000.

Appadurai, Arjun. *Modernity at Large: Cultural Dimensions of Globalization*. Minneapolis: University of Minnesota Press, 1996.

Appiah, Kwame Anthony. *The Ethics of Identity*. Princeton, NJ: Princeton University Press, 2007.

Aranza, Jacob. *Backward Masking Unmasked: Backward Satanic Messages of Rock and Roll Exposed*. Shreveport, LA: Huntington House, 1983.

———. *Making a Love That Lasts: How to Find Love without Settling for Sex*. Ann Arbor, Mich.: Servant, 1996.

Aranza, Jacob, and Theresa Lamson. *Reasonable Reason to Wait*. Lafayette, La.: Huntington House, 1984.

Ariel, Yaakov. *Evangelizing the Chosen People: Missions to the Jews in America, 1880–2000*. Chapel Hill: University of North Carolina Press, 2000.

———. "How Are Jews and Israel Portrayed in the Left Behind Series? A Historical Discussion of Jewish-Christian Relations," in Bruce David Forbes and Jeanne Halgren Kilde, eds., *Rapture, Revelation, and the End Times: Exploring the* Left Behind *Series*. New York: Palgrave Macmillan, 2004.

Arnett, Jeffrey Jensen. *Metal Heads: Heavy Metal Music and Adolescent Alienation*. Boulder, CO: Westview, 1996.

Asad, Talal. *Formations of the Secular: Christianity, Islam, and Modernity*. Palo Alto, CA: Stanford University Press, 2003.

Austin, Andrew. "Faith Matters: George Bush and Providence." Political Research Associates, *Public Eye* (March 18, 2003).

Baker, Phil. "The Hum of the Tuning Fork." *Hindu* (July 1, 2001).

Balmer, Randall. *Blessed Assurance: A History of Evangelicalism in America*. Boston: Beacon, 1999.

————. *Mine Eyes Have Seen the Glory: A Journey into the Evangelical Subculture in America*, 3rd ed. New York: Oxford University Press, 2000.

————. *Thy Kingdom Come: How the Religious Right Distorts the Faith and Threatens America: An Evangelical's Lament.* New York: Basic, 2006.

Balmer, Randall, ed. *Encyclopedia of Evangelicalism*, rev. ed. Waco, TX: Baylor University Press, 2004.

Bangs, Lester. "Bring Your Mother to the Gas Chamber." *Creem* (June 1972).

Barkun, Michael. *A Culture of Conspiracy: Apocalyptic Visions in Contemporary America.* Berkeley: University of California Press, 2003.

Barthes, Roland. *The Responsibility of Forms: Critical Essays on Music, Art, and Representation.* Berkeley: University of California Press, 1991.

Bartkowski, John P. *The Promise Keepers: Servants, Soldiers, and Godly Men.* New Brunswick, NJ: Rutgers University Press, 2004.

Baudrillard, Jean. *Simulacra and Simulacrum.* Ann Arbor: University of Michigan Press, 1995.

Beal, Timothy K. *Religion and Its Monsters.* New York: Routledge, 2002.

Beaujon, Andrew. *Body Piercing Saved My Life: Inside the Phenomenon of Christian Rock.* New York: Da Capo, 2006.

Beck, Ulrich. *Risk Society: Towards a New Modernity.* London: Sage, 1992.

Bellah, Robert. *Varieties of Civil Religion.* New York: Harper & Row, 1980.

Benhabib, Seyla, ed. *Democracy and Difference: Contesting the Boundaries of the Political.* Princeton, NJ: Princeton University Press, 1996.

Bennett, David H. *The Party of Fear: From Nativist Movements to the New Right in American History.* New York: Vintage, 1995.

Bercovitch, Sacvan. *The Puritan Origins of the American Self.* New Haven, CT: Yale University Press, 1975.

————. *The Rites of Assent: Transformations in the Symbolic Construction of America.* New York: Routledge, 1992.

Berry, Colin. "The Mystery of Chick Comics." *Wired* 5:2 (February 1997).

"Bible Belt Pastors Welcome Sinners to a Virtual House of Hell." *Times* (London) (November 1, 2002).

Binder, Amy. "Constructing Racial Rhetoric: Media Depictions of Harm in Heavy Metal and Rap Music." *American Sociological Review* 58:6 (1993): 753–768.

Bivins, Jason C. *The Fracture of Good Order: Christian Antiliberalism and the Challenge to American Politics.* Chapel Hill: University of North Carolina Press, 2003.

————. "Religion in Bush's America." *Sofia* (May 2006).

————. "The Religion of Fear: Conservative Evangelicals, Identity, and Antiliberal Pop." *Journal for Cultural and Religious Theory* 8:2 (July 2007).

————. "Religious and Legal Others: Identity, Law, and Representation in American Christian Right and Neopagan Cultural Conflicts." *Culture and Religion* 6:1 (March 2005).

Blecha, Peter. *Taboo Tunes: A History of Banned Bands and Censored Songs.* San Francisco, CA: Backbeat, 2004.

Blocker, Jack S. *American Temperance Movements: Cycles of Reform.* Woodbridge, CT: Twayne, 1989.

Blumhofer, Edith L., ed. *Religion, Politics, and the American Experience: Reflections on Religion and American Public Life.* Tuscaloosa: University of Alabama Press, 2002.

Bok, Sissela. *Mayhem: Violence as Public Entertainment.* Reading, MA: Perseus, 1998.

Bonta, Steve. "Is It 'Only Rock 'n' Roll'?" *New American* 18:7 (April 8, 2002).

"Booksellers' Group May Expel Chick." *Christianity Today* (October 23, 1981).

Bosman, Judith. "Christian Message, Secular Messengers." *New York Times* (April 26, 2006).

Boston, Rob. "Left Behind." *Church and State* (January 2, 2002).

Bourdieu, Pierre. *Distinction: A Social Critique of the Judgement of Taste.* Cambridge, MA: Harvard University Press, 2002.

Boyer, Pascal. *Religion Explained: The Evolutionary Origins of Religious Thought.* New York: Basic, 2001.

Boyer, Paul. *When Time Shall Be No More: Prophecy Belief in Modern American Culture.* Cambridge, MA: Belknap, 1992.

Brasher, Brenda E. *Give Me That Online Religion.* New Brunswick, NJ: Rutgers University Press, 2004.

Brinkley, Alan. *The End of Reform: New Deal Liberalism in Recession and War.* New York: Vintage, 1995.

Bronfen, Elisabeth. *The Knotted Subject: Hysteria and Its Discontents.* Princeton, NJ: Princeton University Press, 1998.

Brother Randall. "My Dinner with Bob Larson: Interview with Boyd Rice." *Snake Oil,* no. 2 (self-published, 1994).

Brothers, Fletcher A. *The Rock Report.* Lancaster, PA: Starburst, 1987.

Brown, Candy Gunther. *The Word in the World: Evangelical Writing, Publishing, and Reading in America, 1789–1880.* Chapel Hill: University of North Carolina Press, 2004.

Brown, Wendy. *Politics Out of History.* Princeton, NJ: Princeton University Press, 2001.

Brulliard, Karin. "Faith through Fright: Shows Aim to Save by Depicting Hell." *Washington Post* (October 30, 2004).

Bukatman, Scott. *Matters of Gravity: Special Effects and Supermen in the 20th Century.* Durham, NC: Duke University Press, 2003.

Bull, Chris, and John Gallagher. *Perfect Enemies: The Religious Right, the Gay Movement, and the Politics of the 1990s.* New York: Crown, 1997.

Burkett, Larry. *The Illuminati.* Nashville, TN: Thomas Nelson, 1996.

———. *The Thor Conspiracy.* Nashville, TN: Thomas Nelson, 2005.

Burns, Sarah L. *Painting the Dark Side: Art and the Gothic Imagination in Nineteenth Century America.* Berkeley: University of California Press, 2004.

Butler, Jon. *Awash in a Sea of Faith: Christianizing the American People.* Cambridge, MA: Harvard University Press, 1990.

Camp, Gregory S. *Selling Fear: Conspiracy Theories and End-Times Paranoia.* Grand Rapids, MI: Baker Book House, 1997.

Capps, Walter. *The New Religious Right: Piety, Patriotism, and Politics.* Columbia: University of South Carolina Press, 1990.

Carpenter, Joel A. *Revive Us Again: The Reawakening of American Fundamentalism.* New York: Oxford University Press, 1997.

———. "Youth for Christ and the New Evangelicals," in D. G. Hart, ed., *Reckoning with the Past.* Grand Rapids, MI: Baker, 1995.

Carroll, Noel. *The Philosophy of Horror; or, The Paradoxes of the Heart.* New York: Routledge, 1990.

Carwadine, Richard J. *Evangelicals and Politics in Antebellum America.* New Haven, CT: Yale University Press, 1993.

Casanova, José. *Public Religions and the Modern World.* Chicago: University of Chicago Press, 1994.

Chabon, Michael. *The Adventures of Kavalier and Klay.* New York: Picador, 2000.

Chang, Jeff. *Can't Stop, Won't Stop: A History of the Hip-Hop Generation.* New York: Picador, 2005.

Chappell, David. *Stone of Hope: Prophetic Religion and the Death of Jim Crow.* Chapel Hill: University of North Carolina Press, 2004.

Chick, Jack T. *Smokescreens.* Chino, CA: Chick, 1983.

———. *A Solution to . . . the Marriage Mess.* Chino, CA: Chick, 1978.

Chidester, David. *Authentic Fakes: Religion and American Popular Culture.* Berkeley: University of California Press, 2005.

Chireau, Yvonne. "Supernaturalism," in Philip Goff and Paul Harvey, eds., *Themes in Religion and American Culture.* Chapel Hill: University of North Carolina Press, 2004.

Christe, Ian. *Sound of the Beast: The Complete Headbanging History of Heavy Metal.* New York: HarperCollins, 2003.

"Christian Comic Books Hope to Soar." *Christianity Today* (July 19, 1993).

"The Christian Fright." *Harper's* 295:1769 (October 1997).

Clark, Lynn Schofield. *From Angels to Aliens: Teenagers, the Media, and the Supernatural.* New York: Oxford University Press, 2003.

Cloonan, Martin, and Reebee Garofolo, eds. *Policing Pop.* Philadelphia: Temple University Press, 2003.

Cloud, David. *Rock Music vs. the God of the Bible.* Port Huron, MI: Way of Life Literature, 2000.

Colton, Michael. "Cartooning for Christ: Jack Chick's Religious Comics." *Brill's Content* 2:9 (November 1999).

Conkin, Paul. *American Originals: Homemade Varieties of Christianity.* Chapel Hill: University of North Carolina Press, 1997.

Connolly, William E. "The Evangelical-Capitalist Resonance Machine." *Political Theory* 33:6 (December 2005).

Coontz, Stephanie. *The Way We Never Were: American Families and the Nostalgia Trip.* New York: Basic, 2000.

Cooperman, Alan. "Coming Soon to a Church Near You." *Washington Post* (October 21, 2005).

Cordero, Jonathan. "The Production of Christian Fiction." *Journal of Religion and Popular Culture* 6 (Spring 2004): 1–17.

Corrigan, John, ed. *Religion and Emotion: Approaches and Interpretations.* New York: Oxford University Press, 2004.

Cromartie, Michael, ed. *Religion and Radical Politics: The Religious New Right in American Politics.* Washington, DC: Ethics and Public Policy Center Press, 1993.

Cross, Whitney. *The Burned-Over District: The Social and Intellectual History of Enthusiastic Religion in Western New York, 1800–1850.* Ithaca, NY: Cornell University Press, 2006.

Culver, Virginia. "Hell House Outlines Stages of Sin." *Denver Post* (October 6, 2000).

Dahl, Robert. *A Preface to Democratic Theory.* New Haven, CT: Yale University Press, 1956.

Davenport, Kristin. "Church Uses Scare Tactics on Halloween." *Santa Fe New Mexican* (October 27, 1999).

Dawson, Lorne L., and Douglas E. Cowan, eds. *Religion Online: Finding Faith on the Internet.* New York: Routledge, 2004.

de Certeau, Michel. *The Practice of Everyday Life.* Berkeley: University of California Press, 2002.

———. "Reading as Poaching," in A. Bennet, ed., *Readers and Reading.* New York: Longman, 1995.

De Luca, Tom, and John Buell. *Liars! Cheaters! Evildoers! Demonization and the End of Civil Debate in American Politics.* New York: New York University Press, 2005.

Debord, Guy. *The Society of the Spectacle.* New York: Zone, 1995.

Deflem, Mathieu. "Rap, Rock, and Censorship: Popular Culture and the Technologies of Justice." Unpublished paper presented at the Law and Society Association annual meeting, Chicago, May 1993 (rev. March 2001).

Delbanco, Andrew. *The Death of Satan: How Americans Have Lost the Sense of Evil.* New York: Noonday, 1996.

Deleuze, Gilles, and Felix Guattari. *A Thousand Plateaus: Capitalism and Schizophrenia.* Minneapolis: University of Minnesota Press, 1993.

Demos, John Putnam. *Entertaining Satan: Witchcraft and the Culture of Early New England.* New York: Oxford University Press, 1982.

"Denver's Sinners Form Queue for a Ticket to Hell." *Sunday Times* (London) (November 3, 1996).

Dery, Mark. "Fear and Loathing: The Gospel According to Jack." *Village Voice Literary Supplement* (April 1999).

DeSmet, Kate. "Comic Book Series Gets No Laugh from Christian Groups." *Detroit News* (April 8, 1989).

Diamond, Sara. *Spiritual Warfare: The Politics of the Christian Right.* Boston: South End, 1989.

Diggins, John Patrick. *The Rise and Fall of the American Left.* New York: Norton, 1992.

Dionne, E. J. "A Shift among the Evangelicals." *Washington Post* (June 16, 2006).

———. *Why Americans Hate Politics.* New York: Touchstone, 1991.

Djupe, Paul, and Laura Olson, eds. *Religious Interests in Community Conflict: Beyond the Culture Wars.* Waco, TX: Baylor University Press, 2007.

Donohue, William A. "A Survey of Chick Publications." *Catalyst* (October 1996).

Dunn, Charles W. *Faith, Freedom, and the Future: Religion in American Political Culture.* Lanham, MD: Rowman & Littlefield, 2003.

Eagleton, Terry. *After Theory.* New York: Basic, 2004.

Edmundson, Mark. *Nightmare on Main Street: Angels, Sadomasochism, and the Culture of the Gothic.* Cambridge, MA: Harvard University Press, 1997.

Edney, Hazel Trice. "Imus Aftermath: Black Leaders Vow Protest of Rap Industry." *Black Press USA* (June 18, 2007).

Edwards, Rebecca. *New Spirits: Americans in the Gilded Age, 1865–1905.* New York: Oxford University Press, 2005.

Eggen, Dan. "FBI Reports Duct-Taping, 'Baptizing' at Guantanamo." *Washington Post* (January 3, 2007).

Eisner, Will. *Comics and Sequential Art: Principles and Practice of the World's Most Popular Art Form.* Tamarac, FL: Poorhouse, 1985.

Ellis, Bill. *Lucifer Ascending: The Occult in Folklore and Popular Culture.* Lexington: University of Kentucky Press, 2004.

———. *Raising the Devil: Satanism, New Religions, and the Media.* Lexington: University of Kentucky Press, 2000.

Emerson, Michael O., and Christian Smith. *Divided by Faith: Evangelical Religion and the Problem of Race in America.* New York: Oxford University Press, 2001.

Erzen, Tanya. *Straight to Jesus: Sexual and Christian Conversions in the Ex-Gay Movement.* Berkeley: University of California Press, 2006.

———. "Warriors for Christ: The Electoral Politics of the Religious Right." *New Labor Forum* 14:3 (October 2005).

Evensen, Bruce J. *God's Man for the Gilded Age: Dwight L. Moody and the Rise of Modern Mass Evangelism.* New York: Oxford University Press, 2003.

Feldman, Noah. *Divided by God: America's Church-State Problem—and What We Should Do about It.* New York: Farrar, Straus and Giroux, 2005.

Fernando, S. H., Jr. "Back in the Day: 1975–1979," in Alan Light, ed., *The Vibe History of Hip Hop.* New York: Three Rivers, 1999.

Fineman, Howard. "Ties That Bind: Bush and LaHaye Have a History, and Share a Sense of Mission." *Newsweek* (May 24, 2004).

Fiske, John. *Understanding Popular Culture.* New York: Routledge, 1989.

Florio, Gwen. "Giving Them Hell." *Philadelphia Enquirer* (October 23, 1997).

Floyd, Samuel. *The Power of Black Music: Interpreting Its History from Africa to the United States.* New York: Oxford University Press, 1996.

Forbes, Bruce David. "How Popular Are the Left Behind Books . . . and Why?" in Bruce David Forbes and Jeanne Halgren Kilde, eds., *Rapture, Revelation, and the End Times: Exploring the* Left Behind *Series.* New York: Palgrave Macmillan, 2004.

Forbes, Bruce David, and Jeanne Halgren Kilde, eds., *Rapture, Revelation, and the End Times: Exploring the* Left Behind *Series.* New York: Palgrave Macmillan, 2004.

Foucault, Michel. *The History of Sexuality,* vol. 1: *An Introduction.* New York: Vintage, 1990.

———. *The Order of Things: An Archaeology of the Human Sciences.* New York: Vintage, 1994.

Fowler, Robert Booth. *A New Engagement: Evangelical Political Thought, 1966–1976.* Grand Rapids, MI: Eerdmans, 1982.

Fowler, Robert B. *The World of Jack T. Chick.* San Francisco, CA: Last Gasp, 2001.

Frank, Thomas. *What's the Matter with Kansas? How Conservatives Won the Heart of America.* New York: Holt, 2005.

Frankfurter, David. *Evil Incarnate: Rumors of Demonic Conspiracy and Satanic Abuse in History.* Princeton, NJ: Princeton University Press, 2006.

Freud, Sigmund. *The Future of an Illusion.* New York: Norton, 1989.

Frykholm, Amy Johnson. *Rapture Culture: Left Behind in Evangelical America.* New York: Oxford University Press, 2004.

———. "What Social and Political Messages Appear in the *Left Behind* Books," in Bruce David Forbes and Jeanne Halgren Kilde, eds., *Rapture, Revelation, and the End Times: Exploring the* Left Behind *Series.* New York: Palgrave Macmillan, 2004.

Fuentez, Tania. "Church Uses Images of Sept. 11 Terrorist Attacks in Alternative Halloween Tour." *Associated Press* (October 30, 2001).

Fukuyama, Francis. "The End of History?" *National Interest*, no. 16 (Summer 1989).

Fuller, Robert. *Naming the Antichrist: The History of an American Obsession.* New York: Oxford University Press, 1995.

———. *Wonder: From Emotion to Spirituality.* Chapel Hill: University of North Carolina Press, 2006.

Furedi, Frank. *Politics of Fear: Beyond Left and Right.* New York: Continuum, 2005.

Gardella, Peter. "Spiritual Warfare in the Fiction of Frank Peretti," in Colleen McDannell, ed., *Religions of the United States in Practice*, vol. 2. Princeton, NJ: Princeton University Press, 2001.

Gardella, Peter, and Colleen McDannell. "Catholic Horror: *The Exorcist* (1973)," in Colleen McDannell, ed., *Catholics in the Movies.* New York: Oxford University Press, 2007.

Gates, David. "The Pop Prophets." *Newsweek* (May 24, 2004).

Gaustad, Edwin S. *Dissent in American Religion.* Chicago: University of Chicago Press, 1973.

George, Nelson. *Hip Hop America.* New York: Penguin, 1998.

Gibbs, Nancy. "The Bible and the Apocalypse." *Time* (June 23, 2002).

Gibson, James William. *Warrior Dreams: Violence and Manhood in Post-Vietnam America.* New York: Hill & Wang, 1994.

Girard, René. *The Scapegoat.* Baltimore, MD: Johns Hopkins University Press, 1989.

Gitlin, Todd. *The Sixties: Years of Hope, Days of Rage.* New York: Bantam, 1993.

———. *The Twilight of Common Dreams.* New York: Metropolitan, 1995.

Glanton, Dahleen. "Halloween Bedevils Some U.S. Churches." *Chicago Tribune* (October 25, 2004).

Glassner, Barry. *The Culture of Fear: Why Americans Are Afraid of the Wrong Things.* New York: Basic, 1999.

Godwin, Jeff. *Dancing with Demons: The Music's Real Master.* Chino, CA: Chick, 1988.

———. *Devil's Disciples: The Truth about Rock Music.* Chino, CA: Chick, 1986.

———. *What's Wrong with Christian Rock.* Chino, CA: Chick, 1997.

Goldberg, Michelle. *Kingdom Coming: The Rise of Christian Nationalism.* New York: Norton, 2006.

Goldberg, Robert. *Enemies Within: The Culture of Conspiracy in Modern America.* New Haven, CT: Yale University Press, 2001.

Goode, Erich, and Nachman Ben-Yehuda. *Moral Panics: The Social Construction of Deviance.* Oxford: Blackwell, 1994.

Goodstein, Laurie. "Disowning Conservative Politics, Evangelical Pastor Rattles Flock." *New York Times* (July 30, 2006).

Gorenberg, Gershom. *The End of Days: Fundamentalism and the Struggle for the Temple Mount.* New York: Oxford University Press, 2000.

———. "Intolerance: The Bestseller." *American Prospect* (September 23, 2002).

Gray, John. *Black Mass: Apocalyptic Religion and the Death of Utopia* (New York: Farrar, Straus and Giroux, 2007).

Greeley, Andrew, and Michael Hout, *The Truth about Conservative Christians: What They Think and Believe.* Chicago: University of Chicago Press, 2006.

Green, John, Mark Rozell, and Clyde Wilcox, eds. *The Christian Right in American Politics: Marching to the Millennium.* Washington, DC: Georgetown University Press, 2003.

Greider, William. *Who Will Tell the People?* New York: Touchstone, 1992.

Greven, Philip. *The Protestant Temperament: Patterns of Child-Rearing, Religious Experience, and the Self in Early America.* New York: New American Library, 1979.

Gribben, Crawford. *Rapture Fiction and the Evangelical Crisis.* Darlington, England: Evangelical Press, 2006.

Grossberg, Lawrence. *Bringing It All Back Home: Essays on Cultural Studies.* Durham, NC: Duke University Press, 1997.

Gutjahr, Paul. *An American Bible: A History of the Good Book in the United States, 1777–1880.* Palo Alto, CA: Stanford University Press, 2001.

Gutmann, Amy. *Identity in Democracy.* Princeton, NJ: Princeton University Press, 2004.

Gutmann, Amy, and Charles Taylor, eds. *Multiculturalism.* Princeton, NJ: Princeton University Press, 1994.

Gutterman, David S. *Prophetic Politics: Christian Social Movements and American Democracy.* Ithaca, NY: Cornell University Press, 2005.

Gutterman, David S., and Andrew R. Murphy, eds. *Religion, Politics, and American Identity: New Directions, New Controversies.* Lanham, MD: Lexington, 2006.

Hacker, Hans J. *The Culture of Conservative Christian Litigation.* Lanham, MD: Rowman & Littlefield, 2005.

Halberstam, Judith. *Skin Shows: Gothic Horror and the Technology of Monsters.* Durham, NC: Duke University Press, 1995.

Hall, David. "What Is the Place of 'Experience' in Religious History?" *Religion and American Culture* 13:2 (2003): 241–250.

———. *Worlds of Wonder, Days of Judgment: Popular Religious Belief in Early New England.* Cambridge, MA: Harvard University Press, 1990.

Hall, Timothy D. *Contested Boundaries: Itinerancy and the Reshaping of the Colonial American Religious World.* Durham, NC: Duke University Press, 1994.

Harding, Susan Friend. *The Book of Jerry Falwell: Fundamentalist Language and Politics.* Princeton, NJ: Princeton University Press, 2001.

Harris, Ron. "Some Churches Offer Sinful Scare." *Associated Press* (October 28, 1997).

Harris, Sam. *Letter to a Christian Nation.* New York: Knopf, 2006.

Hart, D. G. *That Old-Time Religion in Modern America: Evangelical Protestantism in the Twentieth Century.* Chicago: Dee, 2002.

Hatch, Nathan. *The Democratization of American Christianity.* New Haven, CT: Yale University Press, 1989.

Hatfield, Charles. *Alternative Comics: An Emerging Literature.* Jackson: University of Mississippi Press, 2005.

Haynes, Michael K. *The God of Rock: A Christian Perspective of Rock Music.* Lindale, TX: Haynes, 1982.

Hebdige, Dick. *Subculture: The Meaning of Style.* New York: Routledge, 1981.

Hedgehog Review 5:3 (Fall 2003): *Fear Itself.*

Hedges, Christopher. *American Fascists: The Christian Right and the War on America.* New York: Free Press, 2006.

Heineman, Kenneth J. *God Is a Conservative: Religion, Politics, and Morality in Contemporary America.* New York: New York University Press, 1998.

Heins, Marjorie. *Not in Front of the Children: "Indecency," Censorship, and the Innocence of Youth.* New York: Hill & Wang, 2001.

"'Hell House' Kits Selling Nationally." *Christianity Today* (October 7, 1996).

Heller, Terry. *The Delights of Terror: An Aesthetics of the Tale of Terror.* Urbana: University of Illinois Press, 1987.

Hendershot, Heather. *Shaking the World for Jesus: Media in Conservative Evangelical Culture.* Chicago: University of Chicago Press, 2004.

Heyrman, Christine Leigh. *Southern Cross: The Beginnings of the Bible Belt.* Chapel Hill: University of North Carolina Press, 1997.

Hicks, Darryl E., and David A. Lewis. *The Todd Phenomenon.* Harrison, AR: New Leaf, 1979.

Higginbotham, Adam. "One Hell of a Show." *Daily Telegraph* (November 18, 2002).

Hitchcock, Mark, Tommy Ice, and Tim LaHaye. *The Truth behind* Left Behind: *A Biblical View of the End Times.* Colorado Springs, CO: Multnomah, 2004.

Hitchens, Christopher. *God Is Not Great: How Religion Poisons Everything.* New York: Twelve, 2007.

Hochschild, Arlie Russell. *The Managed Heart: Commercialization of Human Feeling,* 2nd ed. Berkeley: University of California Press, 2003.

Hollander, John. "Fear Itself." *Social Research* 71:4 (Winter 2004).

Holmes, David L. *The Faiths of the Founding Fathers.* New York: Oxford University Press, 2006.

Hoover, Stewart M. "Introduction," in Stewart M. Hoover and Lynn Schofield Clark, eds., *Practicing Religion in the Age of Media: Explorations in Media, Religion, and Culture.* New York: Columbia University Press, 2002.

———. "Visual Religion in Media Culture," in David Morgan and Sally M. Promey, eds., *The Visual Culture of American Religions.* Berkeley: University of California Press, 2001.

Horner, Kim. "A Truly Haunting House." *Dallas Morning News* (October 21, 1999).

Huddy, Leonie. "Fear and How It Works: Science and the Social Sciences." *Social Research* 71:4 (Winter 2004).

Hume, David. *Dialogues and Natural History of Religion.* New York: Oxford University Press, 1998.

Hunter, James Davison. *Culture Wars: The Struggle to Define America.* New York: Basic, 1992.

Hutchison, William R. *Religious Pluralism: The Contentious History of a Founding Ideal.* New Haven, CT: Yale University Press, 2004.

"In Your Face." *Focus on the Family Magazine* (September 1996).

Ingebretsen, Edward J. *At Stake: Monsters and the Rhetoric of Fear in Public Culture.* Chicago: University of Chicago Press, 2001.

———. *Maps of Heaven, Maps of Hell: Religious Terror as Memory from the Puritans to Stephen King.* New York: Sharpe, 1996.

Ito, Robert. "Fear Factor." *L.A. Magazine* (May 2003).

Jackson, Gregory S. "Cultivating Spiritual Sight: Jacob Riis' Virtual-Tour Narrative and the Visual Modernization of Protestant Homiletics." *Representations* 83 (Summer 2003).

Jacobs, Alan. "Apocalyptic President?" *Boston Globe* (April 4, 2004).

Jacoby, Russell. *The Last Intellectuals: American Culture in the Age of Academe.* New York: Basic, 1996.

James, Henry. *The Aspern Papers and the Turn of the Screw.* New York: Penguin, 1984.

Jamison, Sean. "Heaven and Hell." *North Texas Daily* (October 30, 2002).

Jay, Martin. *Downcast Eyes: The Denigration of Vision in Twentieth Century French Thought.* Berkeley: University of California Press, 1994.

Jenkins, Philip. *Decade of Nightmares: The End of the Sixties and the Making of Eighties America.* New York: Oxford University Press, 2006.

———. *Mystics and Messiahs: Cults and New Religions in American History.* New York: Oxford University Press, 2000.

Jones, Gerard. *Men of Tomorrow: Geeks, Gangsters and the Birth of the Comic Book.* New York: Basic, 2004.

Joseph, Mark. *Faith, God and Rock & Roll.* London: Sanctuary, 2003.

Kabel, Marcus. "Texas Church Defends Columbine Scene in 'Hell House.' '" *Reuters* (October 29, 1999).

Kammen, Michael. *American Culture, American Tastes: Social Change in the Twentieth Century.* New York: Knopf, 1999.

Kao, Grace, and Jerome Copulsky. "The Pledge of Allegiance and the Meanings and Limits of Civil Religion." *Journal of the American Academy of Religion* 75:1 (2007).

Kaplan, Esther. *With God on Their Side: George W. Bush and the Christian Right.* New York: New Press, 2005.

Kazin, Michael. *A Godly Hero: The Life of William Jennings Bryan.* New York: Knopf, 2006.

Kearney, Richard. *Strangers, Gods and Monsters: Interpreting Otherness.* New York: Routledge, 2003.

Kellner, Douglas. *Media Culture: Cultural Studies, Identity and Politics between the Modern and the Postmodern.* New York: Routledge, 1995.

Kendall, John. "Lurid Comic Books Attack Beliefs of Most Religions." *Los Angeles Times* (January 25, 1981).

Kendrick, Walter. *The Thrill of Fear: 250 Years of Scary Entertainment.* New York: Grove Weidenfield, 1991.

Kennedy, Pagan. "All about Evil: Jack Chick's Ire and Brimstone." *Village Voice Literary Supplement* (April 1992).

Khatchadourian, Raffi. "Azzam the American: The Making of an Al Qaeda Homegrown." *New Yorker* (January 22, 2007).

King, Richard. *Orientalism and Religion: Postcolonial Theory, India, and "the Mystic East."* New York: Routledge, 1999.

Kintz, Linda. *Between Jesus and the Market: The Emotions That Matter in Right-Wing America.* Durham, NC: Duke University Press, 1997.

———. "Culture and the Religious Right," in Linda Kintz and Julia Lesage, eds., *Media, Culture, and the Religious Right.* Minneapolis: University of Minnesota Press, 1998.

Kirkpatrick, David D. "Club of the Most Powerful Gathers in Strictest Privacy." *New York Times* (August 28, 2004).

Kitwana, Bakari. *Why White Kids Love Hip Hop: Wangstas, Wiggers, Wannabes, and the New Reality of Race in America.* New York: Basic Civitas, 2005.

Kohut, Andrew, et al. *The Diminishing Divide: The Changing Role of Religion in American Politics.* Washington, DC: Brookings Institution Press, 2000.

Konow, David. *Bang Your Head: The Rise and Fall of Heavy Metal Music.* New York: Three Rivers, 2002.

Korpe, Maria, ed. *Shoot the Singer! Music Censorship Today.* London: Zed, 2004.

Kramnick, Isaac, and R. Laurence Moore. *The Godless Constitution: A Moral Defense of the Secular State.* New York: Norton, 2005.

Krims, Adam. *Rap Music and the Poetics of Identity.* Cambridge: Cambridge University Press, 2000.

Kristeva, Julia. *Powers of Horror: An Essay on Abjection.* New York: Columbia University Press, 1982.

Kristof, Nicholas D. "Jesus and Jihad." *New York Times* (July 17, 2004).

Kuebelbeck, Amy. "Under Fire? Is Anti-Catholic Sentiment Increasing? Some Say Yes and Declare They're Not Going to Take It Anymore." *Los Angeles Times* (September 9, 1991).

Kuersteiner, Kurt. *The Unofficial Guide to the Art of Jack T. Chick: Chick Tracts, Crusader Comics, & Battle Cry Newspapers.* Atglen, PA: Schiffer, 2004.

Kugelmass, Jack. *Masked Culture: The Greenwich Village Halloween Parade.* New York: Columbia University Press, 1994.

Kurlansky, Mark. *1968: The Year That Rocked the World.* New York: Random House, 2005.

LaHaye, Tim. *The Battle for the Public Schools.* Old Tappan, NJ: Revell, 1983.

———. "The Colossal Battle." *Esquire* (September 2004).

———. *Faith of Our Founding Fathers.* Brentwood, TN: Wolgemuth & Hyatt, 1987.

LaHaye, Tim, and Greg Dinallo. *Babylon Rising.* Wheaton, IL: Tyndale House, 2003.

LaHaye, Tim, and Jerry B. Jenkins. *Apollyon: The Destroyer Is Unleashed.* Wheaton, IL: Tyndale House, 1999.

———. *Are We Living in the End Times? Current Events Foretold in Scripture . . . and What They Mean.* Wheaton, IL: Tyndale House, 1999.

———. *Armageddon: The Cosmic Battle of the Ages.* Wheaton, IL: Tyndale House, 2003.

———. *Assassins: Assignment: Jerusalem, Target: Antichrist.* Wheaton, IL: Tyndale House, 1999.

———. *Desecration: Antichrist Takes the Throne.* Wheaton, IL: Tyndale House, 2001.

———. *Glorious Appearing: The End of Days.* Wheaton, IL: Tyndale House, 2004.

———. *The Indwelling: The Beast Takes Possession.* Wheaton, IL: Tyndale House, 2000.

———. *Kingdom Come: The Final Victory.* Wheaton, IL: Tyndale House, 2007.

———. *Left Behind: A Novel of Earth's Last Days.* Wheaton, IL: Tyndale House, 1995.

———. *The Mark: The Beast Rules the World.* Wheaton, IL: Tyndale House, 2000.

———. *Nicolae: The Rise of Antichrist.* Wheaton, IL: Tyndale House, 1997.

———. *The Rapture: In the Twinkling of an Eye.* Wheaton, IL: Tyndale House, 2007.

———. *The Regime: Evil Advances.* Wheaton, IL: Tyndale House, 2005.

———. *The Remnant: On the Brink of Armageddon.* Wheaton, IL: Tyndale House, 2002.

———. *The Rising: Antichrist Is Born.* Wheaton, IL: Tyndale House, 2005.

———. *Soul Harvest: The World Takes Sides.* Wheaton, IL: Tyndale House, 1998.

———. *Tribulation Force: The Continuing Drama of Those Left Behind.* Wheaton, IL: Tyndale House, 1996.

LaHaye, Tim, and Bob Phillips. *The Edge of Darkness.* Wheaton, IL: Tyndale House, 2006.

———. *The Europa Conspiracy.* Wheaton, IL: Tyndale House, 2005.

———. *The Secret on Ararat.* Wheaton, IL: Tyndale House, 2004.

Lakoff, George. "Framing the Dems: How Conservatives Control Political Debate and How Progressives Can Take It Back." *American Prospect* 14:8 (September 2003).

———. *Moral Politics: How Liberals and Conservatives Think,* 2nd ed. Chicago: University of Chicago Press, 2001.

Lambert, Frank. *The Founding Fathers and the Place of Religion in America.* Princeton, NJ: Princeton University Press, 2006.

———. *Inventing the "Great Awakening."* Princeton, NJ: Princeton University Press, 2001.

Landres, J. Shawn. "Public Art as Sacred Space: Asian American Community Murals in Los Angeles," in Stewart M. Hoover and Lynn Schofield Clark, eds., *Practicing Religion in the Age of Media: Explorations in Media, Religion, and Culture.* New York: Columbia University Press, 2002.

Lang, Bernhard. *Sacred Games: A History of Christian Worship.* New Haven, CT: Yale University Press, 1997.

Larson, Bob. *Abaddon.* Nashville, TN: Thomas Nelson, 1993.

———. *Hippies, Hindus and Rock & Roll.* Carol Stream, IL: Creation House, 1972.

———. *Larson's Book of Cults.* Wheaton, IL: Tyndale House, 1989.

———. *Larson's Book of Rock.* Wheaton, IL: Tyndale House, 1987.

———. *Rock: For Those Who Listen to the Words and Don't Like What They Hear.* Wheaton, IL: Tyndale House, 1983.

———. *Rock & Roll: The Devil's Diversion.* McCook, NB: Larson, 1971.

———. *Satanism: The Seduction of America's Youth.* Nashville, TN: Thomas Nelson, 1989.

Lawrence, Bruce. *Defenders of God: The Fundamentalist Revolt against the Modern Age.* San Francisco, CA: Harper & Row, 1989.

Layman, Geoffrey. *The Great Divide: Religious and Cultural Conflict in Party Politics.* New York: Columbia University Press, 2001.

Leavitt, Judith Walzer, and Lewis A. Leavitt. "After SARS: Fear and Its Uses." *Dissent* 50:4 (Fall 2003).

Leege, David C., et al. *The Politics of Cultural Differences: Social Change and Voter Mobilization Strategies in the Post–New Deal Period.* Princeton, NJ: Princeton University Press, 2002.

Lefebvre, Henri. *Critique of Everyday Life,* vols. 1–3. New York: Verso, 2002.

"The Legend(s) of John Todd." *Christianity Today* (February 2, 1979).

Levine, Lawrence W. *Highbrow Lowbrow: The Emergence of Cultural Hierarchy in America.* Cambridge, MA: Harvard University Press, 1988.

Lienesch, Michael. *In the Beginning: Fundamentalism, the Scopes Trial, and the Making of the Antievolution Movement.* Chapel Hill: University of North Carolina Press, 2007.

———. *Redeeming America: Piety and Politics in the New Christian Right.* Chapel Hill: University of North Carolina Press, 1993.

Light, Alan. "Public Enemy," in Alan Light, ed., *The Vibe History of Hip Hop.* New York: Three Rivers, 1999.

Light, Alan, ed. *The Vibe History of Hip Hop.* New York: Three Rivers, 1999.

Lindsey, Hal. *The Late Great Planet Earth.* Grand Rapids, MI: Zondervan, 1970.

———. *There's a New World Coming.* Santa Ana, CA: Vision House, 1973.

Linker, Damon. *The Theocons: Secular America under Siege.* New York: Anchor, 2007.

Lipsitz, George. *Time Passages: Collective Memory and American Popular Culture.* Minneapolis: University of Minnesota Press, 2001.

Lott, Eric. *The Disappearing Liberal Intellectual.* New York: Basic, 2006.

———. *Love and Theft: Blackface Minstrelsy and the American Working Class.* New York: Oxford University Press, 1995.

Luhr, Eileen. "Metal Missionaries to the Nation: Christian Heavy Metal Music, 'Family Values,' and Youth Culture, 1984–1994." *American Quarterly* 57 (March 2005).

Luo, Michelle, and Laurie Goodstein. "Emphasis Shifts for New Breed of Evangelicals." *New York Times* (May 21, 2007).

Lyons, Arthur. *Satan Wants You: The Cult of Devil Worship in America.* New York: Mysterious, 1988.

Lyons, Paul. *New Left, New Right, and the Legacy of the Sixties.* Philadelphia: Temple University Press, 1996.

Marcus, Daniel. *Happy Days and Wonder Years: The '50s & the '60s in Contemporary Cultural Politics.* New Brunswick, NJ: Rutgers University Press, 2004.

Marsden, George. *Fundamentalism in American Culture: The Shaping of Twentieth-Century Evangelicalism, 1870–1925.* New York: Oxford University Press, 1980.

Martin, Linda, and Kerry Segrave. *Anti-Rock: The Opposition to Rock 'n' Roll.* New York: Da Capo, 1993.

Martin, William. *With God on Our Side: The Rise of the Religious Right in America.* New York: Broadway, 1995.

Marty, Martin E. *Modern American Religion,* vol. 1: *The Irony of It All, 1893–1919.* Chicago: University of Chicago Press, 1997.

Maske, Monica. "Church Enacts Horrors of the End to Scare Unbelievers Out of Hell." *Star-Ledger* (Calvary, OH) (November 2, 1991).

Massa, Mark S., S.J. "The New and Old Anti-Catholicism and the Analogical Imagination." *Theological Studies* 62 (2001).

Massumi, Brian, ed. *The Politics of Everyday Fear.* Minneapolis: University of Minnesota Press, 1993.

McAlister, Melani. *Epic Encounters: Culture, Media, and U.S. Interests in the Middle East since 1945.* Berkeley: University of California Press, 2005.

———. "Prophecy, Politics, and the Popular: The *Left Behind* Series and Christian Fundamentalism's New World Order." *South Atlantic Quarterly* 102:4 (Fall 2003).

McAllister, Matthew P., Edward H. Sewell, Jr., and Ian Gordon. "Introduction," in Matthew P. McAllister, Edward H. Sewell, Jr., and Ian Gordon, eds., *Comics & Ideology,* vol. 2. New York: Peter Lang, 2001.

McCloud, Scott. *Understanding Comics: The Invisible Art.* New York: HarperCollins, 1993.

McCloud, Sean. *Divine Hierarchies: Class in American Religion and Religious Studies.* Chapel Hill: University of North Carolina Press, 2007.

———. *Making the Religious Fringe: Exotics, Subversives, and Journalists, 1955–1993.* Chapel Hill: University of North Carolina Press, 2003.

McCutcheon, Russell. *Manufacturing Religion: The Discourse on Sui Generis Religion and the Politics of Nostalgia.* New York: Oxford University Press, 2003.

McDannell, Colleen. "Beyond Dr. Dobson: Women, Girls, and Focus on the Family," in Margaret Lamberts Bendroth and Virginia Lieson Brereton, eds., *Women and Twentieth-Century Protestantism.* Champaign-Urbana: University of Illinois Press, 2002.

———. *The Christian Home in Victorian America, 1840–1900.* Bloomington: Indiana University Press, 1994.

———. *Material Christianity: Religion and Popular Culture in America.* New Haven, CT: Yale University Press, 1995.

McGinn, Bernard. *Antichrist: Two Thousand Years of the Human Fascination with Evil.* New York: Columbia University Press, 2000.

McLoughlin, William G. *Revivals, Awakenings, and Reform: An Essay on Religion and Social Change in America, 1607–1977.* Chicago: University of Chicago Press, 1980.

Merback, Mitchell B. *The Thief, the Cross, and the Wheel: Pain and the Spectacle of Punishment in Medieval and Renaissance Europe.* Chicago: University of Chicago Press, 1999.

Merrifield, Andy. *Henry Lefebvre: A Critical Introduction.* New York: Routledge, 2006.

Metz, Gary. "Jack Chick's Anti-Catholic Alberto Comic Book Is Exposed as a Fraud." *Christianity Today* (March 13, 1981).

Michael, John. *Anxious Intellects: Academic Professionals, Public Intellectuals, and Enlightenment Values.* Durham, NC: Duke University Press, 2000.

Michaels, Walter Benn. *The Trouble with Diversity: How We Learned to Love Identity and Ignore Inequality.* New York: Metropolitan, 2006.

Michelson, D. L. *Rock Music: Careful or Carnal.* Orlando, FL: Christ for the World, 1975.

Mickelthwait, John, and Adrian Woolridge. *The Right Nation: Why America Is Different.* New York: Penguin, 2005.

Miller, James. *"Democracy Is in the Streets": From Port Huron to the Siege of Chicago.* Cambridge, MA: Harvard University Press, 1994.

Miller, Perry. *The New England Mind: From Colony to Province.* Cambridge, MA: Belknap, 1983.

Miller, Vincent J. *Consuming Religion: Christian Faith and Practice in a Consumer Culture.* New York: Continuum, 2003.

Minkema, Kenneth P. "Possession, Witchcraft, and the Demonic in Puritan Religious Culture," in Colleen McDannell, ed., *Religions of the United States in Practice*, vol. 1. Princeton, NJ: Princeton University Press, 2001.

Mitchell, W. J. T. *Picture Theory: Essays on Verbal and Visual Representation.* Chicago: University of Chicago Press, 1995.

Moen, Matthew C. *The Transformation of the Christian Right.* Tuscaloosa: University of Alabama Press, 1992.

Moore, R. Laurence. *Selling God: American Religion in the Marketplace of Culture.* New York: Oxford University Press, 1994.

———. *Touchdown Jesus: The Mixing of the Sacred and the Secular in American History.* Louisville, KY: Westminster John Knox, 2007.

Moreman, Christopher M. "Devil Music and the Great Beast: Ozzy Osbourne, Aleister Crowley, and the Christian Right." *Journal of Religion and Popular Culture* 5 (Fall 2003).

Morgan, David. *Protestants and Pictures: Religion, Visual Culture, and the Age of American Mass Production.* New York: Oxford University Press, 1999.

———. *The Sacred Gaze: Religious Visual Culture in Theory and Practice.* Berkeley: University of California Press, 2005.

———. *Visual Piety: A History and Theory of Popular Religious Images.* Berkeley: University of California Press, 1998.

Morgan, Jack. *The Biology of Horror: Gothic Literature and Film.* Carbondale: Southern Illinois University Press, 2002.

Morone, James. *The Democratic Wish: Popular Participation and the Limits of American Government.* New Haven, CT: Yale University Press, 1990.

———. *Hellfire Nation: The Politics of Sin in American History.* New Haven, CT: Yale University Press, 2003.

———. "The Tropes of Wrath." *Dissent* (Spring 2005).

Moynihan, Michael, and Didrik Søderlind. *Lords of Chaos: The Bloody Rise of the Satanic Metal Underground.* Los Angeles: Feral House, 2003.

Murrin, John M. "Religion and Politics in America from the First Settlements to the Civil War," in Mark Noll, ed., *Religion and American Politics.* New York: Oxford University Press, 1990.

Nathan, Debbie, and Michael Snedeker. *Satan's Silence: Ritual Abuse and the Making of a Modern American Witch Hunt.* New York: Basic, 1995.

Neal, Lynn. *Romancing God: Evangelical Women and Inspirational Fiction.* Chapel Hill: University of North Carolina Press, 2006.

Neal, Mark Anthony. *What the Music Said: Black Popular Music and Black Public Culture.* New York: Routledge, 1998.

Neuhaus, Richard. *The Naked Public Square: Religion and American Democracy.* Grand Rapids, MI: Eerdmans, 1986.

"New England News Briefs." *Boston Globe* (April 7, 1999).

Nixon, Elisabeth Ann. "Playing Devil's Advocate on the Path to Heaven: Evangelical Hell Houses and the Play of Politics, Fear, and Faith." Ph.D. diss., Ohio State University, 2006.

Noll, Mark. *The Eclipse of Old Hostilities between and the Potential for New Strife among Catholics and Protestants since Vatican II.* South Bend, IN: Cushwa Center, 1985.

———. *A History of Christianity in the United States and Canada.* Grand Rapids, MI: Eerdmans, 1992.

Nord, David Paul. *Faith in Reading: Religious Publishing and the Birth of Mass Media in America.* New York: Oxford University Press, 2004.

Norris, Christopher. *What's Wrong with Postmodernism? Critical Theory and the Ends of Philosophy.* Baltimore, MD: Johns Hopkins University Press, 1990.

Norton, Anne. *Republic of Signs: Liberal Theory and Popular Culture.* Chicago: University of Chicago Press, 1993.

Nuzum, Eric. *Parental Advisory: Music Censorship in America.* New York: Perennial, 2001.

Oates, Joyce Carol. "Introduction," in Joyce Carol Oates, ed., *American Gothic Tales.* New York: Plume, 1996.

O'Leary, Stephen D. *Arguing the Apocalypse: A Theory of Millennial Rhetoric.* New York: Oxford University Press, 1994.

Olin, Bruce. "From Gentle Jesus to Macho Messiah." *New York Times* (April 9, 2004).

Orsi, Robert A. *Between Heaven and Earth: The Religious Worlds People Make and the Scholars Who Study Them.* Princeton, NJ: Princeton University Press, 2005.

Otto, Rudolf. *The Idea of the Holy*, excerpted in Carl Olson, ed., *Theory and Method in the Study of Religion: A Selection of Critical Readings.* Belmont, CA: Wadsworth, 2002.

Parker, Suzi. "The Real Convention?" *U.S. News & World Report* (August 25, 2004).

Pellegrini, Ann. " 'Signaling through the Flames': Hell House Performance and the Structure of Religious Feeling." *American Quarterly* 59:3 (2007): 911–935.

Perry, Michael J. *Religion in Politics: Constitutional and Moral Perspectives.* New York: Oxford University Press, 1999.

Phillips, Kevin. *American Dynasty: Aristocracy, Fortune, and the Politics of Deceit in the House of Bush.* New York: Penguin, 2004.

———. *American Theocracy: The Perils and Politics of Radical Religion, Oil, and Borrowed Money in the 21st Century.* New York: Viking, 2006.

Pike, Sarah M. "After Columbine: Demonic Teens on the Internet, God's Martyrs in the Headlines." Paper presented at the annual meeting of the American Academy of Religion, November 2001, Denver, CO.

Pinn, Anthony B. *Noise and Spirit: The Religious and Spiritual Sensibilities of Rap Music.* New York: New York University Press, 2003.

Posner, Richard. *Public Intellectuals: A Study of Decline.* Cambridge, MA: Harvard University Press, 2003.

Promey, Sally M. "Religion in Plain View: The Public Display of Religion in the United States." *AAR Religious Studies News* 20:4 (October 2005).

———. "Taste Matters: The Visual Practice of Liberal Protestantism, 1940–1965," in Laurie Maffly-Kipp, Leigh E. Schmidt, and Mark Valeri, eds., *Practicing Protestants: Histories of Christian Life in America, 1630–1965.* Baltimore, MD: Johns Hopkins University Press, 2006.

Prothero, Stephen, ed. *A Nation of Religions: The Politics of Pluralism in Multicultural America.* Chapel Hill: University of North Carolina Press, 2006.

Pustz, Matthew J. *Comic Book Culture: Fanboys and True Believers.* Jackson: University of Mississippi Press, 1999.

Putney, Clifford. *Muscular Christianity: Manhood and Sports in Protestant America, 1880–1920.* Cambridge, MA: Harvard University Press, 2003.

Quinn, Eithne. *Nuthin' but a "G" Thang: The Culture and Commerce of Gangsta Rap.* New York: Columbia University Press, 2005.

Radosh, Daniel. *Rapture Ready! Adventures in the Parallel Universe of Christian Pop Culture.* New York: Scribner's, 2008.

Raeburn, Dan. *The Imp*, no. 2 (self-published, Chicago, 1997).

Rafferty, Terrence. "Bitter Spirits." *New York Times* (January 28, 2007).

Reddy, William. *The Navigation of Feeling: A Framework for the History of Emotions.* Cambridge: Cambridge University Press, 2001.

Reed, Adolph, Jr. "The 2004 Election in Perspective: The Myth of the 'Cultural Divide' and the Triumph of Neoliberal Ideology." *American Quarterly* 57:1 (2005).

Reed, Ralph. "What Do Religious Conservatives Really Want?" in Michael Cromartie, ed., *Disciples and Democracy: Religious Conservatives and the Future of American Politics.* Washington, DC: Ethics and Public Policy Center, 1994.

"Religious Leaflets Stir Anger at Schools." *San Diego Union-Tribune* (November 18, 2000).

Reynolds, Larry J. "American Cultural Iconography," in Larry J. Reynolds and Gordon Hunter, eds., *National Imaginaries, American Identities: The Cultural Work of American Iconography*. Princeton, NJ: Princeton University Press, 2000.

Ribuffo, Leo P. *The Old Christian Right: The Protestant Far Right from the Great Depression to the Cold War*. Philadelphia: Temple University Press, 1983.

Rich, Frank. "A Culture of Death, Not Life." *New York Times* (April 10, 2005).

Roberts, Robert C. *Emotions: An Essay in Aid of Moral Psychology*. Cambridge: Cambridge University Press, 2003.

Robertson, Pat. *The End of the Age: A Novel*. Dallas, TX: Word, 1995.

Robin, Corey. *Fear: The History of a Political Idea*. New York: Oxford University Press, 2004.

Rogin, Michael. *Ronald Reagan: The Movie, and Other Essays in Political Demonology*. Berkeley: University of California Press, 1988.

Roof, Wade Clark. *Spiritual Marketplace: Baby Boomers and the Remaking of American Religion*. Princeton, NJ: Princeton University Press, 1999.

Rose, Tricia. *Black Noise: Rap Music and Black Culture in Contemporary America*. Hanover, NH: Wesleyan University Press/University Press of New England, 1994.

Ross, Robyn. "The Scream Teams." *Austin American-Statesman* (TX) (October 7, 2004).

Rossinow, Douglas. *The Politics of Authenticity*. New York: Columbia University Press, 1998.

Rozell, Mark, and Clyde Wilcox. *Second Coming: The New Christian Right in Virginia Politics*. Baltimore, MD: Johns Hopkins University Press, 1996.

Rubin, Julius H. *Religious Melancholy and Protestant Experience in America*. New York: Oxford University Press, 1994.

Ryan, Terri Jo. "Church's Hell House Draws on Sept. 11 Tragedy." *Waco Tribune* (TX) (October 28, 2002).

Sandage, Scott. *Born Losers: A History of Failure in America*. Cambridge, MA: Harvard University Press, 2005.

Sandeen, Ernest Robert. *The Roots of Fundamentalism: British and American Millenarianism, 1800–1930*. Grand Rapids, MI: Baker Book House, 1978.

Sandler, Lauren. *Righteous: Dispatches from the Evangelical Youth Movement*. New York: Viking, 2006.

Sanneh, Kelefa. "Christian Rock and Mainstream Music Move Closer Together." *New York Times* (April 27, 2006).

Santino, Jack, ed. *Halloween and Other Festivals of Death and Life*. Knoxville: University of Tennessee Press, 1994.

Savelle, Jon. "Hell House Warns against Wayward Path." *King County Journal* (Bellevue and Kent, WA) (October 28, 2002).

Schaefer, William J. *Rock Music: Where It's Been, What It Means, Where It's Going*. Minneapolis, MN: Augsbury, 1972.

Schmidt, Leigh Eric. *Consumer Rites: The Buying and Selling of American Holidays*. Princeton, NJ: Princeton University Press, 1995.

———. *Hearing Things: Religion, Illusion, and the American Enlightenment*. Cambridge, MA: Harvard University Press, 2002.

Sears, Alan, and Craig Osten. *The Homosexual Agenda: Exposing the Principal Threat to Religious Freedom Today*. Nashville, TN: B&H, 2003.

Sharks, Andrew. *Civil Society, Civil Religion.* Oxford: Blackwell, 1995.

Sharlet, Jeff. "Preachers of Doom." *New Statesman* (July 19, 2007).

———. "Through a Glass, Darkly: How the Christian Right Is Reimagining U.S. History." *Harper's* (December 2006).

Shea, William. *The Lion and the Lamb: Evangelicals and Catholics in America.* New York: Oxford University Press, 2004.

Sherman, Dale. *Urban Legends of Rock & Roll.* New York: Collector's Guide, 2003.

Showalter, Elaine. *Hystories: Hysterical Epidemics and Modern Media.* New York: Columbia University Press, 1998.

Shuck, Glenn W. *Marks of the Beast: The* Left Behind *Novels and the Struggle for Evangelical Identity.* New York: New York University Press, 2005.

Sieving, Christopher. "Cop Out? The Media, 'Cop Killer,' and the De-racialization of Black Rage." *Journal of Communication Studies* 22:4 (October 1998).

Skal, David J. *Death Makes a Holiday: A Cultural History of Halloween.* New York: Bloomsbury, 2002.

———. *The Monster Show: A Cultural History of Horror,* rev. ed. New York: Faber & Faber, 2001.

Slotkin, Richard. *Gunfighter Nation: The Myth of the Frontier in Twentieth Century America,* new ed. Norman: University of Oklahoma Press, 1998.

Smith, Christian. *American Evangelicalism: Embattled and Thriving.* Chicago: University of Chicago Press, 1998.

———. *Christian America? What Evangelicals Really Want.* Berkeley: University of California Press, 2000.

Sobel, Mechal. *Teach Me Dreams: The Search for Self in the Revolutionary Era.* Princeton, NJ: Princeton University Press, 2000.

Soocher, Stan. *They Fought the Law: Rock Music Goes to Court.* New York: Schirmer, 1998.

Squire, James, and Jane Smiley. "Fear Factor." *American Prospect* (April 2004).

Standaert, Michael. *Skipping towards Armageddon: The Politics and Propaganda of the* Left Behind *Novels and the LaHaye Empire.* Brooklyn, NY: Soft Skull, 2006.

Stoeffler, F. Ernest. *The Rise of Evangelical Pietism.* Leiden: Brill, 1971.

Stone, Jon R. *On the Boundaries of Evangelicalism: The Postwar Evangelical Coalition.* New York: Palgrave Macmillan, 1997.

Stout, Harry. *The Divine Dramatist: George Whitefield and the Rise of Modern Evangelicalism.* Grand Rapids, MI: Eerdmans, 1991.

Stout, Jeffrey. *Democracy and Tradition.* Princeton, NJ: Princeton University Press, 2003.

———. "The Spirit of Democracy and the Rhetoric of Excess." *Journal of Religious Ethics* 35:1 (March 2007).

Stromberg, Frank. *The Comics Go to Hell: A Visual History of the Devil in Comics.* Seattle, WA: Fantagraphics, 2005.

Styers, Randall. *Making Magic: Religion, Magic, & Science in the Modern World.* New York: Oxford University Press, 2004.

Sullivan, Winnifred F. *The Impossibility of Religious Freedom.* Princeton, NJ: Princeton University Press, 2005.

Szwed, John. "The Real Old School," in Alan Light, ed., *The Vibe History of Hip Hop.* New York: Three Rivers, 1999.

Taibbi, Matt. "The Low Post: The Imus Sanction." *Rolling Stone* (April 18, 2007).

Tate, Greg. *Flyboy in the Buttermilk: Essays on Contemporary America.* New York: Simon & Schuster, 1992.

Taves, Ann. *Fits, Trances, & Visions: Experiencing Religion and Explaining Experience from Wesley to James.* Princeton, NJ: Princeton University Press, 1999.

Thomas, Keith. *Religion and the Decline of Magic: Studies in Popular Beliefs in Sixteenth and Seventeenth Century England.* New York: Oxford University Press, 1997.

Thompson, Father Augustine, O.P. "Should Our Kids Celebrate Halloween?" *Catholic Parent Magazine* (Huntington, IN) (September–October 1995).

Trend, David. *The Myth of Media Violence: A Critical Introduction.* Oxford: Blackwell, 2006.

Trott, Jon. "Bob Larson's Ministry under Scrutiny." *Cornerstone* 21:100 (1993).

Tweed, Thomas A. *Crossing and Dwelling: A Theory of Religion.* Cambridge, MA: Harvard University Press, 2006.

Twitchell, James B. *Dreadful Pleasures: An Anatomy of Modern Horror.* New York: Oxford University Press, 1987.

Unger, Craig. "American Rapture." *Vanity Fair* (December 2005).

Urban, Hugh. "Bush, the Neocons, and Evangelical Fiction: America, 'Left Behind. ' " *Counterpunch* (November 18, 2004). Online at www.counterpunch.org (accessed March 17, 2008).

———. *Secrets of the Kingdom: Religion and Secrecy in the Bush Administration.* Lanham, MD: Rowman & Littlefield, 2007.

von Busack, Richard. "Comic Book Theology: Unearthing Famed Christian Artist Jack Chick." *Metroactive Weekly* (San Jose, CA) (April 2, 1998).

Walser, Robert. *Running with the Devil: Power, Gender, and Madness in Heavy Metal Music.* Hanover, NH: Wesleyan University Press/University Press of New England, 1993.

Walzer, Michael. *Interpretation and Social Criticism.* Cambridge, MA: Harvard University Press, 1987.

Ward, Chip. "Left Behind: Bush's Holy War on Nature." *Nation* (September 16, 2005).

Warner, Marina. *No Go the Bogeyman: Scaring, Lulling, and Making Mock.* New York: Farrar, Straus and Giroux, 1998.

Watson, Sidney. *The Mark of the Beast.* Charleston, SC: Bibliobazaar, 2007.

———. *In the Twinkling of an Eye.* Uhrichsville, OH: Barbour Publishing, 2005.

———. *Scarlet and Purple.* Old Tappan, NJ: Fleming H. Revell, 1933.

Weber, Eugen. *Apocalypses: Prophecies, Cults, and Millennial Beliefs through the Ages.* Cambridge, MA: Harvard University Press, 1999.

Weber, Timothy P. *On the Road to Armageddon: How Evangelicals Became Israel's Best Friend.* Grand Rapids, MI: Baker Academic, 2005.

Weinstein, Deena. *Heavy Metal: The Music and Its Culture.* New York: Da Capo, 2000.

Whitaker, Robert W., ed. *The New Right Papers.* New York: St. Martin's, 1982.

Whitehead, John. *Religious Apartheid: The Separation of Religion from American Public Life.* Chicago: Moody Press, 1994.

Whitehouse, Harvey. "Rites of Terror: Emotion, Metaphor, and Memory in Melanese Initiation Cults," in John Corrigan, ed., *Religion and Emotion: Approaches and Interpretations.* New York: Oxford University Press, 2004.

Wilcox, Clyde. *Onward Christian Soldiers: The Religious Right in American Politics.* Boulder, CO: Westview, 2006.

Williams, Raymond. *The Country and the City*. New York: Oxford University Press, 1975.

Wolfe, Alan. *The Transformation of American Religion: How We Actually Live Our Faith*. Chicago: University of Chicago Press, 2005.

Wolterstorff, Nicolas, and Robert Audi. *Religion in the Public Square: The Place of Religious Convictions in Political Debate*. Lanham, MD: Rowman & Littlefield, 1996.

Wosh, Peter. *Spreading the Word: The Bible Business in Nineteenth Century America*. Ithaca, NY: Cornell University Press, 1994.

Wright, Bradford. *Comic Book Nation: The Transformation of Youth Culture in America*. Baltimore, MD: Johns Hopkins University Press, 2001.

Wuthnow, Robert. *America and the Challenges of Religious Diversity*. Princeton, NJ: Princeton University Press, 2007.

Yonke, David. "Pastor Feels Called to Fight Demons." *Toledo Blade* (February 11, 2006).

Žižek, Slavoj. *On Belief (Thinking in Action)*. New York: Routledge, 2001.

Index

Abbott, "Dimebag" Darrell,
    259n114
abjection, 278n22
abortion, 8, 37, 43, 140, 218, 219
    and Jack Chick, 78
    conservative evangelicalism, 194
    and Hell House, 17, 131, 142, 150, 151,
        152–153, 155, 164, 166, 167,
        266n85
    and Judgement House, 146, 147
    and Timothy LaHaye, 181
    in *Left Behind* series, 197
    and New Christian Right
        organizations, 181
    retribution for, 153, 204
    and Keenan Roberts, 138
Acquire the Fire, 226
Adorno, Theodor, 39, 53
adultery scenes in Hell House, 157–158
Agamben, Giorgio, 221
AIDS scenes in Hell House, 142
Akin, Jimmy, 85, 249n43
Alamo, Tony, 49
Alliance Defense Fund, 230
alterity, 33, 193, 221
American Civil Liberties Union, 80, 162
American Coalition for Traditional
        Values, 181
American Council of Christian Churches,
        29, 47
American Family Association, 95, 254n5
American Tract Society, 44
Amis, Martin, 213
Amos, Book of, 171
Antichrist, 33–34, 41, 140, 174
    and Jack Chick, 59
    contemporary representations of, 176
    and economics, 198, 274n137
    in *Left Behind* series, 186, 187, 192, 210
    and Hal Lindsey, 176

and Marilyn Manson, 112
and Revelation Walk, 133, 145
and Pat Robertson, 270n29
and United Nations, 197
apocalypticism, 169–70, 172, 202, 231,
        232, 233
    and Jack Chick, 59, 86
    Christian, 175, 176
    defined, 202
    and end times, 174, 175
    in fiction, 9, 171, 177, 178, 183, 210, 216
    in films, 3, 19, 175, 177
    in Hell House, 164
    and Timothy LaHaye, 182, 184, 189
    in *Left Behind* series, 20, 171, 191, 198,
        199, 209
    in Book of Revelation, 172
Aranza, Jacob, 20, 90, 93, 98, 99, 103, 109,
        256n57
    biographical information, 95
    on music and the occult, 100, 102
Aranza Outreach, 95
Ariel, Yaakov, 191, 209
Aristotle, 92
Arlington Group, 184
Armageddon, 174, 176, 182, 186, 187
Army of God, 204
Arnett, Jeffrey, 107
Asad, Talal, 15, 83
Asbury, Francis, 32
Ashcroft, Sen. John, 184, 230
Assemblies of God, 46, 134

Back in Control Training Center, 97
backward masking, 75, 94–95, 102, 105,
        109, 126
Baha'i, 101
Balmer, Randall, 28, 177, 224
Baptists, 46
Barton, David, 230